Hypocrisy and the Philosophical Intentions of Rousseau

Hypocrisy and the Philosophical Intentions of Rousseau

The Jean-Jacques Problem

Matthew D. Mendham

PENN

UNIVERSITY OF PENNSYLVANIA PRESS

PHILADELPHIA

Published by
University of Pennsylvania Press
Philadelphia, Pennsylvania 19104-4112
www.upenn.edu/pennpress

Printed in the United States of America on acid-free paper
1 3 5 7 9 10 8 6 4 2

Library of Congress Cataloging-in-Publication Data
Names: Mendham, Matthew David, author.
Title: Hypocrisy and the philosophical intentions of Rousseau : the Jean-Jacques problem / Matthew D. Mendham.
Description: 1st edition. | Philadelphia : University of Pennsylvania Press, [2021] | Includes bibliographical references and index.
Identifiers: LCCN 2020020802 | ISBN 978-0-8122-5283-5 (hardcover)
Subjects: LCSH: Rousseau, Jean-Jacques, 1712–1778. | Rousseau, Jean-Jacques, 1712–1778—Political and social views.
Classification: LCC B2137 .M46 2021 | DDC 194—dc23
LC record available at https://lccn.loc.gov/2020020802

To my parents, Joann and Don Mendham

CONTENTS

ABBREVIATIONS AND CONVENTIONS

Beaumont	*Letter to Beaumont* (1763). (Followed by page in CW:9 / OC:4.)
CC	*Correspondance complète de Jean-Jacques Rousseau: Édition critique.* 53 vols. Ed. R. A. Leigh. Geneva: Institut et musée Voltaire, 1965–1995. (Followed by volume, page.)
Conf.	*Confessions* (ca. 1764–1770, posthumous). (Followed by Book, page in CW:5 / OC:1. Where indicated, the translation of Angela Scholar has been followed [New York: Oxford University Press, 2000].)
Corsica	*Constitutional Project for Corsica* (1764–1765, posthumous). (Followed by page in CW:11 / OC:3.)
CW	*The Collected Writings of Rousseau.* 13 vols. Ed. Roger D. Masters and Christopher Kelly. Hanover: University Press of New England, 1990–2010. (Followed by volume, page.)
Dictionnaire	*Dictionnaire de Jean-Jacques Rousseau.* Ed. Raymond Trousson and Frédéric S. Eigeldinger. Paris: Honoré Champion, 2006.
DOI	*Discourse on the Origin and Foundations of Inequality Among Men*, or second *Discourse* (1754–1755). (Followed by Part, page in EPW / OC:3.)
DPE	*Discourse on Political Economy* (1755). (Followed by page in LPW / OC:3.)
DSA	*Discourse on the Sciences and Arts*, or first *Discourse* (1750–1751). (Followed by Part, page in EPW / OC:3.)
E	*Emile, or On Education* (1762). (Followed by Book [or "SV" for the profession of the Savoyard Vicar], page in *Emile*, trans. Allan Bloom [New York: Basic Books, 1979] / OC:4.)
EPW	*The Discourses and Other Early Political Writings.* Ed. and trans. Victor Gourevitch. Cambridge: Cambridge University Press, 1997.
Julie	*Julie, or the New Heloise* (1761). (Followed by Part, letter number, page in CW:6 / OC:2.)
LdA	*Letter to M. d'Alembert on the Theatre* (1758). (Followed by page in *Politics and the Arts*, trans. Allan Bloom [Ithaca: Cornell University Press, 1960] / CW:10 / OC:5.)
LF	Letter to Mme Dupin de Francueil, 20 April 1751. (Followed only by [paragraph number], based on CW 5:551-52 / CC 2:142-44.)
LPW	*The Social Contract and Other Later Political Writings.* Ed. and trans. Victor Gourevitch. Cambridge: Cambridge University Press, 1997.
LR	*Last Reply* (1752). (Followed by page in EPW / OC:3.)

Malesherbes	"Four Letters to M. le Président de Malesherbes: Containing the True Picture of My Character and the True Motives for All My Behavior" (1762). (Followed by letter number, page in CW:5 / OC:1.)
ML	*Moral Letters* (ca. winter of 1757–1758, posthumous). (Followed by letter number, page in CW:12 / OC:4.)
Mountain	*Letters Written from the Mountain* (1764). (Followed by letter number, page in CW:9 / OC:3.)
Obs.	*Observations* (to Stanislas, King of Poland, 1751). (Followed by page in EPW / OC:3.)
OC	*Oeuvres Complètes*. 5 vols. Ed. Bernard Gagnebin, Marcel Raymond, Jean Starobinski, et al. Paris: Gallimard (Bibliothèque de la Pléiade), 1959–1995. (Followed by volume, page.)
PN	"Preface to *Narcissus*" (1753). (Followed by page in EPW / OC:2.)
Poland	*Considerations on the Government of Poland* (1770–1771, posthumous). (Followed by chapter, page in LPW / OC:3.)
Rev.	*The Reveries of the Solitary Walker* (1776–1778, posthumous). (Followed by walk number, page in *Reveries*, trans. Charles Butterworth [Indianapolis: Hackett, 1992] / OC:1.)
RJJ	*Rousseau, Judge of Jean-Jacques: Dialogues* (1772–1776, posthumous). (Followed by dialogue number [or HPW for "History of the Preceding Writing"], page in CW:1 / OC:1.)
SC	*Of the Social Contract, or Principles of Political Right* (1762). (Followed by Book, chapter, page in LPW / OC:3.)

Where a translation has been modified, this has been indicated, except in trivial cases such as capitalization. Where no English edition is cited, translations are my own. For short titles of the many works titled *Rousseau* or *Jean-Jacques Rousseau*, I refer to their more distinctive subtitles (e.g., Damrosch, *Restless Genius*; Gauthier, *The Sentiment of Existence*).

In keeping with a somewhat common practice deriving from the *Dialogues*, I will often use "Jean-Jacques" to refer to the personal character of Rousseau, as distinguished from the author.

INTRODUCTION

> I loved him very much, but when I saw his *Confessions*, I ceased to esteem him. His soul revolted me, and for me with Jean-Jacques, it was the opposite of what usually happens: After his death, I began to underestimate him.
>
> —Georges-Louis Le Clerc, comte de Buffon

> His sad nature poisoned his life, but posterity will never forget his talents. If he had the too-dangerous art of excusing—even in the eyes of virtue—the faults of a passionate soul, do not forget that he wanted above all to learn to recover from them, and that he constantly made us love this virtue that it is perhaps not given to feeble humanity to follow always.
>
> —Élisabeth-Sophie-Françoise Lalive de Bellegarde, comtesse d'Houdetot

Why did Rousseau fail—often so ridiculously or grotesquely—to live up to his own principles? In one of the most notorious cases of hypocrisy in intellectual history, this champion of the joys of domestic life immediately rid himself of each of his five children, placing them in an orphanage. Some less famous cases are comparably discrediting. He advocated profound devotion to republican civic life, and yet he habitually dodged opportunities for political engagement. As Denis Diderot quipped, "It's a very peculiar citizen who's a hermit."[1] Finally, despite an elevated ethics of social duty, he had a pattern of turning against his most intimate friends and ultimately fled humanity and civilization as such. Again, Diderot touches the nerve: "Only the vicious person lives alone."[2]

It is this striking chasm between principles and life that I dub "the Jean-Jacques problem." Can the two be reconciled? In the not-so-distant past, this question provoked only homages or screeds, and the man and his work were vindicated or cast away with a single thrust. The leading recent interpretations have been more cautious. Some have answered with a qualified "no." Seeing Rousseau's ethical and political thought as lofty, they have cordoned off most of his wayward life as philosophically irrelevant—a view bolstered by his own statements of personal regret. Others have answered with a qualified "yes." Seeing the elevated exterior of the normative writings as misleading, they find his genuine philosophy to be embodied in his anti-political and often amoral autobiographical writings.

It has thus proven possible to explain the Jean-Jacques problem, but at the cost of dismissing the life or downgrading the principles. This book attempts a third way. By showing that Rousseau took this problem more seriously than has been recognized, it also illuminates some of his most elusive stances on the place of virtue, society, and civic engagement in human life. In this reading, the Rousseau of his main normative writings (ca. 1751–1764) was vehemently opposed to intellectual hypocrisy, and he saw himself as engaged in an urgent project of harmonizing his life with his principles. This ranged from repudiating modern luxuries and providing assistance to his poor neighbors, to writing only for the sake of humanity and his homeland with minimal regard to personal consequences. Although this aspirational side of Jean-Jacques has not gone unnoticed, it has never been pursued on anything like the scale necessary to unravel the Jean-Jacques problem—a systematic analysis of his normative philosophy and self-portrayals in view of the often-yawning gap between them.

Our prevailing images of an apathetic, self-absorbed Jean-Jacques emerge mainly from the autobiographies, especially the accessible *Reveries of the Solitary Walker* and the most memorable passages of the longer *Confessions*. By contrast, uncovering this earlier Jean-Jacques will require not only a careful reinterpretation of the autobiographies but also the intellectual context, many untranslated letters, and the full corpus of the normative writings. I argue that, after his expulsion from France (June 1762), especially after the revelation of the secret about his children (December 1764) and his disastrous stay in England (1766–1767), Jean-Jacques began to shrink from the ambitious philosophical life to which he had previously aspired. I link this, in particular, to a new drive to mitigate his culpability for his discarded children, to a new quietism regarding civic engagement, and to a collapse of his sense of social duty.

Prior to his transition, when he most advocated self-command, social dedication, and civic justice, he most aspired to live in accord with these ideals. After this, he sought chiefly to vindicate his lifelong innocence, and the lenient standard of natural goodness came increasingly to prevail over the demanding standard of cultivated virtue. This implies more substantive development than the leading paradigms have allowed. However, far from leading us to dismiss his coherence, a moderate developmental approach allows us to endorse his intellectual and personal self-presentations in each major stage. We thus perceive that in his early work, he did not view his life as cleanly distinct from his nobler principles. Conversely, even as he seems most complacent and narcissistic in his final autobiographies, we should not project that spirit back onto the major normative writings, since the autobiographies themselves indicate the more idealistic aspirations which drove that earlier work.

This study is by no means meant to eliminate the gaps between Rousseau's normative teachings and his conduct. Even at his most aspirational, we will see several weaknesses and failures, some of them bizarre. As a whole, his life is a profoundly mixed affair, while his thought both emerged from it and radically transcended it. By pursuing the dialectic between his principles and his life, I hope to provide a kind of moral biography in view of his most controversial behaviors, as well as a preamble to future discussions of the spirit of his thought.

1. The Jean-Jacques Problem

Edmund Burke saw the moral and political excesses of the French Revolution as resulting from many factors, prominently including their political inspiration by Jean-Jacques Rousseau, "founder of the philosophy of vanity." Burke's criticism remains one of the most influential:

> It is from the same deranged eccentric vanity, that this, the insane *Socrates* of the National Assembly, was impelled to publish a mad Confession of his mad faults, and to attempt a new sort of glory, from bringing hardily to light the obscure and vulgar vices which we know may sometimes be blended with eminent talents. He has not observed on the nature of vanity, who does not know that it is omnivorous; that it has no choice in its food. . . . [It] has driven Rousseau to record a life not so much as chequered, or spotted here and there, with virtues, or even distinguished by a single good action. It is such a life that he chooses to offer to the attention of mankind.[3]

About the most notorious of these faults, Burke observes that the "moral hero" of the French National Assembly exhausts "the stores of his powerful rhetoric in the expression of universal benevolence; whilst his heart was incapable of harbouring one spark of common parental affection.... Without one natural pang, [he] casts away, as a sort of offal and excrement, the spawn of his disgustful amours, and sends his children to the hospital of foundlings."[4]

Burke's case against Rousseau's character would be corroborated by the two major contemporary thinkers whose friendships with him were dramatically ruptured: Diderot and David Hume.[5] In a late, largely autobiographical writing, Diderot appeals to this pattern of ruptured friendships as decisive evidence against Rousseau's character.[6] Upon being publicly repudiated by Rousseau (1758) after fifteen years of friendship, Diderot observed: "This man is false, vain as Satan, ungrateful, cruel, hypocritical and vicious.... Truly this man is a monster."[7] In Madame d'Épinay's partly historical, partly fictional *Histoire de Madame de Montbrillant*, the Diderot character waxes similarly theological about the Rousseau character: "He makes me believe in devils and hell."[8] Similarly, Hume was shocked after Rousseau, in a private letter, accused him of betrayal: "He is surely the blackest and most atrocious villain, beyond comparison, that now exists in the world; and I am heartily ashamed of any thing I ever wrote in his favor."[9] In cooler moments, there was still—in a way—room for doubt about what lay behind Rousseau's behavior. Diderot went to visit him once "to learn if he was mad or vicious."[10] In the same way, to Hume, "It is not a nice problem, whether he be not an arrant villain or an arrant madman or both."[11] Finally, and again like Diderot,[12] Hume thought Rousseau's moral reputation would be devastated by his conduct and thus "blast his writings at the same time."[13]

Are these philosophers behaving badly, dismissing a rival thinker's work through irrelevant ad hominem attacks?[14] Should we not separate the thought from the thinker? Responses could be seen as falling along a spectrum, with "rigorists" or "harmonists" more resistant to this gap, as opposed to "latitudinarians" (a term I borrow from an old theological debate).[15] The latter approach has been explored well in the history of literature. For instance, Marcel Proust strongly rejected the biographical contextualism exemplified by Charles Augustin Saint-Beuve, which came to dominate nineteenth-century criticism. To Proust, "That method which consists of not separating the man from the work ... fails to recognize what any more than merely superficial acquaintance with ourselves teaches us: That a book is the product of a self other than that which we display in our habits, in society, in our vices."[16] He adds that being a close friend of an author, far from providing indispensable guidance to understand his works, might be "a serious hindrance": "For such close friends, the self which produces the works is obscured by the other self, which may be very inferior to the outward self of many other men."[17] Similarly, in philosophy, Voltaire sidestepped the problem of Francis Bacon's alleged "bribery and extortion"—a "crime very unbecoming a Philosopher"—by pointing to his undeniable strengths: "He was so great a man . . . that I have forgot his vices."[18] A general latitudinarianism is stated later: "I consider men after their death in no other light than as they were writers, and wholly disregard everything else."[19] It is not difficult to find other cases where elevated works of genius emerge from persons who are—by many appearances—far less elevated.

Turning to the opposed camp, intelligent "harmonists" need not deny that outstanding work could come from a degraded hand, but they would focus on the broader implications of honoring the resulting chimera. Burke concedes that in a purely technical field like geometry, one might honor the work while cordoning this off strictly from the life. Yet this does not apply in a case like Rousseau's, since he "is a moralist, or he is nothing."[20] Socrates insisted that one's life and teaching should harmonize and that students would be ill-advised to learn under someone who fails in this.[21] Who would qualify? Perhaps no one of clear mind and good will has demanded that moral teachers be flawless, even as far as human nature would allow. Yet it could be a standing norm that no one should aspire to teach about practical ethics who has not distinguished herself comparably in practice. In keeping with this, both John Locke and Rousseau insist that a virtuous tutor is indispensable in the educational process.[22] (For all their differences, Locke and Rousseau each saw ethical formation as the chief goal of education, in repudiation of the scholastic methods that dominated, both then and now.[23]) In a civic context, Rousseau observes: "Wherever the lesson is not backed by authority and the precept by example, instruction remains fruitless, and virtue itself is discredited in the mouth of one who does not practice it" (DPE 22/261; see also *Poland* IV, 190/966f). Similar consistency is also required in domestic education, although here we find the clarification that the tutor will not be morally flawless in reality and should not try to come across as such.[24]

In a moderate harmonist approach, the philosopher might be open about her nonexemplary personal attainments but might focus on her resolution to improve and to show some marks of progress. This is taken up by Seneca (a major source for Rousseau):[25]

> If, therefore, one of those who bark against philosophy like dogs
> should put their usual question: "Why, then, do you speak more

> bravely than you live? . . . Why do you farm more extensively than your natural need requires? Why do you flout your own prescriptions when you have dinner? Why do you own furniture of some refinement?" I shall add weight to your reproaches in due course and take myself to task more than you imagine, but for the present I give you this reply: I am not wise, and, to feed your spite, I shall never be so. And so demand of me, not that I should be equal to the best, but that I should be better than the bad [*malis*]: I am satisfied if each day I make some reduction in the number of my vices and find fault with my mistakes. I have not arrived at good health [*ad sanitatem*], nor indeed shall I; my plan is to alleviate, not to banish, the gout that afflicts me. . . .
>
> "You talk one way," you say, "but you live another." You creatures full of spite, who loathe all men of quality, this was the criticism launched at Plato, yes, and at Epicurus, and at Zeno, too; for they all described, not how they lived their own lives, but how they ought to live them. I speak of virtue, not of myself, and my abuse is directed at vices, especially my own: when I can, I shall live as I should do. And that malice of yours . . . will not discourage me from engaging with what is best . . . , [or] hinder me from . . . revering [*adorem*] virtue and crawling after her, though at a great distance behind.[26]

In this approach, some inconsistencies between teaching and behavior are not marks of hypocrisy in any particularly damaging sense, and those who eagerly seize on these gaps are themselves guilty of another kind of vice. Seneca adds that, to these spiteful critics, it is advantageous "that no one should appear to be good."[27] Common criticisms of Plato, Aristotle, Democritus, and Epicurus are also invoked later, apparently including Plato's failed attempts to educate Alcibiades. This is "vilifying your betters"; "Do you look at other men's pimples when you are yourselves covered with a mass of open sores?"[28]

In Plutarch's *Lives*—the book Rousseau claimed was the most formative to him[29]—important statements of method address this danger. The ancient biographer seeks a delicate balance:

> When painters are faced with a slight blemish of some kind on the beautiful and pleasing figures they portray, we do not expect them either to omit it altogether (which would stop their portraits being true likenesses) or to stress it (which would make them ugly to look

> at). By the same token, since it is difficult—or more probably, impossible—to represent a man's life as entirely free from shortcomings and blemishes, we should supply the truth . . . when dealing with the good aspects of our subject's life. However, the flaws and defects [*fautes et erreurs*] which, prompted by emotion or by political necessity, taint his actions we should regard as lapses from a virtue rather than as manifestations of vice. We should not, then, be particularly eager to overemphasize these flaws in our account, but should write instead as if we felt ashamed of the fact that human nature fails to produce any character which is absolutely good or unequivocally virtuous.[30]

This method serves Plutarch's fundamental purpose, which is to benefit himself and his readers through a better understanding of character, virtue, and vice.[31]

In judging the credibility of a practical philosopher's life, the approaches of Seneca and Plutarch may relieve some pressure. Yet they cannot excuse just anything, and here we speak of Rousseau. We thus introduce as "the Jean-Jacques problem" what has long been discussed *avant la lettre*.[32] Rousseau seems to have written his autobiographies largely to explain himself and to defend his embattled legacy,[33] so we are left with the bitter irony that this endeavor made things worse in several ways. Disturbing facts about his life, which might have remained unknown or the preserve of a few historical specialists, have instead become focal points of undergraduate seminars. Consider the most direct self-defense, *Rousseau, Judge of Jean-Jacques: Dialogues* (written 1772–1776). Although several have defended it for passages of keen insight,[34] overall its obsessive focus on an allegedly universal conspiracy against him makes it his least readable and convincing work. Robert Wokler calls it "infrequently read today, and still more seldom read without pain."[35] Another layer of irony can be added from J. G. Herder. A highly philosophical and sympathetic reader, Herder nonetheless concluded that the *Dialogues* must have been forged by Rousseau's enemies in order to discredit him.[36]

Scholars have understandably been hesitant to represent such a client. From the perspective of this book, the most promising beginnings have been made by Ruth Grant and Joseph Reisert. Although they are each mainly concerned with questions about Rousseau's normative thought, they also address the Jean-Jacques problem. Grant concedes some of Rousseau's important personal failures, but she is unusual in pointing to a few strengths as well. Having established this rough moral stalemate, she concludes that, overall, Rousseau "deserves the benefit of the doubt," and it is "certainly not surprising" that he does not exemplify all the perfections he advocates.[37] The argument that follows in this book is not a direct response to Grant. Her approach is perhaps the most compatible with mine, although I will need to extend and refine it in several ways. Possibly most significant, as this book adds an element of development, many would question the extent to which the later Jean-Jacques is still entitled to Grant's benefit of the doubt.

Reisert takes an alternative approach, which has become fairly common among scholars. Instead of establishing a moral parity, he pleads no contest about Jean-Jacques's virtue. According to Reisert, in the autobiographies, Rousseau conceded that he "utterly lacks" the strength of will that he associated with virtue and duty, but he nonetheless "loves virtue with all his heart."[38] This does seem to be a leading strategy. For instance, Jean-Jacques is struck by "love of virtue" and could not "coldly contemplate virtue in all its beauty" or "portray its most touching charms without being moved by them" (RJJ I, 8/668). However, the practical effects of this seem minimal, since he is also "a man without malice rather than good, a soul healthy but weak, who adores virtue without practicing it, who ardently loves the good and does hardly any" (II, 87/774).[39] All this rings true of the timid, self-absorbed, hermit-like dreamer whom we know only too well from the autobiographical writings. In the same vein, after quoting Burke on Jean-Jacques's lack of a single virtue, Roger Masters and Christopher Kelly observe: "Burke's remark is in complete accord with Rousseau's analysis."[40]

Here, it seems, we have the best defenses of Rousseau's philosophical integrity that can be mustered by himself and his friendliest interpreters. Its core distinction between author and thought has been widely seen as diffusing the Jean-Jacques problem, at least enough to return seriously to the normative writings. This is a latitudinarian approach but perhaps not its most extreme form. For instance, although Rousseau's main thrust is that he is far from virtuous, he insists he is not bad or malevolent—he does not intend others harm and could not be guilty of moral "crime."[41] He sometimes argues that his writings themselves are strong evidence of *some* decency in him, since their moral depth and beauty could never proceed from a base soul.[42] In the major letter to Claude Anglancier de Saint-Germain (1770), Rousseau presents the "living warmth" of his writings as evidence of his good morals, and he cites the depiction of love in the *New Heloise* as a sufficient refutation of the charge that he is debauched.[43] Montaigne takes this approach in absolving Seneca of the charges of hypocrisy: "Seneca's virtue is so evidently alive

Figure 1. On the necessity of reconciling life with principles.

and vigorous in his writings, which themselves provide a manifest defense against such insinuations as his being excessively rich and spendthrift, that I could never accept any witness to the contrary."[44] On these approaches, then, some kinds of writing provide presumptive evidence of sound character; conversely, some forms of demonstrably bad character would give the lie to a professed admiration for virtue.

We might distinguish four alternatives on the relation between life and ethical teaching, as shown in Figure 1. The "admirer" is Jean-Jacques, and the "apprentice" is Seneca.[45] They each "revere," or "adore," virtue, although neither claims to be of Socratic caliber personally. Many readers may be convinced to walk alongside our Roman statesman in "engaging with what is best," despite the teacher's flaws. But who would find gravitas in the mainly internal and abstract transports of our Genevan? Amid this cloud of witnesses, does he not cut a complacent figure? Would Socrates welcome him hardily to the Elysian Fields, seeing him as a worthy inheritor of the tradition of philosophy and the philosophical life?[46] All things considered, this might, rather, lead to a striking novelty—Socrates blushing.[47]

Rousseau runs into additional difficulties if we trace his approach to latitudinarianism beyond his late autobiographical writings. Like the autobiographies, his earlier writings distinguish "faults" from "crimes"; faults are to be met with a certain compassion, given the weakness of human nature.[48] However, at least through the 1750s, he was best known for his severe criticism of the vices he saw around him (represented in our cover image on the left).[49] This is why Diderot compared him with figures even more austere than Socrates: "the Cato and Brutus of our age."[50] What is less well-known is that Rousseau reserved his most withering criticism for certain philosophers and men of letters. In the epistolary novel *Julie* (1761), when the provincial Swiss protagonist first arrives in Paris, he reports on the vices and hypocrisies of high society: "I see a gilt-up man decry luxury, a financier taxes, a prelate unruliness . . . ; I hear a woman of the court discuss modesty, a great lord virtue, an author simplicity, an *abbé* religion" (II.16, 198/241).[51] Among these shameless characters, he singles out one type for flagellation: "It is not even required of an author, and above all a moralist, that he speak as his books do, nor that he act as he speaks. His writings, his words, his conduct are three utterly different things, which he is not obliged to reconcile. In a word, everything is absurd and nothing shocks, because they are accustomed to it, and there is even in such incoherence [*inconséquence*] a sort of stylish appearance in which many people take pride" (II.14, 193/235).[52] Rousseau claims to have been disabused of his own early belief that in reading books of ethics and philosophy, he was seeing "the soul and principles" of their authors. "I looked upon all these grave writers as modest, wise, virtuous, irreproachable men" (PN 95n/962n; cf. *Beaumont* 52/966). Finally, in his critique of philosophical cosmopolitans, their ideas seem faulty above all because they excuse people from real deeds in practice.[53] These are not one-off polemics but are applications of the most central themes in his critique of advanced civilization. Our general problems of insincerity and hypocrisy are seen as particularly acute—and, it would seem, particularly inexcusable—among these opportunistic intellectuals.[54] There may be no philosophical critic who has been less welcoming to latitudinarians.

At this point, troubling metaphors will flood the biographically informed mind. How could this carriage be stopped without a scene of vast intellectual carnage? Why grind an ax so sharp when it is obviously pointed at your own neck?[55] What *is* a petard, anyway?

There are a few ways out. It could be mere charlatanry, or it could be fanaticism and self-deceit on a grand scale.[56] It could be a form of esotericism (the public insistence on virtue, seeking mainly or solely to foster socially beneficial traits among common people).[57] My approach would allow for each of these to some extent, but it would mostly move in another direction. At the beginning of his career, Rousseau was already subject to a manageable charge of hypocrisy (as a learned writer who criticizes learned writers). In the pamphlet where he offered his first sustained response about his person (1753), he claimed, "It would suffice for me to compare the times in order to reconcile the things" (PN 94/962).[58] In other words, look carefully at the ideas and behavior at one time and compare them with those of another time; no troubling contradictions should remain. In our case, I am suggesting that philosophical development needs more careful consideration, in tandem with personal changes.[59] This goes against the grain of the major recent philosophical interpretations, which have been strongly antidevelopmental, even when they do attend to the autobiographies. They point, as we will see, to Rousseau's own claims that his philosophy was deeply consistent from beginning to end.[60]

I seek to "compare the times" in a manner that is respectful to the claims of our author and best suited to the evidence as a whole. I will argue, first, that at least during a substantial period of his normative writing (ca. 1751–1764),[61] Rousseau prominently sought to harmonize his life with his principles. He was, he said, "too sincere with myself, too proud inside to want to contradict my principles by my actions" (Conf. VIII, 299/356).[62] In the case of the early Nietzsche, interest in the philosophical life was linked with skepticism: "In philosophical systems which have been refuted, the only thing that can still interest us is the personal element; for that is eternally irrefutable."[63] He would soon extend this: "The only critique of a philosophy that is possible and that proves something, namely trying to see whether one can live in accordance with it, has never been taught at universities: all that has ever been taught is a critique of words by means of other words."[64] Rousseau has a more limited pessimism about reason's prospects, but he moves in that existential direction by being mainly concerned with the kinds of philosophical truth that can be decisive for human life.[65] He thought the philosophies of his day teach us "to speechify and not at all to live." They reason about "the sovereign good," but they have not found "the art of being happy" for themselves (ML II, 180/1087). In an important retrospective on how he definitively formed his religious and moral ideas in the early 1750s, he argues that contemporary philosophers sought knowledge only to distinguish themselves,[66] not "in order to know themselves" or "to enlighten themselves [*s'éclairer*] within" (Rev. III, 29/1012f). By contrast, he sought a philosophy that was "for me" (32/1016). Hence, most of his lifetime of "studies" might have been done just as beneficially if he were permanently confined to "a desert island" (29/1013). This coheres with his earlier normative advice: "Before daring to undertake the formation of a man, one must have made oneself a man; one must find within oneself the example" (E II, 95/325).

Turning to more concrete means, the *Confessions* discusses—directly, yet mysteriously—a project for "personal reform" (beginning ca. February 1751).[67] As we will see, it faced plenty of setbacks, but, in this period, Rousseau often expresses substantial remorse for his faults (displayed in our cover image on the right, from his *Julie*, with heavy autobiographical overtones).[68] Like our Senecan model, Rousseau seeks to overcome his faults—sometimes, in atypically Christian language, to "atone" or "expiate" for them.[69] Unlike several prominent claims he made in the autobiographies, we will find that for more than a dozen years, he often proclaimed his disinterested devotion to several elevated causes, including neighbors in financial need, the liberty of his homeland of Geneva, and proclaiming harsh yet useful truths to all of humanity.[70]

Discussed in accessible sources like the *Confessions*, some of these aspirational themes have been noticed by scholars.[71] But discussions are normally cursory, whereas this book seeks a systematic interpretation of normative philosophy and philosophical life in view of each other.[72]

The ideal of a philosophical life on a deserted island would suggest that this is an independently sufficient motivation. Yet, we also know that Rousseau was acutely attuned to the public consequences of his conduct. Whereas he found his casually hypocritical contemporaries to neglect this altogether,[73] the rhetorical practices of the ancient Greeks and Romans were very different (E IV, 321-23/645-48, *Essay on the Origin of Languages* XX). They understood the force of character in making an audience—often of limited rational capacity—come to accept or reject a speaker's message.[74] Similarly, the initial spread of Christianity should be attributed mainly to the kind of people chosen to announce its message: "their saintliness, their veracity, their justice, their pure and spotless morals" (*Mountain* III, 167/728).[75] Another example is the Savoyard Vicar, who is introduced as exemplifying "virtue without hypocrisy," allowing for happiness and "so singular a life," despite poverty and persecution (E IV, 264-66/563-65; cf. Conf. III, 77/91f, IV, 99-100/118-19). Truth is different from rhetorical persuasiveness, of course. An impostor may fool good people, and "a good man" may "fool himself, carried away by the ardor of a holy zeal that he mistakes for inspiration" (*Mountain* III, 167/728). But Rousseau sought persuasiveness as well as truth, and he knew his ideas could scarcely be taken seriously if his life was discordant: "I judged that, if I was to be listened to, I must reconcile my conduct with my principles" (Conf. IX, 349/416).[76]

These efforts bore fruit early on. We should recall that the autobiographies were published from 1780 through 1789, after the author's death in 1778.[77] (Notably, the First Part of the *Confessions* was "one of the most widely read books of the 1780s," and its Second Part did not appear until 1789.[78] Although the First Part has its embarrassing revelations, it is only the Second Part that brings us the notorious discussion of the children and the strong marks of paranoia.)[79] This means that before the decisive revelations, the celebrity of Jean-Jacques and his various mythologies—normally either hostile or exuberant—had already percolated for about three decades. These were based on his ideas and prominent self-portrayals in the normative writings, as well as many anecdotes, especially following his persecution of 1762.[80] His distinctive lifestyle—seen as embodying his philosophy—inspired much of his allure (see Conf. VIII, 308/367). This is why he was so often linked with Diogenes the

Cynic—the ancient philosopher most associated with putting radical ideas into personal practice, and with the quest to find a real human being (cf. DOI II, 186/192).

2. Existing Paradigms

Among overall interpretations of Rousseau's thought, the most common—among many specialists and most nonspecialists—offer a fairly straightforward picture, bypassing the question of the gap between life and principles. One group finds a highly austere writer, advocating self-overcoming virtue, devoted republicanism, or a hard-headed and dignified political liberalism. Focusing on normative writings, such as the first *Discourse*, *Emile*, and the *Social Contract*, they either overlook the life and autobiographies or casually posit a continuity.[81] I dub this the "Noble Moralist" interpretation, and it is prominent among political theorists, philosophers, and intellectual historians.

A nearly opposite view is offered in the "Romantic Liberationist" interpretation. Here we find a passionate advocate of subjectivity, authenticity, emancipation from social norms, or the goodness of spontaneous sentiment. Such readings typically focus on the autobiographical works, although they sometimes also discuss the normative writings—normally briefly—as fully in keeping with these emphases.[82] A more rigorous version is offered by Jean Starobinski, the most widely cited biographical interpreter of Rousseau. He draws from the normative writings fluently, but he reads them as expressing straightforward needs of the soul of Jean-Jacques, crying out against an oppressive and artificial civilization.[83] Common in literature departments, Romantic Liberationism can sidestep the prominent hypocrisy problems, since Jean-Jacques's authentic self was not given to lasting commitments of family, friendship, or political community.

Indispensable for this book are the approaches developing sophisticated middle positions between these extremes, fully acknowledging the need to reconcile the unruly autobiographies with the high-minded prescriptions. Closer to the Noble Moralist reading, for some, the autobiographical claims are not Rousseau's most fundamental, lucid, or normative; his genuine philosophical contributions are the teachings on virtue and justice, written mainly prior to the autobiographies. Ernst Cassirer built upon Immanuel Kant to first articulate what I call the "Flawed Moralist" approach.[84] Although Kantians have often followed this path,[85] several who have most effectively subordinated the autobiographies to the normative thought have offered very different accounts of that normative thought—whether largely a form of Platonism,[86] Aristotelianism,[87] humanism,[88] the advocacy of integrity,[89] the aspiration to democracy,[90] or the conscience of the modern age.[91]

By contrast, the Veiled Antinomians emerge closer to the Romantic Liberationists, giving the autobiographies pride of place as interpretive cues. David Gauthier argues that in his life and in implicit indications throughout his writings, Rousseau suggests the failure of his solutions that require duty and virtue, such as Emile's education and republican citizenship.[92] In this view, his final, deepest, and most fundamental redemptive vision is love, understood as union and reciprocal possession without obligation.[93] A range of scholars who have been largely influenced by Leo Strauss also read between the lines, yet find a more individualistic Rousseau. For them, the radical freedom and solitude revealed in the autobiographies and the *Discourse on Inequality* are Rousseau's highest and most philosophical ideals.[94] They diverge more on the standing of the normative writings, but they tend to emphasize the unnaturalness or oppressiveness of the political life[95] and to see the domestic virtue of *Emile* as largely popularizing.[96] Both alternatives are demonstrably inferior to the spontaneous goodness and solitary wholeness of the autobiographical Jean-Jacques.[97] I suggest the following categorization, as shown in Figure 2.

My claim is not that every study of Rousseau's life or work raises these questions or may be placed neatly in one of these categories. Yet, these questions are of intrinsic importance, and those who have assumed or forwarded a clear stance on Rousseau's overall orientation might profitably be understood as falling somewhere along this fluid spectrum. Of course, the influential paradigms have not gone without criticism, and I draw from those offered by Starobinski, Wokler, Céline Spector, and others.[98]

3. Summary Approach

Biographical and psychological approaches once dominated Rousseau studies.[99] For at least two generations, most philosophically oriented specialists have

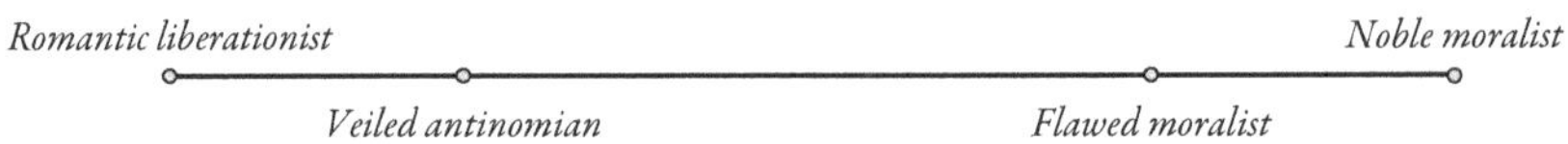

Figure 2. Interpretations of Rousseau's life and thought.

opposed these methods, finding them barren compared to more sympathetic consideration of his actual arguments. Wokler criticizes the common attempt to "trace the main promptings of Rousseau's philosophy to the region of his genitals"; for instance, "his urinary complaint or sexual repressions."[100] Although not a psychological study, at one level, the present book must plead guilty to the charge of biographical distraction. It is not meant primarily as a sustained analysis of what is most valuable in Rousseau's writings—his normative ideas. I have done that kind of work elsewhere and look forward to returning to it, having stumbled into this project through a series of genuine perplexities. Beginners in the philosophical study of Rousseau should focus on his normative writings, and some of the helpful studies about them, with little regard to the immense disruption caused by the massive autobiographical supplement. It remains defensible to bracket the Jean-Jacques problem in analyzing particular books or themes.[101] As Cassirer observes, Kant's analysis of Rousseau's ideas was in some ways better for his having initially read *Emile* with biographical innocence.[102] Yet for more comprehensive studies, it remains the fact that our philosopher dashed out a thousand pages of autobiographical writings, in terms of his own intellectual categories, and largely with the purpose of explaining his other works.[103] By following up on that dialectic, I attempt to provide a prolegomenon to the advanced study of Rousseau, with special reference to the credibility of his normative writings. In this book, I will not plumb the depths of technical normative ideas, such as natural right or the general will, but will present a new approach to the development of the moral and political ideas, as well as the spirit of the whole. I do not claim that biography and autobiography should always play a leading role in the scholarly division of labor, but I do suggest that, in this case, they can provide a useful vantage point for the more strictly normative studies.

I have striven to keep the argument accessible to those who are not well-versed in Rousseau's autobiographies or life history. Nonetheless, beginners may benefit from consulting a summary biography, or life and works.[104] There are also two very good comprehensive biographies in English.[105] In key respects, no secondary work can substitute for the primary sources. Of Rousseau's three autobiographical writings, only the *Confessions* (written ca. 1764–1770)[106] gives a chronological narrative. Its story formally ends with 1765, long before the author's death in 1778, thus leaving his final and most troubled years largely unknown even to many advanced scholars.[107] This book seeks to make these years better known historically and philosophically, and to juxtapose them with the earlier fifteen years (1749–1764) during which Rousseau's self-consciously

Socratic resoluteness and disinterestedness have not been adequately brought to the surface.

Chapter 1 is the first study in English or French to look comprehensively at Rousseau's explanations of his discarded children, as well as to categorize those explanations systematically. I find that he provided nineteen different rationales across his books and letters, and that his core emphasis oscillated across time. Sometimes he sought full exculpation; other times, he sought to "expiate" for actions he deeply regretted; and, still other times, to mitigate his culpability. Viewed contextually, although he plausibly claims that this behavior was common at the time, he implausibly claims that the public institutions in which he placed his children were adequate and healthy.

Chapter 2 considers Rousseau's efforts to harmonize his life with his principles during his main period of authorship. The *Confessions* describes his "effervescence" upon discovering his core philosophical insight (1749), as well as his "personal reform" undertaken to live up to these new principles. However, there are several ambiguities in the *Confessions* account, and scholars have drawn very different inferences about the soul of our author. It remains disputed when these moral changes began, how serious and sincere they were, when they ended, and what the corresponding spirit of his normative writings was. Although I share the currently prevailing aspiration to interpret Rousseau as coherent, my findings here suggest that genuine tensions and developments should not be simply cast aside.

Diderot's charge against the "hermit" Jean-Jacques has been rearticulated by Gauthier, who sees Rousseau's life as "a denial of all citizenship."[108] Defenses of Rousseau's personal citizenship have been few and brief, partly because discussions in the *Confessions* and *Reveries* are unpromising. However, turning to earlier letters and the normative writings, a different picture emerges in Chapter 3. During his main period of philosophical citizenship (ca. August 1754–June 1762), and typically in looking back on it in the *Confessions*, Rousseau justifies his civic behavior in terms of what I call "distant citizenship." He framed himself as needing to live outside his homeland in order to best serve it in his distinctive mission, and this was presented as a painful duty rather than as a pandering to inclination. Moreover, Socratic and Stoic models of civic engagement seem to have provided him with a respectable precedent for avoiding more direct engagement, given the circumstances and his skill set. Until he gave up on Geneva (February 1765), he was interested in behaving in accordance with high civic principles, and he was a leading resource for the republican cause in his homeland.

Whereas during his main period of philosophical authorship (ca. 1751–May 1762), Rousseau avoided concrete criticism of established regimes, he overcame this caution soon after his condemnation across Europe (June 1762), becoming a ringleader for Genevan opposition politics (ca. July 1762–February 1765). Based mainly on the (as yet untranslated) correspondence, Chapter 4 provides the first comprehensive discussion of Rousseau's civic behavior, as well as his self-understanding of citizenship and civic duty, during his only truly activist period. I swim against the main current of the *Confessions*, which treats these activities very briefly, omits some of his most provocative behaviors, and justifies himself in essentially Hobbesian terms, stressing his resistance to political involvement and his advocacy of peace. Finally, I posit a quietist turn in behavior and thought that began around 1766, and I challenge the prevailing scholarly view that, despite his often flamboyant rhetoric, Rousseau definitively opposed revolution.

Chapter 5 shows how, for all the political and religious backlash provoked by the *Letters Written from the Mountain*, it was a brief digression at Voltaire's expense which may have proved the most consequential for Rousseau. Voltaire replied with a devastating, anonymous pamphlet: *The Sentiment of the Citizens* (December 1764). Revealing the great secret about Rousseau's children, it undermined his standing with the pastors and common people of Môtiers enough that, in September 1765, Rousseau had to flee under threat of popular violence. This chapter shows that, even though the pamphlet did not singularly cause the autobiographical turn, it redoubled it and likely altered its character.

Whereas most scholarly disputes focus on the happiness or misery of Rousseau's final solitude, Chapter 6 pursues the various kinds of solitude he depicts, and in what senses he sees them as ethically justified. To Diderot's 1757 charge that "only the vicious person lives alone," Rousseau answered that his positive duties to society (especially assisting his impoverished neighbors) are in fact better fulfilled in his more secluded situation than they could be in Paris. We find evidence of Jean-Jacques's social dutifulness, regarding at least the period ca. 1756–1766. After this, as his sense of persecution increased, we find him periodically claiming exemption from certain duties, such as intellectual labor and service to impoverished neighbors; he also indulges at length in pastimes believed useless, like botany. This puts a new light on some prominent late passages in which he starkly opposes his character to all habits of virtue and duty.

The Conclusion returns to our interpretive debates and the broader implications of this book. The leading interpretive paradigms largely invert each other, and each has its strengths. Veiled Antinomianism illuminates the Rousseau of the last dozen years of his life and the philosophy of natural goodness, but it fails to account for the sincere aspirations to virtue—both to live it and to articulate it credibly—at many earlier points. Conversely, Flawed Moralism illuminates his philosophical intentions during the period he considered his intellectual peak, while exposing some of the more desperate rationalizations of the later period. But it does not account for the subversive elements of the teachings on natural goodness that run throughout his corpus or the ways in which the autobiographies develop these themes in profound and influential ways. My own approach is the "inversion of priorities." A prioritarian reading finds Rousseau developing certain themes across his corpus in accordance with a consistent anthropology, as both major paradigms have established in their various ways. However, the fundamental tone, priorities, and purpose of his writings can shift considerably.

CHAPTER 1

I Could Never Have Been an Unnatural Father

Explaining the Discarded Children (ca. 1746–1778)

Jean-Jacques Rousseau was one of the most eloquent champions of the duties and joys of family life, as well as one of the greatest theorists of educating the young. Yet he immediately consigned each of his own five children to a foundling home. This is widely recognized as the greatest paradox and scandal of his life and one of the most notorious anecdotes in the history of philosophy. Some of his supporters have been so disconcerted by it that they developed several theories—commonly asserted from the 1780s through the 1960s—that the children were not in fact his, due either to his impotence or to the infidelity of their mother, Thérèse Levasseur (1721–1801).[1] In addition to these two theories, some argued that Rousseau invented this as a fable in order to prove his sincerity,[2] and others that Thérèse and her mother successfully duped him about there even being children. After reviewing these four hypotheses, Bernard Gagnebin and Marcel Raymond present the decisive evidence against them, drawn from the admissions of Rousseau, the witnesses of his contemporaries, and documents discovered at the foundling home.[3] Raymond Trousson has recently confirmed that the essential state of the factual question has scarcely changed since the 1959 discussion of Gagnebin and Raymond.[4]

The records are thus clear enough that Rousseau and his cohabitant had five children between approximately 1746 and 1752.[5] What remain highly disputed are the implications for Rousseau's character, his standing as an arbiter of moral and political duties, and his basic intellectual intentions. In various discussions from 1751 to 1778, he grappled with these questions in a manner that was famously ambiguous and ambivalent. The leading biographers and editors of the last two generations have in general been sympathetic to Rousseau, but they have not been impressed by his self-defenses here. R. A. Leigh writes that the relevant pages in the *Confessions* "are certainly the most painful and the most contradictory of his book," and Maurice Cranston describes them as "one of the least compelling passages in that book."[6]

Although the topic has often been sensationalized, informed and sustained discussions are rare. The exceptions are Jean Guéhenno and Lester Crocker, who cite most of the relevant sources, but, I would argue, they are one-sided philosophically. Guéhenno's discussion is peculiar.[7] He concedes that Rousseau shirked his duty and that Rousseau's 1751 letter defending his actions was "base and ignoble."[8] Yet then, explicitly dismissing Rousseau's arguments, Guéhenno attributes the discarding ultimately to fate and the historical necessity of Rousseau obeying his unique genius, to "become himself."[9] History need not respect "our petty rules and petty virtues," and Guéhenno even chides those interested in the topic for wishing to reduce "exemplary men . . . to our own level in order to take our revenge on them for being great."[10] Crocker is nearly comprehensive in terms of the loci from which he draws, but he reveals hostile intent in the arguments he selects for presentation.[11] He, too, quickly dismisses Rousseau's argumentation, explaining the discarding as a result of psychological factors, including "latent homosexuality" and the "compulsive" acts of "the introspective neurotic."[12]

It appears, then, that no near-comprehensive discussion of Rousseau's children exists that is either systematically organized or philosophically oriented to discern the significance of this episode for his life and work. In being the first to present the evidence comprehensively and systematically, as well as to engage seriously with the full range of Rousseau's argumentation, this chapter is meant as a foundation for responsible discussion of this sad and bizarre chapter of intellectual history. It is otherwise restrained in its speculations, especially about possible psychological implications.

Despite the prominence of this issue in Rousseau's history, autobiographical reflections, and reception, many scholars opt to avoid mentioning it altogether. Many others offer brief accounts of the historical facts or some of Rousseau's arguments, without venturing further engagement.[13] Both approaches are perfectly legitimate, and yet, as a cumulative effect, scholars have been left with either unguided curiosity or largely untested assumptions about the complex relations between life and thought here. Of the small number of sustained discussions, most have been biographically and historically oriented.[14] Excellent work has been done in excavating the evidence and delineating its context. In these works and in more philosophical ones, some of Rousseau's rationales have been subjected to strong criticism or have been provided defense (normally in a qualified form). But most of these philosophical reflections have been offered in only a few sentences or paragraphs, and the most extensive discussions have been scattered throughout longer works, as discrete comments on separate passages. Since they have not attempted to present the evidence systematically, their final judgments of Rousseau have not responded to an adequate range of countervailing evidence. Raymond Trousson has perhaps been the most balanced among those who have offered sustained reflections, but even his selection and presentation of evidence elides key difficulties.[15]

Whether historical or philosophical, current stances on Rousseau and his discarded[16] children are tied to broader disputes about the ultimate meaning of his thought. They seem to fall into three main groups. First are those who see Rousseau as embodying extreme subjectivism, individualism, and/or narcissism, and thus appeal to his paternal delinquency as a paradigm of his reckless life and work.[17] Second, some perceive a similar individualism and autonomy in his thought and life, and the discarded children are either a proper way of pursuing his freedom and genius within his context[18] or a profound and consistent expression of modern political philosophy.[19] Third, some argue that Rousseau should be seen as a genuine advocate of virtue and justice in terms of his overall intentions; they see the case of the children as exceptional, and they emphasize his later statements of regret.[20] In each approach, what is taken to be most fundamental about his thought ends up akin to what is taken to be most pertinent about his life. (A logical fourth possibility, of straightforward hypocrisy—that Rousseau fully and consistently believed his rigorous prescriptions about the family but never cared about embodying them in his personal life—does not seem to have any defenders.) Thus, although the genuine meaning of one's philosophy might in principle be separate from any questions about one's personal life, the two have been closely linked in this case. This is especially natural concerning Rousseau, since he defended his personal life on moral grounds and in terms connected (in various ways) with his overall philosophy. Unlike many later interpreters, he did not see this as a curiosity to be sidestepped but as a substantive issue touching upon his credibility as a normative thinker. In responding to it in several different ways across three decades, he provides a unique window into his moral standing in his own eyes, and therefore also his view of what humans owe each other by nature, how this may be altered or distorted by society, and how to cope with moral failures (or apparent failures). For such reasons, carefully tracing the threads of Rousseau's discarded children is not merely for biographical interest, but also sheds light on his broader intentions and proper legacy.

I begin with a new approach—an analytical outline of each rationale Rousseau provided. Future discussions might usefully draw from that categorization, even if some details of the layout, or the implications drawn from it here, are found wanting. I also contextualize this case within eighteenth-century French family life. I then pursue our evidence more thematically than chronologically, beginning with Rousseau's strongest defenses of his decisions and working toward his most remorseful claims. (For those less familiar with the material, it may be useful first to consult the chronological recapitulation in Section 1.7 below.) The strongest defenses were offered in 1751 and 1778. The Second Part of the *Confessions* (1769–1770) is more ambiguous; in private letters of 1769–1770, this ambiguity leans toward remorse. The most complete remorse apparently develops in the period of *Emile* (ca. 1757–1762). In closing, I emphasize the complexity of Rousseau's shifts between defending, atoning for, and partially excusing his behavior, as well as the implications of this for his broader intentions and development. I offer a middle position between those who see his behavior and associated excuses as demonstrating his unchecked individualism and conventionalism and those who ultimately absolve this episode in order to find him a moralist in good standing.

1. Analytical Outline and Historical Context

The rationales may be clustered into five major categories. Specifications and variants are marked as subheadings. Headings and subheadings have been placed in the order in which an argument was first made, whether by the date of writing or—in works with multiple arguments, such as the astounding letter to Madame Dupin de Francueil of 20 April 1751[21]—by its placement within a single work. Dates in parentheses indicate each source that appeals to the argument of the subheading. Two letters from 1770 must be distinguished: to Madame de Berthier, of 17 January (as 1770a),[22] and to Claude Anglancier de Saint-Germain, of 26 February (as 1770b).[23] Posthumous works are referenced by the dates of their writing: Second Part of the *Confessions* (1769–1770), *Dialogues* (1772–1776), and *Reveries* (1778). (Although the *Reveries* was written from 1776 through 1778, this outline only draws from Walk IX, which was apparently written in 1778.)[24]

In addition to the likely birth dates mentioned above (1746–1752), the other pivotal historical event is the public exposure of this great secret in an anonymous pamphlet—now known to be by Voltaire—called *The Sentiment of the Citizens* (December 1764).[25] Among many harsh claims, including some fabrications, one charge pointed to the essential truth: Rousseau's companion (Thérèse) is an "unfortunate woman . . . whose children he exposed [*exposé*] at the door of a hospital."[26] The next month, Rousseau nearly published a response that evaded this charge on what seems to be a technicality: "I have never exposed [*exposé*], nor caused to be exposed [*fait exposer*] any child at the door of any hospital, or elsewhere" (cf. rationale 3.b below).[27] This pamphlet decisively altered Rousseau's accounts of his discarded children. Before Voltaire, we find the strangely moralistic confidence of a 1751 letter and the clear attempts to overcome a regretted past in the writings of 1760–1762. After Voltaire, we find oscillations between qualified excuse-making and typically defensive professions of remorse. The one exception to this late tendency occurs in the *Reveries* (rationale 6), where, at least on the surface, he fully affirms the original discarding. This is included as a sixth rationale to indicate this final shift, but because its content is not new I claim only five "major" rationales.

The rationales may be categorized as follows:

1. I would not have been able to bring them up.
    a. My illness prevented me from expecting a long life. (1751)[28]
    b. I was too poor and depended on precarious work for a living. (1751, 1769–1770 twice, 1770b, 1778)[29]
    c. This poverty is the fault of the rich. (1751)[30]
2. Their family situation would have been unacceptable.
    a. Their illegitimate birth would have brought shame to their mother. (1751, 1769–1770, 1770b)[31]
    b. Their illegitimate birth would have stigmatized them, making their future prospects bleak. (1751)[32]
    c. I needed to shield them from being raised by the indecent Levasseur family. (1769–1770 twice, 1778, cf. 1751)[33]
    d. In hindsight, I thank Heaven that my children were spared knowing me in my misfortunes, especially since my enemies would surely have taught them to hate, and perhaps even to betray, their father. (1769–1770, 1770a, 1770b, 1778)[34]

3. There were adequate public institutions for raising children.
   a. They would be fed better and more securely there than by me. (1751)[35]
   b. They were appropriately deposited there, not "exposed." (1751, cf. 1765)[36]
   c. They would be raised more hardily and usefully there than by me or by aristocrats. (1751, 1769–1770, 1770a, 1770b)[37]
   d. Their upbringing would be comparable to that of the children in the republic of Plato. (1751, 1769–1770)[38]
4. I later came to regret these actions, and to respond appropriately.
   a. *Emile* is an attempt to expiate my old sin (1760);[39] In it, with remorse, I confessed the actions almost openly (1761, 1762),[40] which should spare me the reproaches of decent people. (1769–1770, 1772–1776)[41]
   b. I became increasingly abstinent largely to avoid repeating the offense. (1769–1770)[42]
   c. I would rather expiate my faults than excuse them (1770a, 1770b, cf. 1769);[43] the fault was no doubt grave, and unpardonable, but it was my only one, and I have well-atoned for it. (1770b)[44]
5. If I was mistaken, I should not be fully or harshly blamed for it.
   a. I adopted the maxims and customs of those around me. (1769–1770, 1770b)[45]
   b. It was committed through reason, not from hardness of heart; I could never have been an unnatural father. (1769–1770, cf. 1770b and 1778)[46]
   c. I was acting in good faith; I did not desire to do harm, or see any harm in it. (1769–1770)[47]
   d. It was a fault, not a crime (1769),[48] and it was incomparably less severe than betraying a friend's confidence, as in the publicizing of my secret. (1769–1770, 1770a, 1770b, cf. 1765)[49]
   e. People should be pitied in misfortune, and much more if they are culpable; my duty was neglected through weakness. (1770a)[50]
6. I would do it again, with much less doubt, too, if I had to do it again. (1778)[51]

All told, we find twenty-five rationales; or, counting only the specific arguments of the subheadings, nineteen. Most readers have not found them particularly convincing, despite—or, perhaps, because of—their voluminousness. As Leo

Damrosch observes after a much shorter overview, they seem to be "what a psychoanalyst would call a case of overdetermination."[52]

Turning from Rousseau's shifting argumentation to the historical context mostly adds to our perplexity. Many scholars have contended that, in their setting, Rousseau's actions were not as outrageous as they have seemed in later centuries. Around 1750, the foundling *hôpitals* (hospices or homes)[53] of Paris were receiving around 17 percent of the infants baptized in that region, and these numbers would more than double by 1772.[54] Scholars disagree about the primary factor behind this. Illegitimacy and abandonment rates were evidently rising throughout eighteenth-century Europe, but those rates in France were particularly high, especially in Paris.[55] For instance, in Paris in 1772, 41 percent of the children born were given up to the hospice, and only around one in seven of these children was legitimate.[56] In a recent scholarly analysis, Matthew Gerber acknowledges the roles of poverty and illegitimacy throughout the eighteenth-century French foundling crisis. However, he argues that the spike in *early* eighteenth-century rates of abandonment occurred in a time of low illegitimacy and relative prosperity, and thus should be mainly attributed to legal changes undermining the rights of unwed mothers, as well as to the unintended consequences of the availability of the foundling homes.[57] Gerber also establishes that the unusually high rates in Paris were largely artificial, since, by the second half of the eighteenth century, transporting foundlings from the provinces to Paris had become a minor industry—and a lethal one.[58]

Although abandoning or depositing children was not uniformly prevalent, it was an especially common behavior of the socially marginal, including the "debutant intellectuals" of Paris. Bronisław Baczko maintains that even after "Jean-Jacques permanently acquired a higher social status, he persisted in behavior and attitudes characteristic of [social] marginality, of the vagabond as well as of the *petit intellectuel.* Obviously, we have in mind his affair with Thérèse, the semiliterate servant girl and, especially, his abandonment of their children."[59] Baczko draws from Robert Darnton, from whom I add: "The great figures of the early Enlightenment—Fontenelle, Duclos, Voltaire, d'Alembert—remained bachelors; or, if they fell into matrimony, as in the case of Diderot and Rousseau, it was with someone of their own station—shop girls and servants."[60]

For such reasons, according to Trousson, "Jean-Jacques is a celebrated case, not an exceptional one, and he was not wrong to say that he followed the custom of his country. . . . Female honor, poverty, the absence of contraception, and the insecurity and price of clandestine abortions explain, if they do not justify, these abandonments."[61] Moreover, even Rousseau's distinction that his children were properly "deposited," not "exposed" (rationale 3.b)[62]—though apparently so empty—has significance in its historical setting. Records indicate that in 1746, less than one-third of the children collected by the foundling hospital were properly deposited; most were exposed in streets or on the steps of churches, and thus left immediately to chance.[63] Several contemporary writers make it clear that there was a significant moral difference between this and direct placement in the foundling home. For instance, the relevant articles in Diderot's *Encyclopédie* draw a sharp distinction between, on the one hand, "this barbaric custom" of parents exposing their children outside of their home and, on the other, the easy reception of the infant in the foundling home. More optimistic than our current records, the Enlightenment author adds that the rise of such homes has thus made the crime of exposing infants "no longer heard of in this city."[64]

Although Rousseau may have been adopting the customs of those around him (rationale 5.a), historical evidence has not been as kind to his claims that his children would be raised hardily and usefully (3.c), or like Plato's *Republic* (3.d). In the 1751 letter to Francueil, he claims that his children would be raised, not "delicately" in "softness" but with a robust "rustic education," as honest, obscure "peasants or workers," in favorable contrast with their father (see [5]). The 1770 letters assume that this 1751 projection has come to pass: the children are living in "an obscure estate";[65] they are "workers or peasants" living in "peaceful obscurity."[66] Actually, foundling mortality rates were frighteningly high—of the infants received in 1751, 68 percent did not make it past their first year, compared to general infant mortality rates around 25 percent.[67] Looking at a longer time frame, in 1760 only around 17 percent of the infants received had lived past age five.[68] Damrosch explains why generally high infant mortality rates were much worse for foundlings: "They arrived malnourished and sickly, were crammed together in grossly unhygienic conditions, and were often badly cared for by their rural nurses if they lived long enough to get there."[69] Even for those who did survive, few fulfilled the official charter's promise of becoming soldiers, workers, and colonists. While the administration attempted to place them as servants or apprentices, they "were often ill-prepared for life outside the *Enfans-Trouvés*," "forced by their poverty into lives of libertinage and vagabondage," with tragic ends.[70]

Scholars are divided on whether we might assume that Rousseau was reasonably ignorant of these cruel realities or whether he ought to have known of them. Leigh proffers the charitable assumption, whereas Trousson claims he should have known.[71] Grant, who is, in general, a defender of Rousseau, argues that his intentions here are "suspect": "It would be easier to credit his claim that he truly intended their benefit had he troubled himself to learn (or allowed himself to acknowledge) the conditions in the Foundling Hospital. Knowing that the fate of his children was likely to be a tragic one, we are entitled to say that Rousseau's justifications were rationalizations of a wicked deed."[72]

Turning to hard evidence, the most relevant contemporary document was published anonymously by Charles Arrault in the *Mercure de France* in 1746, and was thus almost certainly known to Rousseau.[73] In general, it is an homage to the foundling home as a humanitarian effort, established by Saint Vincent de Paul in 1640 but increasingly centralized by the king and the Parisian authorities. Arrault clearly argues that this institution offers significant moral and political advantages over the crime of exposing infants in the streets.[74] Gerber also draws from Arrault in discussing the abuses from the earlier "decentralized and disorganized" foundling system: "Children were sold in the streets to beggars who maimed them to elicit public sympathy, to wet nurses who substituted them for their deceased charges, to prominent families who falsely posed them as heirs, and to witches who used them in rituals of black magic."[75] According to Arrault, this institution removes the pretext for this "inhumane and cruel" manner of getting rid of children whom parents believed they could not raise. Through this institution, "nature has recovered its rights in the heart[s]" of the parents, who wish to "preserve the life that they have given" their children.[76] However, Arrault also discusses the insufficiency of the ordinary revenues and the recurring difficulties for infrastructure, given the sharply increasing number of foundlings.[77] Indeed, his document closes with a call for charitable giving in order to rectify inadequacies of space and ventilation that had been responsible for the deaths of a "very great number" of foundling children through communicable sickness in 1739.[78] We might conclude that, despite Arrault's positive stance on the institution and on the superiority of proper depositing over exposition, it seems unlikely that a contemporary reader could be naively confident, and in complete good faith, that this was truly as safe as parental or adoptive care.

For Rousseau's part, in each of his discussions of his own children, he never reveals any awareness of the link between foundling status and high mortality rates. Yet a political fragment (likely dating around 1759) suggests that, at least by that point, the link had become straightforward in his mind. The fragment polemicizes about population and against urbanization, citing statistics on "Paris 1758": 19,148 baptisms (indicating births), among whom were 5,082 foundlings. He reflects that "the state kills them before their birth by making children onerous to their fathers" ("Political Fragments" IX, CW 4:53 / OC 3:528).[79] Consider also his comments, in the context of mothers who have temporarily sent their children out to the country to be nursed, crossed out from the Favre manuscript of *Emile*: "How many times in traveling through the countryside have I groaned at seeing how barbarously the nurslings from the city are treated there."[80]

The intellectual context provides several markers concerning self-justification and hypocrisy. Rousseau shared the moderate Enlightenment's kindness toward human nature, as well as its Malebranchean account of a God who works only through universal laws.[81] The Christian view of grace—of divine forgiveness as a pure gift for certain repentant individuals, even those with profoundly bad character or behavior—was not acceptable for these reasons, among others. But since Rousseau did not share the accommodating standards and easy conscience of many intellectuals of his time, his quest for justification proved harrowing. Perhaps his most fundamental solution is a distinction between moral "crime" (*crime*), which embodies an intention to harm, as opposed to "error," "mistake," "misdemeanor," or "fault" (*faute*), which was inseparable from the weakness of human nature, and should thus not be judged too harshly by God or man.[82]

Since Rousseau typically argued that he was guilty only of faults, we might pause to compare him with Benjamin Franklin, who describes some of his life's foibles as "*errata*"—printer's errors. These "faults," which he would like to correct if he were to repeat his life, can apparently be distinguished from "*wilful* gross Immorality or Injustice."[83] Whereas Rousseau prided himself on his near-flawless avoidance of prostitutes, Franklin's "hard-to-be-govern'd Passion of Youth, had hurried me frequently into Intrigues with low Women that fell in my Way."[84] The passive voice here is worthy of our great confessor, but in general Franklin's higher underlying self-confidence helped him to actually accomplish what Rousseau only claims to: "My present conduct might be blameable, but I leave it without attempting farther to excuse it, my present purpose being to relate Facts, and not to make Apologies for them."[85] And unlike Rousseau's longing for unattainable aristocratic ladies, Franklin ended up settling in marriage for Deborah Read, a dependable but not particularly appealing woman, whom he had previously mistreated.[86] They adopted and raised Franklin's natural son, William.

As we will see, at times Rousseau gravitated toward the more Christian (even Catholic) posture of admitting a truly severe moral failure and believed he might "expiate" or "atone" (*expier*) for it through suffering or good works. But more commonly and typically, he could not follow the model of Augustine, who could argue that he was ashamed of his youthful treatment of his concubine and had made a clean break with that past. (Biographically, Augustine compares favorably with Rousseau for raising his natural son, Adeodatus, until the death of Adeodatus at age seventeen, but he compares unfavorably in sending his concubine away in order to secure a socially and economically desirable marriage.[87] The concubine was among the issues that were being seized upon by Augustine's critics, prompting him to write his *Confessions*.[88]) Rousseau often tried to reform himself, but apparently his anthropology and self-understanding precluded him from denouncing his past behavior in a similar way. Accordingly, it is not repentance but excuses—showing why one's errors (or apparent ones) are understandable or acceptable, given their context and motivations—that usually play the crucial role in his personal appeals. As Karl Barth put it, "It is scarcely possible to find in these confessions an example of a truly undialectical piece of self-accusation."[89] In practice, these appeals could be most aptly compared not with the theological categories of justification and grace in Augustine or Calvin but with the jurisprudential categories of exculpation and mitigation in Grotius or Pufendorf.

The dates in the analytical outline (Section 1.1 above) indicate when each rationale was written down, but context also involves the time when each was supposedly implemented. One major development in Rousseau's thinking is described as occurring during Thérèse's third pregnancy (ca. 1750).[90] According to the *Confessions*, it was around this time that Rousseau was newly inspired to live in accordance with the "heroism and virtue" of his fatherland and his first *Discourse* (VIII, 298/356). The pregnancy thus made him reflect more on his own duties: "to examine my children's destiny and my relationship with their mother according to the laws of nature, justice, and reason, and of that pure and holy religion which is as eternal as its Author" (299/356).[91] This is in contrast with the simple complacency described in Book VII, regarding the first two pregnancies (ca. 1746–1748).[92] This earlier Jean-Jacques was content to follow "the customs of those around me" (rationale 5.a) in order to extricate himself from the "extreme difficulty" (287/342f). He learned these customs at the inn of Madame La Selle, where his refined dinner companions offered the highest praise to the bachelor who had most populated the foundling home (see 288-89/342-44).[93] Regarding this context, Cranston observes, "Before his 'reform,' his scruples, like his ambitions, were those of a young man of the world."[94] Finally, Thérèse's mother played a role; she "feared a new nuisance [*embarras*] of a rabble of kids" and "came to my aid" in convincing Thérèse of this solution, despite the latter's "groaning" (VII, 289/344).[95]

A concession might be made by some, that, for the first two births, insofar as Rousseau had no claim to moral standing but that of a downtrodden Parisian bohemian, our criticism of his behavior might not ultimately be directed against him so much as against the customs of his time and place. For instance, according to current philosopher Vittorio Hösle, "On the basis of an intentionalist ethics one has no choice but to recognize that someone who obeys the immoral norms of his culture bears no guilt, insofar as he had no opportunity to reflect on a possible alternative. The actions . . . must therefore be measured first of all by the norms of his own [culture's] mores; this insight of historicism cannot be surrendered."[96] Henry Chadwick applies similar reasoning to Augustine's case: "For a young man it was a regular custom to take a concubine until such time as he found a suitable fiancée, marriage being understood as a property deal between the two families. The modern criticism is not of Augustine so much as of the total society in which he was a member."[97] Granting all this as a general framework, we are still far from justifying the entire case of the discarded children, since the later ones were born after his personal reconsideration of his new principles.[98]

2. Unashamed Bookends, 1751 and 1778

It is only concerning the period after his reform that Rousseau offers his best-known rationales about the discarded children (Conf. VIII, 299–301/356–59). He mentions the April 1751 letter to Francueil in this context as well, and the timing suggests that the inquiry leading to it may have been prompted by the birth of his third child.[99] As both the letter and the later reflections indicate, although his behavior did not change—at least not at this point—Rousseau's intensified conscience required more elaborate self-defenses.[100] It should therefore not be surprising that, despite the historical proximity, the letter to Francueil does not mention that Rousseau was simply following the customs of those around him. Following the Parisian crowd could no longer suffice, at least not officially. In the above outline (Section 1.1), the later rationales involve the expiation (4) or mitigation (5) of acts which are admitted to be faults or that are, at least, highly questionable. By contrast, the first three rationales seek exculpation. Existing "prejudices" to the contrary notwithstanding, these utilitarian justifications grant no basis for shame or remorse (as distinguished from sadness). The decisions are said to be positively good, whether because of personal necessity in the face of economic injustice (rationale 1), an intolerable family situation (2), or the suitableness of the foundling institutions (3). Remarkably, with two exceptions related to timing,[101] each of the justifications that are documented under the first three headings was included in Rousseau's first statement, of 1751. Thus, the self-exculpation is highly comprehensive in this letter. Alongside the lack of any regretful or ambivalent claims, this accounts for its tone, which is widely described as aggressive or cruel.[102]

The 1751 letter's approaches to marriage and social injustice are especially noteworthy. Rousseau anticipates the objection: Why is he not married? "Ask your unjust laws, madame. It did not suit me to enter into an eternal commitment, and one will never prove to me that any duty obliges me to do so. What is certain is that I have done nothing of the sort and that I do not want to do anything of the sort" (LF [4]). These claims are quite surprising in view of his later defenses of marriage in works such as *Julie* and *Emile*.[103] The "eternal commitment" seems to be the issue, and yet Rousseau seems to be going further than the moderate arguments for divorce in Locke or Montesquieu.[104] This raises the question of whether Rousseau shared the libertinism of Diderot, at least as the latter would come to display it in works such as the *Supplement to the Voyage of Bougainville*—and, if so, when and in what sense the Genevan came to repudiate it.[105] Diderot objects to sexual stigma and to the moral requirement of an eternal commitment.[106] His published writings against "indissoluble" marriage begin around 1759, quite possibly in connection with his unhappy marriage.[107] Nonetheless, he and his wife had a daughter whom he loved deeply and for whom he arranged a first-rate education.[108] In another work of historical fiction, Diderot combines *Bougainville*'s argument about sexual vice as largely a consequence of "our absurd laws," with the observation that probably fewer than two in a hundred men are "faithful to the letter" to their wives, and the corresponding plea not to get overly upset by adultery, "a fault so trivial."[109] In his published writings, Rousseau comes closest to this spirit in the *Discourse on Inequality*, when he discusses "countries where morals still count for something and . . . where the duty of eternal fidelity only makes for adulteries, and where even the laws of continence and of honor inevitably increase debauchery, and multiply abortions" (I, 157/159).

After its repudiation of an eternal commitment, Rousseau's 1751 letter anticipates the objection that one should not have children if one cannot feed them. "I beg your pardon, madame: nature wishes us to have children because the earth produces enough to feed everybody, but it is the social station of the rich, it is your station that robs from my estate the bread of my children" (LF [4]).[110] It does not seem merely coincidental that Rousseau's next major work would be the second *Discourse* (1754–1755).[111] Not only does it powerfully condemn social injustice and stratification, but it argues that a "prodigious" population consistently emerged in a state of nature and among "barbarians" (Note IX, 202f/206f, and Note XVII, 221/222). This is contrasted with the deprivations that arise with "established property and hence society," including the array of "shameful ways there are to prevent the birth of human beings and to cheat nature," including homosexual acts, "secret abortions," or "the exposure [*l'exposition*] or murder of large numbers of children, victims of their parents' poverty or the mothers' barbarous shame" (Note IX, 200/204).[112] The general sociological and victimological approach of the second *Discourse* is also clearly anticipated in the 1751 letter: "If my poverty and my illness deprive me of the power of carrying out such a dear care, it is a misfortune about which I must feel sorry, and not a crime for which I must reproach myself. . . . You take for the dishonor of vice what is only the dishonor of poverty" (LF [1, 6]).

No doubt there was grinding poverty in France at the time, and this surely contributed to the foundling problem. But was Rousseau truly so poor and oppressed that he was incapable of supporting children? He was aware of the difficulties here; earlier in the letter, he offered a trichotomy to defend his course of action. Now working with his hands (in Paris), he scarcely makes enough money to support himself, let alone a family. In order to make more, he could, first, "have recourse to the profession of author," but "the worry [*tracas*] of children" would not leave him "the tranquility of mind necessary to do a lucrative work," and "writings dictated by hunger hardly bring in anything and that resource is soon exhausted." That leaves a second alternative, "to court some low employment," which would require intrigue and infamy in order to be lucrative, forcing him to drain "the life-blood of the needy" (LF [2]).[113] The implied logic is that because these alternatives are unacceptable, it was best to remain a mere copyist and send the children away. As it turns out, at various points in his life, Rousseau's associates took issue with him for refusing to accept honest work that might have provided more securely for Thérèse and others to whom he was obliged.[114] Given his premises about intellectual independence and the economic conditions of Paris, Rousseau would have vigorously denied the honesty of the sorts of work they had in mind. But even granting this, why, we might ask, remain in a region where luxury, population density, and the resulting cost of living make raising one's offspring nearly impossible for the common and upright person? It seems plausible to infer that Rousseau's personal ambitions for intellectual glory were the decisive (albeit conspicuously unspoken) factor here. Leigh, Trousson, and Cranston essentially agree that, despite all the stated rationales, the underlying and most fundamental reason for the decisions—arrived at as a kind of reflex—was the desire to maintain his freedom, and thus his quest for glory, rather than accept the burdens and distractions of a vulgar father.[115] According to Jean Fabre, Rousseau's masterpieces proved that he was right to avoid all personal commitments and cares.[116] Although this may be true from an outside perspective, Rousseau's later view was quite different. We might recall the repeated lament in the *Confessions*—expressed after he attained "celebrity," and it did him so little good—that if in his youth he had only settled in a decent place like Geneva or Fribourg and become a respectable craftsman, he could have been "a good Christian, a good citizen, a good father, a good friend, a good worker, a good man in all ways" (I, 36f/43f).[117] Even before his persecution and the revelation of his great secret, he counseled Antoine-Jacques Roustan that, despite the talent that could allow Roustan to succeed as a man of letters, he should learn from Rousseau's experience and be content with obscurity: "Be a good father, good husband, good professor, good regent, good minister, good Citizen, simple man in everything, and nothing more, and I promise you a happy life."[118]

All things considered, few careful scholars have been inclined to agree with Rousseau's early defense of discarding his children as necessary and proper.[119] More generally, we might concede that there is a third-person empirical plausibility to his "sociological perspective," and we have seen that his behavior was at least somewhat characteristic of economically marginal people during this time.[120] Nonetheless, we might infer from this paradigmatic case that, from a first-person perspective, explaining one's decisions primarily in terms of context might unduly increase reckless and inhumane actions.[121]

The letter to Francueil's confidence in the objective justice of Rousseau's decision appears to be reaffirmed in his last writing. The *Reveries* appeals to many of the older rationales, responding at length to what he saw as an implied slander, that Rousseau must hate children because he abandoned his own.[122] Most pathetically, throughout the extended passage he appeals to his tenderness and not being an unnatural father (rationale 5.b; Rev. IX, 123-25/1086-88). For instance, "It would assuredly be the most unbelievable thing in the world that the *Héloïse* and the *Emile* were the work of a man who did not love children" and "I do not believe any man has ever loved to see little bambinos frolic and play together more than I" (125, 123/1088, 1087).[123] He concludes: "I would do it again, with much less doubt too, if I had to do it again; and I well know that no father is more tender than I would have been toward them, once habit had combined with nature" (124/1087, rationale 6).[124] This marks the only clear endorsement of the discarding—as opposed to his fundamentally good character—besides the 1751 letter. And yet, following three paragraphs of a rambling discussion on how he has come to understand the human heart, and how his misfortunes and his age repel people from him, we seem to find regret and longing assert themselves: "Oh! if I still had a few moments of pure affection which comes from the heart, were it only from a babe in arms; if I could still see in some eyes the joy and contentment of being with me which I used to see so often . . . , for how many ills and sorrows would these short but sweet effusions of my heart not compensate me? Ah! I would not be obliged to seek among animals for the look of benevolence which is henceforth denied me among humans" (126/1089).[125] He then recalls a walk of two years prior, when a boy of five or six years was found "squeezing my knees with all his might while looking up at me in such a friendly and affectionate manner that I was inwardly moved, and I said to myself: 'This is how I would have been treated by my own.' I took the child in my arms, [and] kissed him several times in a kind of rapture" (Rev. IX, 126/1089). The memory turns out to be bittersweet in a few ways, but it is plausible to see in *Reveries* IX an oscillation of guilt, self-defense, and remorse, rather than a definitive statement of serenity or philosophical conviction.[126] Rousseau has thus not fully returned to the confident moral posture that blusters throughout the letter to Francueil. At the same time, his normative philosophy about the justifiability of his original actions is close to the 1751 account—only now, we might infer, he is even more to be pitied, since he is not only deprived of parental joys but haunted by deep loss and loneliness.[127] It is not clear how long held or stable this shift in normative philosophy was; it may have been a momentary oscillation, or an outgrowth of the more antinomian solitude that Rousseau apparently came to embrace in his final years.[128]

3. Ambiguity in the Second Part of the *Confessions*, 1769–1770

The famous rationales of the *Confessions* might best be understood by juxtaposing them with the confident defenses just discussed, especially the letter to Francueil. Readers approaching this issue mainly through the *Confessions* are likely to be struck by Rousseau's leniency with himself and the many (sometimes incompatible) rationales he provides there. By contrast, the memoir claims that he is being highly restrained in mentioning his earlier justifications, both because he does not want to lead young men astray by the reasons that "deceived" him and because his purpose is to write a confession, not to accuse or excuse himself.[129] Remarkably, compared to the 1751 letter, he was highly restrained—at least in terms of exculpatory rationales. For the most part, exculpatory claims are either omitted or spoken of only as his beliefs at the time, not as current judgments of what was objectively moral. His poverty (rationale 1.b), the illegitimacy of the births (2.a), and the greater usefulness of their upbringing as foundlings (3.c) are mentioned only in passing as contributing to his original decision. The famous comparison with Plato's *Republic* (3.d) is also only historical: "I will content myself with saying that my reason was such that by handing over [*livrant*] my children to public education for lack of power to bring them up myself; by destining them to become workers and peasants rather than adventurers and fortune hunters, I believed I was performing an action of a Citizen and father, and I looked at myself as a member of the Republic of Plato" (Conf. VIII, 299/357).[130] In the case of Plato, Rousseau is explicitly speaking only of his beliefs during the depositing of the third child and, by implication (cf. 300/357), the following two. The argument was robustly stated in the letter to Francueil [6], surrounded by arguments that Rousseau has been deprived of "the sweetness of paternal embraces" and that "the prejudices of the world" oppose his decision: "In his republic Plato wanted all the children to be brought up in such a way that each would remain unknown to his father and all would be children of the state."[131]

However, two claims from the first three (exculpatory) headings make their first appearance in the *Confessions*, and they seem to be given current moral weight. The first is that the children would have been atrociously raised by the Levasseur family (rationale 2.c). He claims this was omitted from the letter to Francueil only because it would have compromised Thérèse's mother and family, even though it was the "most decisive" and strongest reason then available to him.[132] (This personal case seems to be in mind in Rousseau's general advice that gentlemen not marry women from the class of people that does not think: "Besides, how will a woman who has no habit of reflecting raise her children? How will she incline them toward virtues she does not know, toward merit of which she has no idea?" E V, 408f/767f).[133] Despite all the ambiguity throughout the *Confessions*, he even seems to affirm that these judgments were prudent, as a better upbringing for the children: "I trembled at the thought of handing them over to this badly brought up family so that they might be even more badly brought up. The risks of having them educated by the foundlings were considerably fewer. . . . One may judge by the morals of [Thérèse's] wretched brother, if ever—whatever else may be said on the subject—I should have exposed my children to an upbringing like his" (Conf. IX, 349/415f).[134] This is the strongest endorsement of the original decisions found in the *Confessions*, and this rationale remains central in the final self-affirmation of the *Reveries*, where he claims that fear for the children of "a fate a thousand times worse" than the foundling home was what "surely most determined" his decision (IX, 79/1087). However, the implications of this exculpatory argument are different from those in the letter to Francueil. According to that early account, anyone financially strained who has public foundling alternatives available would be fully justified in depositing his children. But according to this later argument, one would need to be caught within a very particular and highly corrosive set of familial circumstances. Nonetheless, paralleling what we noted in the case of the letter, even if the abstract reasoning is potentially viable, it remains unclear that Jean-Jacques was in fact so helplessly trapped, whether in terms of changing location,[135] reforming familial dynamics, or avoiding multiple pregnancies.[136]

The second novel exculpatory rationale (2.d) in the *Confessions* is more peculiar, being based on hindsight. Rousseau expresses ambivalence concerning whether the children would have been brought up as decent people under Madame d'Épinay or Madame de Luxembourg, and then continues: "but I am sure that they would have been brought to hate, perhaps to betray their parents: it was a hundred times better they never knew them" (VIII, 300/357). The language is similar in the letter to Madame de Berthier: "I would prefer that they live in an obscure state without knowing me, than to see them, in my adversity, basely nourished by the treacherous generosity of my enemies, ardent to instruct them to hate, and perhaps to betray their father."[137] In the *Reveries*, Rousseau is convinced that "what Muhammad made of Zayd is nothing compared with what [the conspirators] would have made of [my children] on my account" (IX, 124/1087). (In the historically loose account to which Rousseau probably alludes, "Voltaire's Muhammad is an utter scoundrel who tricks Zayd into committing parricide and then kills him.")[138]

Unlike the other exculpatory rationales, this one is not meant to justify Rousseau's decisions on their original bases. But it does alleviate his current experience of guilt, and he even expresses thanks to heaven (*le Ciel*) for his decision to send his children away, thus preserving them and himself from this fate.[139] In this and other contexts, the conspiracy also allows him to make some (rather distasteful) attacks in passing, against those friends who revealed his secret. This treachery, committed against a friend, reveals true "baseness of soul," far worse than his mere "fault," however "great" (5.d).[140] Yet, in stating his case, he finds himself at cross-purposes. For, when arguing against his treacherous friends, he needs to contrast the strong sentiments and obligations deriving from an established friendship, with the relatively weak ones of a father who has never seen his children (Conf. VIII, 301/359). By contrast, when he is establishing that he could never have been "an unnatural father," his sentiments toward his children are exceedingly tender, and it was only his reason that was at fault (5.b). In a long paragraph, he questions whether he might have been one of those "misbegotten individuals, deaf to nature's sweet [*doux*] voice," evincing mere "hardening" (*endurcissement*) and trampling "ruthlessly underfoot that sweetest of duties." Appealing to higher sentiments in him that are incompatible with all this, he boldly concludes that this combination is impossible: "Never for a single moment in his life could Jean-Jacques have been without sentiment, without a heart [*entrailles*], an unnatural father [*pere dénaturé*]. I may have deceived myself, but I could never have hardened myself" (299/356f).[141] In a similar difficulty, whereas here (5.b) he locates his true moral identity and fundamental goodness in his heart as opposed to his reason, when he is comforting himself with hindsight about the conspiracy (2.d), the "regrets of my heart" are overcome by "my reason," which perceives how heaven has "protected [my children] from their father's fate" (299/357).

But these passages are exceptions, and the predominant moral strategy of the *Confessions* regarding the children is not exculpatory but mitigative. The main discussion (VIII, 299-301/356-59) focuses in his current voice almost entirely on rationale 5, that he should not be fully or harshly blamed for his actions. This is apparently the chosen emphasis because he is uncertain whether he still believes the exculpatory rationales and whether they will be convincing to others. He must therefore be convincing at least in establishing that it was the utilitarian—even altruistic—motivation that truly prevailed within him. Thus, the focus on internal factors: his moral influences (5.a), his faulty reason (in contrast with his heart, 5.b), his lack of an intention to harm (5.c), and the difference between a fault and a crime (5.d).

For all its ambiguity, this discussion of the children should be seen as forging a middle position between the objective defense of his actions and the admission of serious guilt alongside a search to compensate. He grants that his decision was highly questionable, and (sometimes) even a great "fault," but somewhat understandable under the circumstances and given his mental and sentimental state. Consider, for instance, the noncommittal opening to the discussion, following the announcement of the third pregnancy and the need to rethink his earlier expedient: "If I was mistaken in my conclusions, nothing is more remarkable than the security of mind with which I yielded to them" (Conf. VIII, 299/356).[142]

Of the mitigative rationales, Rousseau seems the most confident when contending that the desire to harm never entered his heart or mind (rationale 5.c). In the following, he is explaining why he openly shared his secret with several friends: "I truly saw no harm [*aucun mal*] in it. Taken all in all, I chose for my children what was best for them, or what I believed to be so. I would have liked, I still would like, to have been brought up and provided for as they have been" (Conf. VIII, 300/358).[143] Another claim about harm is perhaps the closest that Book VIII comes to a thesis about the children: "My fault was great, but it was committed through error. I neglected my duty, but the desire to harm never entered my heart" (301/359).[144] Despite all the mitigation, he stops short of affirming that he made the right decision or that he would do the same thing again. In these ways, the *Confessions* shows far more ambivalence than the two chronological bookends, which, at least on their face and in their explicit argumentation, claim full moral confidence—the letter to Francueil and the *Reveries*.

More generally, it is these mitigative, subjective lines of argument that have provoked some of the most serious analysts to take issue with Rousseau. According to some, he has a dangerously sharp division between supposed intention and all concrete behavior.[145] In addition, he almost always elides blunt criticism of himself, often by seeing fate as responsible for his actions.[146] This can be seen as part of his general philosophical project of positing the source of genuine evil as being entirely outside of the self,[147] a theme described well by Jean Starobinski: "Rousseau invariably needs to construct an external, exculpatory genealogy of evil."[148] Otherwise put, "Evil originates outside the self and remains external to it."[149]

4. Vacillation Around the *Confessions*, ca. 1764–1770

If the *Confessions* primarily mitigates culpability on the basis of Jean-Jacques's internal states when he made the decisions about his children, many other claims—written around 1759 to 1770—straightforwardly admit the severity of the fault. They do not attempt to justify the objective acts or the subjective states leading to them but, rather, his life as a whole, either by expiating these faults through subsequent actions or sentiments or outweighing them through the overall moral balance of his life (rationale 4). It is this rationale alone that approximates a traditional concept of "confession," stating a condemnable act without reinterpreting it in a favorable light, while also being willing to take decisive action to amend or compensate for it. Although this approach is not entirely absent from the *Confessions*, it is weak there. For instance, his claim that he became increasingly abstinent largely in order to avoid impregnating Thérèse again (4.b) seems to be a kind of repentance. But it is unlikely that he judged this an especially strong factor contributing to his abstinence, compared to his wish to avoid aggravating his urinary condition. The official statement of the rationale contains this ambiguity: "I feared a repetition of the same offence and, reluctant to take this risk, felt that I would rather condemn myself to abstinence than expose Thérèse to finding herself once again in the same situation. I had noticed, besides, that commerce with women aggravated my condition appreciably; this twofold reason had caused me to form resolutions I had sometimes kept badly enough, but in which I had been persisting with greater constancy for the past three or four years" (Conf. XII, 498/594f).[150] The physical explanation stands alone in his 1761 letter to Madame de Luxembourg: "Since my retreat to Montmorency [April 1756 or December 1757], my state of health has forced me to live with her as a sister."[151]

Similarly, there is the discussion of *Emile* in the *Confessions*, offered as a two-sentence aside within a discussion of Thérèse's character and her growing coolness toward Rousseau. Although it mentions remorse, it does so in the past tense, referring only to the time of writing *Emile*. In terms of current sentiments or judgments, it only rebukes those who would still reproach him after the kind of admission he made:

> The decision I had come to with regard to my children, however well considered it had seemed to me to be, had left me with a heart that was not always easy. While contemplating my treatise on education, I had come to feel [*je sentis*] that I had neglected duties from which nothing could absolve me. My remorse finally [*enfin*] became so acute that a public admission of my error [*faute*] was almost torn from me at the beginning of *Emile*, where its application to me is so obvious that it is surprising that, after reading such a passage, anyone should have had the heart to reproach me with it further. (Conf. XII, 497/594)[152]

Peter France cites this passage as an example of confession as a "preemptive strike": "When he has accused himself, no one else has the right to accuse him."[153] The authorial distance formally parallels that taken from the earlier, exculpatory rationales. But while in those cases he was explicitly breaking from rationales he could no longer (fully) endorse, regarding *Emile* it is not clear why he does not confess—in a present voice—his culpability, his guilt feelings, or his labors in expiating that guilt.[154]

By contrast, these more vulnerable, expiatory confessions seem to be a major approach in at least three letters written around the time the Second Part of the *Confessions* was composed, and in the next section we will see that these follow a pattern that began around 1759. In a November 1769 letter to Thérèse, Rousseau combines expiation (rationale 4.c) with the casuistic form of mitigation, that this "fault" was not a "crime" (5.d). Apparently writing to dissuade her from leaving him, he encourages her "to crown an unfortunate but innocent, honest and virtuous life by an end which will honor it and assure us a durable happiness. We have our faults [*fautes*] to lament and to expiate; but, thank heaven, we have in us neither darkness nor crimes [*crimes*] to reproach. Let us not blot out by the imprudence of our last days the sweetness and the purity of those we have passed together."[155] In the January 1770 letter to Madame de Berthier, his plea for mitigation does not come from denying or qualifying the severity of his fault as a father: "Madame, pity those whom an iron fate deprives of such a happiness; pity them if they are only unfortunate; pity them much more if they are culpable" (5.e).[156] The same letter then insists that he would never bend his maxims in order to make them fit his conduct, thereby falsifying "the holy laws of nature and of duty in order to extenuate my faults." He continues, "I would rather expiate [*expier*] them than excuse them;[157] when my reason tells me that in my situation I did what I should have done, I believe it less than my heart, which groans and contradicts it."[158] These last two guilty clauses are repeated verbatim in the letter to Saint-Germain in the following month. He mentions the reasons that made him deposit his children, saying they "prevented me from myself fulfilling the first, the most holy of the laws of nature; in this, far from excusing myself, I accuse myself; and when my reason tells me that in my situation I did what I should have done, I believe it less than I believe my heart, which groans and contradicts it."[159] However, he proceeds with a self-defense of unusual energy. He begins by decrying the art with which "the barbarians" have come to portray his fault: "How they painted me all the more as an unnatural father because I have groaned; how they have sought in the depths of my character a fault [*faute*] which was the work of my misfortune; as if to sin [*pécher*] was not of man and even of the just man. It was grave, no doubt, it was inexcusable; but it was also the only one, and I have well-atoned [*bien expié*] for it. Except this, and vices which have never done any harm except to me, I can expose to all eyes a life irreproachable in every secret of my heart."[160] Along with the exculpatory rationale of "my misfortune," we find here a range of mitigative rationales about the state of his heart, his internal character, and the fallibility of humanity. In addition, we find that this was his only "fault" (4.c)—or perhaps "grave" fault—and he has expiated for it. It is not clear whether the compensation was through active moral labor, through sufferings inflicted upon him, or both. Related ideas had been developed in the First Part of the *Confessions*, even if those discussions of Marion (a fellow servant whom he blamed for his own act of theft) and of Le Maître (a friend abandoned in Lyon) seem to contradict the 1770 letter's claim that he has only committed one serious fault.[161] Especially in the case of Marion, he writes that his guilty conscience has avenged this act every day since (Conf. II, 71/85). But he finally expresses hope that such a crime can be "expiated," and perhaps has been through his many misfortunes and by "forty years of uprightness and honor in difficult circumstances" (73/87). These discussions in the First Part, written from around 1764 through 1767, exemplify the more unqualified sort of confession. Therefore, they might be seen as continuing the spirit that began around 1759 and that was temporarily displaced by the more self-justifying spirit of the Second Part of the *Confessions*.

Many have criticized attempts to discern this kind of shift in Rousseau over time; in the case of his children, however, he directly authorized it. We find this in the *Reveries*, in explaining why he once publicly lied about having had children. He describes a dinner that occurred "some time ago" when he was asked whether he had had any children: "Blushing up to my eyes, I replied that I had not had this good fortune." This lie is described as a mechanical effect of his embarrassment: "Previously, I did not have this embarrassment and I would admit my faults with more frankness than shame, because I did not doubt that people saw what redeemed [*rachetoit*] them and what I felt inside myself. But a mischievous eye distresses and disconcerts me: in becoming more unfortunate, I have become more timid, and I have never lied except due to timidity" (IV, 54/1034f; cf. RJJ II, 190/905). Given the likely timing of this dinner, Rousseau's loss of confidence and increased tendency to lie is portrayed as having commenced a dozen years beforehand—around the time of Voltaire's revelation of the secret.[162]

The Second Part of the *Confessions* seems closest to the more defensive elements of the letter to Saint-Germain.[163] But unlike the discussion of the children in that part of the *Confessions*, the 1769 letter to Thérèse and both 1770 letters mention expiation, while unambiguously expressing remorse. Why such a contrast, in both tone and argumentation? Although there are genuine concerns about appealing to letters in discerning an author's intention, those do not seem pertinent here, partly because Rousseau clearly intended his copy of the letter to

Saint-Germain to be preserved for posterity and partly because the letter to Francueil undermines the possibility that Rousseau is more openly remorseful in his letters and more defensive in his published writings.[164] Insofar as the difference may be based on the form of the writings, it seems more plausible to suggest that he was being more sincere in these letters written to confidants, whereas in the Second Part of the *Confessions* he seems to use sincerity largely as a tool to gain his audience's approval, thus overcoming his enemies' attempts to destroy his reputation (cf. Conf. 229/273). It is at least as likely that these differences in the expression of guilt are rooted in differences across time. According to the most careful study of the manuscripts of the *Confessions*, Rousseau's January letter to Berthier was written after the section on his children in Book VIII, and the letter thus brought back memories of that recent account.[165] That precludes us from reading the 1770 letters as the last expressions of a pattern of higher remorse (which would thus have become more ambiguous with the Second Part of the *Confessions*, and then triumphantly overcome by the time of the *Reveries*). Rather, the *Confessions* represent a temporary oscillation—perhaps through some combination of internal lack of confidence and public defensiveness—away from overt remorse. Remorse would then resurge in the letters written only one to three months later. However, none of these differences should be pushed too far, since in each case from 1764 through 1770, a certain amount of remorse is expressed, and the author attempts to demonstrate—in one way or another—that he is fundamentally good nonetheless.

5. Evolution in *Emile*, ca. 1757–1762

During the period of *Emile* and other normative masterpieces, Rousseau's rationales about the children are exclusively expiatory—striving to compensate for a fault that is clearly acknowledged as severe (rationale 4). These arguments are also the only ones that appeal to his behavior or mental states occurring *after* the discarding, unlike the objective exculpations of the goodness of the act (1-3) or the subjective mitigation of culpability based on mental states at the time of the decisions (5).[166] Although the statement of this rationale in *Emile* itself is straightforward, its development and context raise questions.

According to a 1760 letter, Rousseau's guilt about the children was a leading motivation for writing the *Emile*: "There remains an old sin [*pêché*] to expiate in print; after that the public will never hear of me again."[167] This is a one-sentence aside within a paragraph explaining his plan to retire from the vocation of author. The expiation, apparently, would be that by writing *Emile*, he was extending his time in a craft he finds painful, for the sake of a higher cause. Similarly, in 1761, he believed himself to be dying, and entrusted Madame de Luxembourg with caring for Thérèse upon his death. He revealed to Luxembourg the secret about his children in order to indicate his special obligations to Thérèse, and he mentioned regret for having taken "so little precaution for ever recognizing them afterwards. For several years remorse for this negligence has disturbed my repose, and I shall die without being able to rectify it, to the great regret of the mother and myself. . . . The ideas my fault have filled my mind with have greatly contributed to making me contemplate the Treatise on Education; and you will find, in Book I, a passage which may indicate this disposition to you."[168] This alludes to an indirect avowal in *Emile*, which follows an argument that personally and soundly raising one's children fulfills a man's "triple debt"—to the species, to society, and to the state. "He who cannot fulfill the duties of a father has no right to become one. Neither poverty nor labors nor concern for public opinion exempts him from feeding his children and from raising them himself. Readers, you can believe me. I predict to whoever has a heart [*entrailles*] and neglects such holy duties that he will long shed bitter tears for his offense and will never find consolation for it" (E I, 49/262f).[169] Here we find not only a deep statement of remorse but also a rejection of several rationales that had been offered in the letter to Francueil.

What led to this veiled but unqualified confession? According to the 1761 letter to Luxembourg, Rousseau's remorse largely gave rise to *Emile*. That would trace the remorse at least to 1757, and perhaps as far back as 1754.[170] However, those who have most carefully studied the manuscripts, John Spink and his student Peter Jimack, have argued vigorously against this interpretation. They favor, instead, the later claim in the *Confessions*, that it was "while" writing *Emile* that Rousseau "felt" remorse—perhaps suggesting "came to feel"—and the avowal was "finally" drawn from him.[171] Spink and Jimack find no traces of personal guilt in the earliest drafts of the manuscript. They argue that *Emile* is not the product of the remorse; rather, "It was the composition of the Emile which provoked the remorse."[172] Unlike the impersonal, theoretical treatise it began as, *Emile* comes to develop novelistic elements with an imaginary pupil and Jean-Jacques as the imaginary tutor, who takes up all the duties and rights of fatherhood (E I, 52f/267, cf. Favre, CW 13:16 / OC 4:71). It is apparently through increasingly identifying himself with the tutor that Rousseau began to reconsider the gap between his creation and his actual life. For Jimack, we first find the highly personal elements indicating remorse in a portion written around May 1759.[173] There, the characters refer to each other as "my father" and "my son," and Emile insists that "so holy and so sweet a duty" as raising his own child should be fulfilled only by himself (see E V, 446, 472, 480/820, 857, 867).[174] The famous indirect avowal is inserted even later, as a revision to the penultimate manuscript, thus dating well into 1760.[175]

This argument about the evolution of the text is suggestive and, as far as it goes, convincing. And yet one might reply that it does not prove that guilt was not present prior to 1759, but only that *overt* guilt was not present.[176] For instance, even if it is not stated in the personal way highlighted by Jimack and Spink, the early portion of the Favre manuscript unambiguously asserts the duties of the father as "the true preceptor" of his children, obligated to raise whatever family is given to him.[177] It was also just prior to beginning *Emile* in earnest that Rousseau penned—in 1758—the moving portrayals of domestic education in *Julie*.[178] If he initially avoided sensitive formulations of the topic in the work on education, this might just as plausibly be a reflection of guilt as of true moral confidence. In any case, implications derived from composition and psychological state will always remain disputable. John T. Scott questions Jimack's sort of reading, "which privileges the psychological state of the author and the process of composition over its content."[179]

More certain is that Rousseau's stated philosophy is quite different in the final *Emile* than in the letter to Francueil, both in the sort of duties he defends and in his concessions that he has not lived up to them. Critics such as Crocker have gone to great lengths to deny the moral significance of these sorts of claims: "Although there were a few moments when emotion led him to betray his guilt feelings, the character of his overt defenses is the refusal of guilt."[180] "Far more likely" than these professions being mere image boosting is that Rousseau "felt no guilt at first," but "later, when his inner anguish grew into ever greater turmoil, when he felt himself accused by a whole world of enemies . . . , his conscience was awakened."[181] I would counter that the relevant social hounding cannot be said to have begun until *The Sentiment of the Citizens*, which Crocker knows was published in 1764.[182] Crocker is therefore left with chronological problems about *Emile*. He contends, regarding its indirect avowal, that Rousseau "later claimed [the book] was a compensation for the abandonment."[183] However, the most relevant claims do not come later, but in letters from 1760–1761. Crocker mentions the "great remorse" of the 1761 letter to Luxembourg but interjects that there was "no apology" and ultimately ends up insisting, "*the only act that counted was the first one.*"[184] It would be better to recognize that Rousseau sometimes denies guilt, sometimes mitigates it, and sometimes accepts it fairly severely. Moreover, this last stance arose internally and affected his moral self-understanding and intellectual intention.

How should we explain this development? Having become a "new man" at Vincennes in 1749, is it plausible that Rousseau was still so casual about his fatherly duties through 1759 or just a few years before that? Should we instead conclude that he was always this casual, and that his avowed shift was superficial or insincere? Demonstrable answers cannot be given, but perhaps the most plausible view is that his prolonged lack of remorse—or apparent, or overt, remorse—was linked in a surprising way to his early public philosophy. Previous scholars have considered the puzzle that Rousseau continued to discard his children for some time after his "personal reform." Some have connected this with his early political idea that the public should raise children—and, correspondingly, that individuals have little if any responsibility for their young.[185] In this case, the discarding would not be an embarrassing contrast of low character with high principles but an expression of his "*civisme*."[186] Insofar as he found this a satisfying reconciliation of life and thought, he would have been overlooking the chasm between his ideal of a republic's universal public raising of children and his actual context of a monarchy's ramshackle institutions for the destitute.[187] This reconciliation is unconvincing enough that he may have come to rethink his political ideal alongside his domestic obligations. After 1755, even in his politically oriented writings, he apparently no longer requires that children move out of their parents' home in order to receive public education.[188]

Overall, Rousseau's paternal failures may not be as outrageous as they seem to be to current readers at first glance, given the customs of the time. And, yet, in view of the actual prospects of foundlings amid aristocratic France, the consequences of his discarding were almost certainly dire. This undermines his most ambitious, exculpatory justifications that his decisions were on balance beneficial. His fatherly contrition might reduce the gap between the principles stated in his domestic ethic and those revealed in the autobiographies. Even so, the gap remains large enough to raise serious questions about sincerity and hypocrisy, and, as we will see in the concluding section, the leading interpreters have taken very different approaches here.

6. Conclusion: The Moralist, the Apologist, and the Meaning of It All

The subtlest interpretations of the discarding in relation to Rousseau's thought seem to fall into two major categories.[189] One of these, commonly maintained in the Straussian tradition, is that Rousseau's merely physical relationship with

Thérèse—and his response to their children—is largely modeled on the natural life of the savages. Hence, this is the most extensive relationship that an independent and philosophical type like Jean-Jacques should have with a woman.[190] This reading is linked with a broader methodology opposed to seeing his personality as the key to his thought, or (especially) reducing his thought to supposed psychological tendencies.[191] These scholars instead interpret his philosophical books on their own terms, but Roger Masters explores the additional possibility of reversing the biographical method by interpreting Rousseau's "autobiographical writings and personal actions in terms of his philosophy."[192] His one selected example is the 1751 letter to Francueil, where Rousseau's arguments "flow directly from his radical insistence on the primacy of individual freedom and the artificiality of conventional opinion."[193] On these readings, Rousseau's philosophy is profoundly consistent over the course of his writings and is revealed in its genuine or highest form in his philosophical portrayals of his solitary life. There is no problem in reconciling this with the domestic ethic since philosophical readers could independently perceive it to be merely exoteric.

There are several important observations here, but it may be too strong to say that with Thérèse, Rousseau was approximating the natural wholeness of the savages in accordance with a genuinely normative model.[194] Instead, we might infer that he often found the relationship with Thérèse emotionally and intellectually unsatisfying, and, at many points (both in life and in writing), he accordingly reduced her to merely physical uses.[195] These uses might be justified—or rationalized—by his paradigm of primitive humanity, developed in the *Discourse on Inequality*, which I would argue is primarily *historical* rather than normative. However, this reduction does not appear to be the whole story. Damrosch cites Rousseau's remarks that he never felt a spark of love for her and finds it a much later perspective that is "unconvincing" about their early relationship: "The reality was very different, as his words and actions on many other occasions showed."[196] Yet, even in the best of times, something was plainly lacking. I contend that Rousseau's contractual concubinage was a narrowly targeted exception to a more robust marital ideal in which Rousseau genuinely believed and to which he would have adhered under more favorable circumstances. In particular—as he sometimes suggested—his life would have been quite different had he been united with someone he considered suitable and worthy of himself, such as an unattached Sophie d'Houdetot or a willing Madame de Warens.[197]

In general, here it seems that the gaps between his normative principles and his autobiographical writings are best explained through his casuistry and targeted exceptions, including many inserted plainly within his normative teachings. For instance, masturbation is discussed well by Joel Schwartz, citing the important treatments by Starobinski and Jacques Derrida, and indicating that Rousseau indulged in this vice, away from which he strenuously kept Emile.[198] However, the casuistic exception that (basically) legitimates Rousseau is already included in his public domestic ethic. He prescribes that, after the age of twenty, this sort of continence "becomes a duty of morality," admitting of modifications and exceptions, and "human weakness" may make it the lesser of two evils, a mere "offense [*faute*]" (E IV, 334/663). Such exceptions would not need to be carved out if we were dealing with sweeping public pronouncements put forward only for common minds, and coolly recognized in private as inapplicable to the philosopher.[199]

The issue can never be settled, but looking at the key periods of later writings on the discarded children, from 1759–1762, 1765, and 1769–1770, we have significant evidence that Rousseau was consumed by guilt for the better part of a dozen years. It is difficult to conceive how this happens if one has confidently accepted as uniquely philosophical the view that humans have no objective positive obligations toward their children, and one has only pretended to believe the contrary in order to avoid persecution or promote social utility. Even in the 1751 letter to Francueil, so contrary to conventional and classical ethics in so many ways, Rousseau does assume objective duties: "If a refuge for them did not exist, I would do my duty and resolve to die of hunger myself rather than not feed them."[200] Similarly, he condemns the "unworthy father who could resolve upon that barbarism" of leaving his children "in the streets exposed to perish if chance does not save them" (LF [4-5]). Although this chapter has explored much of the best evidence that Rousseau ultimately did not believe his moralistic teachings, in the end, this seems unlikely as a claim about his overall intentions. Note also that Straussians oppose interpreting philosophy in view of biography primarily because this approach militates against the serious treatment of the philosophy. But the case here is nearly the reverse: I appeal to his biography and the philosophical presentations of it in order to challenge reductive interpretations of the philosophy.[201]

The Straussian approach is the most sophisticated interpretation that makes Rousseau's discarding and later defenses into a paradigm of what is most fundamental in his thought—viewed as a kind of individualism and conventionalism. The most important alternative reverses both premises, seeing him as a profound advocate of virtue and justice and his children as an unfortunate exception that he came to regret as he matured. This is the sort of reconciliation of life and principles pioneered by the Kantians, and, in the case of the children, its best statement might be drawn together from Trousson's biography.[202] Against the fantastical route of salvaging Rousseau by denying his paternity, Trousson observes that this is not only implausible but unnecessary—"as if the bohemian, the mercenary of 1747, had already become the exemplary citizen of Geneva, the virtuous mentor, the director of conscience of the years around 1760."[203] Although this man became "the conscience of modern times," he did not yet exist in 1746, and he would come "to judge himself severely one day: few people have gone through as marked a rupture between the first part and the second part of their existence."[204] Despite the outline given in the *Confessions*, in reality his great "reform" was only progressively realized and was filled with relapses over the course of three or four years.[205] Rousseau's justifying rationales in the letter to Francueil are "curious" and leave a "painful" impression, but his untranquil conscience is revealed by the fact of encoding. In the *Reveries*, he forced himself to say he would make the same decision again, but the realities of guilt, social longing, and his "poisoned wound" soon reveal themselves.[206]

Much can be affirmed from this reading, to which we might add that no one should be expected fully to live up to her own normative ideals.[207] And yet, something seems lost by simply allowing Rousseau to mature (with various setbacks) beyond his youthful waywardness, while seeing in his later discussions regret as the reality, and apologetics as mere appearance. We have seen that he typically precludes himself from relating to his past in the manner of Augustine. In terms of our analysis, his expiatory arguments (rationale 4) move in this direction, but they are the exclusive approach only from 1759–1762, while being appealed to elsewhere only in 1769–1770, and then almost entirely in private letters. This in itself would be no great problem for Trousson's kind of interpretation were it not for the persistent appeals to the more self-justifying rationales throughout the rest of the corpus—exculpatory in 1751 and 1778 and mitigative in the Second Part of the *Confessions* and related letters (1769–1770). Trousson's account of Rousseau's underlying psychology is not implausible—especially after 1764, the proliferation of excuses might be accounted for better through paranoia and obsessive guilt feelings than through newfound sincerity or substantive intellectual development. Moreover, one might plausibly infer that, at the time of inserting his indirect avowal in *Emile*, he may have expected this to be his only public statement on the topic of his children. Thus, the autobiographical turn after 1764–1765 is a truly unfortunate one for those who would prefer to read Rousseau as a moralist in completely good standing. All this being said, the underlying psychology is only one side of the question, and the author's stated rationales are likely the more important side.[208] In this case, these rationales could naturally be used to justify almost any behavior, even if at various points Rousseau offered other principles that might restrain the excessive subjectivity which may result from a focus on intentions and the heart.[209] Overall, it is reasonable to argue that the act of discarding may be considered incidental or peripheral to his thought. Even so, his excuses for it should be considered fundamental, since they express a broad and deep philosophy of natural goodness corrupted through society, the main practical implication of which is greatly to reduce, and often to eliminate, personal responsibility for vice and moral "fault" (albeit not *usually* for moral "crime").[210]

If the Veiled Antinomian reading of Masters and Kelly cannot account for the sincere moralizing phases of Rousseau's development and if the Flawed Moralist reading of Trousson cannot account for its practically demoralizing phases, what remains? We see that Rousseau's discarded children led him sometimes to acknowledge profound remorse and undertake moral labors as compensation, but, at other times, they led him to relentless apologetics and casuistry. These are comparably real aspects of his psychology and life history and are linked with comparably significant aspects of his philosophical

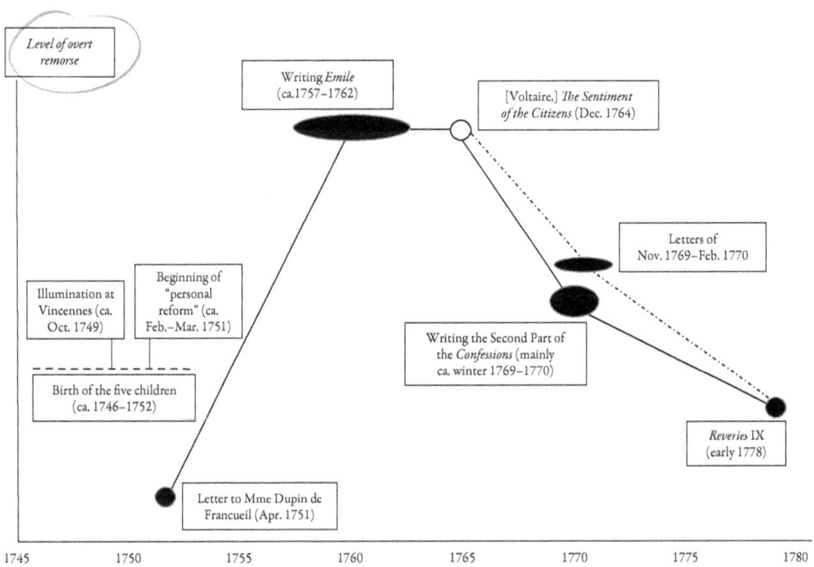

Figure 3. Chronological schematization of Rousseau's discarded children.

argumentation and cultural legacy. While this may seem intuitive as stated, the interpretive traditions have stoutly resisted this combination of theses, instead positing one side as real or fundamental and the other as appearance or peripheral.

Given the contradictory thrusts of his nineteen rationales, one can offer no simple absolution. Rousseau might be pitied for his misfortunes and even his culpability. Yet, his typical hedging of that culpability only enhances the tragedy of this case.

7. Chronological Recapitulation

The story of Rousseau's discarded children is complex, in part because of Rousseau's multiple shifts across time and in part because of his ambivalence at most times. In view of this chapter's thematic structure, a brief chronological summary may be of use. In Figure 3, determining the level of overt remorse requires judgment calls, and little weight should be placed on exact alignments in that dimension. Nonetheless, certain major turning points and shifts of emphasis are apparent. The ovals and circles represent our legitimate data points; the lines are merely placeholders, and might better be envisioned as wavy rather than straight. The dotted lines linked with the letters of 1769–1770 suggest the contrast between these private remarks and the more defensive posture taken in the overlapping period of the *Confessions*.

CHAPTER 2

I Became Another Man

Reforms, Relapses, and the Soul of the Author (ca. 1749–1762)

Having dwelt extensively on the disturbing case of Rousseau's discarded children, for our proceedings to be sound, we must also turn to the kinds of evidence that Rousseau thought pointed in his favor. Perhaps chief among these are the benefits he intended to provide humanity through his writings during his main period of authorship (ca. 1749–1762), as well as the way of life he pursued in order to bring these writings to fruition and to embody their ideals as plausibly as he could. It may seem strange to consider his authorship as ending in 1762, given the output that continued until his death. However, even before his persecution and exile in June, he had planned to retire from writing after the publications of that year.[1] A letter from around this time claims that after "having tried ten years the sad craft [*métier*] of author, for which he was not made, [he] renounces it in the joy of his heart . . . quitting the pen to never pick it up again."[2] A few clarifications are in order. Writing new books, properly speaking, seems to be distinguished from more leisurely or mechanical activities, such as completing lesser manuscripts, assembling collected writings editions, and writing his memoirs (see Conf. X, 432–33/515–17; XI, 469/560f; XII, 521/622). Accordingly, a late retrospective discusses the sense in which *Emile* is his final writing: "the other two writings that he has published since then [i.e., *Beaumont* and *Mountain*] no longer being part of his system and destined only to the personal defense of his homeland and his honor" (RJJ III, 211/933).[3] Finally, considering works published during Rousseau's lifetime, Christopher Kelly and Eve Grace emphasize how, excepting the *Dictionary of Music* (1767), which was "substantially completed five years earlier," Rousseau did not publish or intend to publish any other work after 1765.[4]

Here I argue, contrary to the most common views of Jean-Jacques, that he made concerted efforts to conform his character to his elevated teachings on virtue and duty. Our main source is Books VIII–XI of the *Confessions*, which contain the most official discussion of his motivations and conduct during his main authorship period. He describes his "effervescence" upon discovering his core philosophical insight (1749), as well as his "personal reform" undertaken to live up to these new principles. That much is relatively well-known to specialists. However, there are several ambiguities in the *Confessions* account, and scholars have drawn very different inferences about the soul of our author. It remains disputed when these moral changes began, how serious and sincere they were, and when or in what sense they ended.

Specifically, some have followed the main suggestion of the *Confessions*, in seeing his period of effervescence to be limited to his time in Paris (1749–1756).[5] This centers on "critical" works, such as the first and second *Discourses*. By contrast, others have placed his effervescent period after his departure from Paris (1756–1762), thus associating it with his more "constructive" writings, *Julie*, *Emile*, and the *Social Contract*.[6] A difficulty that emerges, then, is that even though the general idea of a phase during which Rousseau was effervescent with virtue would seem to support more edifying or elevated views of his intentions, the works that best fit these interpretations may not even be included in his own idea of his effervescent stage. David Gauthier—a more subversive interpreter—pursues this, finding that after his departure from Paris, Rousseau returned to his true nature as "an unstable paranoid" and saw that his subsequent works lacked his earlier "celestial fire."[7] Conversely, subversive or reductive interpreters often see the *Discourse on Inequality* as crucial, but the *Confessions* seems to present it as the high-water mark of his enthusiasm for virtue. In the most philosophically substantive analysis of the *Confessions*—*Rousseau's Exemplary Life: The* Confessions *as Political Philosophy* by Christopher Kelly—an indirect answer may be provided. For Kelly, although the illumination at Vincennes gave Rousseau his core discovery about nature,[8] in the enthusiasm that immediately followed his discovery, he actually became "less natural than he had been before." Instead of pursuing the natural life of independence and contentedness, he is led astray by "noble pride," enthusiasm for virtue, and other drives specifically rooted in *amour-propre* and civilization.[9] In this reading, the original human nature of the second *Discourse* is Rousseau's fundamental model, but it took Jean-Jacques years of experience to live in accordance with it. Thus, in this case, his philosophical principles were far ahead of his life.

These moves by Gauthier, Kelly, and others are linked with disputes on the overall coherence of Rousseau's way of thinking, both systematically and over time. Rousseau insisted on his fundamental consistency at several points,[10] and, for more than a generation, the leading philosophical interpretations have followed him.[11] While sharing the aspiration to seek as much philosophical consistency as feasible, my findings here suggest that genuine tensions and developments should not be reduced to a few sentences or footnotes.[12] This would be more in keeping with Robert Wokler and a few others, who maintain a thesis of fundamental unity, while allowing for chronological shifts and development.[13]

1. Resolved in Paris? (1749–1756)

Rousseau's accounts of his character follow the terminology developed in his normative writings, notably a dichotomy between "goodness" and "virtue." The former is natural; primarily passive and negative, it entails a lack of intention to harm others unless this is necessary for one's own preservation (e.g., DOI I, 154/157f; E V, 444/817f). The latter is acquired, active, and rare, entailing a forceful victory over one's affections and passions for the sake of a higher good (e.g., DSA I, 7/8; *Julie* I.39, 97/118; E V, 444f/817f). In the First Part of the *Confessions* (Books I–VI), Rousseau points to various factors that shaped his character. While divulging his gaffes, faults, and peculiarities, he insists upon his decent intentions and sentiments, as well as the history and circumstances that exculpate or mitigate his faults. His most consistent and confident self-portrayal is thus of goodness and of having certain seeds of and longings for virtue, which were planted in him from his early childhood. We see this, for instance, in connection with reading Plutarch with his father (Conf. I, 8/9), and in his discussions with the Abbé Gaime (III, 77/91f). A second layer originates with his return to Madame de Warens, who had moved from Annecy to Chambéry (1732–1741, including summer retreats at Les Charmettes). At this point, he claims, he started becoming virtuous (V, 150/179; VI, 217–21/259–64).

The Second Part of the *Confessions* (Books VII–XII) opens with a long period in Paris (ca. summer 1742–spring 1756),[14] which was professionally undistinguished prior to the first *Discourse* (1750–1751). As we have seen regarding his children, association with urban bachelors and leading men of letters led him to adopt at least some of their more dissolute ways (Conf. VII, 288–89/343–45).[15] During this period before his breakthrough, some of his writings explicitly renounce the ideals of his republican youth. In his "Letter to Parisot" (dated July 1742), Rousseau renounced the "fierce maxims," "sad austerity of the Stoa," and "harshness [*dureté*]" of his republican childhood. By then, he had come to love "humanity" and cherish "gentleness [*la douceur*]," respecting the rank and imitating the virtues of the great (CW 12:17 / OC 2:1140).[16] He even defends luxury and commerce in his (ca. 1741) "Letter to M. Bordes" (see CW 12:11f / OC 1:1131f). Thus, his behavior and outlook may have been difficult to distinguish from mainstream *philosophes*, artists, and their aristocratic patrons. His retrospectives pass over his final "pre-Rousseauian" years (1746–1749) very rapidly—in fewer than ten pages.[17] We are thus left with difficult questions about where to find rupture and where continuity.

Although some historical details and the overall impact of his experience have been disputed, Rousseau famously described how his early moral and intellectual wandering was overturned by his "illumination" at Vincennes (ca. October 1749).[18] Upon reading the Academy of Dijon's question on whether the recovery of the sciences and the arts had contributed to the purification of morals, "I saw another universe and I became another man" (Conf. VIII, 294/351). After referring the reader to the *Letters to Malesherbes* (II, 575–76/1135–36) for the details of the illumination, Rousseau describes the period that followed: "With the most inconceivable rapidity my feelings raised themselves to the tone of my ideas. All my little passions were stifled by enthusiasm for truth, for freedom, for virtue, and what is most surprising is that this effervescence maintained itself in my heart during *more than four or five years* to as high a degree perhaps as it has ever been in the heart of any other man" (Conf. VIII, 295/351, emphasis added). Unfortunately, Rousseau's accounts of his effervescence for virtue are difficult to align. He has a tendency, which has often been observed, to speak in absolute and irreconcilable ways about becoming an entirely different man, becoming happy or miserable for the first time, or having his fate decisively settled by a given event.[19]

For instance, when did these great changes begin? The above passage mentions an immediate change of "feelings" as well as ideas, but behavior and character seem to have lagged behind. Following the account of Vincennes, he admits, in the *Confessions*, that even after writing the *Discourse on the Sciences and Arts* (October 1749–March 1750), "false shame" and fear of ridicule prevented him from living in accordance with his principles and openly attacking the prevailing maxims of his age. But upon hearing that he won the prize (July 1750), "This news reawakened all the ideas that had inspired it, gave them a new lease on life, and at last caused to germinate in my heart that first seed of heroism and virtue which my father and my fatherland and Plutarch had sown there during my childhood" (Conf. VIII, 298/356).[20] Nonetheless, it was only another public success—the publication of that *Discourse* (January 1751)—which prompts his "personal reform." Traditional accounts follow the *Confessions* in linking this with the resignation of his position as cashier to the Dupin de Francueil household (304/362), which they place around February–March 1751.[21] He then resolved to earn his living with his hands, as a copyist of music (304–5/363–64). Other sources also link the first stage of his reform to the resignation of "the post I then held" and the shift to copying music (Rev. III, 31/1014f).[22] However, the spur to this is also said to be the arrival of his fortieth birthday (June 1752),[23] and Leigh places the actual resignation from the cashier position still later (October–November 1752).[24] For our purposes, nothing great seems to hinge on these details. It may be best to follow Leigh in seeing the retrospective accounts as "simplified" or "stylized" narratives, whereas historically there were several major starting points to the personal reform.[25] Moreover, even in the *Confessions*, there are several important cases of aligning or reconsidering his behavior in view of the newly adopted principles, which apparently occurred before what he *calls* the beginning of the reform.[26] It seems, then, that he gives "personal reform" a somewhat narrow meaning, perhaps especially linked to public comportment and vocation. Therefore, any inquiry focused on the broader question of adherence to principles—or attempted, or perceived adherence—must look beyond the explicit reform to the broader moral changes undertaken around this time. For simplicity, to remain closer to Rousseau's most sustained narrative (the *Confessions*), I will refer to February–March 1751 as the main beginning of the reform. Even if Rousseau was mistaken about the timing of the cashier position, it appears that he accurately linked the publication of the first *Discourse* to significant personal resolutions.[27]

Like the beginning point of these changes, their overall direction is multifaceted and somewhat murky. Rousseau resigned from his position with the Dupins for various reasons, including his belief in his impending death, as well as the profession's repugnancy, unsuitability, and inconsistency with his recently adopted "stern principles" (Conf. VIII, 303–4/361–62). Renouncing all thought of fortune or preferment, he was determined to live in independence and poverty, "breaking the shackles of opinion" and undertaking an objective which was "perhaps the greatest, or at least the most useful to virtue, that a mortal has ever conceived" (303f/362).[28] His reform began with his appearance—he gave up his sword, gold trimmings, and white stockings; he sold his watch, and adopted a short, simple wig.[29] By contrast, in Venice a decade before, he was conspicuously stylish, parading a sword at his side.[30] Although he initially kept his more refined clothing, his sumptuary reforms were inadvertently aided when someone—evidently Thérèse's brother—stole his fine linen shirts (305/364).[31] Another outward expression was fearlessness in trampling proprieties while socializing, although he grants that these efforts were somewhat feigned and "so contrary to my natural disposition [*mon naturel*]" (309/368f).[32] After similarly discussing "the epoch of my external and material reform," the parallel *Reveries* account describes that of "my intellectual and moral reform" (III, 33/1016). This leads to an important discussion of how he settled his "opinions and principles once and for all" (33/1016), and in particular his religious views, culminating in "approximately" what he wrote in the "Profession of Faith of the Savoyard Vicar" (34/1018).

Our author claims that the Second Part of the *Confessions* is full of errors, and he did not even have time to reread it (Conf. 229/273).[33] This may partially explain why in Book IX, after describing his move from Paris to the Hermitage (April 1756), Rousseau provides a full reprise of his earlier transformation, which was discussed extensively in Book VIII. Here the transformation is casually placed around the time of the first *Discourse*:

> Up until then I had been good; I now became virtuous, or at least intoxicated with virtue. This intoxication had begun in my head, but it moved to my heart, where, upon the debris of my uprooted vanity, the noblest pride sprang up. This was no act; I became in reality what I appeared to be, and, for the *four years at least during which this state of ferment continued at its height*, there was nothing fine or great that can enter the heart of man of which I would not, with heaven's help, have been capable. This was the source of the sudden eloquence, of that truly celestial flame which, setting me on fire, spread through all my early works, and of which not one single spark had escaped during the previous forty years, because it had not yet been kindled. (Conf. IX, 350/416)[34]

This condition was "most contrary to my natural disposition," and yet it lasted "almost six years" (350/417). We thus find two more estimates of the effervescent period, in addition to the "more than four or five years" from Book VIII (295/351), which was said to begin either with Vincennes (ca. October 1749) or with the "personal reform" (ca. February–March 1751). In any case, after Jean-Jacques became "truly transformed," his friends and acquaintances could no longer recognize him. The timid and easily ashamed man had become audacious, intrepid, and proud, scorning the manners and prejudices of his age—and "crushing their little witticisms" like insects. This was quite different from the tongue-tied man Paris knew "two years previously" (350/416f).

Before turning to its denouement, we pause to ask, what are we to make of this intellectual and moral ferment? Jean Starobinski and Christopher Kelly are among the few who have offered sustained philosophical discussions of it.[35] Although very different in intellectual method, they each offer what might be called deflationary readings, based on arguments that the effervescent stage was fundamentally out of keeping with Rousseau's genuine character (Starobinski) or his philosophy (Kelly).

For Starobinski, even though at one point Rousseau had some desire to embody his self-made public image as the virtuous Roman citizen or the "great soul who suffers at the sight of corruption and iniquity," eventually he returns to his "'true nature,' which is weaker, more sensual, more contradictory."[36] Starobinski focuses on the tensions in the retrospectives: The fervent Jean-Jacques is said to be in "the state most contrary to my nature," yet "I became in fact what I appeared to be"; Rousseau praises "the noblest pride" in this transformation, while on the same page "he describes his enthusiasm for virtue as 'foolish pride.'"[37] To Starobinski, this indicates that he was not lying or putting on a mask, but that "he believes in his lies."[38] While later writing the *Confessions* at Wootton or Monquin (1766–1770), Rousseau comes to believe that this "enthusiasm of truth, freedom, and virtue" had in fact "done violence to his spontaneous nature."[39] In retrospect, the "intoxication" with virtue appeared parallel to the conspiracy: As an "alien force" which "compelled him to betray his true self."[40] His "own inner truth" is compounded of "weakness, fickleness, and instability."[41] Overall, "in his private life—concubinage with Thérèse, abandoned children—Rousseau knows that, despite his justifications, the being does not coincide with the appearance: he does not resemble the virtuous fathers of ancient Rome. And one knows that later on Rousseau will cease to claim virtue, which demands an effort he feels unable to make. It will be enough for him to claim pure and natural spontaneity, goodness, innocence, or in any case nonmalfeasance which can go along with weakness."[42] For Starobinski, the effervescence and reform were a half-hearted and, in some cases, insincere posture of virtue; it is no surprise that they were short-lived and later renounced.

Among interpreters who are fundamentally critical of Rousseau, Starobinski is unusual in maintaining the respect of scholars in the field, who tend to be (at least at some basic level) more favorable to their subject. Although he has justly earned this respect, in some cases his generally negative judgment and his thesis about Rousseau's overarching psychological unity may lead him to overstep his mark. Specifically, Starobinski allows for chronological development on a few points, such as the main emphasis across Rousseau's writings.[43] However, in terms of Jean-Jacques's overall character and ethical orientation, Starobinski tends to infer continuity, on the model of the lowest moments and latest phases. Regarding effervescence and reform, Starobinski is right to point to a critical distance between the author of the *Confessions* and the earlier Jean-Jacques portrayed. That author knew that the burning enthusiasm of those years had not sustained itself and that his intellectual project was devastating for his happiness. Even so, this critical distance does not seem to be as sweeping as Starobinski perceives. For instance, it is not his "enthusiasm for virtue," which Rousseau describes as "foolish pride"; instead, he claims it was "the illusion of my foolish pride" that made him believe "I was made to dispel" all the illusions of our wise men and social order (Conf. IX, 349/416).[44] Similarly, the project of *Julie* to promote religious toleration had "little sense [*peu sensé*]," since it "assumed good faith among men" (366/436).[45] An early statement of doubt about his project is in an important letter of 1762: "It is one of the things which has made me the most tepid and discouraged during my brief literary career, to feel that, even supposing I had all the talents which I would need, I would attack fatal errors fruitlessly, and that if I would be able to vanquish them, things would not become better."[46] Overall, he comes to view his earlier project as quixotic, but he still insists that it is the public whose unreason is greater.[47] The public's illusions and fatal errors also had more staying power, and capacity for vengeance, than the young idealist seems to have imagined.[48] He deeply regrets its personal results, without castigating the genuineness of the transformation or suggesting that it was a form of self-inflicted violence.

More generally, Starobinski raises legitimate questions about the sincerity and genuineness of these changes; we know that many of Rousseau's contemporaries harbored similar doubts.[49] His own retrospective seems to perceive more mixed motives than his earlier self did, while still insisting that what happened was uniquely powerful in its effects (cf. Conf. VI, 218/260). This, too, has contemporary support. Consider d'Alembert, writing in 1762: "One has to have known Rousseau, as I did, to see how the courage to defy everything made his spirit take off. Fifteen years ago I saw him circumspect, timid, and almost a flatterer, and what he wrote was mediocre."[50] Many questions remain about Rousseau's public self and relations with virtue. Yet the theory of a simple mask leaves unexplained this period of historic intellectual achievement. It is more likely that—as with many cases of genius—mind, sentiment, and conduct reinforced one another in a unique way, generating results that are far more distinguished than many contemporary minds of impeccable talent and burning ambition.

If the bedrock of Starobinski's interpretive strategy is Jean-Jacques's psychology, for Kelly it is Rousseau's philosophical principles, which are taken as the purpose of the autobiographical project, and interpreted in the light of them.[51] Overall, for Kelly, the *Confessions* is the story of how Jean-Jacques, though misguided in his imagination and education, was able—through personal peculiarities and a series of accidents—to break free from the illusions of civilization and discover the nature which civilization had so profoundly distorted and covered for so long.[52] In addition to showing how this was possible, the *Confessions* is meant to portray Jean-Jacques as a new "exemplary life," replacing the earlier, limited models of Socrates, Cato, and Jesus.[53] However, his path of return is circuitous. Although he discovers nature intellectually at Vincennes, in practice he does not return to a "natural or quasi-natural condition" of contented independence, as he had briefly experienced at Les Charmettes after becoming disillusioned with Madame de Warens (*Confessions* Book VI).[54] Rather, Jean-Jacques becomes "drunk with virtue" and filled with "the most noble pride" (Conf. VIII, 350/416).[55] For Kelly, the lack of tranquility in the soul and the noble pride—a form of *amour-propre*—are indications that "the discovery of nature does not return his feelings to a natural state."[56] Similarly, "That the discovery of nature causes an intoxication with virtue indicates that there is no necessary relation between knowing what nature is and living according to it."[57] Although Jean-Jacques makes "continuous efforts" during this period of effervescence to "reform his personal life to make it compatible with these new ideas and feelings," in his enthusiasm "for truth, for liberty, for virtue," he was attempting to combine "incompatible elements."[58] Although being turned into "another man" reveals how he discovers his system, it also makes him "less natural than he had been before."[59]

I agree with Kelly that Rousseau's accounts of his life can be read as expressing his philosophy and that gaps between his life and his philosophical teachings should be accounted for. Nonetheless, it seems that Kelly, in keeping with the strictest Straussian readers, is overly rigorous in positing the primitives of the second *Discourse* as Rousseau's most authoritative standard, and this leads him at times to mistake the intentions of the *Confessions*. As some have argued at length, primitive natural simplicity constitutes one standard frequently used by Rousseau, but in *Emile*, *Julie*, and even in the *Social Contract* and other political writings, he gives highly sophisticated accounts of how lives can be richer and fuller within society and by adhering to virtue, and how this can be natural in a qualified sense.[60] This reading of his normative thought seems to cohere better with the retrospectives on Vincennes. For, if his discovery plainly revealed that the only philosophically justifiable life is one of natural independence, on the basic model of primitive humanity, how did Jean-Jacques end up aspiring enthusiastically "for truth, for liberty, for virtue"? Why did this effervescence go on for several years "to as high a degree perhaps as it has ever been in the heart of any other man" (Conf. VIII, 295/351)? This moves beyond the problem of an effect without a cause, since the effect and the cause move in opposite directions. The whole trajectory that made him a historic figure would be not only unexplained but additionally clouded by the retrospective account.

Moreover, this would not be a mundane case of hypocrisy, where principles are offered that are somehow nobler than the speaker's practice. It would be a case of acting and feeling far above the moral level that one's principles would justify, and doing so not as a strategic compromise with the realities of society[61] but in a kind of rapture. We know that Rousseau often expresses embarrassment or regret at the gaps between his principles and his practice, often attributing the failures to circumstances, personality, earlier habits, or the influence of old friends. But does he ever express embarrassment over acting more demandingly than his known principles could justify?

Admittedly, Rousseau does think it is *possible* to behave in a more demanding and elevated manner than one's principles would justify. This is portrayed by Wolmar, the eventual husband of the heroine of the novel *Julie*. As a religious skeptic, he "does not believe any of what gives a value to the virtues," and thus even as he does good, he is "insensible to everything that makes doing good agreeable, and by the oddest inconsistency [*inconséquence*] thinking like the impious [*en impie*] and living like a Christian" (*Julie* V.5, 481, 484/588, 591).[62] This seems to result from an early life spent in countries with nearly universal religious hypocrisy (482f/588f), alongside a highly unusual disposition, which is cold and obeys reason alone, doing good by inclination and without expectation of reward.[63] Thus, this kind of inverted hypocrisy seems to be portrayed as unique. Moreover, this disposition is very different from St. Preux's character, which is the one signaled as autobiographically based (Conf. IX, 362/430).

If Jean-Jacques is no Wolmar, what were the forces behind his change? On deflationary readings, their effects would be similar to what Rousseau alleges of Molière and other intelligent satirists: "They are men who, at the most, sometimes make fun of the vices without ever making virtue loved—men who, as one of the ancients said, know how to snuff out the lamp but who never put any oil in it" (LdA 35/276/32).[64] No doubt, there are many civilized passions that

Rousseau would prefer to snuff out. Yet the early philosopher, like his early works, seems somehow to have found morally elevated sentiments, principles, and ways of life that were worthy of dedication, and even enthusiasm.

2. Collapsed in Montmorency? (1756–1762)

Having outlined the kind of moral enthusiasm that changed Rousseau's outlook, we have already seen a related problem. The discussions of effervescence in Books VIII and IX of the *Confessions* are perhaps most surprising for how much they differ from a fairly intuitive understanding of the course of Rousseau's authorship, which is perhaps most clearly articulated by Kantian approaches. On these readings, after the "critical" warm-up of the early discourses, Rousseau came to express his mature views on virtue, duty, and freedom in his "constructive" masterpieces.[65] Although he was ambivalent about *Julie* (1761),[66] and the *Social Contract* (1762) has a somewhat fragmentary status,[67] it is now well-known that he declared *Emile* (1762) his "best," "greatest," and "most important" book.[68] He was also proud of the *Letter to d'Alembert* (1758), especially in hindsight.[69] Based on the content of the writings, if he was ever a "friend of virtue," it would seem to be during this period. Some scholars have accordingly described 1756–1762 as the period of effervescence or intoxication with virtue.[70] This would cohere with seeing the departure from Paris as the most public expression of the embrace of virtue and natural simplicity, escalating the personal and intellectual break from the *philosophes*.[71] However, what we have seen in the *Confessions* suggests that 1755 or 1756 concludes the period of effervescence, rather than initiates it. Thus, if the more reductive or deflationary interpretations have difficulties with the Parisian period, it is the more constructive or elevated interpretations that are on the defensive here. David Gauthier, a reductionist, has seized this opportunity. Since on Rousseau's own accounts, his reawakening lasts only until he left Paris (April 1756),[72] for Gauthier, the subsequent works are gentler, but, as we have seen, they lack the "celestial fire" of his Parisian ones.[73] He adds: "Rousseau was right to think that he had become a different man in the aftermath of his illumination, a man whose trajectory led him to be the Citizen whose task it was to expose the injustice of the existing social order, but that after his departure from Paris, he lost the zeal of that different man."[74]

At one level, this seems correct. However much oscillation and qualification Rousseau provided about the onset and peak of effervescence, in multiple passages he presents its dissipation as straightforwardly linked with his departure from Paris. Scholars have also plausibly established that, at the time of writing *Confessions* Book IX,[75] he wanted to emphasize the "second revolution," associated with the move to the Hermitage, as disastrous for his personal aspirations and happiness. Yet, we will need to take a closer look at what I will refer to as the broader Montmorency period (April 1756–June 1762). This period includes the time at the Hermitage of Madame d'Épinay (April 1756–December 1757), and then at the Montlouis of the Luxembourgs, with periodic stays at their Petit Château (December 1757–June 1762).[76] This analysis again complicates Rousseau's development, shedding a different light on his intellectual achievements and moral outlook during this period.

As we have seen, after describing his move to the country, he reprises his earlier intoxication with virtue (Conf. IX, 350/416).[77] He had become "someone else" for "almost six years," and this change

> perhaps would be lasting still but for the particular circumstances that cut it short and restored me to nature, above which I had tried to rise.
>
> This change began as soon as I had left Paris and as soon as the spectacle of that great city's vices no longer fuelled the indignation it had inspired in me. When I no longer beheld men, I no longer despised them; when I no longer beheld the wicked, I no longer hated them. My heart, which was not made to hate, could henceforward only lament their wretchedness, from which it no longer distinguished their wickedness.[78] This gentler but much less sublime mood soon dulled the ardent enthusiasm that had transported me for so long; and, almost without noticing it myself, I became once again fearful, obliging, timid; in a word, the same Jean-Jacques I had been before. (Conf. IX, 350/417)[79]

He is ceasing to be "someone else"; we see a change in mood, somehow connected with a change in social manner.[80] The next paragraph adds to a sense of decline: "If this revolution had done no more than restore me to myself [*à moi-même*], and had stopped there, all would have been well; but unfortunately it went further and carried me rapidly to the other extreme. Since then my restless soul has swung endlessly backwards and forwards through the line of repose, and its oscillations, continually repeated, have never allowed it to come to rest. Let us look in detail at this second revolution, a terrible and fateful epoch in a fate completely unprecedented among mortal men" (351/417f).[81] In combination with the previous paragraph, this appears to suggest that after the Parisian years, Rousseau became gentler but also lost his intellectual fervor and his happiness. For Kelly, even though Rousseau is cured of his initial intoxication with virtue, his "unnatural, social desires led him into a series of failed attempts to achieve social rather than natural wholeness."[82] As for the "other extreme" to which Rousseau was carried, Gauthier suggests that this refers to his becoming "the paranoid who saw himself [as] society's victim."[83] Here I will offer an alternative reading of these changes, suggesting a kind of extension to the effervescent period.

Rousseau never specifies the "other extreme" into which he is plunged (Conf. IX, 351/417). However, paranoia is not the likely explanation, if for no other reason than that he rarely attributed this to himself, especially not for the period under discussion. (More commonly, he insisted that he was overly *trusting* by nature, and only became suspicious in a given case after enduring extreme woes, atrocities, and betrayals.[84]) Another difficulty is that, just before alluding to this "other extreme," he had also mentioned becoming "fearful, obliging, timid," as he had been "before" (350/417). So there are several moving parts here. It may be that Rousseau is offering a set of three character types, parallel to Aristotle's theory of the mean, here in regard to something like friendliness in social relations.[85] The first extreme flowed from the Parisian effervescence: He scornfully combated the "morals, maxims, and prejudices of my century" (350/417).[86] There he was "audacious, proud, intrepid" (350/417). Although it is not presented as a normative median point (as with Aristotle), the psychological and social middle is somehow Jean-Jacques's most authentic nature ("fearful, obliging, timid"). Here he may be invoking his childhood and a calmer and freer kind of desire that he felt with Madame de Warens.[87] In addition, the context may point to his earlier nature in Paris, including the period before Vincennes, when he combined domestic and sexual relations with Thérèse that fell far short of the passion of love, along with a more passionate search for intimate friendship among the *philosophes* (348–49/414–16). He thus wants to suggest that there is no full precedent for the "other extreme" into which he soon became launched, which we might call *wistful, ardent, and doting*.[88] This shift begins prior to his time with Sophie d'Houdetot, but that was its peak.

In this context, it is worth recalling that in his normative writings he often distinguishes "love" or (more precisely) "true love" from many other intimate, affectionate relations that we would normally call love. Rousseau's "true love" is a delirium or "unbridled ardor" and—he argues—ultimately a chimera. One passage in *Emile* refers to the argument of the second *Discourse*, as establishing that the sentiment of "true love" (*l'amour véritable*) is "not as natural as is thought." It continues: "There is a great difference between the sweet habit which makes a man affectionate toward his companion and that unbridled [*effrénée*] ardor which intoxicates [*enivre*] him with the chimerical attractions of an object which he no longer sees as it really is" (E V, 430/798).[89] This seems to be the context for his repeated claim that he only ever knew love with Sophie.[90]

How costly was this plunge into romantic passion for his effervescence and intellectual life? Perhaps not as bad as he initially suggests. First, just one paragraph before describing the dulling of his "ardent enthusiasm," and apparently in referring to his newly found eloquence and bold writing, he claims that this phase ended "ten years afterward" (Conf. IX, 350/417)—suggesting a date around 1760–1762, rather than 1756. Earlier in Book IX, he claimed that readers could not conclude that he had been living in idleness if they took measure of his writings during "the six years I spent at the Hermitage and Montmorency," despite many distracting obligations (339/404). This longer time frame is also supported by the later perspective of the *Dialogues*, where he again invokes the "unfortunate question" from the Academy of Dijon, which suddenly made "the scales fall" from his eyes.

> From the lively effervescence that developed then in his soul came those sparks of genius that have glittered in his writings during *ten years of delirium and fever*, but of which no vestige had appeared before then and which presumably would not have sparkled subsequently if, once this surge had passed, he had wanted to continue to write. Enflamed by the contemplation of those great objects [e.g., societies of simple, wise, happy people], they were always present in his thought, and comparing them to the real state of things, he saw them each day in relations that were totally new to him. (RJJ II, 131/829)[91]

At this point, whether because his understanding of his history had changed or because he had broadened the meaning of "effervescence," we see a longer period of "delirium and fervor," which includes the broader Montmorency period. It lasts ten years, thus bringing us to some range as 1750/1752–1760/1762.[92] In related passages, his "period of effervescence" spanned ten years, with a consistent passion, energy, and vehemence, during which everything from his pen had a coloration that "no other will ever match" (II, 164/871f; III, 217f/940f). Near the beginning of the *Dialogues*, "Rousseau" had found it inconceivable that Jean-Jacques could be an "enemy of all rectitude, all justice, all goodness," if he could have "imprisoned himself for ten to twelve years in the course of writing fifteen volumes speaking the sweetest, purest, most vigorous language of virtue," and "pitying human miseries," among many other achievements (I, 22/687).[93] Here this elevated state lasts for the whole period of his main authorship. The twelve years cited would be the most happily all-encompassing claim, spanning 1749–1761. (Having already submitted *Emile*, the finishing touches on the manuscript of the *Social Contract* were submitted to his publisher in November 1761.[94] This makes 1761 a sufficient end date for the main period of authorship, even though *Emile* and the *Social Contract* were published the following year.)

Thus, the descriptions in *Confessions* IX of the "second revolution" and the dulling of the "ardent enthusiasm" (350f/417) are unlikely to indicate the sort of psychological collapse they might initially suggest, pace Gauthier. There must, rather, have been a *shift* in Rousseau's mental state, at least somewhat exaggerated in some passages due to the foreboding personal troubles. This is confirmed elsewhere. For, from the perspective of the *Confessions*, April 1756 was the beginning of his great misfortunes, but according to the *Letters to Malesherbes* (January 1762)—written near the completion of this period but before his exile from France—"I began to live only on April 9, 1756" (III, 577/1138). To be sure, the claim in the *Malesherbes* is also partly polemical, needing to defend his present state of solitude. But even in the *Confessions*, the Montmorency period had much to recommend it, despite the misfortunes to which it gave rise.

3. Conclusion: Vestiges of Vincennes

Having come to terms with several accounts of effervescence, what shall we say of the "personal reform" and the broader enterprise of living in accordance with the "stern principles" of Vincennes? This has largely dropped out of our account and seems to be only a subtle undercurrent in the post-Parisian narrative of the *Confessions*. The answer would need to be pieced together from the component parts of the reform. We have seen suggestions of Jean-Jacques losing his former sternness, in terms of boldly opposing the witticisms of Paris; he also ridiculously allowed himself to be overcome by tenderness and romantic love (see Conf. IX, 358f/427). In these ways, he did not sustain—or even fully develop—the more Roman and civic sides of his character to which he initially aspired. In the "foolish pride" passage, he concludes by reflecting that his "singular course . . . might finally have made me respectable, if it had been possible for me to persevere with it" (349/416). More generally, he sometimes claims he never developed strength of will—something central to his formal definitions of virtue.[95] However, with much less fanfare than the collapse into persecution and misery, we find several aspects of the reform continuing well into the Montmorency period and beyond.

With regard to Sophie, he points to some elements of virtue in their restraint during the height of their affair. Their character was revealed in that they never transgressed the limits they set for themselves, despite their intimacy (373, 388/443, 462).[96] After it was resolved that they could be no more than friends, their meeting shows he had overcome his senses and "reacquired ascendency over myself" (401–2/478–80). He concludes that the uniquely strong passion he had for her will always do credit to them "by the rare and painful sacrifices made by both of us to duty, to honor, to love, and to friendship" (402f/480).[97] In overcoming this intoxication, he "worked on my own heart with more courage and more success," in particular taking advantage "of the leisure and independence . . . to take up my works again with more consistency" (X, 420–21/501–2).

Perhaps the most significant vestiges of reform are linked with *amour-propre*. A central part of Rousseau's idea of the good life is avoiding its tyranny—its deference to arbitrary human opinion, and its drive for comparative self-advancement. On these counts, Rousseau seems to believe his reform had substantial staying power. Although he sometimes enjoyed the friendship and support of the wealthy and great nobles, he lived moderately, having "renounced my greatest extravagances, those that pay heed to public opinion" (Conf. IX, 337/402).[98] He calls others to witness whether, during his time with the Luxembourgs and many other nobles, he was ever "for one moment dazzled by this brilliance," letting the flattery go to his head, becoming less simple in his manners, "less affable with the ordinary people," or "less ready to render any service to anyone that was in my power" (X, 442/527).[99] These personal virtues were necessary for him to advance his principles consistently; related professional virtues were needed in order to write with integrity. The "station of author . . . could not be illustrious and respectable except to the extent that it was not a profession [*métier*]" (IX, 338/402f; cf. E III, 197/473). Therefore, throughout his life, whenever possible, he retained the determination he took upon resigning the cashier position, to earn his daily bread as a music copyist (Conf. VIII, 304/363).[100] He identified himself as a copyist rather than an author,[101] although a few of his books did generate some money, which allowed him to copy at his own pace and "provided some security against hardship" (IX, 337f/402). The core distinction seems to be that he had a profession that allowed him to live even if his books did not sell. He could thus write only for the common good, rather than from the need to "please the multitude" and write best sellers (338/402). He does, however, begin to show an interest in generating revenue from his books once his health makes him plan for retirement from both writing and copying. In a 1762 letter, he claims that *Emile* is "my last work . . . , and it must provide my bread for the little time that remains for me to live, since from now on I am beyond the condition of earning it."[102]

In contrast to his fundamental approach, Rousseau saw Hugo Grotius and the great majority of modern intellectuals as offering essentially Hobbesian accounts of political authority, betraying the people in order to pander to the existing powers (E V, 458/836; SC II.2, 59/370f). Without entering this question of motive, there is evidence supporting Rousseau's account of the general tenor of political thought during this time. According to Helena Rosenblatt, "Both Grotius and Pufendorf were, in fact, absolutists like Hobbes: for them social contract theory principally served as the foundation for absolute monarchy."[103] More generally, in their "historical application," "at least in Geneva," the early modern natural-law theories of Grotius, Samuel Pufendorf, Jean Barbeyrac and Jean-Jacques Burlamaqui "were used *against* the forces of democratization."[104] It is also the case that several of these authors were rewarded handsomely for their submissive political teaching.[105] This backdrop explains Rousseau's prominent refusals of pensions from monarchs.[106] Although this strikes many as merely peculiar now, David Hume—before his quarrel with Rousseau—considered it unusually virtuous behavior for an intellectual.[107] For instance, he describes how Frederick of Prussia and Lord Keith offered to provide Rousseau a home and "all his necessaries" as "gratuities." Rousseau refused these "with his usual dignity" but inquired how he could earn funding to purchase them by "the fruit of his own industry." Hume comments: "I think this instance of conduct a kind of phenomenon in the republic of letters, and one very honourable for M. Rousseau."[108]

As Rousseau saw it, personal independence was a precondition for truthful writing, which must be undertaken boldly and with little regard for personal consequences. He often described his mission as speaking harsh yet useful truths to all the established factions.[109] Although bold disinterestedness seems crucial to his self-understanding, this also raises questions. Here I can demonstrate how his idea of boldness was seen as fully compatible with not seeing himself as obligated to speak all truths for all purposes at any risk.[110]

He was tested on these matters at the height of his authorship and revealed a distinct sense of vocation in his principled statements, even if he was not above personal fears. During his time in Paris, he collaborated closely with Diderot. The latter was precocious and more radically opposed to the religious establishment, leading to early legal troubles. Notably, he was imprisoned, then confined to the château of Vincennes; it was on his way to visiting him that Rousseau claims his famous "illumination" occurred.[111] Among the strategic lessons Diderot passed on to Rousseau was the limitation of political writing to general principles.[112] This became a well-established aspect of our citizen's writings through 1762; exceptions were few, minor, and soon regretted.[113] For instance, soon after the publication of the *Social Contract*, Rousseau reassured its publisher that it examined governments "only by their principles," never passing "the limits of a purely philosophical and political discussion."[114] Yet it was only very late in the editorial process that he brought a footnote on the marriage of Protestants fully into line with this policy.[115] This episode shows that fear for personal security sometimes played a significant role, at least in reinforcing his principled commitment not to intervene in concrete political disputes.

Religious persecution was in the air in France at this time. It would soon prompt Voltaire to redefine himself as a humanitarian writer and activist, defending particular victims of injustice.[116] By contrast, Rousseau declined urgent pleas for his aid in a case of religious persecution (October 1761–March 1762) and has been criticized for this.[117] In one response, he raises questions about the merits of the case, but, more fundamentally, he appeals to his purpose as an author:

> The friends of truth are not welcome in courts, and should not expect to be. Each person has his vocation on earth, mine is speaking harsh but useful truths to the public. I try to fulfill it without worrying about the evil that the wicked want to commit against me, and which they do commit when they can. I have preached humanity, gentleness and toleration as far as it is up to me; it is not my fault that people have not listened. As for the rest, I make myself one law, to always limit myself to general truths—I make neither libels nor satires, I do not attack a man, but men, not an action but a vice. I would not know, sir, how to go beyond that.[118]

This clarification of his mission was expressed when *Emile* had been submitted to the press, and the *Social Contract* was nearly so.[119]

Here one might object, how could Rousseau claim indifference to being harmed by the wicked? In his autobiographies, we see timidity and paranoia, which often become crippling. A relevant comparison would emerge less than one month after the above statement of purpose. He began writing a series of frenzied letters to the censor Malesherbes and to the publisher of *Emile* (November–December 1761), fearing that delays in the printing of that book were the result of a Jesuit conspiracy.[120] Strikingly, one of the most desperate letters was sent on the very day (18 November) that an order was signed banishing the Jesuits from France.[121] This led Rousseau to a rare acknowledgment—that he had been a victim of an "unhinged imagination."[122] He apologized profusely, but similar fears would soon reemerge.[123] This is not one of the impressive parts of Rousseau's personality, but it is important to recognize that these fears were not *entirely* the result of irrational fear. Heinrich Meier has documented many pirated editions and forged letters that were targeted against his works and reputation.[124] As it has been observed in connection with Richard Nixon, "even paranoids have enemies." Maurice Cranston similarly observes: "Rousseau was correct in believing he had enemies, but he was strangely inept . . . as to the identity of those enemies."[125] And this episode is minor compared to the fears that would follow, beginning especially after his time in England (1766–1767).[126]

Regardless of their varying bases in reality, it is difficult to see how these crippling outbursts of fear could coexist with the noble self-image he was presenting around the same time. One plausible solution is that—at least as an ideal—he seems to have made a firm distinction between fearing for his personal safety and fearing for the authentic preservation of his books. Regarding his safety, he strove to make no concession beyond limiting his public statements to general principles. Regarding his books, no moralistic restraints seemed to apply. In fact, he claims virtue and honor *require* him to be deeply concerned about any distortions of his useful writings[127] and the permanent blackening of his image that would result. Thus, in the case of the Jesuits and *Emile*, he thought publication was being delayed until his (imminent) death, when the book could be manipulated until "a Jesuit doctrine [would] appear under the name of J.-J. Rousseau."[128] Accordingly, even when writing the *Confessions*, and perceiving "the most dreadful plot" in history unfolding against his reputation, he claimed he was still in better condition than while *Emile* was delayed in the press: "I will die with an easier mind, secure in the knowledge that I am leaving in my writings a witness to myself that will sooner or later triumph over the conspiracies of men" (Conf. XI, 475/568).[129] He similarly describes his decision (around 1762) to retire from writing: "Although in abandoning the world I was leaving my enemies a clear field, I was leaving behind me, too, in the noble enthusiasm that had dictated my writings and in the uniform consistency of my principles, a witness to my soul that would correspond to that offered by my whole conduct on behalf of my character [*mon naturel*]" (XII, 535/639).[130]

My theory—that he combined fretfulness about the preservation of his books with boldness about his personal security—is confirmed in an exchange with Paul-Claude Moultou of February 1762, a few months after the Jesuit fear first emerged. Moultou had been entrusted to read—and protect from manipulation—the manuscript we know as the "profession of faith of the Savoyard Vicar." In addition to praise and sympathetic criticisms regarding this piece,[131] Moultou expressed deep concern for the author: "Your cowardly enemies, having uselessly tried to make you drink from the cup of ridicule, will they not move heaven and earth to make you drink that of Socrates? My God, I tremble for you!"[132] He was not the only friend who voiced astonishment at Rousseau's boldness in moving to publish his major statement on religion.[133] Yet the citizen remained fairly confident about his personal safety throughout this time. Biographers have established that some of his grounds for this turned out to be mistaken, including his trust in the effectual support of Malesherbes and the Luxembourgs.[134] To this I would add that in his response to Moultou, Rousseau offered another principled statement, which he likely understood to be the most fundamental ground of his boldness:

> I am touched by your concern for my safety, but you must understand that in the condition I am in,[135] there is more frankness than courage in speaking useful truths, and from now on I can state the worst to men without having much to lose. . . . One could not attack me justly, and this suffices for my tranquility. All the prudence of my conduct has always been to act so that no one can harm me without having wronged me. . . . Wanting to shield oneself from injustice—that is to attempt the impossible, and to take precautions that would never end. I add that, honored in this country by public esteem, I have a great defense in the uprightness of my intentions which are felt in my writings. The Frenchman is naturally humane and hospitable; what would be the point of persecuting a poor, sick man who is in nobody's way and preaches only peace and virtue? So long as the author of the

> book *de l'esprit* lives at peace in his fatherland,[136] J.-J. Rousseau may hope not to be persecuted there.
>
> So calm yourself on my account, and be assured that I risk nothing.[137] But as for my book, I admit that it is now in a state of crisis which makes me fear for its fate. . . . I will let them remove what they will from the first two volumes, but I cannot endure them touching the profession of faith. . . . The copy which is in your hands gives me courage.[138]

The threat to the manuscript leads to a dread perceived as justified, whereas the threat to his person leads to serene resolution. In the latter case, he embraces Moultou's comparison with Socrates, depicting it as a long-settled policy. Thinking he was gripped by fatal illness put Rousseau in a similar position to the aged Socrates, both believing they had nothing great to lose by an early, unjust death.[139] Moreover, Rousseau follows Socrates' moralized idea of prudence—being nearly indifferent about personal safety, while supremely concerned about never making it possible to be *justly* harmed by another (see Conf. IX, 356/424).[140] The idea is anticipated by Rousseau as early as the "Preface to *Narcissus*" (1753): "While it does not matter to me whether I am thought of well or ill, it does matter to me that no one have the right to think ill of me" (92/959). Similarly, a few years later, we find the following in a (highly autobiographical) discussion of the so-called misanthrope: "Having declared war on the vicious, he must expect that they in turn will declare it on him. If he had not foreseen the harm that his frankness would do him, it would be a careless mistake and not a virtue. . . . He knows men" (LdA 40/280/37).[141]

He reaffirmed this willingness to suffer for truth, and the duty and honor of doing so, as persecution was imminent in June 1762. After the publisher of *Emile* in Amsterdam expressed alarm about the contents of the Profession of Faith, Rousseau responded:

> I am very sorry about the trouble that the "Profession of Faith" is giving you, but I must say to you, once and for all, that no interdiction, no danger, no violence, no power on earth would ever make me retract one syllable. . . . In giving glory to God and speaking for the true good of men I have done my duty. Whether they benefit by it or not, whether they condemn me or approve of me is their business, and I would not give a blade of grass to change their blame into praise. As for the rest, suppose they do their worst; what will they do to me that nature and my own ill health will not achieve soon without them?[142]

Even after hearing of the writ of his arrest, he claims he waited patiently, happy "to be called to the honor of suffering for the truth." In the end, he only decided to flee in order not to compromise Madame de Luxembourg—thus sacrificing "my glory to her tranquility" (Conf. XI, 485–86/579–80). This reasoning reaches a high point in the major letter to Saint-Germain: "No, I find nothing so great, nothing so beautiful, as suffering for the truth. I envy the glory of the martyrs. If I do not have in everything the same faith as them, I have the same innocence and the same zeal, and my heart feels worthy of the same prize."[143] Amid a retrospective list of traits he thought would ultimately disprove his slanderers, he claims he was in all things "sincere to the point not only of imprudence but of the most unbelievable disinterestedness" (Conf. XII, 536/640).[144] In a book that allots considerable space to many ambiguities, and some notorieties, in this unusual man, here we might have established something that has not found many observers in recent decades, despite many fair treatments of his thought: a demonstrably impressive side of his character.[145]

Not only in the *Confessions* but also in the two other major autobiographical works, letters, and several "occasional" reflections,[146] we behold the ostensible soul of our author. Scholars have been led in very different directions, based on the cross-cutting emphases in Rousseau's accounts of his moral and psychological history throughout his main period of authorship. We find a somewhat disillusioned author of 1769–1770, looking back on the two most consequential periods of his life, in both of which he was quite a different man than what, perhaps especially in hindsight, seemed to be his most authentic nature. In Books VIII–XI of the *Confessions*, the emphasis is on the revolutions in his circumstances and character, and their disastrous consequences for his happiness. Nonetheless, a patient reading can show that his changes during the Parisian period (ca. 1749–1756) were not as feigned or philosophically groundless as some have argued. They were out of keeping with his earlier nature, but they seem to be understood as appropriate responses to the illumination. As for the broader Montmorency period (1756–1762), despite the initial suggestion that his effervescence collapsed, in the end we find it expressing itself with greater moral and psychological balance, grounding his writings that he most strongly endorsed (the *Letter to d'Alembert*, *Emile*, and, in more qualified senses, *The Social Contract* and the latter parts of *Julie*). As for personal reform, while some of the early Roman civic aspirations seem to dissipate, several reforms continue through 1762 and until Rousseau's final years, especially regarding labor, luxury, and speaking harsh yet useful truths at considerable risk to himself.

CHAPTER 3

It's a Very Peculiar Citizen Who's a Hermit

The Question of Civic Devotion (ca. 1754–1762)

Apart from the discarded children, civic behavior may present the most difficult case of the Jean-Jacques problem. Philosophers, political theorists, and intellectual historians would often know Rousseau best for his theory of the general will, advocating republican citizenship as disinterested devotion to the good of the whole polity.[1] He often skewered the intellectuals of his time for professing elevated moralities while living egotistically: "Distrust those cosmopolitans who go to great length in their books to discover duties they do not deign to fulfill around them. Such a philosopher [*Tel philosophe*] loves the Tartars so as to be spared having to love his neighbors" (E I, 39/249).[2] It is natural to infer that empty claims of civic republicanism would fare no better than empty claims of cosmopolitanism, and yet Rousseau's practical citizenship is eminently questionable. Denis Diderot was able to expose the hypocritical nerve in one sentence. The once-intimate friends had fallen into a controversy about solitude soon after Rousseau's move (in April 1756) to the Hermitage. The main quarrel (February–April 1757) was sparked by Diderot's claim in *The Natural Son* that "only the vicious person lives alone" (see Conf. IX, 382–84/454–57).[3] In an otherwise somewhat conciliatory letter, Diderot closed with a painful barb: "Adieu, Citizen—and yet it's a very peculiar citizen who's a hermit."[4] Similarly, after their break, Diderot privately invoked Juvenal when reflecting on his estranged friend's relations with Thérèse: "*curios simulant et vivant.*" More fully, Juvenal's critique of philosophical hypocrisy reads: "One longs to escape from here . . . when some people dare to pronounce on morality—those who affect the Curii's style while living a Bacchic orgy."[5] Concerning the Jean-Jacques problem, we may also think of the Roman's overall lament on his times: "It is difficult *not* to write satire."[6]

Most scholars seem to have sided with Diderot in finding Jean-Jacques's civic devotion uncompelling, if not absurd. David Gauthier has stated the case well. Among the main contentions of *Rousseau: The Sentiment of Existence* is the insignificance of citizenship in the deepest thoughts and commitments of the "Citizen of Geneva." Based on an analysis of the political writings, Gauthier suggests that Rousseau "knew, in himself, that the alleged freedom of the ideal citizen was a false freedom." However, it is only in Rousseau's "autobiographical self-understanding" that Gauthier finds this decisively confirmed.[7] Thus, "It is only at the end of his life that Rousseau is finally able to say who he is."[8] These later works reveal "more clearly" that "his life is a denial of all citizenship, of any attempt to force him into the dependence on his fellows that true citizenship would demand."[9] Gauthier draws from the claim in the *Confessions* that Voltaire's move to Geneva (February 1755) was a major factor deterring Rousseau's return, after his visit there (June–October 1754).[10] For instance, if Rousseau lived in Geneva, he would have needed to combat Voltaire "ceaselessly," and "would prove to be 'an unbearable pedant,' unless he allowed himself to be 'a lax and bad citizen.'"[11] To Gauthier, this episode reveals that Rousseau "had come to have no stomach for what he recognized as the demands that real citizenship would put upon him."[12] Moreover, once he left Paris for the Hermitage (April 1756), he "showed not the slightest yearning to reside in or even visit his *patrie*," and he lost the zeal of "the Citizen whose task it was to expose the injustice of the existing social order."[13] Gauthier mentions an apparently more civic claim in the *Confessions*, that to write for the good of the fatherland, one must live outside of it.[14] He dismisses this on the basis of the shift we have seen: "Rousseau himself notes a difference in tone" between the effervescent Parisian writings (ca. 1749–1755) and the later ones. "Elsewhere in the *Confessions*, he speaks of both 'the bile' (VIII, 309/368) and the 'truly celestial fire' (IX, 350/416) that were present in his first Parisian writings; his post-Parisian works, by contrast, 'breathed a gentleness of soul' (X, 420/503) that surely excludes bile and celestial fire alike."[15] Finally, for Gauthier, we find the clearest, implicit response to the idea of "Citizen of Geneva" in a passage from the *Reveries*. There, Rousseau explains that he has "never been truly suited for civil society where everything is annoyance, obligation, and duty and . . . my independent natural temperament always made me incapable of the subjection necessary to anyone who wants to live among men" (Rev. VI, 83/1059).[16] Gauthier is not alone in seeing here a repudiation not merely of the abuses of civil society but of citizenship as such, as well as the social "as the realm of duty and obligation."[17]

Beyond the question of personal character, the claims of Diderot and Gauthier also raise questions about intention and experiential credibility. One of the leading defenses of republican virtue would be depleted insofar as Rousseau's claims may be taken as a form of propaganda, offered without sincere commitment. And if he advocates civic devotion largely for its sweet taste,[18] and yet actually finds these duties distasteful and unnecessary, it suggests that his central political appeals may be based more in imagination than reality, as liberal critics have often charged. Overall, if the great modern with "the soul of an ancient"[19] were in fact, from the beginning, an Epicurean finding public duties irreconcilable with personal happiness[20] or a prototype for Alexis de Tocqueville's "individualism,"[21] then his legacy may be more justly linked with self-absorption than civic devotion.

Defenses of Jean-Jacques as citizen have been few and brief, due largely to the *Reveries* and the sparseness of civic discussions in the *Confessions*. James Miller's "dreamer of democracy" is exhilarated by his (largely projected) visions of civic life in Geneva but ends up being close to the Jean-Jacques of Diderot and Gauthier, in preferring "the retirement of solitude to the responsibilities of citizenship."[22] Ernst Cassirer disagrees more strongly with Diderot's quip: "Rousseau was just such a *citoyen bien singulier*. From the outset he stood in a paradoxical relation to society: he had to flee from it in order to serve it and give it what he was capable of giving."[23] Beyond this brief response, the debate has been one-sided, since most who forward a more civic or duty-driven Rousseau seem to have avoided questions of his personal citizenship. Yet, there is something to be said on behalf of Cassirer's stance, insofar as it aligns with the explanation Rousseau most frequently gave of his life as a citizen, especially during his main period of writing political philosophy.

In contrast, during an interlude following his exile from France (June 1762), Rousseau was drawn into a leading role in concrete Genevan political controversies, a period I call "the activist moment" (ca. July 1762–February 1765). As I will argue in Chapter 4, this approach was atypical and soon gave way to an unprecedented apolitical shift.

In this chapter, however, I focus on the period from the restoration of Rousseau's Genevan citizenship to the publication of *Emile* (August 1754–May 1762), including his subsequent reflections on this period. He then defended his indefinite absence from his homeland as a form of what I call "distant citizenship," where, because of his personal history and distinctive mission, he could be more useful to his fellow citizens from afar. During this period, his distance from his homeland was presented as painful to him, yet as resulting from zealous pursuit of duty. This subtly differs from the portrayal of the same period in later autobiographical reflections (1769–1770).[24] Then his earlier deferrals of civic engagement are presented as deriving not mainly from consideration of duty but from inclination and temperament. However, this seems to be fully compatible with objective, positive civic duties, unlike the better-known ("Kantian") analysis of the *Reveries* (1776–1778). Whereas these avoidances of civic engagement may naturally be read as Epicurean, I show significant parallels with Socratic and Stoic models of philosophers declining to engage in civic life in some circumstances, which indicate that this can be objectively justifiable, even on civic grounds.

1. The Zealous, Distant Citizen

Gauthier rightly claims that Rousseau's justifications for not residing in Geneva were sometimes unconvincing, and that our citizen often seemed to find fault with any scheme for return.[25] Yet Gauthier himself mentions the puzzle that, if Rousseau lost the zeal of citizenship in 1756, it is not clear why he continued to publish as "Citizen of Geneva" until March 1763.[26] I add that Rousseau's longstanding self-assessment is also difficult to reconcile with Gauthier's reading, that the Genevan embodied a lifelong repudiation of citizenship, and that he had no stomach for "what he recognized" as its real demands.[27] Instead, during the period in question, he presents himself as zealous in his intentions to serve his homeland and variously defends his absence as a historical accident, an unfortunate necessity, or the natural precondition of his distinctive usefulness. These explanations have often been overlooked and make it difficult to dismiss his civic behavior summarily. Nonetheless, ambiguities remain and, as we will see in the next section, even Rousseau came to question whether these nobler ideals were his fundamental motivations.

Gauthier focuses on two episodes. First, there was the main decision not to reside in Geneva (in the spring of 1755)[28] and, second, the refusal even to accompany Madame d'Épinay during her journey there (October 1757).[29] The second decision can be dealt with briefly. Gauthier claims that "his reasons were strictly personal" and "the connection between Geneva and Rousseau as citizen had been abandoned."[30] He cites Cranston: "As usual, when any scheme was suggested to Rousseau that might facilitate his return to Geneva, he immediately found fault with it."[31] Yet Cranston points to a less idiosyncratic explanation elsewhere: d'Épinay was apparently pregnant by her lover Grimm, and our protagonist did not want to put himself in a position where he would be assumed to be the father.[32]

The first decision deserves closer attention. After the success of the *Discourse on the Sciences and Arts*, but before the publication of the *Discourse on Inequality*, Rousseau made a high-profile journey to Geneva (June–October 1754). Restoring his legal claim to Genevan citizenship was a leading motivation. He had lost that claim upon converting to Catholicism in 1728 (Conf. II, 57–58/68–70). During his journey, he seems to have been sincerely investigating the prospects for permanently resettling in Geneva, and, when he arrived, "I abandoned myself entirely to patriotic zeal" (VIII, 329/392). This retrospective seems accurate, based on letters from the time,[33] as well as on public statements.[34] For instance, we find in a letter to Madame Dupin: "This is certain, that this city seems to me one of the most charming in the world, and its inhabitants the wisest and happiest men that I have known."[35] Around this time, he put some finishing touches on a Dedicatory Epistle for the *Discourse on Inequality*: "To the Republic of Geneva."[36] It explains his distance from his homeland as a historical accident. He would have wished to live "peacefully in a sweet society with my fellow-citizens" (DOI 117/115).[37] But if, "less happy or too late grown wise, I saw myself reduced to ending a lame and languishing career in other countries," he would at least address them as he is doing, "imbued with tender and selfless affection for my distant fellow-citizens" (118/115).[38] As R. A. Leigh observes, this is the posture of a prodigal son returning.[39] A few pages later in the Dedication, Rousseau discusses the truths learned from his father—through authors including Tacitus, Plutarch, and Grotius—in a similar manner, even though it may be that "the excesses of a foolish youth caused me to forget such wise lessons for a time" (120/118).

Nonetheless, before publishing the Dedication, it had become clear that its publication would not be approved by the Small Council, and that it may provoke the hostility of that patrician governing body. (Among the factors provoking the hostility of the partisans of the aristocracy was writing the dedication to the Republic, rather than to "the Council" or "the Senate.")[40] A letter from soon after the journey (November 1754) shows his awareness of the likely reception, alongside a willingness to endure increased alienation from Geneva if it might benefit the city. "Believe that I want to be—until the grave—honest, true, and a zealous citizen;[41] and that, if I must deprive myself on this occasion of the sweet abode of the fatherland, I would thus crown the sacrifices I have made to the love of men and of truth, with that which would pain my heart the most, and consequently honor me the most."[42] According to the *Confessions*, he received a poor reception, and this was a leading reason he did not resettle in his homeland.[43] This account has been disputed—according to Richard Whatmore, Rousseau strove to ensure that the Dedication would not undermine his standing with the magistrates, and thereby complicate his return to citizenship. Moreover, he was "initially pleased at the reception of the *dédicace*."[44] However that may be, for a decade following the Dedication, his published works and many letters follow the self-definition that emerges with this post-journey letter—less as the once-prodigal penitent and more as the currently devoted citizen. While continuing to invoke historical misfortune as a reason for his absence, this is prominently framed in terms of duty and sacrifice.

The most authoritative statement of this "distant citizenship"[45] is in *Emile* (published May 1762). It follows the important distinction that even though—despite extensive travels across Europe—Emile could not find a fatherland (*patrie*) of true liberty and justice, he nevertheless has a country (*pays*).[46] The tutor then advocates the duty of "attachment to the place of your birth," and living among those compatriots (E V, 473/858):[47]

> You ought to live amidst them, or at least in a place where you can be useful to them insofar as you can, and where they know where to get you if they ever have need of you. There are circumstances in which a man can be more useful to his fellow citizens outside of his fatherland than if he were living in its bosom. Then he ought to listen only to his zeal and endure his exile without grumbling. This exile itself is one of his duties. But you, good Emile, on whom nothing imposes these painful sacrifices, you who have not taken on the sad job of telling the truth to men, go and live in their midst, cultivate their friendship in sweet association [*un doux commerce*], be their benefactor and their model. (474/858f)

We are to infer that our author is a legitimate exception to a general affirmation of positive civic duties, which are to be locally discharged. But this typical or prima facie obligation is itself justified by the broader normative principles of service to one's country, and—perhaps—to all of humanity ("the truth to men").[48] On that basis, Rousseau's exemption from local civic duty seems justified by his devotion to a broader, more unusual form of service, which is better pursued from a distance. The resulting duty is experienced as a sacrifice, apparently contrary to inclination.[49]

The *Emile* does not explain why Rousseau's writing is better done from afar, but this theme is developed elsewhere, including in the *Letters to Malesherbes* (January 1762), written when *Emile* was forthcoming. In defending his solitude more generally, Rousseau claims to be more useful from his retreat. "I would be much more useless to my fellow citizens if I lived in their midst than I can be from my retirement when the opportunity presents itself. What does it matter in what spot I live, if I act when I ought to act?" (*Malesherbes* I, 580/1143).[50] Similarly, "It is something to have been able to contribute to preventing or at least putting off the pernicious establishment in my fatherland that d'Alembert wanted. . . . If I had lived in Geneva I would not have been able either to publish the dedicatory epistle of the *Discourse on Inequality*, or even to speak against the establishment of the theater in the tone that I did" (IV, 580/1143). The *Letter to d'Alembert* directly claims to have been written as a duty of citizenship,[51] and contemporary letters suggest that Genevan opponents of the theater found it of great service in their civic cause.[52] Geneva's longstanding rejection of the theater—deriving from republican, Platonic, Christian, and distinctly Calvinist influences—had come under considerable stress by this time.[53] Moultou proclaimed of Rousseau's missive: "Your book is the rallying signal of all good citizens, the disgrace and fright of the wicked."[54] A letter from Jean-Louis Mollet also confirms the notion of distant citizenship: "There is, *Monsieur*, an invisible chain between you and us which attaches you very sincerely to all your fellow-citizens."[55]

In addition, the claim in *Malesherbes* about the ability to speak boldly in service of Geneva is emphasized in the passage in the *Confessions* defending distant citizenship: "Unless one is a man of intrigues, if one wants to dedicate books to the true good of the fatherland, one must not compose them in its bosom" (Conf. IX, 341/406).[56] Living as a foreigner in France was "very favorable for daring to speak the truth," and this "consideration very much contributed" to Rousseau's acceptance of Madame d'Épinay's entreaties to settle at the Hermitage rather than in Geneva (Spring 1756; Conf. IX, 341/406). Living in his homeland, he would have been far more constrained by censorship.[57] He also apparently thought that copying music, although an honorable profession for him in France, would be frivolous and contemptible in Geneva.[58] Finally, although he would not claim to be a lawgiver (*législateur*) for Geneva—that title goes chiefly to Calvin—his arguments here on the favorable conditions for speaking the truth parallel those in the *Social Contract* on the benefits of a lawgiver being of foreign origin. Such a lawgiver is less prone to having his legislative vision tainted by particular passions and factions (SC II.7, 69f/382).

In all of this, we find a highly principled explanation of Rousseau's civic devotion to his home country, in both its results and its motivations. Although some tensions can be discerned, distant citizenship should not be dismissed as a casual or peripheral stance. It is a firm orientation in his epistolary self-conception, in his stated intentions in normative writings, and in the perceptions of his political allies. Any balanced assessment of Jean-Jacques as citizen must consider that. Nonetheless, ambiguities begin to emerge even in the *Letters to Malesherbes*, and these increase with the relevant parts of the *Confessions* (1769–1770), written after Rousseau's decisive break with Geneva (February 1765). In these retrospectives on his earlier period (1754–1762), his sees his civic usefulness as far more limited and his motives as far more mixed.

2. Following Inclination, Fulfilling Duty

At the time of the *Letters to Malesherbes*, Rousseau was anticipating a peaceful retirement from serious authorship and, apparently, the sort of public burdens that go with it.[59] Instead, as we will see, he was plunged into two and a half years of the most intense civic activity of his life, followed by thirteen years of wandering and autobiographical prolixity. Yet, before this dramatic turn, these 1762 letters give us a first retrospective on what he thought he had accomplished, both intellectually and personally, during his main authorship. The letters also begin offering frank admissions of the limits of his devotion, which would become a prominent theme in the later autobiographies. In the first of the *Letters to Malesherbes*, he explains his retirement to the country, and the "disgust I have always experienced in the company of men," on psychological grounds. The decisive factor is revealed to be "an indomitable spirit of freedom"—one that comes "less from pride than from laziness" and that makes "the lesser duties [*les moindres devoirs*] of civil life" unbearable (*Malesherbes* I, 573/1132).[60] Here we have an anticipation of the well-known passage from the *Reveries*, against all the restraints of citizenship.[61] Not only does it contrast with the general pattern of this period, but, as we have seen, it is also in the *Letters to Malesherbes*—in the fourth letter—where he provides a robust justification of his solitude in terms of its usefulness to Geneva (580/1143).[62] Peculiar though it seems, the very presence of both explanations in the same series of letters suggests that Rousseau saw no contradiction here—that any tension could be explained. Most likely, in *Malesherbes* (unlike, for instance, in *Emile*), personal inclination is framed as his (most) effectual motive; however, this inclination is seen not as contrary to duty but as potentially compatible with it and, in some cases, the best way to fulfill it.

This awkward conjecture is confirmed in the cases of major civic encounters with Geneva and Corsica, as recounted in the *Confessions*. There, besides the duty-centered factors we have discussed regarding Geneva, Rousseau openly indicates how personal factors, rather than optimal usefulness to the fatherland and truth alone, at least partially motivated him. For instance, he claims to have been highly averse to any involvement in civil strife in his homeland ever since he first witnessed disturbances in 1737; he even swore an oath not to be involved in them.[63] Reflecting on the main period when resettling in Geneva was a real possibility (1755–1756), the *Confessions* focuses on Voltaire's presence just outside of that city (since March 1755). Rousseau claims that moving to Geneva would have drawn him into the sort of controversies for which he had no taste, or any likelihood of prevailing (Conf. VIII, 332–33/396–97). For instance, "What could I have done alone, timid and speaking very poorly, against an arrogant, opulent man backed up by the influence of the great, with a brilliant ostentatious eloquence, and already the idol of the women and young people?" (333/396f). He concludes: "I was afraid of exposing my courage needlessly to danger; I listened only to my peaceable nature, to my love of repose.... If I had retired to Geneva... I doubt whether, for all my ardent and patriotic zeal, I could have done anything great and useful for my country" (333/397).[64] The effectual motive is granted to be personal disposition, but, with a rather un-Kantian complacency, he does not present this as conflicting with any objective duties.

This argument from the likely futility of relocation in pursuit of civic duty reemerges with the Corsica affair, which occurred a decade later (September 1764–ca. September 1765).[65] Asked by a leading Corsican to serve as "a legislator" for the newly independent island,[66] Rousseau responded with great enthusiasm, despite his sense of significant obstacles: "It is superfluous, sir, to try to excite my zeal for the enterprise that you propose to me. The very idea elevates my soul and transports me. I would believe the rest of my days very nobly, very virtuously, very happily spent; I would even believe I have redeemed the uselessness of the others if I could render these sad remains good in some way to your brave compatriots, if I could contribute by some useful counsel to [their] plans."[67] Another letter written a few months later indicates his strong assumption of a positive duty to do civic good where feasible. He responded to a friend who had tried to dissuade him from this venture: "Far from thinking that one must not mix oneself in human affairs, in order to avoid doing something reproachable, on the contrary, I think that one prepares oneself very much for reproach when one neglects to do good, or at least to attempt it when there is some hope of success."[68]

Among the difficulties he initially mentioned was the need to travel to the island, which would be far more instructive than all the documents he was also requesting: "Six months passed on the place would instruct me more than a hundred volumes."[69] The *Confessions* attempts to rehash some of his enthusiasm for Corsica, but it mostly explains the ultimate failure of his endeavor to settle there. He came to hope Corsica might be a refuge from his persecutions in Môtiers. However, his desire to settle there was "very much cooled" by the "horrible depiction" of the Corsicans and Corsica provided to him by one correspondent, Captain Hyacinthe-Antoine d'Astier (Conf. XII, 544/649; see also 545f/651). Although the nature of the Corsicans is never presented as decisive in the *Confessions*, he had signaled as much in a 17 February 1765 letter to d'Astier: "The explanations you have kindly given me on Corsican affairs have made me absolutely abandon the project of going to that country."[70] In addition, and apparently more decisive, was "the ineptitude and aversion I have always had for the active life to which I was going to be condemned" (Conf. XII, 544/650). Attempting public life would thus be "completely contrary to my taste," and it would discredit him in the eyes of the Corsicans (544/650). He concludes: "If the greatness, the beauty, and the utility of the object gave me new courage, the impossibility that the great cost would be rewarded with success deprived me of it absolutely. . . . Twenty years of profound meditation with only myself for company would have cost me less than six months of active life spent in the midst of men and their affairs, and in the certain expectation of failure" (545/650).[71] Futility thus seems to nullify a potential duty and confirm the call of inclination. He then describes another reversal, prompted by a plan of his that would have supported his "beloved solitude" in Corsica. He would promise to write only their history, while considering the prospects for secretly writing a constitution (545/651).[72] His final, official rationale for abandoning the move to Corsica, "my cherished project," was the arduousness of the journey itself, which would have been impossible to plan given his short-notice eviction from the Island of Saint-Pierre (545–46/ 651–52). However, it was writing a "plan of government" or "plan of institution" that was requested of Rousseau—not traveling to the island—and contemporary evidence suggests that he saw the persecutions of Môtiers as interrupting this project, rather than ending it.[73] It was not until May 1768 that the project became moot, when Corsica was ceded to France and occupied.[74]

In the Corsican and Genevan cases, there seems to be an assumption that, in following his interests and tastes, he was not failing in his positive civic duties, which he also acknowledged. There is, of course, nothing peculiar in thinking one's interests and tastes may converge with one's duties. Demonstrating the supreme personal benefits that derive from virtue or justice is the basic premise of Greek eudaimonism, and much in modern as well as ancient normative philosophy seeks to establish political circumstances in which individual interests would align with the public good.[75] And yet, in ethics, this tradition largely amounts to advocating the direct and supreme pursuit of virtue and justice, resulting in a subtler and more indirect concern about personal results.[76] At least in principle, this is very different from following an intuitive or calculated sense of personal interests or preferences, while blithely assuming their compatibility with the morally appropriate. In seeming here to take the latter approach, Rousseau opens himself to an Athenian sarcasm against their rivals' claim to virtue: "Of all the people we know, the Spartans make the most blatant equation of comfort with honor, and expediency with justice."[77] Rousseau is presenting what we might call a moral "compatibilism," and it seems highly susceptible to self-deceit and mere pretenses of fulfilling basic duties. Would he follow personal inclination when it is known to be contrary to duty, or should reasonably be known to be such? His assumption in the *Letters to Malesherbes* and the *Confessions* seems to be far more sanguine—that he did have objective duties as a citizen, and he fulfilled them at least tolerably well under the circumstances, even while (at least often) yielding to inclination.

It remains unclear whether we should grant this assumption. For now, we may conclude that in his earlier autobiographical retrospectives (ca. 1762, 1769–1770), he did not suggest his inclinations were out of keeping with his duties. This contrasts, on the one hand, with the more dutiful and disinterested interpretation offered in his earlier normative writings and personal letters (ca. 1754–1762) and, on the other hand, with the well-known, theoretically Kantian passage in the *Reveries* (written 1776–1778): "Virtue consists in overcoming [our inclinations] when duty commands in order to do what duty prescribes, and that is what I have been less able to do than any man in the world" (VI, 77/1053).

3. Conclusion: Socrates, Seneca, and the Semi-Civic Jean-Jacques

By what historical standard might we judge Rousseau's civic behavior? Although he praises some of the great statesmen, such as Lycurgus and Cato,[78] he seems to be aware that his own more distant or indirect acts of citizenship preclude him from strict legitimation through those models. More plausible comparisons could be made with others he admired who were mainly dedicated to the philosophical life and who reflected at length on the civic duties of a philosopher, notably Socrates, Plato, Seneca, and Plutarch. As is well-known, Socratic and Platonic philosophy emphasizes the pervasive corruption of political life in Athens and most (if not all) contemporary polities. Accordingly, in the typical case, for a wise and just person to engage in politics would be futile and would likely provoke a very early death.[79] However, the qualifications and exceptions to this stance are equally significant. In several important cases, Socrates and Plato put positive civic ideals into practice.[80] At his trial, Socrates appealed to "not words but what you esteem, deeds."[81] Similarly, according to Plutarch, in considering his Syracusan venture, Plato was ashamed "lest it should seem that he was all mere theory [*que ce n'étaient que paroles de lui*]."[82] Turning to the specific accomplishments, Socrates was distinguished for courage during his military service,[83] and prominently resisted two instances of illegal or unjust activities under the Athenian democracy and the oligarchy.[84] Plato's attempts to establish philosophical rule in Syracuse were also well-known to Rousseau, and they parallel in some ways his own Corsican episode. Although Plato was deeply disappointed by the results he attained in Sicily, he defends the manner of death of his protégé Dion, since "it is altogether noble and right to suffer whatever may come while aiming at the highest for oneself or one's city."[85] Plutarch frames Plato's intervention more positively, in view of the long-term effect of bringing down an unusually powerful and corrupt tyranny.[86] Although the Genevan ended up leaving himself more open to the charge of being merely theoretical, he and Plato were each ambivalent about his undertaking, considering the great nobility of the project if successful, weighed against the low probability of success and the high personal risk.[87]

In cultivating a subtler idea of the prima facie duties of political engagement, Seneca is also significant. Although sometimes faulted as a luxurious hypocrite beneath a veil of philosophy, in the interpretation likely to have been favored by Rousseau, he was an exemplary philosopher, forced to cope with unusually corrupt circumstances.[88] He often sought "retirement" from public life, and several of his writings dedicated to a defense of solitude and a private life were dear to Rousseau.[89] Seneca was aware that this retreat from politics may seem Epicurean, but he insisted that, despite some partial overlap in practice, there was an underlying principled difference: "Epicurus says: 'The wise man will not go into public life, unless something interferes.' Zeno says: 'He will go into public life, unless something impedes.'"[90] The duty is substantial but only presumptive: "When we enjoin service to the state, we do not mean to just any state, nor that one must serve at all times or without ending."[91] We find, first, the Platonic justification of nonengagement that we have seen, that a particular public realm is "too corrupt to be helped"; in these cases, "the wise man will not struggle pointlessly nor squander himself to no avail."[92] To this, Seneca adds more personal causes: "If he has too little authority or strength, if the public realm will not accept him or his health impedes him."[93] Turning to Socrates, at least on some accounts, he encouraged or discouraged others from entering political life, depending on whether they had those particular skills.[94] As for Plutarch, although he strongly opposes Epicurus's general stance of avoiding public service, he factors in whether a public career is "particularly right" for the skills of the person in question, and sees illness, exile, or loss of fortune as a potential "passport to philosophical leisure."[95] These are, of course, the kinds of extenuating circumstances that Rousseau appealed to—sometimes too prolifically—concerning relocation to Geneva or Corsica.

All told, the structure and preoccupations of Rousseau's personal citizenship seem closest to a Stoic and Senecan model—presupposing serious political duties as a kind of default but also the legitimacy of extenuating circumstances, both personal and political. The flexibility of the Stoic model might be seen to encompass not only his major disengagements from citizenship but also the useful acts of distant citizenship he engaged in from 1754 through 1762, and the draw of Corsica in 1764–1765. At times, no doubt, he may stretch that model too far and conclude too readily that circumstances vindicated his privatizing inclinations. Nonetheless, it seems that—as we have also found in the case of the discarded children—the very proliferation of excuses most likely indicates a presumption of prima facie duties and a conscience that was highly stimulated, even if sometimes less effectual than it should have been.

We should perhaps not go so far as Cassirer in proclaiming Rousseau a "very peculiar citizen" who had to flee from society in order to "give it what he was capable of giving."[96] This would take Rousseau too much at his word—or his earlier words—privileging his most dutiful self-interpretation to the exclusion of others. The friends of Citizen Jean-Jacques should make several concessions. For most of his life as philosophical author and citizen, this civic engagement was minimal and threatened to belie his self-proclaimed title. Gauthier is right that he promptly declined civic opportunities (at least in some notable cases), and this raises lasting questions about his most fundamental commitments.[97] It must be concluded—to the surprise of almost no one who has read his autobiographies—that Rousseau was often undistinguished in his direct civic engagement.

However, there is countervailing evidence, to which the debunkers of our citizen have not given adequate weight. Even omitting our "activist moment" (ca. July 1762–February 1765), during his main period of philosophical citizenship (ca. August 1754–June 1762), and typically in looking back on it in the *Confessions*, he justifies his civic behavior in terms of a "distant citizenship." He framed himself as needing to live outside his homeland in order to best serve it in his distinctive mission and, at least until an initially private letter of 1762, this was presented as a painful duty rather than a pandering to inclination. If his retrospectives are often most striking for their lengthy explanations of civic passivity, he nonetheless typically seems to assume that his inclinations led him to decisions that were compatible with objective, positive civic duties. Moreover, Socratic and Stoic models of civic engagement seem to have provided him with a respectable precedent for avoiding more direct engagement, given the circumstances and his skill set. Although at times he was more peculiar than a citizen, until he gave up on Geneva (February 1765), he was interested in behaving in accordance with his high civic principles, and he was a leading resource for the republican cause in his homeland.

CHAPTER 4

A Lover of Peace or a Vile Insurgent?

Confronting the Genevan Patriciate (ca. 1762–1768)

During his main period of philosophical authorship (ca. 1749–1762), Rousseau cautiously distanced himself from direct political behavior—especially any concrete criticism of the French and Genevan regimes.[1] This formal caution proved insufficient, given the subversiveness of his general political and religious principles, as well as the audacity of signing such books under his own name.[2] Disaster struck him in June 1762. Already by 13 May, word reached his publisher that Malesherbes would not tolerate the importation of the *Social Contract* into France.[3] Yet the real explosions occurred with *Emile*. Copies of it were available in Paris on 24 May 1762; on 9 June, the Parlement de Paris condemned it and ordered the arrest of its author.[4] On 19 June, the Small Council of Geneva condemned *Emile* and the *Social Contract*, adding a secret rider that the author would be arrested if he entered Genevan territory.[5] Maurice Cranston observes that, whereas in France the main initial concern was with *Emile* and religion, in Geneva the *Social Contract* was the main fear since "the preoccupations of the patrician government were firmly political."[6] Accordingly, *Emile* was ordered lacerated and burnt in France and Geneva; the *Social Contract* was so only in Geneva.[7]

Soon after this, Rousseau overcame much of his strategic caution, centrally contributing to Genevan opposition politics (ca. July 1762–February 1765). He became a ringleader for the political causes of his allies, alternatively referred to as the reformers or the bourgeois, popular, or liberal party; they were soon to be known as the "remonstrators" (*représentants*).[8] (The latter term refers to the *représentations*—remonstrances or appeals—submitted against perceived abuses by the magistrates.)[9] Although in some way drawn in to vindicate his own name against the dishonor inflicted upon him by the government, Rousseau saw himself as decisively motivated by his duties to his homeland, and restoring "the liberty and rights of the bourgeoisie."[10] The controversies induced him to abdicate his long-cherished Genevan citizenship (May 1763) and culminated with a major political work that would remain prominent in Genevan politics for another two turbulent decades: the *Letters Written from the Mountain* (December 1764). According to the magisterial editor of Rousseau's correspondence, Ralph A. Leigh, this was "designed to make a specific impact on the course of events in Geneva"; it "represents the high point of Rousseau's political activism, and is the most caustic and aggressive of all his works."[11]

Book XII of the *Confessions* surveys the entire Swiss exile (June 1762–October 1765). It is the only book that deals with a portion of his life after genuine disaster struck, and it is one of the longest in the *Confessions*.[12] Despite this, it dedicates fewer than five pages to Jean-Jacques's Genevan political activities. It also omits some of the most significant episodes, such as his explosive (and essentially public) letter explaining his abdication of citizenship, which prompted several major protests against patrician rule and was decried by the establishment as "the tocsin of sedition."[13] The cursory treatment in the *Confessions* seems to justify his behavior solely on the grounds of his resistance to political involvement and his advocacy of peace.[14] Written around the time of the *Confessions* account, the major letter to Saint-Germain (1770) responds to allegations that he sought to establish a "pure democracy" in Geneva and that he excited quarrels there: "Not only have I always criticized the quarrels of Geneva, but I have spared nothing for bringing the remonstrators to peace."[15] Remarkably, the author of the *Discourse on Inequality* and the *Social Contract* had come to justify himself in essentially Hobbesian terms.[16] (This may be an important departure from his original normative emphasis, even if scholars have rightly pointed to some theoretical similarities between the two authors on issues such as the nature of sovereignty, the relation between reason and the passions, and civil religion.)[17] He thus also misses a compelling opportunity to respond to the charges we have seen—that this hermit could not engage in practical acts of citizenship or interest himself in real politics[18]—and may even be seen as pleading no contest. This is puzzling, and here we find ourselves in the uncomfortable position of needing to swim against the main current of the great autobiographical retrospective. I will suggest that a very different spirit may be found in the writings of this "activist moment." Then he was concerned not only—or even mainly—with respecting public order, although that was important. Instead, his primary intentions can be seen as closer to those of the Rousseauian Machiavelli—a republican primarily devoted to the public liberty, both intellectually and personally.[19]

There are two main contemporary sources of Rousseau's political outlook and behavior during this period. First is *Letters Written from the Mountain*, which has only recently become the object of serious study and remains far less read than the major theoretical works that preceded it, or the autobiographical works that followed. Second is a substantial correspondence, which has never been translated. Accordingly, this period is relatively unknown to most students of Rousseau, and there seems to be no Anglophone account offering a comprehensive discussion of Rousseau's civic behavior, as well as his self-understanding of citizenship and civic duty, during his only fully activist period. Christopher Brooke also indicates the limits of current scholarship on these matters, since "Helena Rosenblatt's excellent book on *Rousseau and Geneva* ends its historical presentation with the *Contrat social*, declining to say much of significance about the period surrounding the *Lettres écrites de la montagne*, Rousseau's major engagement with Genevan politics."[20] Rosenblatt's epilogue has nonetheless remained the best starting point in English for a philosophically minded, chronological overview of Rousseau's civic behavior in this period.[21]

After offering a clear narrative, I engage the important revisionist account of Richard Whatmore, who calls attention to a brief revival of engagement with Genevan politics around 1768. Whatmore argues that Rousseau came to be seen as "a lover of peace rather than liberty,"[22] and, even concerning the earlier stages, was always more peaceably deferential to the authorities, and distant from the remonstrators, than scholars have suggested. In challenging Whatmore, I emphasize a major shift in Rousseau's thinking that began around 1766. I thereby also challenge the prevailing scholarly view that, despite his often flamboyant rhetoric, Rousseau definitively opposed revolution. My approach provides another explanation of Rousseau's claim about his treatment of "natural and political right" in the *Social Contract*: "Locke in particular treated them exactly in the same principles as I did" (*Mountain* V, 235f/812). As Brooke has shown, this claim "has mostly been rejected by those commentators who have considered it."[23] Yet Brooke was able to apply it seriously to Locke and Rousseau on popular sovereignty and on the relation between religion and politics.[24] Here, on the right to resisting authorities, I follow Brooke's advice to extend their connections in other fields.[25] A parallel influence treated here is Algernon Sidney, who had been "under the eyes" of Rousseau as he composed the Second Part of the *Discourse on Inequality*.[26]

1. From the Exile to the *Letter to Beaumont* (June 1762–March 1763)

Rousseau was deeply surprised and disappointed by the condemnation of *Emile* and the *Social Contract*. As he was forced to flee France and seek refuge across various Swiss states, he initially counseled his political sympathizers in Geneva to be highly restrained about his case. For instance, in June and early July 1762, he urged minister Paul-Claude Moultou to "stay silent" and "respect the decisions of the magistrates,"[27] apparently believing direct intervention would be not only dangerous but unnecessary: "The more I weigh all the considerations, the more I am confirmed in the resolution to maintain the most perfect silence. For, finally, what might I say without renewing the crime of Ham? I will stay silent, dear Moultou, but my book will speak for me."[28] (The "crime of Ham" alludes to Genesis 9:20–27, on the duty to respect one's father—and thus here, one's fatherland—even in a drunken and naked state.)[29] The retrospective similarly claims he thought the initial rulings would be reversed in due time (Conf. XII, 508/606f). In later letters, Rousseau would consent to Moultou publishing a pamphlet in his defense but then had second thoughts, being afraid of the risks his friend would run.[30]

As for the Genevans, many had become ambivalent at this point, even among those who were normally well-disposed toward Rousseau. In his favor, many saw the main political argument of the *Social Contract* as an unusually clear and powerful articulation of their cause.[31] As Moultou wrote to Rousseau: "Our bourgeois say no less than that this Social Contract is the arsenal of liberty, and while a small number rages, the multitude is triumphant. It almost pardons your religion in view of your patriotism."[32] Moultou also rejoiced that this work was "read avidly" and "ought to terrify all tyrants."[33] More generally, Rousseau's strong distinction between "Sovereignty" and "Government" placed the ultimate locus of legal authority in the direct voice of the citizen body, with the Government merely enforcing the Sovereign's laws (the general will, i.e., the will of a majority oriented toward the common interest).[34] Here I have no intention of reducing or limiting the *Social Contract* to its Genevan context, but one purpose that was widely recognized at the time was its defense of an embattled model of the Genevan constitution.[35] Placing "Sovereignty" firmly with the people rebuked the "patrician" or "oligarchic" Small Council (*petit conseil*).[36] The patricians (or *haute bourgeoisie*) were not an official rank, but they dominated the political system by Rousseau's time; they amounted to less than 6 percent of the total population.[37] At least according to the liberal or democratic interpretation, the patricians had increasingly encroached on the General Assembly of the citizens and bourgeoisie, leaving the latter groups with only a nominal sovereignty.[38] According to Leigh, although the claims of the "Genevan radicals" appeared subversive, in offering this historical interpretation, they claimed to be the true constitutional party, in this way paralleling "some of their English contemporaries."[39]

Given its centrality to Rousseau's practical politics, we might pause to discuss the historical context of the General Assembly (or General Council). Being a full "citizen" was relatively rare and a high honor in Geneva; the *bourgeois* were the next tier down, who had purchased their letters of bourgeoisie, at increasing cost in the seventeenth and eighteenth centuries.[40] The *bourgeois* belonged to the General Council but were ineligible for high office; their Genevan-born children were citizens. The less wealthy newcomers were *habitants*, and their children *natifs*.[41] Until the mid-1760s, the conflicts were between the patrician magistrates, on the one hand, and the citizens and bourgeois, on the other; by the early 1770s, the *natifs* (then around 80 percent of the population) were incorporated into the bourgeois cause.[42] Given the close alliance of citizens and bourgeois for our period, I follow Rosenblatt in using the terms synonymously.[43]

Rousseau had often been asked to help bolster the theoretical argument of the bourgeois ever since his visit of 1754, and he was often praised by its leading figures.[44] He may also have become politically bolder and more aligned with the group of bourgeois radicals in 1759.[45] The patricians, having been somewhat disturbed on occasion by his earlier writings,[46] found it necessary to respond decisively to the *Social Contract*. According to the Procurator General, Jean-Robert Tronchin, claiming a right for "periodic assemblies" to revoke "at their pleasure" their "constitutive laws" or their governing officials would lead to an "extreme freedom" even more "crushing than servitude."[47]

If the political reception of the *Social Contract* fell along predictable lines in Geneva, its civil-religion chapter, as well as the profession of faith in *Emile*, led many sympathetic figures to question Rousseau's thinking or publicly distance themselves from him.[48] Accordingly, some of his most prominent advocates during this time criticized *Emile* or certain arguments in the *Social*

Contract, while protesting against the unjust treatment of the author, and asking that he be left in peace. Colonel Charles Pictet spoke against the unjust procedure used against Rousseau in Geneva, and was punished. Victor de Gingins, Seigneur de Moiry, the prefect to whom Rousseau wrote in Yverdon (in Bernese territory), asked that the author be allowed to live there in peace. This was to no effect.[49] Rousseau expressed his gratitude publicly to de Moiry[50] and more generally sought to mollify the religious situation. Although often annoyed by many requests to clarify his religious positions (expressed anxiously by political well-wishers who were more orthodox and Calvinist), he partially conceded to them in a declaration of August 1762. Written to his local pastor and published by his friends in Geneva, it claims that his profession of "the reformed Christian Religion" is all the less suspect, since having long lived in France, he would have only needed to keep silent about religion "in order to enjoy the civil advantages from which I was excluded by my religion. I am attached in good faith to this true and holy religion, and I will be so until my last breath."[51] Although this declaration provoked the disgust of d'Alembert and Madame de Boufflers, it drew a positive response from the Calvinists and proved politically embarrassing for the Small Council and its supporters.[52] Similarly, in his *Letter to Beaumont* (published March 1763),[53] Rousseau's religious polemic was framed against a Catholic archbishop, again largely pleasing his Genevan associates.[54] However, according to Leigh, the *Beaumont* only polarized Genevan opinion—fomenting enthusiasm among his partisans, while fortifying reprobation among his adversaries. At the same time, it seems to be the least discussed of all Rousseau's writings, indicating that censorship had largely succeeded at this point in making him "a clandestine author."[55]

Amid this controversy, we find Rousseau increasingly collaborating, through meetings and correspondence, with the opposition leaders. Ambiguities abound, since he had a frequent tendency to draw back after initiating an adversarial approach.[56] It seems sensible, though, to follow Raymond Trousson in considering 24 July 1762 as the main turning point.[57] Unlike the highly cautious and passive approach Rousseau had counseled since his exile, he then drafted a list of grievances for potential circulation, adding: "Do not be surprised to see me change tone." He mentions his 9 July expulsion from the Canton of Berne—instigated by Geneva—as what justifies this change.[58] He understands that attaching his name to such a list might "harm my interests" in Geneva, but he counsels Moultou not to be concerned about that.[59] He goes on to explain that he will henceforth judge with *sang-froid* all the follies committed by the Genevan authorities, "as if it were not a question of me."[60] Slightly later, this indifference is grounded in the hopelessness of his cause there: "Regarding Switzerland and Geneva, I have ceased taking interest in what they think of me there. Those people are so hypocritical, or so false, or so stupid, that one must give up on enlightening them."[61]

Writing to a more distant ally in August, he resumes a more passive voice, but with the same willingness to take personal heat for the political cause: "If, then, you believe that in the manner of discussing my case, there is some means which tends to restore the liberty and rights of the bourgeoisie, use it, act in my name . . . , but remain tranquil about what can only have a bearing on me. For whatever you may believe, my honor does not depend on the procedures of the magistrates of Geneva."[62] He was also highly involved in strategizing for the November 1762 election,[63] in which his allies opposed the reelection of Procurator General Tronchin, who was seen as having driven the indictment of the *Social Contract* and *Emile*.[64] (We now know that although Tronchin sought to condemn the books, he advised *against* the course taken, of issuing a warrant for the author's arrest.[65] To Leigh, the fact that the Small Council overruled their legal adviser indicates "their sense of urgency and danger.")[66] In the election, Tronchin prevailed by 800 votes to 400. This gravely disappointed Rousseau, but Jacques-François Deluc and others saw grounds for hope, since the majority favoring Tronchin had been heavily reduced since the previous election.[67]

2. Abdicating Citizenship as Civic Duty (April–September 1763)

What might be called a second round of direct civic activism was apparently triggered on 29 April 1763, when the Small Council forbade the printing of the *Letter to Beaumont* in Geneva (a decision triggered by pressure from the resident French diplomat).[68] Rousseau was again dismayed, not only by the legal action but by the lack of public protest against it.[69] Although he was consistent in publicly stating the rulings of 1762 as the cause,[70] apparently this response to the *Beaumont* was the immediate cause of his formal abdication of his right of Genevan citizenship (12 May 1763).[71] Although privately considered for some time,[72] this remained shocking. According to Trousson, here Jean-Jacques "slapped Geneva in the face" in front of all of Europe; it was "the first time in history" that "an illustrious writer rejected his fatherland, declaring it unworthy of him."[73] In its direct claims, the brief official letter avoids public insult, focusing instead on personal pain. The abdication has been prescribed to him by "honor and reason, however dearly it costs my heart." Having loved his fellow citizens, but so badly failed to make them love him, he is making them this "last sacrifice" to please them "even in their hatred."[74] Even the cessation of citizenship, then, is presented as an act of devotion, and he would restate this in the *Letters Written from the Mountain*: "Far from the ostracism that forever exiles me from my country being the result of my faults, I have never fulfilled my duty as a Citizen better than the moment I ceased to be one, and I would have deserved this title by the act of making myself renounce it" (V, 226/801).[75]

Scholars are divided about Rousseau's civic claims here. Rosenblatt's interpretation is favorable: "Close friends realized that this was another strategic political move." She quotes minister Antoine-Jacques Roustan: "You are, I think, the first person who does his duty by avenging himself, and who makes himself useful to his fellow-citizens by ceasing to be one of them."[76] By contrast, for Trousson, Rousseau's adversaries could rejoice at being "finally rid of this troublesome preacher," whereas his friends and sympathizers were appalled and dismayed.[77] The latter ask, for instance: "Did the great Cato resign forever his quality of Roman citizen?"[78] And: "How does vengeance accord itself with grand principle?"[79]

Trousson's argument may be bolstered by an earlier exchange. Nine months beforehand, Rousseau had written to Isaac-Ami Marcet de Mézières (1695–1763), an old friend of his father, who was also one of the heads of the bourgeois protesters during the troubles of 1734.[80] Rousseau confided his resolution to eventually renounce his citizenship: "I am ill, dear friend, I need rest, I love peace; I will never find it in Geneva or among the Genevese. I have therefore decided to renounce my fatherland, and even to renounce it publicly; but as I intend to consider only my own convenience and my honor, I will patiently await the favorable moment, and until then will let [my enemies] triumph in peace. This renunciation is the last writing with which I want to finish, and I will try to render it still useful to my former fatherland [*ancienne patrie*]."[81] It is personal interests rather than civic duty that play the leading role here, although they are presented as compatible. Marcet's response was in no way receptive: "Jean Jacques, my very dear Jean-Jacques, son of Isaac, you have blamed philosophers because they were only reasoners and not wise [*Sages*]; you have tried to be wise and become a reasoner! Vulgar man, the faults of others overwhelm you, and exude you."[82] Marcet saw renouncing his citizenship as a simple capitulation to unlawful force.[83] In his reply,[84] and at a few other points in his Genevan quarrel, Rousseau does not present himself as having exemplary civic motives but as morally free to move on from a painful relationship, having fulfilled whatever duties he may have had to his "ungrateful fatherland" (cf. Conf. XII, 510/609). Thus, in the letter of abdication: "Having fulfilled to the best of my ability the duties attached to this title [of citizen], while enjoying none of its benefits [*avantages*], I do not believe I am at all indebted [*en reste*] to the state, in leaving it."[85] In closing the *Mountain*, he claims he has "fulfilled my final duty toward the fatherland," and now "I take leave [*congé*] of those who live there" (IX, 306/897).[86]

The scholarly divide derives partly from the ambiguity of Rousseau and Roustan when they present the abdication as civic duty. The Roustan letter, which is cited by Rosenblatt and Trousson, each to her or his own purposes, is in fact highly ambivalent. Roustan begins by citing "this fatal letter" of renunciation, and claiming that, knowing how strongly "patriotic fire consumes your heart, I did not presume that you would ever be able to win such a cruel victory over [your fatherland]." He grants that it is "still a service that you render them," and, following Rosenblatt's quote,[87] he continues: "The only side of it which does me some pain, is that the small number of your friends are the ones the most afflicted."[88] To Roustan, the act seems to be civically dutiful and potentially useful, yet still somewhat rash and selfish. He also indicates the complexity of the patrician response: "Your Tartuffes of enemies still do not know if they should be saddened or delighted, on the one hand they are charmed to be dispensed from giving you justice"; on the other hand, they fear that the political demands for change will only increase.[89]

In some later accounts, the former citizen insists that his intent was to remove his case from public controversy, thus restoring calm to the city. In a 1768 letter to Moultou, he proclaims that "the misfortune in which I have been implicated, in the commencements of your [city's] troubles, makes it my duty, from which I will never depart, to be neither the cause nor the pretext of their continuation. . . . This is what made me renounce my citizenship."[90] This seems difficult to square with the contemporary record. As Leigh comments, the 1768 letter's claim is "a bit idealized. . . . Rousseau did not renounce his citizenship in order to slow down the political activity of the remonstrators. Much to the contrary, the first remonstrances were posterior to the letter of abdication. If Rousseau renounced his citizenship, this was in part due to the indignation inspired by being the victim of injustice and in part in order to reproach his fellow citizens for their inactivity."[91] Rousseau in fact was nudged by the leading activist, Deluc, and leveraged the abdication to launch a major political campaign.[92] This would prove comforting to his previously dismayed friends. Overall, the evidence in this phase suggests a very human political figure, roughly equidistant from the heroic activism portrayed by some of his advocates, and the simple, self-absorbed capitulator perceived by some of his critics.

In Rousseau's first draft of the 12 May 1763 letter of abdication, he had written, "I will be quiet, out of respect, about the reasons for this, they are only too well known; and I leave them for the public and posterity to judge."[93] No sentence corresponds to this in the version of the letter that was sent, likely indicating that Rousseau came to think even this was too provocative.[94] He thus intentionally refrains from any political justification of himself in the official letter of abdication. However, this was supplied in the letter (of 26 May) that followed Deluc's prompt.[95] Although ostensibly private, Rousseau apparently anticipated that it would find broad circulation, and he even ensured that it would.[96] It explains the abdication as the only tolerable path available: "Publicly stigmatized [*Flétrir*] in my fatherland without anyone calling out against this mark of crime [*flétrissure*]; after ten months of waiting, I had to come to terms with the only option likely to preserve my honor, so cruelly offended."[97] It goes on to explain the role of the Genevan citizens in this dishonor,[98] given that no remonstrances had been submitted on his behalf:

> If I were stupid enough to want to persuade the rest of Europe that the Genevans had disapproved the conduct of their magistrates, wouldn't they take me for a fool? Do we not know, they would say, that the bourgeoisie has the right to make remonstrances on every occasion it believes the laws have been offended against, and when it disapproves of the conduct of the magistrates? What has it done when you have waited nearly a year?[99] If only five or six bourgeois had protested, it might be believed. . . . This course was easy, legitimate, and not at all troubling to public order[100]—why has it not thus been taken? Doesn't the silence of all refute your assertions?[101] Show us the signs of the disavowal you ascribe to them. Monsieur, this is what has been said to me, and rightly said: People are not judged by their thoughts, but by their actions.[102]

Rhetorically and strategically, it is significant that this incitement is placed in the mouth of hypothetical interlocutors. Nonetheless, it is this letter that was denounced by the establishment as "the tocsin of sedition."[103] The citizens indeed sprang into action at this point, writing four remonstrances on behalf of Rousseau and other perceived victims of injustice (June–September 1763).[104] Rousseau saw these actions as doing them honor and was persuaded that if he could ever be useful to the Genevans, he could be more so from afar than living among them.[105] However, unlike our theme of "distant citizenship" from Chapter 3, in this case, the distance seems merely geographical, since he was involved in the drafting and publishing of some remonstrances. For instance, in a letter to Deluc, Rousseau volunteers to handle the publication of the remonstrances and any related documents.[106] Cranston discusses a case of advising on strategy around August 1763.[107] There were also extensive machinations involved in setting up a meeting with his Genevan allies at Thonon, in the territory of Savoy, in June 1764.[108]

This letter explaining his abdication is altogether omitted in the *Confessions*, which attributes the remonstrances only to the letter of abdication and the citizens' concern for their interests.[109] More generally, these early phases of post-exile Genevan activism are covered in only two pages of the *Confessions*; again, they stress only his resistance to political involvement and his advocacy of peace (see XII, 510–11/609–10). Concerning the final stage to which we now turn, he does express pride in the *Letters Written from the Mountain* for supplying pivotal arguments and strategy to the remonstrators. However, having fulfilled "this duty" and having "served the fatherland and their cause to the end," "I no longer involved myself in their affairs except by ceaselessly exhorting them to peace" (Conf. XII, 522/624).[110] Again, this more passive and Hobbesian approach of the retrospective ought to be compared with the original documents.

3. The Last Charge of the Former Citizen (September 1763–February 1765)

Our third, and final, positive phase of Genevan civic activism ends in disaster for Rousseau, both politically and personally. The magistrates were concerned about the unrest surrounding the abdication and the remonstrances that followed. The remonstrances were quickly dismissed in the formal process,[111] but they provoked a more consequential response from Jean-Robert Tronchin. Published anonymously, his *Letters Written from the Country* (September–October 1763) systematically defended Genevan institutions and the legality of the Small Council's actions.[112] He claimed that even though the General Council was in principle sovereign, it was a mark of prudence that these powers were transferred by contract to the Small Council and were not regularly challenged.[113] Geneva avoided the anarchy of a pure democracy by having a balanced constitution, comparable to Britain's, as well as by maintaining the necessary societal subordination.[114] Whatmore adds: "The central pillar of Tronchin's text was a defense of the *droit négatif*, the right of the Council of Twenty-Five to veto proposals that were put to it, rather than having all proposals evaluated by the General Council, including . . . représentations."[115] This was seen as an imposing work.[116] Deluc and others appealed to Rousseau as their only hope: "Your virtuous fellow-citizens" are persuaded that only you could respond suitably, "as much for your particular defense as for that of our remonstrances."[117] He quickly set to historical research and writing, admitting a poor understanding of the history of Genevan institutions and requesting documents from key allies.[118] But political events were turning against him. As Cranston describes Tronchin's impact: "A solid majority of the citizens at the Genevan Assembly in the New Year 1764 voted sheepishly for the candidates for public office drawn up by the Small Council."[119]

Rousseau's efforts resulted in the *Letters Written from the Mountain*, published in December 1764, in time to influence the following election.[120] Its First Part begins with sustained—and, as we will see, often very heterodox—defenses of the religious and political claims of *Emile* and the *Social Contract* (Letters I–III, VI). Even assuming the ideas in these books to be harmful or false, the procedures used against him would have been unlawful (Letters IV–V). Banning the books is one thing, but stigmatizing the books and threatening the author go further (*Mountain* I, 137–39/691–93). The latter presume a harmful intention, which must be established with clear evidence and sound procedure, "as an accuser must convict the accused before a judge" (139/693). Yet all this was passed over in his case, where the books were judged rashly, and the author was judged without hearing him, by a body that was not authorized to do so.[121] Moreover, the citizen in question had lived an honorable life, with a distinctive record of taking public responsibility for his writings, which were intended only for the public good (V, 218–21/791–95). He asks, "Must one begin by dragging an irreproachable citizen into the prisons like a scoundrel? And what advantage will public esteem and the integrity of an entire life have then before the judges, if fifty years of honor over against the slightest evidence do not save a man from any affront?" (221/794).[122] Throughout the *Mountain*, there is a curious dialectic of writing extensively about himself and his honor,[123] while also claiming to be writing disinterestedly for the sake of Geneva, as well as humanity as such.[124] One intended reconciliation is that the injustices of his case illustrate the general importance of seriously tending to the public liberty, including the adjudication of remonstrances. Hence, the Second Part (Letters VII–IX) shifts from his own case to the political affairs of Geneva (I, 135/688).

As we will also see, among the leading topics are Geneva's historically democratic constitution, its recent subversion by the Small Council, the peaceable and commercially focused character of the Genevan citizenry, and the future prospects of Genevan liberty.

Leigh, letting his own sympathies show, calls the *Letters Written from the Mountain* "a wholesale onslaught on the Genevan oligarchy which rocked it to its foundations and completely annihilated Tronchin's skillful presentation of its case."[125] Similarly for Trousson, the Small Council's "champion, the invincible Tronchin, has bit the dust, and the magistrates were left hesitant, lost, and stunned by this crushing blow."[126] However that may be in terms of objective argumentation, the contemporary reception was far more mixed. Rousseau knew he was writing boldly, but apparently he did not know he had set himself up for his second (and final) round of legal fallout.[127] The *Mountain* was quickly burned in Paris and the Hague; the Genevan Small Council denounced it, declaring it "unworthy to be burned by the executioner."[128] Its religious argument seemed to reverse the conciliatory trend of the somewhat Calvinist-friendly *Letter to Beaumont*, surpassing even *Emile* in the blatant heterodoxy of its arguments on revelation and miracles (*Mountain* III). Many moderate citizens and bourgeois abandoned a name that had become toxic.[129] As for politics, Rousseau had now published a book that went far beyond general principles and alarmed not only the Genevan establishment but also "aristocrats and administrators everywhere" for wanting "to overthrow an established government."[130] According to doctor Théodore Tronchin, "The miserable Rousseau, who had the black project of overthrowing his fatherland in order to avenge himself, is currently the object of contempt and public hatred."[131] By contrast, a Genevan ally reports: "Our people say openly [*hautement*] that your book is the gospel that we should follow, others that it is the torch of liberty, others that it is a firebrand in the middle of a powder magazine."[132] The book proved pivotal in a significant political episode: The candidates the Small Council put forward for magistracies were confirmed by only paltry majorities in the New Year's elections of 1765.[133] The citizens and bourgeois seemed finally on the brink of victory,[134] yet the magistrates retained key structural advantages. They demanded a vote of confidence, upon threat of mass resignation. In the 7 February election, the citizens capitulated at a high rate.[135] The episode may seem strange to us, but Linda Kirk finds in it "what we can now identify as the problems of a one-party state," which cannot develop the idea of a loyal opposition. This also proved difficult for the "American and French republics at the end of the eighteenth century."[136] Rousseau was disgusted—as Leigh puts it, Rousseau thought the citizens had "missed their opportunity" and that this capitulation was "disloyal and ungrateful after his labours on their behalf."[137] Later in February, and likely in combination with increasing personal troubles, he swore off all involvement in Genevan politics.[138] Despite his own withdrawal from the field, his political legacy remained substantial from 1765 through 1782, when citizens repeatedly opposed the Small Council, leading to several threats of civil war, and ending with a democratic revolution that was overturned by France.[139] Several allies and former allies came to appropriate his political arguments without reference to him;[140] meanwhile, the magistrates would long continue to present him as the malcontents' ringleader and sole instigator.[141]

4. Peace Versus Liberty

The above narrative of an activist moment (ca. July 1762–February 1765), when Rousseau came to march directly with Geneva's reformers against its magistrates, can be plausibly inferred from the usual historical accounts. More recently, Whatmore has offered a learned revisionist interpretation. He shows that, beginning in the late 1760s, a new generation of reformers expressed significant opposition to Rousseau's politics, as someone who was insufficiently democratic and who preferred peace to liberty.[142] In addition, despite his emphatic break from Genevan politics, he was induced to a brief engagement near the end of the constitutional crisis of 1766–1768. He counseled the reformers to seek peace and reconciliation with the magistrates, thus discrediting himself in the eyes of several of them.[143] The particular advice was backed by general principle in a few significant letters: "Entirely persuaded as I am that there is nothing here below that is worth purchasing at the price of human blood, and that there is no longer liberty on earth except in the heart of the just man; I indeed sense, nonetheless, that it is natural to men of courage who have experienced liberty to prefer an honorable death to the harshest servitude."[144] He then counters that, even in "the clearest case of the just defense of yourselves," it is certain that the Genevans would make themselves worse off even if they were victorious in their struggle (this apparently alludes to the threat of French intervention). He goes on to offer the extraordinary advice that "instead of soiling your hands in the blood of your fellow citizens," they should all entirely abandon the city of Geneva, leaving it to be no longer anything but "a den of tyrants."[145] In another letter, he contends "that peace is better than liberty, and that the only asylum for liberty that remains on earth is in the heart of the just man, and that it is not worth the trouble to fight for the rest."[146] Then, according to Whatmore, "When agreement was reached, he was delighted with the compromise, on the grounds that he saw 'subordination and confidence' restored; the veneration of magistrates was the essence of republican glory."[147]

Some scholars have suggested a certain change of mood or tone in these remarks. To Judith Shklar, "In his last years Rousseau felt that under prevailing conditions peace was worth even more than freedom. For freedom existed only in the heart of the just man."[148] James Miller describes it as a new "pose of conciliator" or of "peacemaker," part of a larger shift away from interest in Geneva, politics, and even justice.[149] By contrast, Whatmore seems to view them as highly consistent with Rousseau's earlier political philosophy, which he presents as more averse to democracy, and more insistent upon public order and deference to governing authorities, than has been understood. According to Whatmore, our citizen had always sought a middle way and distanced his political philosophy from the often reckless remonstrators.[150]

What is normally seen as a high point of populist-republican activism would, on this reading, amount to a far more Hobbesian approach to citizens and subjects. Do these letters of 1768, and the broader history of dispute with the remonstrators, show us most clearly who Rousseau has been all along? Whatmore offers many important corrections to simplified accounts of Rousseau as radical democratic activist. These can be added to the long-standing qualification that, even though much of the remonstrators' *language* is highly populist and democratic, the remonstrators are speaking for the interests of the citizens and bourgeois, which are themselves exclusive groups.[151] Nonetheless, I would question Whatmore's account of the general orientation of the *Letters Written from the Mountain* and of the preceding decade of political writings and correspondence. Overall, it is difficult to read the *Mountain* as mainly intended to stake out a genuine mean between the extremes.[152] Near the end, after strong criticisms of Tronchin and the magistrates, Rousseau grants that it is a coarse sophism to "assume all the abuses in the party one is attacking and none of them in one's own.... One must assume abuses on both sides ... but that is not to say that their consequences are equal" (*Mountain* IX, 300f/890). He thus seems to be acknowledging and defending, under the circumstances, the writing of a book that is fundamentally partisan.

On the central question of the right of the Small Council to control what proposals are placed before the General Council ("*le droit négatif*"), it is true (as Whatmore claims) that Rousseau concedes it is sometimes appropriate

(*Mountain* VIII, 261f/843). And perhaps this would have been shocking to some remonstrators.[153] Nonetheless, Rousseau himself insists that the appropriate form of this—concerning new legislative proposals—is not what is at stake in the current quarrel. What is at stake is another use of the "negative": The Small Council unilaterally and summarily dismissing complaints against political innovations and injustices *committed by itself.* The two possible purposes of remonstrances are "to make some change in the law" or "to correct some transgression of the law" (*Mountain* VIII, 264/846; see 261–65/842–47). As for the second, it is "a question of preventing anyone from innovating. . . . *That is what the Citizens and Bourgeois,* who have such a great interest in preventing all change, *propose in the complaints about which the Edict speaks.* . . . It would be against all reason, it would even be indecent, to wish to extend the negative right of the Council to that object" (265/847).[154] To Rousseau, as to the remonstrators, the council's behavior is constitutionally novel and contrary to the basic principle, which precludes being the supreme judge of one's own case (265–66/847–48f; IX, 287/873f).[155] To the remonstrators and Rousseau, the constitutional right to protest would be meaningless if the Small Council can thus reject remonstrances against itself.[156] By contrast, for Tronchin, allowing this judgment in one's own case is inseparable from instituting government, and, with it, a final human authority.[157]

In the cases of democracy and populism, the *Mountain* shows very little interest in counseling us against their dangers. Whatmore summarizes an argument from the *Mountain,* warning against democracies giving "excessive authority to the people as a body": "The people . . . were always poor judges, and would either elect a despot or continue to abuse liberty themselves."[158] It is difficult to discern what in this passage Whatmore is describing. It claims, for instance, that "the democratic constitution is certainly the masterpiece of the political art" (*Mountain* VIII, 257/838). The sovereign is distinguished from the government, as in the *Social Contract,* and the burden of the argument is to blame self-interested oligarchs (and their supporters) for failing to grasp this feature of democratic states like Geneva (see 257/837f). Elsewhere, we do find anti-populist remarks about the poor capacities of the people to understand international relations (VII, 248/826f; cf. IX, 291/878; SC II.2, 58/370). Even here, though, the inference Rousseau draws is not that the people are incapable of exercising sovereignty but that declarations of war and peace are not truly functions of sovereignty. Locke makes a parallel distinction, since international relations are like a state of nature and thus "much less capable to be directed by antecedent, standing, positive Laws."[159]

Instead of warning us against democracy and populism, the main story of the *Mountain* is the one Rousseau sees as the natural inclination of all governments—persistent encroachment by the powerful against the public liberty and the interests of the whole (*Mountain* VI, 232–33/808–9; VII, 238–39/815–16; cf. SC III.10). Given the well-known passage in the *Social Contract* repudiating democratic government, one of the surprising features of the *Mountain* is how often it casually refers to Geneva as being (historically and properly) a democracy or democratic constitution, using the term in a positive sense. This is because it is presented as democratic regarding Sovereignty, but not Government (thus aligning with the *Social Contract*).[160] Rosenblatt usefully argues that Rousseau's criticisms of "democracy" apply only to the administration of government. Since the Genevan bourgeoisie had never aspired to this, these criticisms merely adopt the anti-democratic "language of his adversaries and turn it against them."[161] Overall, there may be some distancing from some Genevan remonstrators, but it remains the case that for Rousseau—as for Locke—popular sovereignty plays a central and indispensable role in just politics.[162]

Finally, the question of peace versus liberty raises major difficulties. Whatmore's revision finds support in the *Mountain*. First, in its accounts of Jean-Jacques's own civic behavior, peace is the main emphasis. It claims that, during the recent quarrels, he was often solicited to return to Geneva in person, but he knew that by appearing he would have caused a stir and likely vindicated his rights (VIII, 269/852).[163] Nonetheless, "I preferred perpetual exile from my fatherland; I renounced everything, even hope, rather than risk public tranquility. I deserve to be thought sincere, when I speak in favor of it" (269/852).[164] Second, it includes direct strictures against political violence, and even Leigh—whose Rousseau is far more activist than Whatmore's—sees one of these strictures as foreshadowing the absolute prohibition of civic bloodshed that we have seen in the letters of 1768.[165] The *Mountain* claims that for the bourgeois in the present conflict, "There was no question . . . of tumults or of violence." Even if Tronchin writes several times that "everything is permitted in extreme evils," for Rousseau "violent means do not suit the just cause" (269/851f). Similarly, "Even liberty is too expensive" at the price of "the blood of our brothers" (256/836). All of this would be in keeping with the recent majority position among scholars as diverse as Judith Shklar, Arthur Melzer, Robert Wokler, and Istvan Hont—contrary to the earlier, frenzied Jacobin picture of Rousseau—that he explicitly, decisively repudiated revolution.[166] Notably, Wokler emphasizes a 1766 letter to "the mysterious republican comtesse de Wartensleben," which contains "one of the finest pages of eighteenth-century French prose."[167] He cites this letter's claim "that the liberty of the whole of humanity could not justify shedding the blood of a single man" as central support for his own conclusion that "it cannot be stressed too strongly that [Rousseau] wished to avert rather than promote revolution and spurned the idea of overthrow, through violence, of any government of his day."[168]

Although Richard Tuck does not link it with debates over the right to revolution, he has recently presented contrary evidence. He cites the testimony of "an English visitor in 1776" that Rousseau "fully supported the Americans."[169] In particular, the visitor reports Rousseau saying that "the Americans . . . had not the less right to defend their liberties because they were obscure or unknown."[170] They were discussing Thomas Day's *The Dying Negro*, which expressed a contrary view of the Americans, based on their hypocrisy about slavery, and this had offended Rousseau.[171] Although from a secondhand source, this is potentially significant, not only concerning revolution but also in view of Melzer's sound generalization that Rousseau's "writings contain not a single reference" to England's American colonies.[172]

5. An Earlier Right to Revolution

I argue that the counsels of restraint are highly significant to Rousseau's project, but, taken on their own, they likely distort his intentions in the *Mountain*, as well as his previous political writings. One difficulty is that polemicizing for peace and against tumult can easily serve as cover for reactionary authorities seeking to squelch a justified and restrained dissent. Rousseau faults Tronchin's critique of the Roman tribunes for exactly this authoritarian tendency (*Mountain* IX, 291–92/879–80).[173] In the actual Genevan context as Rousseau sees it at this time, the main political threat is surely popular complacency rather than disorder.[174] One of the book's most-cited passages—which apparently derides the commercial Genevans for being so unlike the civic Spartans—seems in fact mainly intended to suggest that *this* citizenry is very far from the excess agitation attributed to it by the magistrates (see 292f/881). Their strong commercial priorities make them the "polar opposite" of a "restless, unoccupied, turbulent people always ready" to be politically engaged; such a people needs to be able to rectify governmental abuses with lighter civic effort (see 293/881). He lists several historical incidents, leading to the conclusion that the bourgeoisie of Geneva, far from being "turbulent and seditious," has never even been "vigilant, attentive, [or] easily stirred up to defend its best established and most openly attacked rights" (298/887).[175] In a commercial society, citizens of middling means will be tempted to avoid the persecution that may come for speaking out against political abuses—they thus "sacrifice everything to peace," preferring safety to liberty (299/888).[176] Here we might recall that in his earlier political treatises, Rousseau would often invoke the tradition of thought that the "order" imposed by despotism entails a psychological and civic death and, accordingly, it is proper to sacrifice *some* (ostensible) peace, thereby enduring some (occasional or moderate) instability for the sake of liberty: "Riots [*émuetes*], civil wars, greatly alarm chiefs, but they do not cause the true miseries of peoples. . . . A little agitation energizes souls, and what causes the species truly to prosper is not so much peace as freedom" (SC III.9, 105–6n/420n).[177] Rosenblatt sees this note as a response to "the patriciate's Hobbesian harping on the need for peace and security."[178]

Well-known from Machiavelli's analysis of tumults in the *Discourses on Livy*,[179] we find a systematic version of the argument in Sidney. He first insists that "seditions, tumults, and [civil] wars" are less common in popular and mixed governments.[180] Yet, more to Rousseau's later point, Sidney also maintains that "seditions, tumults, and wars" are not the worst things that can proceed from a government, but rather, it is "worse to bring nations to such misery, weakness and baseness, as to have neither strength nor courage to contend for anything; to have nothing left worth defending, and to give the name of peace to desolation."[181] This form of killing takes "from men the means of living," thus preventing marriage and births.[182] In the same way, although Locke's *Two Treatises* generally avoid political psychology, he makes observations "by the by" linking absolute monarchy and diminishing population.[183] Finally, this civic and psychological death is prominent in Montesquieu's analysis of despotism: "While the principle of despotic government is fear, its end is tranquility; but this is not a peace, it is the silence of the towns that the enemy is ready to occupy."[184]

In view of Rousseau's analysis and his strong association with this agonistic political tradition, it seems too simple to say that liberty is not worth a drop of human blood. Most scholars would agree that for Rousseau, the maxim would be meant only to apply to domestic politics, and foreign conquerors could still be forcibly resisted. But then, would a successful conquest imply an absolute duty of submission by the conquered and their descendants? The Genevan is certainly aware of this problem. A letter primarily arguing against conspiracy and bloodshed mentions, as an apparent exception, the case of Pelopidas (d. 364

BC), who delivered his native Thebes from the yoke of the Spartans.[185] Since Plutarch dedicates a life to Pelopidas, Rousseau would likely have considered this case since his childhood. The *Geneva Manuscript* argues that the state of war between a conqueror and the conquered does not end except "by means of a free and voluntary convention." Thus, "the moment the subjugated people can shake off a yoke imposed by force . . . , it should" (I.5, CW 4:93 / OC 3:302). Similarly, from his fragmentary "The State of War," on the Spartans and the Helots: "They were necessarily in a state of war with one another, simply because they were the masters and the others the slaves. There is no doubt that since the Lacedaemonians killed the Helots, the Helots had the right to kill the Lacedaemonians" (LPW 176 / OC 3:608; see also SC I.1, I.4, esp. 48/358). Overall, this is likely another case where he follows Sidney, Locke, and Montesquieu, in greatly limiting the supposed rights of conquerors.[186] Sidney, for instance, insists on the rights of a "subdued nation" or "conquered people"[187] and includes Pelopidas in his pantheon of Greek, Roman, and biblical leaders who delivered their people from "their oppressors," avenging "the injuries received from foreign or domestic tyrants [*Tirans Domestiques ou Etrangers*]."[188]

Parallel questions can emerge within any community. For instance, if a government violently suppresses peaceful protesters, must the latter permanently capitulate or be blamed for any further bloodshed? For Locke, in the case of an unjust attack, "the safety of the innocent is to be preferred."[189] Similarly, denying the right of revolution because of the need for peace is like saying "that honest men may not oppose robbers or pirates, because this may occasion disorder or bloodshed."[190] Rousseau seems to raise this question within the very passage of the *Mountain* that swears off "violent means." Although there was no question of "tumults or of violence" for the Genevan bourgeoisie in the recent cases, he describes these recourses as "sometimes necessary but always terrible, that have been very wisely forbidden to you. Not that you have ever abused them, since on the contrary you never used them except in the final extremity, only for your defense, and always with a moderation that perhaps ought to have preserved the right of arms for you, if any people could have it without danger" (VIII, 269/851). So extrajudicial force is apparently "sometimes necessary," especially "for your own defense"—thus raising the very Lockean possibility that a government might put itself in a "state of war" against its own people.[191] The remark on "forbidden to you" apparently refers to specific legal prohibitions from the 1738 Mediation (see *Mountain* VII, 250/829f). The loss of the "right of arms" occurred soon after 1738. Having played a triumphant role in the earlier civil conflict, the "bourgeois militias" were disbanded.[192] This provides a more provocative context for the well-known, effusively patriotic reminiscence of the bourgeois military exercises, near the end of the *Letter to d'Alembert* (135–36n/351n/123–24n; cf. *Poland* XII, 236/1016).

We find similar conclusions when Rousseau fills out some of the history that is alluded to in this passage. He describes a famous Genevan episode from 1734. In response to a firm assertion of their rights by the citizens, certain magistrates wove a "conspiracy." They prepared barricades at a high point of the city and began transporting weapons and munitions "in order to subjugate the whole people from there" (see *Mountain* IX, 294, 294n/882f, 882–83n). Linda Kirk describes this episode, known as the "*tamponnement*": "About twenty cannon, so placed that bourgeois insurgents could have made effective use of them, were rendered inoperable by having wooden plugs hammered into them." Meanwhile two large guns were spotted being secretly transported to a strategic patrician area.[193] Roussseau presents the citizens' response as morally straightforward: "The plot is discovered; the bourgeois are forced to take up arms, and by that violent undertaking the [Small] Council loses a century of usurpation in a moment" (294/882f).[194] The bourgeois practiced extraordinary restraint following their victory. They sought no vengeance against the conspirators, whereas, "In any other country the people would have begun by massacring these conspirators, and pillaging their houses" (see 294n/883n; cf. VII, 243f/821).[195] This was part of their larger tendency: "Look in your history to see whether all the plots haven't always come from the side of the magistracy, and whether the Citizens have ever had recourse to force except when it was necessary to protect themselves against it" (IX, 300/890).

This pattern extends to all peoples, according to Rousseau: "Never has the people rebelled against the laws when the leaders did not begin by breaking them in some respect" (*Mountain* VIII, 262n/843n; cf. *Beaumont* 61/978). He goes on to argue that China flourishes compared to Europe in terms of population, because, in spite of "oriental despotism," it always responds to a local revolt by first "punishing the governor." Europe's adherence to "the opposite maxim" explains its steadily diminishing population (*Mountain* VIII, 262n/843n).[196] Here, again, we might see Rousseau joining Locke against Hobbes. For Locke, it seems evident that more disorder has emerged from "the ruler's insolence" than from "the people's wantonness."[197] For Hobbes, "The condition of man in this life shall never be without inconvenience; but there happeneth in no commonwealth any great inconvenience, but what proceeds from the subject's disobedience and breach of those covenants from which the commonwealth has its being."[198]

In all this, the Genevans' aspirations for constitutional change were limited. Yet, in the tumults or violence passage, Rousseau briefly asserts a general principle: "When the excess of tyranny puts the one who suffers it above the laws, it is still necessary that what he attempts in order to destroy it leave some hope of succeeding" (269/851f).[199] This might cause us to rethink some of his cautious claims about revolution in his earlier political writings, where he often refrains from advocating it directly, but lays out the conditions when it becomes empirically inevitable and normatively irreproachable.[200] For instance, in the *Discourse on Inequality*, we see a final return to "the sole law of the stronger and consequently to a new state of nature" (DOI II, 171–72, 179, 185–86/175–76, 184, 190–91). And in the *Social Contract*, there is a time when ordinary citizens are "restored by right to their natural freedom, and forced to obey but not obligated to do so" (III.10, esp. 108/423).[201] The best-known claim (of "the age of revolutions") is merely a prediction, but it could be connected with the logic of being restored to natural freedom under extreme conditions (see E III, 194, 194n/468, 468n).

None of this suggests that Rousseau would support the attempt to forcibly and drastically transform a large aristocratic and commercial monarchy into a republic—he would reject that for many reasons. In general, the prospects for transforming corrupt societies are bleak.[202] In part because of the degradation that despotism generates, in almost all cases revolutions only increase oppression.[203] Yet, several of the passages making these arguments also suggest that there are exceptions. Melzer cites much evidence to demonstrate "that Rousseau genuinely opposed revolution."[204] Similarly, for Wokler, "Of course Rousseau proposed no revolutionary transformations of corrupt society into new republics of virtue."[205] Both Melzer and Wokler may conflate the prospects for widespread European regeneration through revolution, with a normative question of political right—whether it is ever permissible to use force against one's existing regime.

While eschewing the prospects for European regeneration, our evidence indicates that Rousseau's general principles on the domestic use of extrajudicial force are further from Hobbes, and significantly closer to Locke, than the established scholarly positions would allow. His counsels against this force are more stringent than Locke's, at least in all cases where discretion is still possible. Yet, in the last resort, it is the practical feebleness and normative groundlessness of tyranny, rather than the unacceptability of ever responding with force, that is his stance.

Nonetheless, it remains the case that he clearly does not advise the Genevans to a forcible overthrow of their government in the *Mountain*. Despite a few heated claims that their tyranny could not become worse, many of the conditions of liberty and justice remain there (cf. VII, 237, 254f/813, 835; IX, 304/894–95).

Moreover, as Whatmore has established, Rousseau is aware of the likelihood of French intervention if the bourgeoisie push their political cause too far or too violently. As he writes, "In your position every false step is fatal, everything that might lead you to take it is a trap, and if you were the masters for an instant, in less than fifteen days you would be crushed forever" (*Mountain* VIII, 269/852). It seems most plausible to see Rousseau here as counseling extreme restraint with regard to violence, but not (pace Whatmore) capitulation about their just cause concerning remonstrances. They are not seeking to be "masters" but only to have a feasible mode of legal redress for perceived injustices.[206] This international context makes prudence especially necessary. However, the present goals of the citizens are justified and attainable enough that continued agitation is more than called for: "All means of protesting against injustice are permitted when they are peaceful," especially the legally authorized ones pursued by the remonstrators (IX, 305/896). In context, the claim seems to be advising the citizens to vote against the tyrannically inclined members of the government (see 305/895f). This was what they nearly achieved in January 1765.[207]

6. A Quietist Turn (ca. October 1766–March 1768)

If a more populist republican emphasis remains the best reading of the *Letters Written from the Mountain*, how should we explain the later falling out with the remonstrators? It seems that, through 1764, whatever political differences existed between them and Rousseau must have been subtle enough that they did not lead to substantial political ruptures. As Whatmore himself suggests, part of the issue is the rise of a new generation in Geneva, but, for our purposes, it is most notable that one of these figures "traced Rousseau's apostasy to February 1768, when he had advised the *représentants* to yield to the patricians or leave their homeland."[208] Whatmore quotes François d'Ivernois, who faults Rousseau for using "all the arts of eloquence and friendship to persuade the *représentants* that tranquility was yet more precious than liberty, and that they ought to think themselves happy to purchase peace by any sacrifice."[209] Leigh describes the 1768 context: "During the siege of Geneva he begged the Citizens to capitulate; and at a later stage, he even urged a mass exodus of Citizens from the city, with their wives, their children, and their possessions, leaving the Petit Conseil to rule over a ghost town. Finally, when the Citizens were actually poised for victory, he urged them to settle for much less than they eventually obtained. His advice was disregarded."[210]

We might ask, then, whether the young remonstrators needed to reject Rousseau's political philosophy as such, or whether he made some later shift or isolated pronouncement that is to blame. Unlike Whatmore, Leigh finds a shift beginning around February 1765, when Rousseau "came to feel that the cause of the Citizens was hopeless," given that the Small Council proved "so obdurate," and "could always rely on French bayonets."[211] Overall, we have independent evidence for an apolitical turn in Rousseau, occurring soon after the *Letters Written from the Mountain*.[212] This is commonly indicated in biographical discussions, but here we suggest a corresponding philosophical shift—a "quietist" turn around this time. For it is one thing to shy away from political controversy, but it is quite another to counsel those who are politically engaged to opt for a peace amounting to capitulation.[213] Rousseau's teaching seems to have shifted ambivalently in this direction in 1766–1767. Consider, especially, the 27 September 1766 letter to the comtesse de Wartensleben. Its best-known sentence opposes any revolutionary bloodshed.[214] However, in context, the claim is subtly qualified, and it is unclear how the general stances relate to personal preferences:

> *Conspiracies may be heroic acts of patriotism*, and there have been some of those; but *almost always* they are only punishable crimes, whose authors think much less of serving their fatherland than subjugating it. . . . *As for me*, I declare to you that for nothing in the world would I have wanted to dip myself in *the most legitimate conspiracy*; because finally these sorts of enterprises cannot be executed without troubles, disorders, violences, sometimes without effusions of blood, and that in my opinion the blood of a single person is worth much more than the liberty of the entire human race.[215]

Much ambivalence is also on display in 1767. One letter begins with deep praise for the bourgeoisie, whose courageous and firm resistance has the unusual merit of remaining "wise and moderate amid great dangers."[216] Then, in a separate section, written eight days later, having been informed of the extremities to which "your poor people are reduced," he changes tune. It is, "according to me, time to concede," "since resistance is useless, and you should [concede] to preserve what remains afterwards of your laws and your liberty."[217] By contrast, a few months later, he indicates that he would not make a good arbitrator, since "I would fear that the love of peace was no longer as strong in my heart as that of liberty."[218] Then, in 1768, we find a decisive quietism concerning Genevan affairs, clearly framed by general principles.[219]

Admittedly, the later stance has some continuity with a strand of Stoicism in the original normative teaching, maintaining that the wise person can find (some degree of) happiness and freedom anywhere on earth. However, that seems to be presented as a qualified happiness, to be sought under lamentable circumstances.[220] Moreover, the Rousseau of 1768 seems highly exposed to the anti-quietist polemic of the *Social Contract*, where the hapless Christian, convinced that the world is inevitably a vale of tears, cares little for political liberty and leaves his community to be preyed upon by domestic charlatans and foreign conquerors.[221] This is in keeping with the satires of Pauline and Hobbesian quietism in the opening chapters of the *Social Contract*—surely some of the most pugnacious writing of any major political philosopher before Marx. Although it is conceded in some way that superior power must be submitted to, this is purely a question of fact rather than right (SC I.3, and III.6, 99/413).[222]

Before closing, we turn to a statement of this Genevan quietism that is in the *Confessions*, and thus far better known than the letters of 1766–1768. Like the *Letters Written from the Mountain*, the *Confessions* discusses the crisis of 1734–1738. Yet, whereas the *Mountain* praises the restraint of the bourgeoisie amid their use of force, the *Confessions* discusses Rousseau's own visit to Geneva in 1737 in very different terms. He claims he witnessed a father and son leaving the same house toward their rival camps, "certain of finding each other face to face two hours later, putting themselves *at risk of* slitting each other's throats" (V, 181/216).[223] Thus, even the near potential for this bloodshed proved decisive for our observer: "This awful spectacle made such a deep impression on me that I swore never to be involved in any civil war [*guerre civile*] and never to uphold liberty within the state by arms, either in person or by my approval" (181/216).[224] In a parallel passage, he links this with his refusal, in 1763–1764, to follow his friends' advice to return to Geneva to reclaim his rights: "The fear of the disorder and troubles that my presence might cause kept me from acquiescing"; he thus remained "faithful to the oath I had previously made of never being a party to any civil dissension [*dissention civile*] in my country" (XII, 510/609).[225] Note that the passage written later, on avoiding any "civil dissension," goes further than the earlier passage, on avoiding any "civil war" (V, 181/216).

Although these passages were written around 1766–1770[226]—overlapping with the quietist turn posited here—they claim a fundamental continuity from 1737, thus challenging any developmental model. I respond, first, that even the *Confessions* does not claim a full continuity, since it concedes that he was far from truly "Genevan" in 1737, in terms of republicanism and patriotism. He even admits to giving away sensitive plans for the fortification of Geneva to Sardinia, Geneva's "oldest enemy" (Conf. V, 181–82/216–18).[227] Second, and conversely, our developmental account is not meant as an absolute dichotomy, and, insofar as the vow reported in the *Confessions* indicates a strong resistance to employing violent means in Geneva, it would largely overlap with the restrained activism we saw in the *Mountain*. However, an absolute renunciation of force would go further. Such a renunciation may, in fact, be suggested in an earlier draft of the *Mountain*. He offers an account—similar to the later *Confessions*—of the "awful spectacle" he witnessed in 1737, of a father and son perhaps meeting face to face and "reduced to slitting each other's throats." He describes the vow he made, but he avoids making any substantive political stance, instead claiming only that he would "testify to the horror which it had inspired in me." He concludes: "Genevans, I fulfill my vow today. If it is possible, restore your liberty; but be slaves rather than parricides. Shed enemy blood—with painful groans—if it is necessary; never that of your fellow citizens."[228] This would confirm an important continuity of sentiment across the periods in question. However, in terms of political teaching, it is significant that this passage was omitted from the final version and replaced with the passage we have seen, praising the restrained self-defense of the bourgeoisie (*Mountain* VIII, 269/851).[229] I conjecture that, in making revisions, he came to see that he could not allow his personal distaste to lead to such a sweeping political conclusion.[230] For that would empower any oppressive establishment to call the bluff of any indignant citizenry and know it can violently suppress them with impunity. The official version of the *Mountain* allows these regimes no such confidence.

As for the major political writings through 1762, we would perhaps do better to read them in the light of this cautious yet firmly resistant stance, rather than the settled preference for peace over liberty that—we have reasons to believe—began developing around 1766. This trend would perhaps culminate in a well-known passage of the *Dialogues*, which is often taken as decisively showing that he repudiated revolution. "Rousseau" laments the public perception of Jean-Jacques as "a promoter of upheavals and disturbances," since he is in reality "the one man in the world who maintains the truest respect for laws and national constitutions, and who has the greatest aversion to revolutions and conspirators of every kind" (RJJ III, 213/935).

7. Conclusion: The Activist Moment

This and the previous chapter have pulled together many historical and philosophical threads, but perhaps they have raised as many questions as they have answered. More consistency in Rousseau's political behavior, and constancy in his motives, would have lightened the efforts of author and reader alike. A few broad trends and generalizations may be indicated. I find a decisive turn to direct political activism in Genevan affairs, here called the "activist moment," around July 1762–February 1765. Like his more abstract writings, his accomplishments during this period remain controversial, although, for the Genevans, much more was immediately at stake. It seems fair to read his behavior and writings of this period as pleasing to the Genevan "left,"[231] as well as to sympathetic recent historians such as Leigh, Trousson, and Rosenblatt. He was thus equally abhorrent to the Genevan establishment. Moreover, this was a time when a considerable swath of enlightened opinion turned against him and some became more aggressive in their opposition.[232] Voltaire advocated the utmost severity: "If one lightly chastises an impious novelist, one punishes capitally a vile insurgent [*un vil séditieux*]."[233] By comparison, Diderot was considerably warming to Jean-Jacques during this period, largely due to his sympathetic identification with any philosopher persecuted by the ignorant and the superstitious.[234] Politically, however, he remained unimpressed. He now contrasts the author of the *Letters Written from the Mountain* with several of the great political leaders of Athens who were betrayed by their homelands (Cimon, Themistocles, Aristides, Miltiades).[235] (Diderot's inclusion of Themistocles seems odd, given the latter's eventual service of the Persian Empire. However, Marcet had also pointed to Themistocles as a model under Rousseau's circumstances, referring to his eventual decision to commit suicide rather than fulfill his promise to aid the Persians against the Greeks as "the most beautiful [way to] take leave of his fatherland.")[236] Although the contributions of these Greeks to their homelands had been far greater than Rousseau's, Diderot claims that their response to "their ungrateful fatherland" was more restrained: "Has anyone caught sight of them avenging themselves, of arming citizen against citizen, of bathing the streets, public places, and temples in blood?"[237] The charge is exaggerated and may still indicate traces of personal animus. Even though I have argued for a relatively pugnacious Rousseau in the *Letters Written from the Mountain*, any fair reading would indicate its insistence on orderly procedure and restraint among his followers, especially concerning violence. But Diderot was far from alone. An early friend and leftish figure, the Abbé de Mably condemned Rousseau directly: "I pitied you in your misfortunes, as I pitied Socrates; but permit me to say it to you: In order to avenge himself against his judges, Socrates did not try to stir up a rebellion [*une sédition*] in Athens."[238] David Hume was personally sympathetic yet politically conservative and was not amused: "I disapprove particularly of the seditious purpose of the last letters, which have succeeded but too well at Geneva: for the magistrates of that city, which the author had formerly celebrated with reason as one of the best governed, are in mortal fear every hour of being massacred by the populace."[239] This reception is likely another reason that Rousseau's later retrospectives were coy about his political activities during this period.[240]

Regardless of the wisdom of Rousseau's political stances or strategies, there can be no doubt that he was highly political from around July 1762 through February 1765. The period could be seen as indicating his potential to fulfill a normal range of concrete political duties. If this had been the usual pattern of his life, he would not have been open to the easy dismissals of Diderot or David Gauthier.[241] Yet, as it is, this is a brief phase within a long career, and its political intensity was largely covered up in his own retrospectives. Hence, our final judgment of citizen Jean-Jacques must also hinge on the more elaborate justifications of the "distant citizenship" period (1754–June 1762),[242] as well as the far more isolated period which began in 1765. Chapters 5 and 6 further explore this last period.

Turning from political stances and behavior to self-representation and stated ideals, the Rousseau of the activist moment usually seems more ambitious than the earlier, devoted (albeit distant) citizen. Apart from the brief period leading to the publishing of *Emile*, in this activist phase Rousseau's boldness and willingness to risk himself are more prominent and recurrent. Yet, in both cases, we cannot be certain how far the principled Socratism extends or to what extent it could be explained as a certain obliviousness about how crushing the ancien régime responses would be. (In the case of *Letters Written from the Mountain*, Cranston observes that both Rousseau and his ally, Captain d'Astier, were surely "most unworldly in having ever expected the Inquisitor [at Avignon] to sanction a book in which St. Paul is described as a 'natural persecutor' and Christian miracles are dismissed as illusions.")[243] An ultimate judgment of his character would require a careful inquiry, at psychological and social levels, about how far the abdication of citizenship was a painful sacrifice to him, motivated mainly by public liberty and justice, rather than a gratification of personal drives to be left alone, to defend his honor, or even to exact vengeance. Rousseau lacked the decisive evidence that Socrates was required to give—the virtuous death which "ought to give weight" to all his other instructions, and which alone distinguished his life and thought decisively from the sophists.[244] Therefore, Rousseau's embraces of this parallel opened him up to new mockeries of extravagant self-regard. Friedrich Melchior Grimm observes that the author of the *Mountain* reveals "a very great naivety about his own merit, and about the respect and gratitude which the human race owes him. He also says that Cicero is only a rhetor, that Voltaire is an Aristophanes, and he, Rousseau, a Socrates."[245] Similarly, before the publication of the *Letter to Beaumont*, Voltaire was eagerly anticipating the "Letter to Christophe" but, upon seeing it, was very disappointed that Rousseau spoke unceasingly of himself.[246] At this point, Rousseau and his associates embraced the exacting, Socratic standard, but, as we shall see, continued personal disaster—both imposed and self-inflicted—would lead him to seek lesser standards of comparison.

In this chapter, I have pursued three main objectives. First, in laying out a comprehensive narrative of Rousseau's political activities and self-justifications during his "activist moment," I have filled a gap in the *Confessions* and countered its surprisingly Hobbesian emphasis on his peaceableness. Second, in engaging the learned and provocative revisionism of Whatmore, I offer a more democratic and activist Rousseau. The latter should not be seen as staking out a middle position between the Genevan remonstrators and the patricians but, rather, strongly weighing in on the remonstrators' side regarding the "negative right," the relative merits of popular sovereignty, and the remonstrators' right to pursue their cause at some risk to the public tranquility. Third, I challenge the recent majority position among scholars concerning Rousseau and revolution. Once it is acknowledged that he shifted in a quietist direction around 1766–1768, his earlier thinking emerges as a subtle variation on the Lockean defense of revolution. Overall, the activist moment (ca. July 1762–February 1765) represents a major shift in the political behavior of Rousseau, while its aftermath represents a shift in the opposite direction, with significant implications for his thought about political resistance.

CHAPTER 5

Excursus

The Revenge of Voltaire and the Autobiographical Turn (ca. October 1762–February 1765)

For all the political and religious polemics in the *Letters Written from the Mountain*, and the resulting fallout, it was a brief digression at Voltaire's expense that may have proved the most consequential for our former citizen. He had long been frustrated at the Genevan patricians' tolerance for Voltaire's blasphemous satires, while his own earnestly religious works were burned (*Mountain* I, 136/690). This pattern of censorship leads to a comparison with Athens, in which Voltaire seems to play the role of Aristophanes: "It is with these same ways of thinking that the Athenians applauded the impieties of Aristophanes and had Socrates put to death" (V, 224/797).[1] Alluding to the friendship between Voltaire and the Genevan ruling class, he asks why Voltaire "has not inspired them with that spirit of toleration that he preaches endlessly, and that he sometimes needs" (224f/799). Rousseau had similarly alleged hypocrisy in a 1764 open letter, in another aside calling Voltaire "the most ardent, the most adroit of my persecutors."[2] If this weren't enough, the *Mountain* also included a mock speech by Voltaire that takes credit for one of his anonymous religious satires, *The Oath of the Fifty* (225/799). This outraged Voltaire. In addition to the risks it might bring, this violated his ethic of authorial anonymity, which was very different from Rousseau's approach to his own works.[3] Relations between the two thinkers had severely declined since at least 1760. Notably, in discussing the publication of his letter on providence, Rousseau sent a "rude and tactless letter" to Voltaire on 17 June 1760.[4] Rousseau transcribes the letter in *Confessions*, including the offending final paragraph: "I do not like you at all, Monsieur.... You have ruined Geneva.... I hate you" (X, 453/541f). According to R. A. Leigh,

Rousseau "was blissfully unaware of the probable repercussions of his gratuitous sally in a mind permanently acclimatized to the conventions of polite mendacity."[5] Against this backdrop, it is no surprise that the digression in the *Mountain* drove Voltaire to fury.

He replied with a devastating pamphlet: *The Sentiment of the Citizens* (December 1764).[6] It was published anonymously, imitating the style of Genevan pastors so effectively that Rousseau would forever remain duped. The latter publicly attributed the pamphlet to Jacob Vernes, his former friend and more recent critic, and persisted in this belief throughout his life, despite Vernes's credible denials.[7] For his part, Voltaire denied authorship emphatically, but clear evidence to the contrary was later offered by Jean Louis Wagnière, his secretary at this time. He testified it was written by Voltaire, who was "justly irritated" and "avenging himself" for the injuries done to him by Rousseau.[8] Robert Wokler notes the resistance of eighteenth-century publishers and a few recent Voltaire scholars, including the editor of Voltaire's correspondence, Theodore Besterman, to include this "scurrilous" attack among Voltaire's works.[9]

Framed as the Genevan pastors' response to the *Letters Written from the Mountain*, the *Sentiment* claims they have lost patience and pity for this former citizen, whose "madness" has turned into "rage," bringing shame to a city once known only for "pure morals" and "solid works."[10] He "ragefully offends" against the Christian religion, our ministers, and "all the bodies of the state."[11] The pamphlet outlines some religious offenses and describes the turmoil he foments in Geneva for merely egotistical purposes. The quarrels and disturbances had died down, but Rousseau seeks to turn the city "upside down," merely "because a bad book has been burned at Paris and Geneva."[12] In its crucial section, the pamphlet lodges the charge that has tainted Rousseau's name ever since. The citizens ask what kind of man it is who is mistreating our pastors, while teaching us "about the duties of society."

> Is it a scholar who is disputing against scholars? No, it is the author of an opera and of two comedies that were hissed at. Is it a good man who, deceived by a false zeal, is making indiscreet reproaches to virtuous men? We admit, blushing and with sorrow, that this is a man who still bears the marks of his debaucheries, and who, dressed up as a street-swindler,[13] drags with him from village to village, and from mountain to mountain, the unfortunate woman whose mother he killed, and whose children he exposed at the door of a hospital, rejecting the cares that a charitable person wanted to provide them,

> and renouncing all the feelings of nature, as he casts off those of honor and religion.[14]

Some of the charges were mere libels, including the one about killing Thérèse's mother (who was, in fact, alive).[15] Wokler describes Voltaire's overall justification of this strategy: "In his commitment to the cause of reform, Voltaire felt free to employ every artistic stratagem, every sarcastic distortion of the aims of his reactionary foe . . . , which he supposed might take seed or bear fruit."[16]

The charge of debauchery leading to sexually transmitted disease was also particularly horrifying to Rousseau, and he returned to it many times from this point on (e.g., "he is rotting with syphilis," according to "the Frenchman": RJJ II, 168/877). Jean Starobinski maintains that, if the sexual adventures in the *Confessions* are "hardly of the sort to boast about," Rousseau is thereby "demonstrating and defending his timidity. Recounting without shame his autoerotic behavior and his failures with women" enables him to rebut this slander.[17]

For all Voltaire's distortions, as we have seen in the case of the children, an exaggerated charge pointed to a secret of great importance. The impact on Rousseau was manifold. Personally, and in combination with the religious arguments of the *Mountain*, this pamphlet undermined his standing with the pastors and common people of Môtiers enough that, within the year, he had to flee under threat of popular violence. His home was stoned the night of 6-7 September 1765; on 9 September he arrived at the Island of Saint-Pierre, later immortalized in *Confessions* XII and *Reveries* V.[18]

Some biographers and historians see the pamphlet as a psychological turning point, when Rousseau's mental capacities began a decisive decline. According to Maurice Cranston, from the day that Rousseau read this pamphlet, his "capacity for clear judgment faltered."[19] Richard Whatmore observes, in connection with Rousseau's false identification of Vernes as the author of *Sentiment*: "The persecution mania that dogged Rousseau's final years began to take hold."[20] Mental decline remains a disputed question, and it is not a direct concern of this book.

Politically, it seems likely that, despite the recent gains of his cause in Geneva, and a few hopeful weeks at the beginning of 1765, the pamphlet played a role in his final surrender. Following another political setback in early February,[21] Rousseau wrote to his leading Genevan associates with new resolutions: "Not only do I no longer want to meddle in the affairs of Geneva, or even to hear them spoken of, but this time I quit the pen and am sure that nothing will make me pick it up again."[22] He explains his new approach: "I will act like children or drunks who simply let themselves fall when someone pushes them, and don't get hurt at all."[23] A more thorough explanation is given slightly later: "The turn which your affairs have taken, Messieurs, and mine, the persuasion that truth and justice no longer have any authority among men, the ardent desire to spare a few moments of repose at the end of my sad career, have made me take the irrevocable resolution of renouncing henceforth all interaction with the public, all correspondence outside of the most absolutely necessary, especially to Geneva."[24] Finally, to the Delucs, he irrevocably breaks off their correspondence and all discussion of Geneva on the following grounds: "Since with such pure intentions, since with so much love for justice and for truth I have done only harm on this earth, I want to do no more of it, and shall retire within myself."[25] With regard to Genevan politics and withdrawing into himself, these are resolutions he substantially kept.[26]

As for never picking up his pen again, something rather different is suggested by the more than one thousand pages of posthumous autobiographical books that we find in the *Pléiade* edition. In January 1765, just before declaring his civic surrender to his Genevan associates, he had explained to Charles Duclos in France his resolution to write about his life.[27] For such reasons, a traditional view is that Voltaire's attack gave birth to the autobiographical project, but that has been proven an exaggeration.[28] Rousseau had long considered writing memoirs and had often been asked to do so. An important 31 December 1761 request by his publisher, Marc-Michel Rey, had been long preceded by others, and Rousseau had apparently resolved to write his memoirs in Spring 1759.[29] An early statement, dating around 1758–1762, is found in "My Portrait": "I am approaching the end of life and I have not done any good on earth. I have good intentions, but it is not always as easy as one thinks to do good. I conceive a new sort of service to render to men: it is to offer them the faithful image of one among them so that they might learn to know themselves" (CW 12:36 / OC 1:1120). While planning his retirement from serious writing in Montmorency (ca. spring 1759–June 1762), he considered this compatible with writing his memoirs, since this was at least initially seen as something that would be taken up at his leisure.[30] The Neuchâtel Preamble (1764) to the *Confessions* claims to offer "a portrait, not a book"; it would disguise him if it were "a carefully written work like the other ones" (CW 5:589 / OC 1:1154).[31] In addition, given its truthful portraits of many other people, it would be wrong to publish it during their lives.[32] In several letters, he presents others' interests or rights (what we would call privacy rights) as a major obstacle to undertaking the project sincerely and therefore properly. He suggests posthumous publication—perhaps even with a ten-year delay[33]—as the only possible solution.

Biographers typically speak in general terms of 1762, or the move to Switzerland, as marking the autobiographical turn,[34] or a turn to writings defending his own integrity.[35] There is an upsurge of relevant activity following the catastrophe of June 1762. In October, he wrote to Malesherbes, urgently requesting copies of the letters that he had sent him in January: the "four consecutive letters on my character and the history of my soul."[36] Leigh comments: "This request shows that JJ was thinking actively of his *Confessions*."[37] Rousseau set apart the copy of the letters sent to him with a small band of paper, on which he wrote "Four Letters . . . Containing the true picture of my character and the true motives for all my behavior."[38] In November, the catastrophe would be invoked with his publisher in connection with the memoirs: "Six months ago my life unfortunately became a work of importance that calls for time and reflection."[39] The letter goes on to claim that he lacks the necessary leisure at this point, although he has "despite himself taken up the pen again," alluding to the *Letter to Beaumont*.[40]

In early 1763, he ordered three books that seem to be of special importance for this endeavor: Pascal's *Pensées*, La Bruyère's *Oeuvres* (including the *Characters*), and a Latin edition of Kempis, *The Imitation of Christ*.[41] Bernard Gagnebin and Marcel Raymond describe these as "books of earthly exile."[42] Kelly points out that, although in the *Confessions* Rousseau is silent about Augustine's *Confessions*, its "most famous predecessor in autobiography," he does offer a lengthy quote from this predecessor in the *Letter to Beaumont*, "written immediately before his resumption of the autobiographical project."[43] He told Moultou that writing his life was "the only thing that remains for me to do."[44] Nonetheless, other projects interrupted him, and it is difficult to establish when serious writing commenced. By the end of 1764, it seems that at least painstaking preparations had been made for the whole First Part (Books I–VI) of the *Confessions*, and the Neuchâtel Preamble was written.[45]

We know, then, that Voltaire did not cause the autobiographical turn. It seems, nonetheless, that he probably redoubled it, and perhaps changed its character. A letter written to Duclos soon after the "dreadful libel" describes how false friends and "the furor of my enemies" have greatly facilitated "the enterprise of writing my life, which you exhorted me to undertake."[46] In March 1765, Rousseau mentioned to Rey "the great enterprise of my life" and that "the work has already commenced."[47] By April, he would describe the uniqueness of his enterprise to his publisher, resolving, "I am making of it an object so important that I consecrate the rest of my life to it."[48] By October, the entire First Part was sketched.[49] As Cranston observes of the *Confessions,* Voltaire provided "the stimulus that produced, at a time when Rousseau had written himself out as a philosopher, his greatest literary achievement."[50] The work would remain his only urgent intellectual endeavor—whenever he was capable of intellectual endeavors—until late 1770.[51] More generally, after 1764, with only a few exceptions, he would not return to the fundamentally normative, theoretical, and religious writing that was his staple since the *Discourse on the Sciences and Arts.* The main exceptions are the *Constitutional Project for Corsica* (worked on mainly during the autumn and winter of 1764–1765, and perhaps continued through the autumn of 1765),[52] and the *Considerations on the Government of Poland* (written ca. October 1770–June 1771, in response to a request from a Polish nobleman and in connection with a temporary resurgence of moral and intellectual determination).[53]

As for changing the character of the memoirs, this is a complex and disputed question. Careful scholars have rejected sharp dichotomies, which contrast an early approach that is "psychological," or based on "self-knowledge" or "reminiscence," with a later approach that is "apologetic," "confessional," or focused on "self-justification."[54] Gagnebin and Raymond respond to Albert Schinz's case that Rousseau shifts, after his quarrel with Hume, from a "psychological" to an "apologetic" conception of his memoirs: "The great difference of material and tone which separates the preamble of Neuchâtel from the definitive preamble may support this point of view. . . . But one would be mistaken to absolutely oppose two conceptions of autobiography in this connection."[55] Similarly, Trousson challenges the view that one must "oppose" the two preambles, "the first expressing a serenely humanistic purpose, the second serving an aggressive apologetic."[56]

Nonetheless, as Gagnebin and Raymond concede, there are considerable differences of tone as we move from 1763 to 1765, not to mention 1770 and beyond (bearing in mind that many other slanders, both real and imagined, would proliferate). In the earlier letters, as well as the retrospective on how the project was conceived in Montmorency, this was not only a leisurely endeavor but also one justified in terms of its general philosophical usefulness. Since, before the catastrophe, his life had not been "very interesting as far as the facts went," they could become so only through an unprecedented "frankness" and "veracity" "so that for once at least a man might be seen just as he was inside" (Conf. X, 433/516).[57] This is the context of the following well-known criticism: "I had always laughed at the false naivety of Montaigne, who, while pretending to confess his faults, is very careful to give himself only lovable ones; whereas I, who had always believed myself and who still believe myself to be, all in all, the best [*meilleur*] of men, felt that there is no human being whose interior, however pure it may be, will not reveal some odious vice" (433/516f).[58] Unprecedented veracity remains the justification of the memoirs in the key 1763 letter: "The history of a man who will have the courage to show himself *intus et in cute* may be of some instruction to his fellow beings."[59] This Latin phrase, meaning "inside and under the skin," would become the epigraph of the *Confessions*.[60] Similarly, in the April 1765 letter to his publisher, he explains that without the openness that could only come with posthumous publication, he could only "write an ordinary life, masked and plastered," as opposed to "something unique and, I dare say, something truly beautiful."[61] Shifting, then, to the 1765 letter on the memoirs as his response to the "dreadful libel," he claims: "I will say everything, I will not omit one of my faults, not even one of my bad thoughts. I will paint myself just as I was, just as I am; the bad will almost always obscure [*offusquera*] the good, and despite this, I can scarcely believe that any of my readers will dare say to himself, I am better than that man was."[62] The method of openness is retained, but it is now linked, not with general philosophical usefulness, but with urgent personal vindication. Insofar as the *Confessions* and the *Dialogues* pursue the latter objective, in contrast with the earlier letters and the magnificent Neuchâtel Preamble to the *Confessions* (1764), we may again have Voltaire to thank.

CHAPTER 6

Only the Vicious Person Lives Alone

Social Duty and the Varieties of Solitude (ca. 1756–1778)

Does Rousseau stand for community or solitude? Are the moral demands of society, everything considered, a blessing or a curse? And is retreat from it a cause of incurable sadness or profound delight and contentment? His readers have long diverged widely on these points. In recent debates, scholars have often appealed to one of two striking passages, which suggest a definitive solution. The better known is from Walk V of the *Reveries of the Solitary Walker* (written 1776–1778), describing his moments on the island of Saint-Pierre (1765), when his soul transcended the "continual flux" and "transitory pleasure" of the earth. In such a state, the soul thinks not of past or future, pleasure or pain. It has no other sentiment

> except that alone of our existence, and having this sentiment alone fill it completely; as long as this state lasts, he who finds himself in it can call himself happy, not with an imperfect, poor, and relative happiness such as one finds in the pleasures of life, but with a sufficient, perfect, and full happiness which leaves in the soul no emptiness it might feel a need to fill. . . . What do we enjoy in such a situation? Nothing external to ourselves, nothing if not ourselves and our own existence. As long as this state lasts, we are sufficient unto ourselves, like God. (Rev. V, 68f/1046f)[1]

This has long been a celebrated passage, and many scholars have placed it near the center of Rousseau's normative thought, understood as radically individualistic and modern.[2] Our second, contrasting, passage is found in the less well-known *Rousseau, Judge of Jean-Jacques: Dialogues* (written 1772–1776). In this curious book, Rousseau's contemporaries are said to universally slander him as a monster of *amour-propre*, pride, wrath, plagiarism, and vicious morals in his personal life and writings. To answer such charges, our author uses a fictional character, "Rousseau," who is "Rousseau as he would be if he had read but not written his books and had only recently arrived in France," in conversation with a "Frenchman," to investigate "Jean-Jacques," a character representing the actual Rousseau.[3] (Patrick Riley calls this "schizophrenia turned into a literary genre").[4] In one passage, we find "Rousseau" commenting on "Jean-Jacques," who is said to have lost all "the sweet things of human society":[5] "I know that the commotion of the world frightens loving and tender hearts; that they withdraw and constrict themselves in the crowd. . . . But I also know that absolute solitude is a state that is sad and contrary to nature: affectionate feelings nourish the soul, communication of ideas enlivens the mind. Our sweetest existence is relative and collective, and our true *moi* is not entirely within us. Finally, such is man's constitution in this life that one is never able to enjoy oneself without the cooperation of another" (RJJ II, 118/813).[6] Scholars find here late confirmation of a Rousseau who is fundamentally in favor of society—and, therefore, it would not be difficult to argue, also an advocate of virtue, duty, community, and justice.[7]

Is any adjudication possible? Must we revert to the older view of Rousseau as simply incoherent, driven mainly by erratic emotions? To begin, a closer look at these paradigmatic passages reveals them not to support their respective positions nearly as strongly as they seem to, taken in isolation. It has been observed that the *Reveries* passage is surrounded by other claims pointing to sociable occasions. Discussing the island of Saint-Pierre, Rousseau observes that this sort of reverie "admittedly was done better and more pleasurably on a fertile and solitary island . . . where the society of the small number of inhabitants was sociable and sweet [*liante et doux*], without being so interesting as to occupy me continuously" (Rev. V, 70/1048).[8] He also points to the "fictions" of human companions in his mind. For Michael O'Dea, it is not clear that *Reveries* V "should be read as describing a semi-mystical state, far beyond the type of reverie in which Rousseau lives out his fantasies surrounded by a host of ideal creatures."[9]

Meanwhile, the statement in the *Dialogues* seems to be largely a setup, which is immediately countered by the secure happiness that Jean-Jacques finds in his "imagination" and "happy fictions" (see RJJ II, 118–19/813–14). Immediately after the quoted passage, "Rousseau" links the argument about "absolute solitude" with many caricatures, which are plainly refuted in the discussions that follow: "Solitary J.J. therefore ought to be somber, taciturn, and always discontent with life. In fact, this is how he appears in all his portraits, and this is how he has always been depicted to me since his misfortunes. He is even made to say in one published letter that he has laughed only twice in his whole life, and both times it was a wicked laugh" (118/813).

So the supremely happy Jean-Jacques of the *Reveries* is actually not so solitary, and the absolutely solitary Jean-Jacques of the *Dialogues* is actually not so miserable. Our definitive solutions slip away.

Rousseau's unusual imaginative life is a common factor in each of these extended passages, and this is difficult to categorize.[10] One of his recurring later themes is that his heart was preeminently made for friendship, and in profound need of intimate union.[11] Yet he was uniquely unfortunate: "I have spent my days searching in vain for solid and lasting attachments" (Conf. X, 446/533).[12] Responding to many such frustrations throughout his life, he sought many "compensations" or "supplements" to partially fill that void. This includes, as we have seen, masturbation.[13] We have also seen Thérèse Levasseur discussed as a supplement,[14] whose mind was impossible to cultivate, and with whom he was unable to genuinely fill his void.[15] He surely has his own case in mind when he advises educated men not to marry a woman from among the uneducated laborers: "The greatest charm of society is lacking to him when, despite having a wife, he is reduced to thinking alone" (E V, 408/767).[16] In addition, he would daydream about human communities worthy of his heart and seek out "imaginary friends" after searching for them "in vain" among men (Conf. IX, 359/427; RJJ II, 127/824). He also shows a special fellowship with animals across his career. In 1754, his habit of feeding fish by hand added to "his reputation as a friend of humanity."[17] At Montmorency (1758–1762), he "tamed" many birds, was very close to his dog and cat, and once claimed that he found "more" friendship in his dog than in humans, while still mentioning a few human friends.[18] A late fragment states, "Being neither a traitor nor a scoundrel and never affectionate from duplicity, a dog is much closer to me than a man of this generation."[19] Finally, there is the late botanical craze. The character "Rousseau" claims that Jean-Jacques found the contemplation of nature to be "a supplement to the attachments he needed," but that he would "gladly leave the society of plants . . . for that of men at the first hope of finding it again" (RJJ II, 103/794). Considering all these cases, some are initially attributed to misfortune or the transitory status of all human things. But as we enter the time of exile (1762) and especially the increased sense of universal persecution (ca. 1766–1776), it is the concerted cruelty of humans toward him that drives his search for compensations and his resolutions no longer to pursue human society.

That Jean-Jacques was reluctant to give up on human fellowship is not especially controversial. Yet its normative significance remains unclear. Despite such professions of social longing throughout the autobiographical works, those who see his ultimate ideal as solitary sometimes appeal to his idea that he was compelled to fully pursue the way of life entailed by his philosophy. To reapply his controversial political phrase, he was "forced to be free."[20] He learned only "too late" to look within himself for all his nourishment, and he owes these enjoyments "to my persecutors" (Rev. II, 13/1003). He now becomes indifferent to glory, infamy, and the like; "this indifference is not the work of my wisdom; it is that of my enemies" (VIII, 117/1081). On these readings, then, any difficulty reconciling life with principles amounts to Jean-Jacques continuing to be personally influenced by aspirations that his philosophical discoveries had revealed to be lacking, merely conventional, or suited only to lesser minds.[21] For Christopher Kelly, when Rousseau discusses the longings of "the heart," this is meant to indicate a departure from his philosophical standard of "complete natural independence"; it is "a specifically civilized version of the desire for wholeness."[22]

The debate over his preferred scope of community may never come to a solid resolution. Unlike many of the paradoxes in his normative thought, in these cases he often fails to provide qualifying remarks or indications of overarching principles that might ground coherent, comprehensive interpretations. Thus, in this case, I suggest an exception to Kelly's solid observation: "Rousseau is characteristically precise in the terms of his praise and in the identification of his different criteria for judgment."[23] Regarding solitude, mere oscillation between conflicting stances seems undeniable at times. For instance, regarding the island of Saint-Pierre, he claims, "I should like to have been so confined on my island that I need have no further commerce with mortals, and I certainly took every measure imaginable to relieve myself of maintaining any" (Conf. XII, 534f/638).[24] Yet, not long before describing his time on Saint-Pierre, he laments his loss of Lord Keith, while disparaging his entire future: "My last happy memories are of him; the whole of the rest of my life has brought me nothing but affliction and anguish" (501/599).[25] Rather than a consistent approach to society and happiness, this seems to be part of the tendency we have seen, to state repeatedly that he was now happy for the first time or that multiple points were the true beginning of his inevitable train of miseries.[26] Also, in view of the human interaction he did enjoy on Saint-Pierre, even according to the *Confessions*, a more accurate statement of his antisocial longing may have been made in the later account of Saint-Pierre. There he longs to go end his days "on this beloved island without ever . . . seeing there any *inhabitant of the continent* to remind me of all the different calamities" (Rev. V, 71/1048).[27]

In pursuing a solid theoretical account in this chapter, I turn away from the strong focus of recent scholarship, on the happiness of solitude. Instead, I turn to the neglected topics of the various kinds of solitude Rousseau depicts and in what senses he sees them as *ethically* justified. I put his prominent advocacy of community, justice, and virtue in the normative writings into a dialogue with his own behavior as analyzed by him and his contemporaries. Beginning soon after his move to the Hermitage (1756) and Diderot's charge that he was not fulfilling his duties toward society, Rousseau offered substantive defenses of his own behavior, explaining how positive duties to society are in fact better fulfilled in his more secluded situation than they could be in Paris. This corresponds with his constructive thought's portrayal of "solitude" as a form of rustic sociability, which alone allows us to fulfill our duties without harming others. However, across the period of 1765–1778, his idea of solitude became more absolute. I then find increasing tendencies to claim absolution from certain duties, such as intellectual labor and service to his poor neighbors, which had previously been fundamental to his self-justification. Although it is fairly common to point out how Rousseau became more socially isolated in his final years, here I establish related developments that have not been sufficiently appreciated: How his sense of personal duty became truncated in those years and how far he justified this in view of his new circumstances. Since he also rejected virtue and duty in some prominent late passages, I also ask how that relates to his ideas and behavior during the height of his authorship.

1. A Friend of Humanity in the Desert?

From an early point in Rousseau's career, his approach to social duties—to neighbors and society at large—was vigorously questioned. As "the Frenchman" would observe later, Jean-Jacques "flees everyone without exception, disdains every caress, rejects all overtures, and lives alone like a werewolf" (RJJ II, 168/877). The common charges of a misanthropic soul and an antisocial philosophy could be seen as mutually reinforcing. If humans have no natural or proper orientation to others or to the broader society, in a philosophical view it would be difficult to see how they could have duties to others, especially positive duties.

Three charges from contemporaries illustrate this. The earliest is from Voltaire, during a stage when his and Rousseau's relations had been respectful.

In his letter (1755) acknowledging a complimentary copy of the *Discourse on Inequality*, he famously dismissed Rousseau's "new book against the human race," which incites "the desire to walk on all fours." He continues: "Never has so much intelligence been used in seeking to make us stupid [*Bêtes*]."[28] He would increasingly see Rousseau as embodying bestial rage against the higher, distinctively human aspects of civilization, interpreting this as a debased version of ancient cynicism—by 1759, Jean-Jacques had become "that bastard of Diogenes' dog."[29]

If this rift with a thinker who conceived of philosophy and progress so differently was perhaps inevitable, far more concerning was the criticism from Diderot, a close friend of fifteen years, who retained major philosophical affinities, including a lack of sympathy for the apologists of luxury.[30] Not long after Rousseau's departure from Paris for the Hermitage (April 1756), Diderot published *The Natural Son* (February 1757).[31] The *Confessions* notes that among its comments against solitaries is the dictum that "only the vicious person [*le méchant*] lives alone" (IX, 382/455).[32] Based on the play, it was not unreasonable for Jean-Jacques to fear he was being targeted, although scholars dispute how directly Diderot was aiming at his friend.[33] Dorval, the title character, has suffered great misfortunes, and concludes: "I hate the interactions of people [*les commerce des hommes*], and I sense that it is far from those who are dear to me that peace awaits."[34] Others implore that this cannot bring tranquility. According to Constance, who has long known unrequited love for Dorval:

> In order to be tranquil, one must have the approval of his heart, and perhaps that of men. You will not obtain the latter, and you will lose the first, if you quit the post that has been marked for you. You have received the rarest talents, and you owe society an account of them. That crowd of worthless beings who move without object, and who clutter up society without serving it—they may move away from it, if they wish. But you, I dare say to you, you are not able to without crime.... You, renounce society! I appeal to your heart, ask it, and it will say to you that the good person lives in society, and that it is only the vicious person who lives alone [*qu'il n'y a que le méchant qui soit seul*].[35]

This final line was deeply wounding to Rousseau, and, in the next months, their relationship became highly strained, as Diderot did not seem sufficiently willing to reject the claim or exempt his friend from it.[36] It is fair to see Jean-Jacques as oversensitive throughout the episode and incapable of acknowledging the element of playful banter in his friend's letters. However, Arthur Wilson suggests that we might reasonably question Diderot's motives for the original claim about solitude and for "harping upon the fate of Mme Levasseur" (Thérèse's mother).[37] Among these motives seem to be the philosophes' perception of the move from Paris as "a standing reproach to them" and "their mode of life."[38] In addition, according to Jean-François Perrin, "Diderot did not support his brilliant friend retiring from the battlefield of the *Encyclopédie*."[39] Thus began the chain of events leading eventually to Rousseau's public disavowal of Diderot (October 1758).[40] Rousseau had already departed in key ways from the highly sociable recent model of the philosopher, who should be comfortable in "the world" (*le monde*; i.e., high society).[41] The break from Diderot reinforced Rousseau's isolation from the philosophes, both personally and ideologically.

Our final charge (1759) is from Théodore Tronchin, a Genevan doctor whose friends included Louise d'Épinay and Voltaire (the doctor is not to be confused with Jean-Robert Tronchin, the procurator general discussed in Chapter 4). He probed a sensitive area while responding to Jean-Jacques's request for medical advice for his neighbors. Expressing disappointment that he now hears so little from Rousseau and following up with a diagnosis of his "indifference," Tronchin asks: "How is it that the friend of humanity is hardly any longer the friend of men?"[42] Here we find the specters of hypocrisy as well as misanthropy. Tronchin actually seems to be prodding Rousseau to move to Geneva, where he could benefit from living near estimable, virtuous people.[43] He had made concerted efforts for this previously.[44] The appeals failed and, following this letter, several other heated letters were exchanged, leading to another lost friendship.[45] It may also be Théodore Tronchin who passed the secret about Rousseau's children on to Voltaire, having learned it from d'Épinay.[46]

In the (much later) autobiographies, there seems to be no response to Tronchin, and Voltaire's letter is only briefly referred to (in Conf. VIII, 333/396). Evidently, Diderot's barb reverberated the most. The best-known responses to it are in *Emile*, the *Confessions*, and the *Dialogues*. There Rousseau seems content with the brief—almost tautological—response that the solitary person cannot be truly vicious or wicked (*méchant*), since he cannot do harm to others.[47] However, for much of the period in question, his responses were of greater substance, providing defenses of the semi-secluded life in terms of fulfilling positive duties to humanity. Across much of the corpus, he also expresses a long-standing taste for a rustic life,[48] and explains how quiet reflection is central in the search for truth and perceiving one's duties.[49] In a fragment of 1753, while living in Paris, he pointed to an advantage of his independent character: "A solitary who enjoys living by himself naturally acquires a taste for reflection, and a man who takes a lively interest in the happiness of others without being in need of them for his own does not have to spare their false delicacy."[50] This analysis is extended in a fragment from the winter of 1756–1757: "In the cities only an external and apparent order reigns, disorder and fatal passions reign there in the depths of all hearts; it is only in the peace of solitude that one learns to order one's soul and one's will in accordance with the genuine laws of universal harmony."[51] Rousseau believes the wise have long treasured this kind of solitude and, before Diderot, the "love of seclusion" had been taken as a clear mark of a peaceful, healthy, and wise soul (Conf. IX, 382/455; RJJ II, 99/789). Despite the prevalence of related themes in Rousseau's earlier thought, it seems to be only in response to Diderot that the links between solitude and duty are first weaponized (seen, of course, as merely *defensive* weapons).

The first response of philosophical significance is found in a 1757 letter, written for Diderot, but unsent, upon the advice of d'Épinay.[52] Diderot's previous letter had referred to "twenty poor people" on a rampart in Paris "who were dying of hunger and cold, and who were waiting for the liard that you used to give them. . . . It is better to be dead than a rogue [*fripon*]; but unfortunate is the one who lives and who has no duties to which he is subjected [*esclave*]."[53] Rousseau's response pointed to the objectively greater needs in Montmorency, and continued:

> There is a good respectable old man here who, after having passed his life working, is dying of hunger in his old age because he is no longer able to work. My conscience is more satisfied with the two sous that I give him every Monday than with the hundred liards I would have distributed to all those beggars on the rampart.[54] You are amusing, you philosophers, when you regard all the inhabitants of the cities as the only men to whom your duties connect you.[55] It is in the country that one learns to love and serve humanity; one learns only to despise it in the cities. I have duties to which I am subjected, and it is for them that I do not want to impose others on me that would take away my power to fulfill them.[56]

In a related letter, he refers to Diderot and Grimm as "philosophers of the cities," exclaiming that "if these are your virtues, you greatly console me for being only a vicious person."[57] Their characters have changed with success. As he put it in a letter to d'Épinay: "Believe me, my good friend, Diderot is now a man of the fashionable world [*un homme du monde*]. There was a time when the two of us were poor and unknown and we were friends. I could say the same of Grimm. But they have both become important people, while I have continued to be what I was, and we suit each other no longer."[58] This is a curious line of argument, given that Rousseau had initially been the minor disciple in his friendship with Diderot and had recently attained greater fame.[59] However, according to Lilti, Diderot was at this point opting for the cultivation of powerful alliances in the salons: "In 1757–58 he had chosen his camp, broken with Rousseau, and, under the guidance of his friend Grimm, embraced a career as a man of letters and was received as a guest by Madame d'Épinay, the baron d'Holbach, and Madame Necker. . . . Unlike Grimm, however, Diderot was no more at ease in the salons than his old friend was."[60] He "remained haunted by a Rousseauist remorse."[61] His increasing discomfort with the society of the great would culminate in a remark in the *Essai sur les règnes de Claude et de Néron* (1782): "Whatever the advantages attached to commerce with *gens du monde* for a scholar, a philosopher, and even a man of letters . . . , I dare believe that his talent and his morals will find themselves better from the society of his friends, from solitude, from reading the great authors, from the examination of his own heart, and from frequent consultation with himself."[62] Despite this apparently Rousseauist turn, Diderot continues to be concerned about the dangers of solitude, as when someone "withdraws into the forest from vanity or misanthropy" and quickly becomes a "ferocious beast" and "*un méchant*."[63]

In his letters responding to Diderot, Rousseau presents himself as embodying a philosophy of the country and therefore of humanity and its duties, which naturally flourish there. The first public statement of this response is in the *Letter to d'Alembert* (1758). Among its arguments for the corruptive impact of the theater is a sustained analysis of Molière's masterpiece, *The Misanthrope*.[64] Molière's title character, Alceste, is comparable to Diderot's Dorval, in that Alceste repeatedly declares that all of humanity has become such a disgrace that he must flee from them "to live alone in some deserted spot."[65] To Rousseau, Molière's need "to make the audience laugh" leads him to portray Alceste inconsistently. This alleged misanthrope is at bottom "a good man who detests the morals of his age and the viciousness [*méchanceté*] of his contemporaries; who, precisely because he loves his fellow creatures, hates in them the evils they do to one another and the vices which produce these evils" (LdA 37/277/34).[66] "There is no good man who is not a misanthrope in this sense," whereas the greatest "enemy of man" is he who "encourages the vicious [*méchans*]" and "flatters the vices" (38/278/35). Authentically portrayed, the good man might fall into unjustified anger and exaggerated claims at times (37f/278/34f), and his frankness will readily offend the false politeness of the outwardly decent, yet fundamentally egotistical, people of *le monde*.[67] The autobiographical resonances are reinforced by the *Letter*'s earlier claims that solitude "calms the soul," placing us "far from the vices which irritate us"; and "Since I see men no more, I have almost stopped hating the wicked [*méchans*]" (7/256/7). Malesherbes supports this interpretation of Jean-Jacques when he compares him to Heraclitus, who weeps at the ills and vices of humanity, in contrast with Democritus, who laughs at them.[68] This was meant to explain Rousseau's solitude: "Being unfortunate enough to often see as horrors what Democritus had only seen as ridiculous, it is straightforward that you have fled to the deserts in order to no longer witness them."[69]

Finally, in his immediate response to Théodore Tronchin's charge of indifference to particular humans, Rousseau thunders back: "If since my birth I have done the least harm to anyone on earth, may the evil come down on my head. If I refuse to do anyone any good I might do, or any service I could render without harming another, then let me suffer the same refusal in my time of need! May God grant that the earth become covered with enemies of men who may, each to himself, make the same imprecation in such good faith."[70] The challenge is stronger than what we would have expected, given the harms revealed in the *Confessions*. As Leigh puts it, "The *Confessions* does not uphold this thesis in such an absolute form. There was for example a certain Marion."[71] Rousseau's claim is heated and perhaps misguided; in fairness, however, he is claiming not that he would suffer no harm from such immediate divine justice but only that he would come out well, all things considered. In any case, this defense is also stated robustly at the end of the Montmorency period, in the *Letters to Malesherbes* (January 1762): "Your literary people have shouted as much as they could that a man by himself is useless to everyone and has not fulfilled his duties in society. I myself consider the peasants of Montmorency to be members of society more useful than all those heaps of idlers paid by the fat of the people to go six times a week to chatter in an academy, and I am more content to be able to give some pleasure to my poor neighbors when the opportunity presents itself than to help enrich the crowds of petty intriguers of which Paris is full" (IV, 580/1143).[72] It is difficult to say when this behavior and related self-defense ceased, although many readers will be familiar with the very different approach to charitable giving that we find in the *Reveries*.[73] The *Confessions* only directly covers his life through 1765, and seems to affirm the continuation of this behavior through that point. He ought "to have been loved by the people of this region [i.e., Neuchâtel in Switzerland], as I have been by all those where I have lived, for my open-handed distribution of alms, for never leaving any pauper around me without assistance, for not refusing any service to anyone that it was within my power and the limits of justice to render" (XII, 523/624).[74] A letter from Pastor Montmollin supports these claims for this period, claiming that Rousseau "has made himself loved and respected in these cantons by his sweetness, his affability, his moderation, his silence and by benefactions made without ostentation."[75] Montmollin affirmed this even after his "heart had been sickened" from reading the *Letters Written from the Mountain*—Rousseau had "always been most dutiful in performing religious duties, both in giving alms and in receiving the sacraments."[76] We also have evidence that this behavior continued during his time in England (1766–1767).[77]

Rousseau's political writings strongly criticize inequality—at least in its typical, extreme forms—as undermining personal independence and thus the conditions for public liberty (SC II.11, 78/391f). His normative thought is well-known for opposing privilege and defending the unfortunate—he is "the Homer of the losers," as Judith Shklar would have it.[78] However, Rousseau was also aware of the limited prospects for republican justice in the world he knew, and he seems to have developed a largely independent ethic for alleviating suffering and degradation within Europe as we normally find it. During the same period, when he repeatedly defended himself as fulfilling substantive duties to his neighbors, he was also offering sustained philosophical guidance on the personal response to poverty, especially in the *Moral Letters* (written ca. winter 1757–1758), *Julie*, and *Emile*. Ruth Grant is a significant exception to the general neglect of this theme: "Though the possibilities for effective public action may be severely limited, personal integrity remains a possibility everywhere and always."[79] According to Grant:

> On the small scale of the local community, a great deal of good can be done without compromising one's integrity. Émile and Sophie engage in a variety of humanitarian projects to improve the lives of the peasants among whom they live [E V, 435–36/804–5; see DOI I, 153f/156]. Rousseau advises Sophie d'Houdetot to work among the poor [ML VI, 201–3/1116–18]. Julie's work with local peasants is directed precisely toward preventing the corruption of young people tempted by city life and bourgeois manners [*Julie* V.2, 438–40/534–37]. Rousseau sees the opportunity to do good for others as one element of a happy life [see Rev. VI, 75/1051, and DOI II, 187/192f].[80]

Consider, too, the training of the young Emile in personal service to the unfortunate, above all by witnessing these behaviors in his tutor (E II, 95, 103–4/326, 338–39). All this is summarized in a general principle of beneficence: "The most vicious [*méchant*] of men is he who isolates himself the most, who most concentrates his heart in himself; the best is he who shares his affections equally with all his kind" (LdA 117/337f/107).

Although it has been called into question,[81] we might have found a rare example of Rousseau's life being substantially reconciled to his principles. At least for the time being.

He considered himself as having duties to society besides beneficence, particularly in writing useful truths. This is a delicate topic, since we have seen that, as 1762 approached and without anticipating the expulsions that would occur, he was planning on retiring from authorship, properly speaking.[82] This raises the question of whether he would be sufficiently repaying his broader debts to society or whether he would be subject to the well-known judgment in the *Reveries*: Society was wrong to "proscribe me from it as a pernicious member," but it would not have been wrong to turn him out "as a useless member" (VI, 84/1059). His approach in his main authorship period seems rather different. The *Reveries* passage has been juxtaposed with one from the first *Discourse*: "Not to do good is a great evil, and every useless citizen may be looked upon as a pernicious man" (II, 17/18).[83] Despite the apparent rigorism of many of his exhortations to serve society, he also subtly pointed to exceptions. Edward compares the moral course of life with a day's tasks: "Did Heaven not assign to you along with life a task to fill it? If you have done your day's work before evening, rest for what remains of the day, that you can do; but let us have a look at your work" (*Julie* III.22, 319/388).[84] This invokes the long tradition of a worthy retirement from public life, including Seneca, Plutarch, and Montaigne.[85]

Rousseau applied these principles to his own case when discussing his imminent retirement from writing in 1762. He claims that he has "done everything I could for society in accordance with my reach; if I have done little for it, I have demanded even less, and I believe I am so well-parted from it in the position I am in, that if I could henceforth rest completely and live for myself alone I would do so without scruple" (*Malesherbes* IV, 581/1144).[86] The strange "done little" is likely connected to long-standing concerns about whether speaking on behalf of truth, liberty, and virtue could truly impact the contemporary public or the philosophical mind. We see, for instance, in the *Moral Letters*: "After so many days lost in pursuing a vain glory, by telling the public truths it was in no condition to understand, I finally see myself proposing a useful object . . . I shall look after you, your duties" (I, 176/1082).[87] Yet, the scales of his fulfillment of duties toward society still pointed substantially in his favor. The argument seems to suggest his intention to retire from his hitherto special vocation of writing for truth and for country,[88] as well as his right to retire from economic labor if that became feasible (see *Malesherbes* IV, 581/1144). This concludes an economic argument: "Since I eat only as much bread as I earn, am I not forced to labor for my sustenance and to pay society for all the need I might have for it?" (581/1143). Consider, too, that, in the original normative argument against living entirely from one's inheritance, this applies to the heir but not to the original earner: "'But my father, in earning [his riches], served society . . .' So be it; he has paid his debt, but not yours. . . . He who eats in idleness what he did not earn himself steals it" (E III, 195/469f).[89] However, this potential liberation from ongoing economic labor does not seem to extend to everyday human duties, such as service to neighbors in need.[90]

Despite these plans, June 1762 intervened, and his retirement was far from smooth. He had several reversals about his intentions to continue writing and, in some cases, took up the pen again in connection to higher duties. However, this should be distinguished from broader duties to—and engagement with—society, since, in principle, retirement from writing was credibly seen, during his peak philosophical period, as compatible with the most admirable and desirable kind of life.

2. Now Alone on Earth

As we have seen, the *Confessions* (written ca. 1764–1770) emphasizes Rousseau's persistent (and typically frustrated) search for intimate friendship. His aspirations were chastened following ruptures with d'Épinay, Diderot, and Sophie d'Houdetot (1757–1758), through the conclusion of its narrative with the departure from the Swiss countries (October 1765). However, it seems that a much more desolate solitude was yet to come, if we compare the *Confessions* account with the final autobiographical works, the *Dialogues* (written 1772–1776) and the *Reveries* (written 1776–1778). Charting the exact course of this development is difficult, since, for the last dozen years, we lack the comprehensive history of his soul aspired to in the *Confessions*.[91] Yet, alongside the other autobiographies, and a correspondence that mushroomed during the years of exile,[92] some important shifts in circumstances, behavior, and perspective can be documented. Although the pattern is jagged, Rousseau's sense of isolation seems to have intensified with the "stoning" in Môtiers (September 1765), the disastrous English exile under the protection of Hume (1766–1767), and other periods, notably 1769–1771 and 1776.

The *Confessions* portrays a strategic social retreat occurring around 1758. Rousseau then attempted to "cure" himself not only of his "insane passion" for Sophie and of finding a complete lover, but also of the "chimera" of friendship.[93] In one of the most sustained discussions of this transition, he also suggests an alternative to his earlier, all-or-nothing approach to intimacy. Soon after discussing his break with Sophie and the new, mild spirit underlying the *Letter to d'Alembert*, he writes:

> Now that I had shaken off the yoke my tyrants had imposed on me, I was leading an even and peaceful enough life; deprived of the charm of friendships that had become too intense [*trop vifs*], I was free, too, of the burden of their chains. Disenchanted with the patronage of friends who insisted on taking charge of my destiny and on subjecting me against my will to their supposed favors, I was determined henceforward to be satisfied with relationships of simple good will, which, while restricting no one's freedom, are the great blessing of life, based as they are on an equal investment on both sides. I already had as many of these as were needed for me to taste the sweet things of society[94] without suffering its disadvantages, and, the moment I tried this kind of life, I felt immediately that it was the most conducive at my age to letting me end my days in peace, far from the storms, the quarrels, and hassles in which I had just been half submerged. (Conf. X, 421f/503)[95]

This resolution seems aimed to escape the excessive intensity of the relations with Sophie (and perhaps Diderot), as well as the constraining dependence on d'Épinay, while still avoiding complete isolation. It is unclear whether Jean-Jacques fulfilled this resolution or even continued to take it seriously for the duration of the period discussed in the *Confessions*. He portrays himself as more guarded in some respects, but he also mentions that he allowed himself to be drawn too far into friendship with the Luxembourgs.[96] Throughout, we find him drawn into more relationships, since his "heart never gives itself by halves,"[97] and he even refers to "friendship" with several people he met during the Swiss exile (June 1762–October 1765).[98] He advises "Henriette" around this time to guard herself against what we can see are his own tendencies: "Be certain that you will be content with others only when you do not need them any longer, and that society will become agreeable to you only when it ceases to be necessary for you."[99]

Perhaps the most sympathetic interpretation would be that these friendships, around 1758–1765, were real and satisfying, while generally not involving the kind of emotional abandonment to another that proved so costly after his departure from Paris (April 1756). It seems to be, then, that only the most intimate form of friendship is considered an "illusion," and this is quite possibly true only for the unfortunate Jean-Jacques. He expressed hope to be permanently cut off from society (or at least the society of the continent) after the stoning at Môtiers, during his time at the island of Saint-Pierre (September–October 1765).[100] Yet sentiments of friendship would remain important during his time in England (January 1766–May 1767).[101] This remains true even after he came to see Hume as a traitor involved in a plot against him (May–June 1766).[102] For instance, in an important personal letter to the elder Mirabeau (January 1767), it is his friends—albeit in a "very small number"—whom he says he wishes to live for.[103]

For all their disappointment, self-pity, and developing sense of persecution, the writings and letters through this point do not share the global social despair of the last autobiographical works.[104] We need not multiply examples. Consider the famous opening lines of the *Reveries*: "I am now alone on earth, no longer having any brother, neighbor, friend, or society other than myself. The most sociable and loving of humans has been proscribed from society by a unanimous agreement" (1/995).[105] And, similarly, from the *Dialogues*: "Everything around him is snares, lies, betrayals, darkness. He is absolutely alone and has only himself as a resource; he must expect neither aid nor assistance from anyone on earth. Such a singular position is unique in the existence of the human race" (I, 81/765). Even though he faced severe persecution in 1762–1765, and did have enemies then and later, these later claims are quite mistaken and may be linked with the episodic paranoia that many scholars find in his last dozen or so years.[106] Multiple scholars attest that he was the most celebrated writer in Europe at the time,[107] but that "he turned a deaf ear to all the proofs of devotion, of admiration, even of enthusiasm which poured in from all sides."[108] Moreover, he still had the faithful solicitude of Thérèse and several friends, old and new.[109] Nonetheless, these succors never become even a side note in the final works, in contrast with what we have seen in the *Confessions*.

When did these perceptions become so all-encompassing? Some point to the quarrel with Hume as the first clear case of universal conspiratorial thinking.

Drawing on a sophisticated analysis of the published writings and correspondence, O'Dea argues that after the period in England, "Rousseau will consistently claim that there is a universal plot against him. This drama brings out all the darker characteristics that are evident in the second volume of the *Confessions* and the other late writings but that find their first expression in the letters of 1766 and 1767."[110] More specifically, John Scott and Robert Zaretsky point out that, in Rousseau's first accusations against Hume (of June and July 1766), he saw all of Hume's friends as being in league against him, once charging Hume as being in a "triumvirate" with Voltaire and d'Alembert.[111] However, this is different from a truly "universal plot," which is apparently first alleged in August.[112]

Another important upsurge of fear occurred when writing the Second Part of the *Confessions*. According to Raymond Trousson, Rousseau began writing the Second Part as the weather became cold in 1769, and his "obsessions came back in force," partly due to his "discovery" in November 1768 of some missing documents and of a perceived plot behind their disappearance.[113] According to Bernard Gagnebin and Marcel Raymond, it is probable that the Second Part of the *Confessions*, excluding Book XII, was written and found its definitive form in only four months (especially November 1769–February 1770).[114] These fears left marks in some of the more disturbing passages of that work, as well as in the major letter to Saint-Germain (26 February 1770). These cases show an increasing fear of persecution, but giving up hope on society is a further step. At one point, our author claims this did not occur until mid-1771. In the *Dialogues*, according to "Rousseau," for the first year after Jean-Jacques returned to Paris (June 1770), he sought relationships among old friends and other apparently decent people, without any success. He thus stopped making visits and resumed "in the capital the solitary life he had led for so many years in the country"; "he extinguished his lantern and shut himself up completely within himself" (II, 101–2/791–92).[115] Similarly, "I saw him in a unique, almost unbelievable situation, more alone in the middle of Paris than Robinson on his island" (128/826; cf. 117/812). To Lilti, this is the key turning point, since Rousseau had previously seen the conspiracy as a limited circle "concocted by his enemies," from which he could appeal to his readers for justice.[116]

Although in some ways he continued to defend his condition, he distinguished this absolute, recent version of solitude from the more social version he enjoyed in earlier years. Of Jean-Jacques we are told: "In his youth and during his brief periods of prosperity when he did not yet have anyone to complain about, he didn't like retreat [*la retraite*] any less than he likes it in his wretchedness. He then divided his delectations between the friends he believed he had and the sweetness of meditation. Now that he is so cruelly disabused, he completely surrenders to his dominant taste" (RJJ II, 150/854; see also 117/812). Here "retreat," or "solitude," apparently suggests a temporary pause from social interaction; it is used to indicate a sociable country life with Madame de Warens in the *Reveries* (X, 141/1099).

In the final stages, hopes for enjoying society are framed as long past, and the newer developments concern hopes for justice in his posthumous reputation. Whereas the *Reveries* frames his loss of interest in future repute as beginning only two months earlier (I, 3f/997f), he had lost all hope in finding happiness from present society "at least a few years" ago (II, 12f/1002). By contrast, the eventual vindication of his honor officially animates the *Dialogues*. It had long been an aspiration of his, and he had previously been confident he would attain it. After completing his great constructive works, he claimed to "hardly care" about his "reputation among his contemporaries," in contrast to "the sole glory that has ever touched my heart, the honor that I expect in posterity and which it will render to me because it is due to me, and posterity is always just" (*Malesherbes* IV, 582/1145; cf. I, 573, 574/1131, 1133). By the time of the *Dialogues*, he seeks vindication against daunting odds.[117] We find another turn in the Postscript to that work, "History of the Preceding Writing," which centers on a disturbing episode of February 1776,[118] in which he was (by some mysterious blow of providence) prevented from depositing his manuscript on the altar of Notre Dame (RJJ HPW 246–49/977–81). After finding no person worthy of being trusted with it, he made a desperate attempt to hand out a circular letter on the streets of Paris, addressed "To all Frenchmen who still love justice and truth" (249–51f, 256–57/981–84, 990–91). Finally, he gave up all concerns for "the senseless judgments of men," in this and future generations. He will "return within myself," and mortals will no longer have any "hold by which they can still disturb my heart's repose" (252–53/985–86). Nonetheless, he goes on to say that he still has a "duty" to leave others "the means to return to [the truth] insofar as I am able" (253/987). This approach is anticipated late in the main text, even if the lack of any hope was then exaggerated. The author replies to the claim that, in the face of the conspiracy, Jean-Jacques should remain completely immobile and not act at all: "I cannot allow myself to follow this advice as regards the just defense of my honor. Until the end I must do everything within my power, if not to open the eyes of this blind generation, at least to enlighten one that is more equitable. All the means for doing so have been taken away from me, I know. But without any hope of success, all efforts possible even though useless are nonetheless my duty, and I will not stop making them until my final breath is drawn. *Do what you ought, come what may*" (RJJ III, 234n/962n1).[119]

The *Reveries* famously claims to emerge from a new serenity, based on a recent renunciation of all hopes from other humans in the present and future generations (I, 3f/997f).[120] Another mysterious event plays the decisive role, but this time it is undisclosed. This event was "not quite two months ago . . . as sad as it was unforeseen" (Rev. I, 3f/997). Some scholars agree that the likeliest possibility is the death of the prince de Conti on 2 August 1776, which removed Rousseau's hope that the 1762 warrant for his arrest might be dismissed.[121] He explains that the hope in the judgments of "a better generation" is what "made me write my *Dialogues*" and, although "remote," that hope "held my soul in the same agitation as when I was still looking for a just heart in this century" (Rev. I, 4/998). Being stated in a far more readable and sometimes sublime book, this contrast has often been given full credence, even if careful readings have shown substantial continuities between the two works.[122] Rousseau seems, more precisely, to be picking up exactly where the *Dialogues* left off, only having made progress in his earlier resolution to find repose in this new indifference to opinion. The efforts to preserve his writings are now decisively judged pointless, and no exceptions for his duties emerge. Unlike the many efforts he took to preserve the *Confessions* and the *Dialogues* from his persecutors, he now knows these efforts "would be useless. And now that the desire to be better understood by men has been extinguished in my heart, only profound indifference remains about the fate of my true writings and of the testimonies to my innocence—which have perhaps already all been forever reduced to nothing" (Rev. I, 7/1001).[123] However, this alleged serenity has its limits, as we see in the exaggerated fears that display themselves in the aftermath of the Great Dane incident.[124] Consider, too, the circumstances that led him to his final reflection on his children. He was told of d'Alembert's eulogy for Marie-Thérèse Geoffrin, connecting her love of children with good character; Rousseau wildly infers from this and the fact that the reading was brought to him, that he must be the actual target (IX, 123/1086).[125]

3. To Abstain Has Become My Sole Duty

What other duties were cast aside in these final years? Two central cases are traced here: Intellectual duties (which are at odds with laziness and the craze for botany) and positive duties toward fellow humans in need. Our chronology remains rough and speculative, since there is some obscurity and oscillation involved, but we find a strong overall pattern of a decreasing sense of social duty. This is basically in tandem with the decreasing sense of social connection we found in the previous section, and is often specifically excused on that basis.

Rousseau'a self-proclaimed laziness seems to apply only to his frequent aversion to intellectual labor and not to physical or economic labor. Physical labor, in the forms of copying music or weaving ribbons, seems, in fact, to have been a major outlet for preventing boredom, despite his periods of intellectual idleness.[126] The *Confessions* describes some tendencies toward laziness even in the broader Montmorency period (1756–1762), but, at least in this stage, these were compatible with extraordinary bursts of creative effort and are probably better described as an independent spirit than true idleness (cf. IX, 337/402).[127] It seems to be after the frustration of *Letters Written from the Mountain* and *The Sentiment of the Citizens* that he first vows to "quit the pen" (February 1765), not from a sense of completion and physical exhaustion but from failure and persecution. This actually led to a redoubling of efforts on the memoirs, but another noteworthy case of idleness occurred on the island of Saint-Pierre (September–October 1765), following the next round of persecution. There he was thrilled to "give myself up all day long, without obstacle or care, to the preoccupations of my liking or to the softest idleness [*la plus molle oisiveté*]" (Rev. V, 70/1048).[128]

In England, intellectual idleness seems to become a more official stance, even though Rousseau made considerable progress on the *Confessions*. After the quarrel with Hume, in the personal letter to Mirabeau (January 1767), he responds to the charge that "to be good only for oneself, is to be good for nothing."[129] The implication is similar to the charges of Diderot and Tronchin in the previous decade, but the response reveals far humbler aspirations. Most directly, "Whoever is truly good for himself is in some ways good for others."[130] In his own case, in view of his infirmities and persecutions,[131] he has been "given my leave by nature and by men; I have taken it and wish to profit from it." He hopes the public may forget him as he forgets it, with one apparent exception: "If the example of an innocent and simple life is useful to people, I can still provide that good for them; but that is the only one, and I am quite determined to live no longer except for me and my friends, in a very small number, but proven, and who suffice for me."[132] Here, it seems for a brief juncture, we see Jean-Jacques aspiring to a genuinely Epicurean life, which contrasts with his broader sense of duty beforehand, and what he later took to be a hopelessly friendless condition.[133]

(I call it an "Epicurean life," without implying an Epicurean philosophy, because he appeals to special conditions that have given him "leave" [*congé*] from positive duties that might otherwise apply.)

As for the intellectual life, he describes his current distaste for "all reading" and painful fatigue caused by any orderly thinking. He claims he has gotten rid of "all my books": "I have taken on all reading with such distaste that it is not possible to reread any of my own writings. The fatigue even of thinking becomes more painful for me each day. I love to dream [*rever*], but freely, in leaving my head to error, and without being enslaved to any subject. . . . This idle and contemplative life, which you do not approve and which I do not excuse, becomes more delicious to me each day."[134] Similarly, before their quarrel, Hume observed that Rousseau "has now totally renounc'd all Reading."[135] While fleeing England (May 1767), the latter would claim that, after the "last blow" of the quarrel with Hume, he feels it would be "impossible" to continue his memoirs.[136] The next month, he was back in France, and, in response to requests from Mirabeau to read some books of the Physiocrats, Rousseau insisted that he had sworn off all reading—especially "anything likely to reawaken his 'extinct ideas' concerning politics."[137] After more entreaties, he succumbed, and eventually sent the well-known political letter of July 1767.[138] Its political argument strongly criticizes the "legal despotism" of the Physiocrats and famously claims to see "no tolerable mean between the most austere democracy and the most perfect Hobbesism" (LPW 270 / CC 33:240). It closes by imploring Mirabeau "to leave my dying head in peace. . . . Love me always; but do not send me any more books" (LPW 271 / CC 241). Lilti generalizes for the following period: "Everyone who visited him in the 1770s reported the same thing: Rousseau insists that he is no longer writing, refuses to speak about his books, and refuses to read the books that have been given to him."[139] There are exaggerations here, in view of the writing of the *Dialogues* and *Reveries*,[140] but they likely point to some real truths.

Botany plays a leading role in our last phase of the conflict between intellectual labor and laziness. Having first taken hold in 1764, Jean-Jacques's predilection is familiar from *Reveries* Walk VII, as "a study for an idle and lazy *solitaire*" (98/1069).[141] But few know that this was the last stage of a genuine struggle. There was a resolution in November 1769: "I renounce it henceforth for many reasons, but especially because I have sensed that it absorbs me completely, that it slackens my heart, attaches me too much to the solitary and idle life, and prevents me from fulfilling indispensable duties that I may not neglect without failing myself."[142] He adds that he wishes to get rid of his herbarium and botanical books, "in order to remove any occasion to fall back into this obsession."[143] A week earlier, to Du Peyrou, he declined an opportunity for a visit, being "called by great and sad duties and the most necessary cares."[144] Although it is not known what gave rise to this "admirable reseizing" of intellectual determination,[145] we do know that chief among the duties alluded to is the resumption of the *Confessions* (becoming its Second Part).[146] Following the renunciation of May 1767 (when fleeing England), he resumed the memoirs in Tyre until November, putting Book VI into its final form, before another personal panic led to a long pause until November 1769.[147] Apparently, the latter resurgence of energy on behalf of his righteous vindication continued through mid-1771. After completing the *Confessions*, or at least most of it, he rushed to Paris (arriving June 1770), eager to read selections of it in public, and thus earn justice for his cause. Readings in elite homes went on from December 1770 to May 1771, when the police shut them down, at the insistence of Madame d'Épinay.[148] The *Poland* was written from around October 1770 through June 1771,[149] undertaken "with the most perfect disinterestedness, and for motives of the purest virtue" (RJJ III, 235/962f).[150]

There were more oscillations between intellectual labor and botanical indulgence over the next several years, until the final botanical upsurge in 1777 and its immortalization in the *Reveries*.[151] This sheds light on that final, apparently carefree depiction of this extravagant "infatuation" which "makes even me laugh" (Rev. VII, 89/1060). "I give myself up to it nonetheless, because in my present situation, I no longer have any other rule of conduct, than in everything to follow my propensity without restraint. I can do nothing about my lot. I have only innocent inclinations; and all the judgments of men being null for me henceforth, wisdom itself wills that in what remains within my reach I do whatever gratifies me, either in public or alone, without any rule other than my fancy and any limit other than the little strength I have left" (89/1060). The botanical enterprise is presented as entirely amoral but not contrary to any duties that apply to him in his condition. (Despite its opening presentation as simply a frivolous indulgence, as the Walk continues it becomes clear that botany also plays a therapeutic role: it "makes me forget men's persecutions, their hatred, scorn, insults": 103/1073.)[152] This broader amoral tendency recalls several other passages, apparently beginning late in the *Dialogues*, in which our author simply abandons himself to any present impulse, claiming justification by his situation and his harmless nature (RJJ HPW, 253/986f; Rev. VIII, 118–19f/1082–83). Tzvetan Todorov cites related passages, arguing that Rousseau has "changed greatly" since he condemned "this very doctrine, attributed (probably justly) to Diderot," of following one's passions in everything.[153]

If the most important turns regarding idleness and intellectual labor occurred in Switzerland and England, the turns in charitable giving seem to occur soon after this. In discussing his current behavior in the *Dialogues* and the *Reveries*, he claims to persist in some charitable acts but apparently no longer sees them as concrete duties or as a part of his identity. A revealing argument is in the *Dialogues*, where he laments that the common people surrounding him no longer show him the esteem, attachment, and even veneration that was felt for him everywhere he used to live, such as Montmorency and Wootton (II, 190–91/905–6).[154] Even if we "assume for a moment" that he now fulfills "with all his strength the duties of humanity, charity, [and] beneficence" such that anyone could witness it, the conspiracy would prevent any public acknowledgment of this. But "he was beneficent and good when, left unhampered to his own nature, he followed his own inclinations in total freedom" (194/910).[155] Similarly, "He must no longer be judged by his present works, even if it were possible to have a faithful account of them. It is necessary to go back to the time when nothing prevented him from being himself, or else to fathom him more intimately, *intus et in cute*" (190/905).[156] Returning to his present condition, "Rousseau" claims he saw Jean-Jacques "refrain despite himself from an opportunity to do a good deed," since he was in a busy neighborhood of Paris and could not endure the "hostile gaze" of the crowd (195f/912). These passages suggest a continuing good nature and generosity, largely prevented from expressing itself due to perceived hostility, as well as conspirators' traps or other fraudulent claims of need.[157] The reasoning is similar in an important passage of the *Reveries*. Although doing good is "the truest happiness the human heart can savor," it has long been out of his reach "to perform wisely and fruitfully a single really good action," and thus his only remaining good is "to abstain from acting" (VI, 75/1051). More fully: "No longer able to do any good which does not turn to evil, no longer able to act without harming another or myself, to abstain has become my sole duty and I fulfill it as much as it is in me to do so" (I, 6/1000).[158] In addition, we find a new fear, which has earned him a certain notoriety, that he now avoids many charitable acts because repeating them might become a duty—something he cannot endure (VI, 74–78/1050–54). He quips that even the sweetest enjoyments become a burden for him when they become a duty, such that he would have been "a bad husband among the Turks" at the hour when the public cry called them to fulfill their sexual duties to their wives (76/1052).[159]

Very often in these last works, his claims to goodness and innocence amount to refraining from harming others, or at least *intending* to refrain.[160]

His benevolence seems to be defended, not in terms of positive duties of virtue or even internal affections but by affections that he *naturally* had previously. If Théodore Tronchin would have lived to see these final writings, he could surely feel a sense of triumph over the great man who once defended himself as a "friend of humanity" in far more robust terms.[161] Voltaire might have again sneered—with more plausibility this time—about "your new book against the human race." This again suggests that the autobiographies have done much to secure Rousseau's reputation for literary brilliance but at significant cost to ideas of his character,[162] and perhaps even to understanding the original spirit of his philosophical project.

4. Conclusion: From the Accuser to the Accused

Looking back at our earlier stage (ca. 1756–1764), Rousseau was the agent, choosing to keep misguided forms of society at a distance, while selectively pursuing its more natural and satisfying forms. In our later stages (ca. 1765–1778), he is the patient or victim, wondering how society could have cast him out so violently and universally. Historically, much of what we have seen in this chapter can be summarized as Jean-Jacques Rousseau (the person and the philosopher) shifting from "the accuser" to "the accused." These phrases are borrowed from Jean Starobinski, who emphasizes a continuity underlying both postures: A narcissistic tendency to perceive "universal evil" in the social world outside himself, and thus either to attack it while exempting himself from it or to feel persecuted by it and passively retreat.[163] We need not follow this psychological diagnosis, but it calls attention to the radicalism of both phases, with a criticism of society whose intensity has seldom been surpassed in the history of philosophy. In addition, Starobinski's emphasis on this continuity is in keeping with his generally critical assessment of Rousseau's life and work.[164] My own emphasis has been on development and, since most recent philosophical interpreters have emphasized the consistency of his thought,[165] my alleged developments should be stated clearly.

This chapter has found the mature, semi-secluded Rousseau (ca. 1756–1764) to be nearly as confident in his character and behavior as he is in his ideas and principles. He was merciless in exposing what he took to be the empty posturing of the contemporary philosophical elite: "Distrust those cosmopolitans who go to great length in their books to discover duties they do not deign to fulfill around them" (E I, 39/249).[166] He posits intellectual failures as largely emerging from personal failures of omission. Whereas the ad hominem argument is now seen as mere fallacy, Rousseau's contemporaries "took seriously the ancient idea that a man's philosophical principles could be shown to be unworthy of serious attention if his life did not put them into practice. . . . There was nothing obviously fallacious or unfair, in other words, about arguments *ad hominem*."[167] To Rousseau, an authentic philosopher would fulfill substantive positive duties, and here we have uncovered many contemporary letters, retrospectives, and outside observers that confirm Jean-Jacques's performance on this front (regarding the period at least ca. 1756–1767). Next, we turn from these dusty volumes of letters to the glimmering *Reveries*. Its author has not been "permitted" to do all the good he has intended, but he can at least offer the author of his being "a tribute of frustrated good intentions, of healthy feelings rendered ineffectual, and of a patience impervious to the scorn of men" (II, 14/1004). Long past flagellating his opponents for their omissions, he is now reduced to licking his wounds over his own omissions. If his original response to Diderot insisted that he is not really alone and he *is* fulfilling his essential social duties, his final narrative is that he really *is* alone and has been forcibly prevented from fulfilling those duties.

In emphasizing this element of change, I do not mean to reject readings of Rousseau's thought as fundamentally systematic and consistent.[168] In principle, differing self-assessments need not have a bearing on one's normative or theoretical philosophy. Moreover, the analysis here provides some confirmation for systematic readings. For in many of his moralistic prescriptions of the duties of individuals to their countries (even outside genuine republics), he framed this in reciprocal, quasi-contractual terms. That is, we know that the decent person owes much to her society, precisely because it is so unlikely that someone could have *become* decent if her society had not been doing some important things well enough.[169] This is a moderate and even conservative layer of Rousseau's thinking, which should be seen as a qualification to the frequent, often savage dismissals of mainstream civilization that are highlighted by scholars like Starobinski. It is not clear that Rousseau ever explicitly appeals to these arguments in defending his final way of life, but the structure of argumentation applies. What does *this* man—exiled or outlawed across much of Europe, and (as he sees it) unjustly scorned and libeled by a whole generation—owe to *his* society? He may reminisce about the debts he accrued in more fortunate times, which allowed him to accomplish what he did in his main authorship (ca. 1749–1762). Yet those days are long past, as a cumulative effect of what he published for no other purpose—he often insisted—than devotion to truth and the public good. Eventually, he reached the point where he no longer owed anything beyond living from the bread he has earned, and refraining from harming others.[170] It is, then, at least roughly the same principles that strongly bound him to others in the 1750s and early 1760s, which seem increasingly to absolve him in the 1770s. These theoretical principles can thus have a high level of formal consistency and yet, with a modest change of contextual emphasis, can lead to practical conclusions that are nearly opposite. This is another reason to pay some attention to developments over time.[171]

If this sounds like a brief for the final Jean-Jacques's moral character, it may be taken as such in response to simple and sweeping dismissals of him. Yet in seeking to judge him by his own principles, and finding so much wiggle room for behavior that is often so extravagant, one might just as naturally censure the thought as acquit the man. Even during the quarrels over friendship and gratitude in 1757–1758, d'Épinay, Grimm, and Diderot noted the capacity of Rousseau's "monstrous system" to sound so elevated, yet always provide the necessary sophism to justify his dishonorable behavior.[172] We have seen related scholarly assessments of his thought, which fault it for positing the source of evil as fundamentally external to the self, or focusing on internal, abstract intention in excusing actual behavior.[173] Consider also Adam Smith's argument on how our moral sentiments direct us against being satisfied with mere "indolent benevolence," or considering oneself "the friend of mankind," "unless he has actually produced" effects "in the external circumstances of the world."[174]

Jean-Jacques's social isolation became more extreme over time; I have argued that his sense of duty was proportionally truncated. Early on, his ideal of solitude was domestic and private yet explicitly social, and it could not be justified apart from broader social duties. But as his persecution—real and perceived—increased, his notion of solitude became more absolute and, in defending his later life, the emphasis shifts toward merely not harming others. As has often been observed, this final solitude has important parallels with the earliest humans of the second *Discourse*, including this emphasis on merely not committing harm. In the Conclusion that follows, we return to the scholarly debates on whether it is this pre-moral and post-moral solitude or a life of virtue and duty that is most fundamental to his thought.

CONCLUSION

So why did Rousseau's life deviate so sharply from his principles? As we have seen, interpretive schools have taken very different approaches.[1] For the better "moralistic" interpreters of Rousseau, beginning with Ernst Cassirer, the usual way out has been to cordon off the major philosophical writings from the personal Jean-Jacques. Normative thought need not be tainted by whatever peculiarities their author may have exhibited, especially when these flaws are regretted.[2] Moreover, late works such as the *Reveries* should be taken not as expressing an ideal but as describing a behavioral logic resulting from his own exceptional circumstances.[3] There is a lack of lucidity in his late claims that he has no need of others.[4] On these grounds, the genuine Rousseau can remain a perceptive defender of justice, virtue, and community.

Conversely, for the better "antinomian" interpreters, discordant and subversive undercurrents run beneath the placid, edifying surface of the major normative writings. Given these fundamental tensions, these interpreters see the autobiographical writings as providing decisive evidence, revealing the deeper intentions of the corpus as a whole. As Eve Grace observes: "When read in the context of Rousseau's thought as a whole, the *Reveries* forms the last and central piece of a puzzle, which, when fitted in, helps to make the whole picture leap into view."[5] The radically solitary happiness of *Reveries* V develops the anthropology of the *Discourse on Inequality* and is the highest way of life for the philosophical mind.[6] Although the autobiographical writings often complain about the injustices done to Rousseau and about his corresponding isolation, in the end they also reveal how these misfortunes "forced him to be free." He had to break away from the distorting forces of civilization, as well as the misguided aspects of his own education, in order to live in accord with his own deepest insights.[7] In such ways, the high normative ideals can be framed as more of a popular appearance than as a philosophical reality.

Although this is not the place for a full assessment,[8] here I provide brief responses with a view to sketching a hybrid approach.

1. The Friend of Virtue and the Specter of La Rochefoucauld

Thinking of the corpus as a whole, much of the Flawed Moralist interpretation amounts to the argument stated well by Joseph Reisert, that Rousseau was a useful and genuine friend of virtue, even if not himself virtuous.[9] Consider how a person who is morally undistinguished might with minimal hesitation be embraced by aspiring communities if that person could usefully articulate norms that advance justice and the common good, while he remained discreet about his personal life. During Rousseau's earlier career, many in Geneva seem to have weighed the practical consideration that their community, at least when facing special challenges, would need allied talent of Rousseau's caliber, despite his ambiguous connections with their ideology and way of life. For instance, Maurice Cranston describes the apparent eagerness of Genevan leaders to readmit Rousseau to citizenship during his visit in 1754, including perhaps light questioning about his religious orthodoxy.[10] Insofar as Rousseau claimed only to serve as a friend of virtue, his approach would parallel the famous claim of La Rochefoucauld, that "hypocrisy is an homage which vice renders to virtue."[11] Of course, Jean-Jacques would resist the suggestion that he embodied *vice* paying homage, but on this reading he would grant that he intentionally praised characters and ideals far better than what he could attain. It would not have been difficult for him to establish that he was regretfully prevented from acting in accordance with his teachings because of contingent factors such as his long wanderings outside his homeland and his residency in a servile environment. None of this would seriously undermine the likelihood that his normative teachings were sincere convictions and rigorous expositions about the best ways of life for humanity.

This accommodation of weaknesses seems especially plausible when dealing with a thinker's past, prior to intellectual maturity or whatever kind of moral maturity his thought may require. Thus, in the case of Rousseau's discarded children, we have seen that, in some respects, he seems scarcely more blameworthy than the parallel case of Augustine and his dismissal, before his conversion, of his concubine of many years.[12] When *Emile* strongly suggests that its author failed in his fatherly duties and has suffered grievously and incessantly for it,[13] we might conclude that this episode was a very sad and disappointing personal failure but without consequence for his later character or thought. Personal struggles may also provide unique insights. For instance, it has been suggested that Rousseau's experience with his children may underlie the turmoil expressed by the character Julie, as she describes her moral decline prior to the transformation that had recently occurred at her wedding ceremony.[14] She observes, "One strays for a single moment in life, deviates by a single step from the straight path. . . . He finally falls into the chasm, and awakens horrified to find himself covered with crimes, having a heart born for virtue" (*Julie* III.18, 291/353). Although there is pity for natural weakness, Julie shows how it can be overcome by firm resolution. In these respects, we must agree with Ruth Grant, that Rousseau has ample resources for overcoming the tendencies toward subjectivity and excuse-making—tendencies often criticized in ethical theories like his, which are based on intention.[15]

Nonetheless, there are other cases when the confrontation with crimes, or mere vices and faults, leads Rousseau not to open remorse or deep aspiration but to endless casuistry and the embrace of authenticity as such. This is one side of the tension that has been discerned in him between "authenticity as submission to universal laws of reason and authenticity as honoring the idiosyncrasies of individuality."[16] We saw, for instance, that the regrets in *Emile* were the fundamental posture toward the discarded children during an important yet brief period (ca. 1759–1762). We also saw that, for longer periods, he dealt with that challenge through justifying the objective standing of those acts, or subjectively mitigating his fault in them. And while this case was exceptional in terms of the actions explained, in other cases, such as Marion and the ribbon, it has been compellingly argued that the rationalizing follows the broader philosophy of natural goodness.[17] We thus wonder if Rousseau ever linked himself with another observation of Julie: "Virtue is so necessary to our hearts, that once genuine virtue has been abandoned, we invent ourselves another after our own fashion, and cling to it all the firmer, perhaps because it is of our own choosing" (*Julie* III.18, 284f/346). Here we cannot say that Rousseau was the best critic of his own vices but that he *potentially* might have been, while often failing to make the final application to his own case. This parallels what was noticed about him personally by troubled friends. During a quarrel with Grimm, Madame d'Épinay challenged Jean-Jacques: "Does a man like you harden himself in his wrongs by means of his sophisms?"[18] Evidently, she thought he was doing so, and our evidence suggests that this was not unusual for him. One might conclude, then, that Rousseau has ample resources not only for resisting subjectivity and excuse-making but also for embracing them. To return to the thread from Reisert, I endorse the possibility of a highly flawed person paying homage to virtue. A person who made grave mistakes in his youth but came to regret them and strove to balance his moral account, can without much hesitation be considered a friend of virtue.[19] Virtue has often condescended to work constructively with well-disposed people who do not live up to her standards. Yet she may feel betrayed by a purported friend who cannot resist publicly revealing his most questionable behaviors, while offering countless excuses in their behalf, alongside a well-packaged ideology enabling others to do the same. This is another point that would have been well-known to Rousseau through La Rochefoucauld: "Nothing is so contagious as an example, and we never do any great good or any great evil which does not produce similar ones. We imitate the good actions through emulation, and the bad ones through the malignity of our nature that shame kept prisoner, and that an example sets free."[20]

If Rousseau had been content as merely a friend of virtue, there would be strong scholarly justification for philosophers and political theorists to leave the personal questions aside and focus only on his normative writings. However, it is often the case that his autobiographies not only depart from but positively undermine this humble posture. For, in many theoretically vigorous and sustained passages, he could not help but pay more intensive homage to goodness than to virtue. And this goodness needed to be defined in such a way that—despite his many vices and faults—no one could dare claim, "I was better than that man" (Conf. I, 5/5).

Finally, as we have seen, in the normative writings, Rousseau is an especially strong critic of the hypocrisy of intellectuals—he is far from "latitudinarian."[21] I add that in those same writings, he groomed political communities to reject these impostors. They have no need for La Rochefoucauld's preferred hypocrisy, whereby a person respects social norms to which she does not firmly adhere. They will not need to compromise their standards in order to recruit or maintain unusually talented people in their communities: "When the citizens love their duty . . . public morals take the place of the chiefs' genius; and the more virtue reigns, the less the need for talents" (DPE 15/253f).[22] This will make them less susceptible to supremely hypocritical characters, such as Catiline and Oliver Cromwell, who reveal their true natures only when they have proven themselves to be violent usurpers (see SC IV.8, 148/466). The latter "was recognized as a tyrant only after he had, for fifteen years, been taken to be the avenger of the laws and the defender of religion."[23] A "clever knave or insinuating talker" like him could persuade Parisians or Londoners of much nonsense, but

"Cromwell would have been condemned to hard labor by the people of Berne" (IV.1, 121/438).[24] Hypocrisy is thus normally discussed not as a case of one's moral reach exceeding her grasp or polite deference to established customs but as an intentional and self-interested fraud, characteristic of Paris or the darkest moments of political history.[25] By contrast, Rousseau's moral and political communities will have a sincere communion of hearts, largely because they have nothing to hide.[26] I conclude that the ideal Rousseauian community—while meeting under oak trees in their rustic simplicity—wouldn't have taken long to send a talented yet self-absorbed and hypocritical "friend of virtue" packing. As we have seen, there is substantial explanatory power in the friend-of-virtue approach,[27] but as it contrasts in some ways with the related stances of the normative writings, some supplement is needed to explain the whole.

2. An Earlier Exemplary Life

Others have been much more welcoming to Jean-Jacques at his most wayward. Although they move in different directions, several of the most influential philosophical interpreters of the autobiographies—including Leo Strauss, Christopher Kelly, Laurence Cooper, and Heinrich Meier—have seen the *Reveries* as providing strong confirmation that Rousseau ultimately opted for a superior way of life, at least for the extraordinary few who are capable of it.[28] In intentional contrast with Cassirer, Strauss's Rousseau sees an "insoluble conflict" between the individual and society, and the autobiographies show how he sided with the individual.[29] I also list David Gauthier as a Veiled Antinomian, even though to him the highest ideal is free and spontaneous love, rather than solitude. To him, the *Reveries* reveals, in a more indisputable way than other sources, that Jean-Jacques had no sincere personal interest in civic life or moral virtue.[30] Indeed, the *Reveries* claims directly that Jean-Jacques has never been suited for "civil society" and that he has been less able to overcome his inclinations "when duty commands"—i.e., to be virtuous—than "any man in the world" (VI, 83, 77/1059, 1053).[31] For Kelly, this is the culmination of the process depicted in the *Confessions*, in which Jean-Jacques becomes a necessary modern alternative to previous exemplary lives, including Socrates, Cato, and Jesus.[32]

We thus find a stark contrast with Flawed Moralist accounts, where Rousseau presents his life as unique, regrets it in many respects, and presents his genuine model in works such as *Emile*.[33] I do not believe this debate can be fully resolved, but, by paying attention to possible shifts, a layer can be added to the discussion.

We find that, in a few passages, he does explicitly present his life as a model to others. But these do not seem to be in the latest autobiographies, or concerning the latest parts of his life. In presenting the solitary dreamer as the major alternative to civic virtue, Stephen Salkever cites a passage from the *Letters to Malesherbes* (1762) as one of a few where "Rousseau refers to his own solitary life as exemplary."[34] The claim seems to hold up, since a universal model is suggested: "It is something to give men the example of the life they should all lead" (*Malesherbes* IV, 580/1143). However, this paragraph defends Rousseau's life not as an isolated dreamer but as an aid to his poor neighbors in Montmorency, as a writer of useful truths defending his fatherland, and the like.[35] Similarly, the *Confessions* describes the need to resign his position with the Dupins (ca. 1751) in view of his recently adopted "stern principles": "I would cut a fine figure, would I not, a cashier to a tax-collector preaching disinterestedness and poverty?" (VIII, 303/362).[36] In the same period, he was increasingly harassed by his intellectual friends: "What attracted their jealousy was not so much my literary fame as my personal reform; they . . . could not forgive me for offering by my conduct an example that might prove inconvenient to them" (304/362).[37]

We recall Edmund Burke's chiding of the French National Assembly, for choosing Rousseau as "a model," even though he is "by his own account without a single virtue."[38] This assessment has been endorsed by some leading scholars.[39] However, I would argue that during the period when Rousseau sometimes appealed to himself as a model, he also accounted himself as having significant virtues.[40] Consider, for instance, his rebuttal in the "Preface to *Narcissus*" (1753) of the charge of "contradiction and incoherence [*inconséquence*]" within the first *Discourse*, as well as between it and his life (PN 105/973). Most of the "Preface" shows the frivolousness of the charge by clarifying the subtler normative implications of the *Discourse*. For instance, it is permissible to write plays for Parisians, since diversions are necessary where virtue is no longer possible (104/972). However, near the end he also moves beyond his earlier, easier approach of simply dismissing personal charges against him.[41] For even if personal inconsistency does not prove the falseness of the principles or the writer's insincerity,[42] he comes to insist that there are some personal inconsistencies that would undermine the credibility of his broader philosophical endeavor: "It matters to the truth I have upheld that its defender not be justly accused of having lent it his assistance on a mere whim or out of vanity, without loving or knowing it" (92/959).[43]

> If they ever see that I am starting to crave the public's favor . . . , or that I seek to undermine my rivals' fame, or that I presume to speak ill of the great men of the age in order to raise myself to their level . . . , or that I aspire to positions in academies, or that I court the women who establish the fashions, or that I fawn on the foolishness of great nobles, or that I become contemptuous of the craft I have chosen and strike out in quest of wealth, no longer wishing to live by the work of my hands, *in a word if they notice that the love of reputation causes me to forget the love of virtue*, I beg them to warn me, even publicly, and I promise instantly to commit my writings and my books to the flames, and to concede all the errors they may wish to reproach me with. (105/973f)[44]

We note, on the one hand, that many of these vices are connected with *amour-propre* and comparative standing. Rousseau's insistence on avoiding these has clear links with sustaining naturalness, and he would continue to emphasize this in his final writings, after he had largely ceased to claim virtue.[45] He claims, for example, "forty years of uprightness [*droiture*] and honor in difficult circumstances" (Conf. II, 73/87).[46] More generally, he may fall into anger or fury at times, but, because of his lack of *amour-propre*, he does not fall into hatred or the desire for vengeance (Conf. IX, 396n/472n; XI, 490/585; RJJ II, 116/810). On the other hand, this early "love of virtue" has substantive consequences—it is a matter of deeds, not mere sentiments or intentions. The implication is that maintaining his way of life amid the world of Parisian ambition is difficult, and yet he possesses the self-command of virtue in these regards.[47]

This disinterestedness is also highlighted in a letter of November 1754, explaining his rationale for enduring the troubles that may come from publishing the Dedication to the *Discourse on Inequality*: "I suppress all personal considerations which may concern me, because they should never enter the motives of a good man who works for the public benefit. If the detachment of a heart which values neither glory, nor fortune, nor even life may make it worthy of announcing the truth, I dare believe myself called to this sublime vocation. It is for making men good according to my power that I abstain from receiving these things from them and that I cherish my poverty and independence."[48] These affirmations persist after his departure from Paris (1756), when the peak period of his effervescence had subsided. He emphasizes the path of virtue in a letter to Sophie d'Houdetot, during what proved to be their final quarrel: "You speak to me, in a reproachful tone, of faults and weaknesses [*de fautes de foiblesses*]. I am weak, it is true; my life is full of faults, because I am a man. But what distinguishes me from all the other men I know, is that with all my faults, I have always reproached myself for them, and that my faults have never made me despise my duty or trample on virtue; and, moreover, that I have struggled for virtue and conquered at times when everyone else has forgotten it. May you always find men as criminal as that."[49] Whereas the *Reveries* divulges uniqueness in his incapacity to overcome himself, this letter insists on uniqueness (within his milieu) in some actual self-conquest. A similar argument had been written for Sophie, without the exasperated tone, in the slightly earlier *Moral Letters* (ca. winter 1757–1758): "If my heart ever went astray in wishes about which you have made me blush, at least my mouth did not attempt to justify my going astray, reason dressed up in sophisms did not lend its service to the error; humiliated vice fell silent at the sacred name of virtue . . . by abstaining from giving decent names to my faults I kept decency from leaving my heart" (I, 175/1081).[50]

A final example comes from July 1766, not long after the onset of the autobiographical phase. Rousseau writes in his major letter accusing Hume of treachery:[51]

> Yes, Mr. Hume, you *have me*[52] by all the ties of this life, but you have no power over my probity [*vertu*] or my fortitude [*courage*], which, being independent either of you or of mankind, I will preserve in spite of you. . . . Mankind may say and do what they will, it is of little consequence to me. What is of consequence, however, is that I should end as I have begun, that I should continue to be upright and true [*droit et vrai*] to the end, whatever may happen, and that I should have no cause to reproach myself either with cowardice in adversity, or insolence in prosperity.[53]

In a letter written soon after this (January 1767), we have found evidence of Rousseau backing away—perhaps for the first time—from claiming to be a substantive model for others.[54] Yet, given the earlier correspondence and writings, our finding from Chapter 2 is less surprising. That is, unlike the usual approach of the *Dialogues* and the *Reveries*, the *Confessions* provides repeated examples of Rousseau's virtuous actions, and tries to explain the "seeds" of virtue that had been planted in him.[55]

This is another way in which the earlier Rousseau had a far more ambitious self-understanding than what is now well-known from the later autobiographies. To the earlier discussions that he rejected intellectual hypocrites, had great aspirations for virtue, and had a mystique of virtue during his lifetime, I now add that, by his own estimates, he had substantial success for at least a dozen years (1753–1766).[56] This challenges not only antinomian models, which assume his most fundamental intentions are post-moral,[57] but also moralistic approaches, which have normally sought to quarantine the life. Instead, we should see practical philosophy and the philosophical life as sister aspirations flowing from a common vision, albeit aspirations that fluctuate over time.

3. The Inversion of Priorities

The existing paradigms largely invert each other, and each has its strengths. Viewed thematically, Veiled Antinomianism illuminates the Rousseau of the last dozen years and the philosophy of natural goodness, but it fails to account for the sincere aspirations to virtue—both to live it and to articulate it credibly—at many earlier points. Conversely, whereas Flawed Moralism illuminates Rousseau's philosophical intentions during the period he considered his intellectual peak, while exposing some of the more desperate rationalizations of the later period, it does not account for the subversive elements of the teachings on natural goodness that run throughout his corpus, or the ways in which the autobiographies develop these themes in profound and influential ways.[58] The Antinomians fail to account for genuine change and tension across the corpus, while the Moralists fail to account for the depth and consistency of a certain strand of unedifying thought. Hence, the Moralists are largely correct on Rousseau's chronological development and biographical context, but they overstep in dismissing the last phase of his writings as merely biographical. Conversely, the Antinomians helpfully develop Rousseau's claims that his writings constitute a coherent system, but they overstep in reducing any tensions to a consistent underlying meaning, while also negating the shifts across time that he explicitly signaled. Notably, in the often cited passage claiming his unique lack of virtue, Rousseau also describes why he has "greatly modified *the opinion I long had of my own virtue*" (Rev. VI, 77/1052f).[59] This new opinion may be more accurate, but as it is explicitly a reinterpretation of his character, it directly undermines any attempt to read this self-interpretation back into the works which precede this shift.

Insofar as my interpretation is convincing, the genuine and philosophical Rousseau was more conflicted in his intentions than the leading paradigms allow. Then, too, on purely historical and interpretive grounds, one could no longer present Rousseau (*simpliciter*) as essentially a champion of the Moralists' justice and duty or of the Antinomians' modern sincerity, philosophical skepticism, and radical solitude. There would, nonetheless, remain a place for a more qualified form of appropriation, especially if it were acknowledged as such.[60] For instance, a revised Flawed Moralist approach could plausibly argue of the autobiographical goodness—not that it is not sane or truly philosophical—but that, on independent grounds, the interpreter finds the teachings on virtue and the just community more persuasive. In the same way, the Veiled Antinomian approach could be revised to claim not that the teachings on political and domestic virtue are not sincere or truly philosophical but that, on independent grounds, the interpreter finds the teachings on natural goodness, solitary contentment, or obligation-free love more persuasive (or at least more coherent with the deepest premises of modern political philosophy).[61] On this basis, a broad range of scholars could continue to indicate what may be learned by engaging carefully with Rousseau, while also acknowledging other ways in which he would continue to challenge their primary historical or philosophical narrative.

Having placed so many interpreters in boxes of my own design, I may be asked for a positive formulation of my own. I suggest the "inversion of priorities." A prioritarian reading maintains that Rousseau develops certain themes across his corpus in accordance with a consistent anthropology, but it does not reduce the dialectical tension between goodness and virtue to a consistent philosophical or practical intention.[62] Both goodness and virtue are highly integrated throughout his works, and the advocacy of one element is very rarely made in direct contradiction to the other element. At the same time, the fundamental tone, priorities, and purpose of his writings can shift considerably. Focusing on these issues of tension and priority within a largely coherent system[63] may leave us with a figure who is less iconic, but it helps explain why so many thoughtful scholars have been able to shed so much light on him, while leaving us with two almost opposite images of his intentions and genuine legacy.

The priorities seem to be inverted during the intensification of his personal crisis, spanning from Voltaire's *Sentiment of the Citizens* to the rupture with David Hume (December 1764–June 1766). Prior to this, he presents himself chiefly as a lover and representative of virtue, and secondarily as a defender of oppressed natural goodness. After this, he presents himself chiefly as a defender and representative of oppressed goodness, and secondarily as a friend of virtue. The practical normative emphasis is reversed. This inversion of priorities contrasts with the leading paradigms, which ultimately appeal to one of these strands as the philosophical reality and the other as a merely popularizing appearance or personal deviation. My approach involves philosophically substantive development, while avoiding absolute dichotomy or rupture across stages.

The *Discourse on Inequality* (1754–1755) seems anomalous for our theory. In its sustained positive portrayals of an original—prerational and premoral—humanity, in contrast with civilized debasement, on many recent readings it has been seen as questioning the desirability or naturalness of virtue and citizenship as such. A full assessment would find important subversive elements in this work. Yet in terms of his later self-understanding, Rousseau sees the second *Discourse* as the high mark of his Parisian period—the time of effervescent virtue. He also partially distances himself from this period in general and this work in particular, since the spectacle of Paris's vices sometimes filled his mind with indignation and an excessive "black bile."[64] Yet, whatever subversive or excessive elements there may be, it is mainly said to explore the pseudo-progress of civilization and modernity, which subvert natural goodness, and thus the necessary conditions for simple decency, virtue, and citizenship alike.[65] In the final writings, a parallel emphasis on goodness over virtue would again predominate, this time driven not by virtue's anger at the general state of society but by the unjustified persecution of the good and innocent Jean-Jacques. The *Considerations on the Government of Poland* (written ca. October 1770–June 1771) is the major exception for this stage, but, as we have seen, it is part of a broader campaign—rare in the last dozen years—to restore command over himself and to reestablish his public reputation.[66]

More typically, for that last dozen years, our author gave up on the sort of writing that he thought gave him a purpose far beyond the ambition and vanity of other intellectuals, and he turned to another sort which shocked many early readers for its vanity and extensive display of faults that did him no credit.[67] This likely undermined the legacy that he was trying to defend.[68] The autobiographical project may also have been quite different had he limited himself to brief character sketches like the *Letters to Malesherbes* or followed Plutarch's model of admitting to weaknesses and vices but not dwelling on them.[69] In this way, even in the case of his children, his offense against philosophy and the philosophical life may perhaps be found more in his excuses than in the deeds themselves.[70] A more Plutarchian and less defensive model would be in keeping with the disinterested philosophical justification of autobiography in the Neuchâtel Preamble to the *Confessions* (1764)—to provide the first genuine portrait of a human life. The final dozen years thus present us with another tragic dimension, increasingly marked by such excuses for the past, as well as by various forms of desperation, despair, and apathy in the present. The abundant testimony from this period has made it impossible for most to perceive that Rousseau had long striven toward an unusually ambitious philosophical life, understood in terms of virtue, citizenship, and benefit to humanity.

As a whole, Rousseau's life is a profoundly mixed affair, while his thought both emerged from it and radically transcended it. Amid lengthy discussions of the odious and the excellent in him, I hope to have offered a preamble—and not a catechism—on the Jean-Jacques problem. Some will be, above all, appalled by his soul, while others may be challenged by a strange yet penetrating man's aspirations to defend and embody a better life.[71] Those impressed by this figure will have confronted some of his all-too-human shifts and tensions, ending in a substantial collapse of those aspirations. Conversely, some may justly find themselves "better than that man," but they will have considered not only his notorious failures but also his civic and humane commitments, which were long maintained amid challenging circumstances.

NOTES

INTRODUCTION

Epigraphs: Buffon, according to the testimony of Hérault de Séchelles (CC 38:317–21, at 318); also discussed in Raymond Trousson, "Buffon," in *Dictionnaire*, 120.

From her note, apparently written several decades after her relationship with Rousseau ended, and inserted in the copy of *Julie* that he had transcribed for her by hand (CC 5:272, with R. A. Leigh, 272 note 1). For her better known (and more critical) retrospective on Jean-Jacques, see Leo Damrosch, *Jean-Jacques Rousseau: Restless Genius* (Boston: Houghton Mifflin, 2005), 282f.

1. Letter to Rousseau, 10 March 1757, CC 4:168–69, at 169.

2. *Le fils naturel, ou Les épreuves de la vertu* (1757), in *Le drame bourgeois, Fiction II*, ed. Jacques Chouillet and Anne-Marie Chouillet (Paris: Hermann, 1980), 13–82, at IV.3, 61f; also quoted in Conf. IX, 382/455 (translation modified).

3. "A Letter to a Member of the National Assembly" (1791), in *Further Reflections on the Revolution in France*, ed. Daniel E. Ritchie (Indianapolis: Liberty Fund, 1992), 29–72, at 48f.

4. Ibid., 49; see 47–50. For similar criticisms of Rousseau's treatment of his children, see below, Chapter 1, note 17.

5. On the break with Diderot (1756–1758), see Arthur N. Wilson, *Diderot* (New York: Oxford University Press, 1972), 293–304, and below, Chapter 6, with notes 31–40. On the break with Hume (1766–1767), see below, Chapter 6, note 102.

6. *Essai sur les règnes de Claude et de Néron* (1782 edition), in *Oeuvres*, 5 vols., ed. Laurent Versini (Paris: Robert Laffont, 1994–1997), 1:971-1251, at I.61, 1030, I.66–67, 1035-36; cf. "Les Tablettes" (written ca. October 1758), in CC 5:281-86, at 282. In his final years, Diderot became increasingly (sometimes obsessively) concerned about Rousseau's forthcoming memoirs (see Wilson, *Diderot*, 608, 610, 691, 704–5, and Versini, Introduction to *Essai sur les règnes*, 969).

7. "Les Tablettes," 282–83.

8. This is in a forged letter, undoubtedly by Diderot according to Leigh (CC 4:444b), allegedly of 5 December 1757 (in CC 4:443–45, at 443). For the fictional elements of *Montbrillant*, see Leigh, *Unsolved Problems in the Bibliography of Jean-Jacques Rousseau*, ed. J. T. A. Leigh (Cambridge: Cambridge University Press, 1990), 134.

9. Hume to Blair, 1 July 1766, *Letters of David Hume*, 2 vols., ed. J. Y. T. Greig (Oxford: Clarendon, 1932), 2:57, also discussed in Robert Zaretsky and John T. Scott, *The Philosophers' Quarrel: Rousseau, Hume, and the Limits of Human Understanding* (New Haven: Yale University Press, 2009), 171.

10. "Les Tablettes," 282, referring to a trip to the Hermitage.

11. Hume to Adam Smith, ca. August–September 1766, in *Letters*, 2:82-83, at 82, also discussed in Dennis Rasmussen, *The Infidel and the Professor: David Hume, Adam Smith, and the Friendship That Shaped Modern Thought* (Princeton: Princeton University Press, 2017), 143.

12. "I esteem the writer, but I do not esteem the man. . . . And the more he has become famous for his talent and the alleged austerity of his morals, the more it seems important to me to break the silence" (*Essai sur les règnes*, I.67, 1036, and cf. II.17, 1131).

13. Hume to Smith, ca. August–September 1766, *Letters* 2:82f, discussed in Rasmussen, *The Infidel and the Professor*, 142f.

14. For the prevalence of the ad hominem in the eighteenth century, in connection with the ideal of the philosophical life, see below, Chapter 6, with note 167.

15. Deriving from debates in the seventeenth-century English Church, "latitudinarian" means "Allowing, favouring, or characterized by latitude in opinion or action, especially in matters of religion" (*Oxford English Dictionary*).

16. "Against Sainte-Beuve" (written ca. 1908–1909), in *Against Sainte-Beuve and Other Essays*, ed. and trans. John Sturrock (London: Penguin, 1988), 3-102, at 12 / "Contre Sainte-Beuve," in *Contre Sainte-Beuve, précédé de Pastiches et mélanges*, etc., ed. Pierre Clarac (Paris: Gallimard, 1971), 211-312, at 221f, translation slightly modified.

17. Ibid., 13/222, translation slightly modified.

18. *Letters Concerning the English Nation* (1733), ed. Nicholas Cronk (New York: Oxford University Press, 1994), XII, 50 / *Lettres philosophiques* (1734), in *Mélanges*, ed. Jacques van den Heuvel (Paris: Gallimard, 1961), 33f. Although Bacon accepted some gifts as Lord Chancellor, the charges against him were strongly politically motivated as well. For differing assessments, see Markku Peltonen, Introduction to *The Cambridge Companion to Francis Bacon* (Cambridge: Cambridge University Press, 1996), 14, and Quentin Skinner, "The Advancement of Francis Bacon," *New York Review of Books*, 4 November 1999, 53-56, at 54b-55a.

19. *Letters Concerning the English Nation*, XXI, 106/93.

20. "A Letter to a Member of the National Assembly," 47.

21. See Plato, *Laches*, 188c-89b, 193d-94a (all Plato references are to *The Complete Works of Plato*, ed. John M. Cooper [Indianapolis: Hackett, 1997]). On the more general need for harmony and the priority of deeds over speeches, see, e.g., *Apology*, 32d-33a, and Xenophon, *Memorabilia*, trans. Amy L. Bonnette (Ithaca: Cornell University Press, 2001), I.5.6, and IV.4.10. See the discussions in John Sellars, *The Art of Living: The Stoics on the Nature and Function of Philosophy* (Bristol: Bristol Classical Press, 2009), 20, 25, and James Miller, *Examined Lives: From Socrates to Nietzsche* (New York: Farrar, Straus and Giroux, 2011), 172. Very similar are the approaches of Seneca (Miriam Griffin, *Seneca: A Philosopher in Politics* [Oxford: Clarendon, 1992 (1976)], 8) and Plutarch (Ian Kidd, Introduction to *Essays*, ed. Kidd, trans. Robin Waterfield [London: Penguin, 1992], 9-11). Cf. Aristotle, *Nicomachean Ethics* I.3, 1095a.

22. See John Locke, *Some Thoughts Concerning Education* (1693–1705), ed. John W. Yolton and Jean S. Yolton (Oxford: Clarendon, 1989), §§71, 89, 117; cf., on the potential impact of servants and others, §§68, 76.

23. This continues a Renaissance polemic, which is also in Montaigne, "Of Schoolmasters' Learning" (in *Complete Essays* [1580–1595], trans. M. A. Screech [New York: Penguin, 2003], I.25, 153-54). See Locke, *Education*, §§70, 94, 147, and Rousseau, e.g., DSA II, 23/25, LR 65/73f, PN 98/966.

24. For necessary flaws, see E II, 94, 97/325, 328, and IV, 334f/664. For the general point, see E II, 95, 120f/325f, 363f; III, 179/446f; SV, 310/629; and V, 378, 388, 447/721f, 738f, 821. See also

Joseph Reisert on the need to see the tutor as a friend (*Jean-Jacques Rousseau: A Friend of Virtue* [Ithaca: Cornell University Press, 2003], ch. 7).

25. See below, Chapter 3, notes 88-89.

26. *On the Happy Life* [17-18], in *Dialogues and Essays*, trans. John Davie (New York: Oxford University Press, 2007), 99-100 (translation modified, in view of the Loeb text and the translation by James Ker). For the likely context of this "disarming" concession, see Miller, *Examined Lives*, 128; for parallel passages in the *Letters on Ethics*, see Griffin, *Seneca*, 302, as well as *Letters on Ethics*, ed. and trans. Margaret Graver and A. A. Long (Chicago: University of Chicago Press, 2015), 27.1.

27. *On the Happy Life* [19], 101. Cf. Tacitus on the prevalence of invective (*Agricola* [1-2]).

28. *On the Happy Life* [27], 110f.

29. E.g. Conf. I, 8/9; *Malesherbes* II, 574/1134; Rev. IV, 43/1024; and several other passages discussed in Bernard Gagnebin and Marcel Raymond, OC 1:1237-38, note 2 to p. 9. Quotations are checked against the translation Rousseau used: *Les vies des hommes illustres*, 2 vols., trans. Jacques Amyot (1559), ed. Gérard Walter (Paris: Gallimard, 1951).

30. *Cimon* [2] in *Greek Lives*, trans. Robin Waterfield (New York: Oxford University Press, 1998), 119-20/[5] in *Les Vies*, 1:1079. See also Plutarch, "On Being Aware of Moral Progress," 84f-85b, in *Essays*, ed. Kidd, 143-44. *Cato the Elder* displays this approach to flaws (see [5, 24], in *Roman Lives*, trans. Robin Waterfield [New York: Oxford University Press, 1999], 12-13, 31-32).

31. On Plutarch's edifying purposes, see *Pericles* [2], in *Greek Lives*, 145, and *Timoleon* [1], in *Plutarch's Lives*, trans. John Dryden, ed. and rev. Arthur Hugh Clough [1864], 2 vols. (New York: Modern Library, 2001), 1:325. On biographical method, see also *Nicias* [1], in *Greek Lives*, 185, and Kidd, Introduction to *Essays*, 3. For his best-known statement of method (on the significance of casual actions for revealing character), see *Alexander* [1], in *Greek Lives*, 312. Rousseau invokes this principle and provides several illustrations from Plutarch, including a devastating one about the vain ambition of Julius Caesar, in E IV, 240f/531 (see *Caesar* [11], in *Roman Lives*, 310f).

32. Others have used similar terms while discussing different problems. Ernst Cassirer's *Das Problem Jean Jacques Rousseau* (1932) deals with the significance of Rousseau's thought as a whole, arguing that biographical matters should be essentially bracketed (discussed below, Conclusion, with note 2). Peter Gay's translation alters "the problem" to *The Question of Jean-Jacques Rousseau*, 2nd ed. (New Haven: Yale University Press, 1989). For Istvan Hont, "The Jean-Jacques Rousseau Problem" is the contrast between his republican politics and his epicurean moral anthropology (*Politics in Commercial Society: Jean-Jacques Rousseau and Adam Smith*, ed. Béla Kapossy and Michael Sonenscher [Cambridge: Harvard University Press, 2015], ch. 1, esp. 18-21).

33. On this judicial function of the autobiographies, see Jean-François Perrin, "Lire *Les Confessions* avec la correspondance de Rousseau, II: Les *Lettres à Malesherbes*," *Méthode* 22 (2013): 147-58, at 151a, 154a, 155b, esp. 153a.

34. It was a 1962 preface by Michel Foucault that was the first serious study of the *Dialogues*, and this contributed to a revival of scholarly interest (Antoine Lilti, "The Writing of Paranoia: Jean-Jacques Rousseau and the Paradoxes of Celebrity," *Representations* 103 [2008]: 53-83, at 56). Lilti also affirms "an extremely rigorous argumentative structure, replete with eloquent passages" (74). The strongest defense is Masters and Kelly, Introduction to CW 1, esp. xviii-xxi.

35. Robert Wokler, *Rousseau: A Very Short Introduction* (New York: Oxford University Press, 2001), 146. See also Lilti, "The Writing of Paranoia," 53-57, and Rousseau's own lament about the book, RJJ Pref. 5/664.

36. Lilti, "The Writing of Paranoia," 56.

37. For weaknesses, see Ruth Grant, *Hypocrisy and Integrity: Machiavelli, Rousseau, and the Ethics of Politics* (Chicago: University of Chicago Press, 1997), 91, 111-13 (discussed below, Chapter 1, with note 72). For character strengths, see 74-77, 113 (discussed below, Chapter 2, note 145), and cf. below, Chapter 6, note 64.

38. *A Friend of Virtue*, 176. For the need to distinguish personal character from moral teachings, see 22n51, 28, 80-81, 89n15, 110n6, 115-16, and, esp., 176-81.

39. On the love of virtue, see also RJJ II, 127/824; *Beaumont* 24/931 ("a friend of virtue"); and Section 2.1 below. On mere goodness, see Chapter 6, especially Sections 6.3–6.4.

40. Introduction to CW 1:xxi. Masters and Kelly differ from Reisert and Grant, however, in that this lack of virtue is not discussed in terms of a genuine gap between life and principles, given the nature of those principles (cf. note 72 below). Cf. Laurence Cooper, who lists among several fundamental paradoxes of Rousseau that he may be "the least virtuous sincere exponent of virtue" (review of *On the Happiness of the Philosophic Life*, by Heinrich Meier, *History of Political Thought* 39.1 [2018]: 189-92, at 189).

41. See Chapter 1, note 82 below.

42. See Conf. IX, 339/404; RJJ II, 101, 149/791, 852. Diderot questions this method: "In order to assure me of the sublime virtue of Jean-Jacques, one sends me back to his writings; this is like sending me to the sermons of a preacher to assure me of his morals and of his faith" (*Essai sur les règnes*, I.61, 1031).

43. 26 February 1770, CC 37:248-71, at 255-56; for the charge, see below, Chapter 5, with note 17.

44. II.32; *Essays* 818 / *Les Essais*, ed. Pierre Villey, rev. V.-L. Saulnier (Paris: Presses Universitaires de France, 2004), 722. Conversely, Rousseau finds Cicero wanting on both fronts—he is a "rhetorician" and a "lawyer" whose moral insights are largely derived from Plato (E IV, 343/676; *Mountain* III, 166n/728n).

45. Miller similarly describes Seneca as "a man of authentically Socratic *aspirations*," despite his deep awareness of his own imperfections (*Examined Lives*, 136).

46. This seems to be the assumption of Jean-Michel Moreau, in his remarkable 1782 engraving, "*Arrivée de J.-J. Rousseau aux champs élisées*" (Rousseau's arrival at the Elysian Fields). See the historical discussions in Gordon McNeil, "The Cult of Rousseau and the French Revolution," *Journal of the History of Ideas* 16.2 (1945): 197-212, at 199, and Louisa Shea, *The Cynic Enlightenment: Diogenes in the Salon* (Baltimore: Johns Hopkins University Press, 2010), 96.

47. Cf. Plato, *Republic* I, 350c-d.

48. Chapter 1, note 82 below.

49. Derived from "Justice and Liberty hanged, while Voltaire rides monster Humanity and Jean-Jacques Rousseau takes his measure," the frontispiece to Henry Fuseli's *Remarks on the Writings and Conduct of Jean-Jacques Rousseau* (1767). The artist is an expatriate from Switzerland who anglicized his name, Johann Heinrich Füssli. For historical discussion, see Ourida Mostefai, *Jean-Jacques Rousseau, écrivain polémique* (Leiden: Brill/ Rodopi, 2016), 144-46.

50. Diderot, *Essai sur la Peinture* (1765), quoted in Damrosch, *Restless Genius*, 217.

51. Translation modified. For the critique of high society more generally, see below, Section 6.1.

52. Translation modified. Similarly, "most modern books" are so cold because their authors believe nothing of what they say ("Biographical Fragment" [ca. winter 1755–1756], CW 12:30 / OC 1:1113).

53. See E I, 39/249 (discussed below, Chapter 3, with note 2).

54. See Michael Locke McLendon, *The Psychology of Inequality: Rousseau's* Amour-Propre (Philadelphia: University of Pennsylvania Press, 2019), 34-40.

55. It would be a case of what Vittorio Hösle describes as "meta-hypocrisy," emerging from a source that staunchly rejects hypocrisy (*Morals and Politics*, trans. Steven Rendall [Notre Dame: University of Notre Dame Press, 2004], 580).

56. All these factors are at the heart of Lester Crocker's interpretation of Rousseau (see below, Chapter 1, with notes 11-12 and 180-84). For charlatanry, see Grant's discussion of Molière's *Tartuffe*. She helpfully distinguishes Tartuffe's cynical and intentional hypocrisy from other kinds, including the "unselfconscious," or self-deceived, hypocrite (*Hypocrisy and Integrity*, ch. 3, esp. 67-68, 88-89, as well as 171-72).

57. On esotericism, see below, Chapter 2, note 61, and Section 2 of the Conclusion.

58. My translation. His earliest approach was to dismiss charges of personal inconsistency as philosophically irrelevant. For his mature approach, see the Conclusion, with notes 41-44.

59. I am arguing only from a parallel with the "Preface to *Narcissus*," not from its authority, since it is only contrasting himself before and after his major philosophical breakthrough of 1749. I will be arguing for additional, subtler changes that occurred later.

60. See below, Chapter 2, notes 10-11, and Section 3 of the Conclusion.

61. This is meant as a minimal estimate; by more flexible standards, 1750–1766 would be acceptable. Following major personal reform efforts beginning in 1751–1752 (Section 2.1 below), a strong public claim of several virtues is in PN 105/973f (published January 1753; quoted below, Conclusion, with note 44). In the *Observations* (October 1751) he had claimed, "I adore virtue," but he distinguished this clearly from "the conduct that makes for a virtuous man" (EPW 35 / OC 3:39). For 1764 as the rough end date, see Chapter 5 and Sections 6.2–6.4. 1766 may be a better end date concerning his own perceived virtue (Conclusion, note 56).

62. Translation modified.

63. Nietzsche, *Philosophy in the Tragic Age of the Greeks* (1873), as translated in Jonathan Barnes, "Nietzsche and Diogenes Laertius," *Nietzsche-Studien* 51.1 (1986): 16-40, at 21.

64. *Schopenhauer as Educator* (1874), VIII, in Nietzsche, *Untimely Meditations*, ed. Daniel Breazeale, trans. R. J. Hollingdale (Cambridge: Cambridge University Press, 1997), 187. Cf. *Beyond Good and Evil*, ed. Rolf-Peter Horstmann and Judith Norman, trans. Judith Norman (Cambridge: Cambridge University Press, 2002), §4.

65. This would be supported by Jason Neidleman, *Rousseau's Ethics of Truth: A Sublime Science of Simple Souls* (London: Routledge, 2017), esp. ch. 3, and Ryan Patrick Hanley, "Rousseau's Virtue Epistemology," *Journal of the History of Philosophy* 50.2 (2012): 239-63.

66. See also "Biographical Fragment," CW 12:30 / OC 1:1113; E SV, 268f/569.

67. See Chapter 2 below, especially Section 2.1.

68. See St. Preux's account of the night he was lured into a brothel (*Julie* II.26), resulting in "the despair of feeling as guilty [*coupable*] as I could possibly be" (244/297; see also Julie's response in II.27; cf. E IV, 335/664). Among the autobiographical allusions, St. Preux's male associates mocked his resistance as "retaining in Paris the simplicity of ancient Helvetic manners" (*Julie* II.26, 241/294f; for St. Preux as largely autobiographical in general, see Conf. IX, 362/430). The *Confessions* confirms that the episode is modeled on the one infidelity that Rousseau committed against Thérèse (VIII, 297-98/354-55). This apparently occurred in late 1749 or early 1750, after he wrote the first *Discourse* but before his personal reform (see below, Chapter 2, with note 20).

69. See Chapter 1 below, notes 43-44.

70. See below, Section 2.3, Chapter 3, and Section 6.1.

71. E.g., the brief comments in Lilti, "The Writing of Paranoia," 62f, 72-73.

72. A few scholars casually appeal to inspiring images of Jean-Jacques (the "Noble Moralist" interpretation, below, note 81). Systematic discussions have been offered by Jean Starobinski and Christopher Kelly. However, as we will see, their syntheses almost nullify the elevated aspirations of our previous two paragraphs, in view of other, more reductive elements in Rousseau's psychology (for Starobinski) or thought (for Kelly). We return to them both in Section 2 of the Introduction, as well as Section 2.1.

73. *Julie* II.16, 198/241; Rev. III, 32/1016.

74. Best known from Aristotle (*êthos*, *pathos*, and *logos* in *Rhetoric* I.2; see also II.1), this argument was also importantly stated by Plato (see note 21 above). Plutarch develops it as well, while counseling not to be deceived by appearance, and that "philosophical arguments must be examined entirely on their own merits, with no reference to the speaker's reputation" ("On Listening," 41b-c, in Plutarch, *Essays*, 35; see also *Rules for Politicians*, 800-801, in *Selected Essays and Dialogues*, ed. and trans. Donald Russell [New York: Oxford University Press, 1993], 143-45).

75. Translation modified. For comment, see Heinrich Meier, *On the Happiness of the Philosophic Life: Reflections on Rousseau's* Rêveries *in Two Books*, trans. Robert Berman (Chicago: University of Chicago Press, 2016), 20, and Christopher Kelly, *Rousseau's Exemplary Life: The* Confessions *as Political Philosophy* (Ithaca: Cornell University Press, 1987), 62-63.

76. Following Scholar, 406, modified. See also RJJ III, 227n/952n.

77. The First Dialogue of RJJ appeared in 1780. Several important works first appear in the Geneva edition of 1782, including the other two dialogues of RJJ, the First Part of the *Confessions* (that is, Books I–VI), and the *Reveries* (Leigh, *Unsolved Problems*, 114, see also 135).

78. Leigh, *Unsolved Problems*, 136.

79. See below, Section 1.4 and Chapter 5.

80. For his celebrity in this later period, see below, Chapter 6, with note 107.

81. For republican versions, see Helena Rosenblatt, *Rousseau and Geneva: From the* First Discourse *to the* Social Contract, *1749–1762* (Cambridge: Cambridge University Press, 1997), 37-39, 47, 178, and Graeme Garrard, *Rousseau's Counter-Enlightenment: A Republican Critique of the Philosophes* (Albany: State University of New York Press, 2003), 33-35, 117-19, cf. 153n11; cf. Maurice Cranston, *The Noble Savage: Jean-Jacques Rousseau, 1754–1762* (Chicago: University of Chicago Press, 1991), 188, 312-13. For a liberal version, see Ethan Putterman, *Rousseau, Law, and the Sovereignty of the People* (Cambridge: Cambridge University Press, 2010), Introduction and ch. 1. Neidleman extends across disparate themes, including citizenship and reverie, but he sees them all as diverse paths for communion and truth-seeking (*Rousseau's Ethics of Truth*, esp. 5-9, 36-37, 75-76, 97-100, 107, 232, 235-37).

82. For sympathetic versions, see Damrosch, Introduction to *The Essential Writings of Rousseau*, trans. Peter Constantine (New York: Modern Library, 2013), xvi-xvii; Damrosch, *Restless Genius*, 63, 243, 444, 483, 494, cf. 294-95; Karen Pagani, *Man or Citizen: Anger, Forgiveness, and Authenticity in Rousseau* (University Park: Pennsylvania State University Press, 2015), 6-9, 14, cf. 129-33. For a critical version, see Ann Hartle, *The Modern Self in Rousseau's* Confessions*: A Response to St. Augustine* (Notre Dame: University of Notre Dame Press, 1983), 1-3, 30-31, 143-57.

83. Esp. *Jean-Jacques Rousseau: Transparency and Obstruction*, trans. Arthur Goldhammer (Chicago: University of Chicago Press, 1988 [1957]), 21, 30-34, 78-80, 198-99, 294-95; Starobinski, "La pensée politique de Jean-Jacques Rousseau," in *Jean-Jacques Rousseau*, ed. Samuel Baud-Bovy (Neuchâtel: La Baconnière, 1962), 81-99, at 86, 92, 97-98. Cf. Judith Shklar, *Men and Citizens: A Study of Rousseau's Social Theory* (Cambridge: Cambridge University Press, 1969), 1-2, 16, 30, 41-46, 99-103, 133-37, 163-64, and, on Starobinski, 230-31.

84. Cassirer, *The Question of Jean-Jacques Rousseau*, 39-40, 127-28; Cassirer, "Kant and Rousseau" (1945), in *Rousseau, Kant, and Goethe*, trans. James Gutmann et al. (New York: Harper and Row, 1963), 1-60, at 55-59.

85. E.g., Nicholas Dent, *Rousseau: An Introduction to His Psychological, Social, and Moral Theory* (Oxford: Basil Blackwell, 1988), 2-3, 6-8, 36, 52, 88-89, 113; John Rawls, *Lectures on the History of Political Philosophy*, ed. Samuel Freeman (Cambridge: Belknap–Harvard University Press, 2007), 192-94; Frederick Neuhouser, *Rousseau's Theodicy of Self-Love: Evil, Rationality, and the Drive for Recognition* (New York: Oxford University Press, 2008), 18-19, 35, 35n13, 85-87; Joshua Cohen, *Rousseau: A Free Community of Equals* (New York: Oxford University Press, 2010), 7-9.

86. David Lay Williams, "The Platonic Soul of the *Reveries*: The Role of Solitude in Rousseau's Democratic Politics," *History of Political Thought* 33.1 (2012): 87-123, esp. 105; Williams, *Rousseau's Platonic Enlightenment* (University Park: Pennsylvania State University Press, 2007); cf. Williams, *Rousseau's* Social Contract: *An Introduction* (Cambridge: Cambridge University Press, 2014), 217-20, 263-64.

87. Reisert, *A Friend of Virtue*, esp. 9-14, 55-56, 80-81, 176-78.

88. Tzvetan Todorov, *Frail Happiness: An Essay on Rousseau*, trans. John T. Scott and Robert D. Zaretsky (University Park: Pennsylvania State University Press, 2001), 57-58, and ch. 3, esp. 34, 49-53; Todorov, *Imperfect Garden: The Legacy of Humanism*, trans. Carol Cosman (Princeton: Princeton University Press, 2002), 97-105, esp. 99.

89. Grant, *Hypocrisy and Integrity*, esp. 58-62, 74-77, 91, 111-13.

90. James Miller, *Rousseau: Dreamer of Democracy* (New Haven: Yale University Press, 1984), esp. 2 on the more psychological, authoritarian, or pessimistic interpretations that had recently prevailed.

91. Raymond Trousson, *Jean-Jacques Rousseau* (Paris: Tallandier, 2003), esp. 188-90, 227-29.

92. *Rousseau: The Sentiment of Existence* (Cambridge: Cambridge University Press, 2006), esp. 4, 38-42, 50, 73, 80, 86, 139, 173-77.

93. Ibid., esp. 12, 46, 80, 99-100, 122, 136-37, cf. 188-89.

94. Strauss, *Natural Right and History* (Chicago: University of Chicago Press, 1953), 264, 271, 282; Strauss, *What Is Political Philosophy? And Other Studies* (Chicago: University of Chicago Press, 1959), 52-53; Eve Grace, "Portraying Nature: Rousseau's *Reveries* as Autobiography," in *Autobiography as Philosophy: The Philosophical Uses of Self-Presentation*, ed. Thomas Mathien and D. G. Wright (New York: Routledge, 2006), 141-67, at 142-43; Meier, *Happiness of the Philosophic Life*, esp. 17, 98-99, 124-26, 136, 187, 279.

95. Strauss, "On the Intention of Rousseau," *Social Research* 14.4 (1947): 455-87, at 481-82; Arthur Melzer, *The Natural Goodness of Man: On the System of Rousseau's Thought* (Chicago: University of Chicago Press, 1990), ch. 8; Meier, *Happiness of the Philosophic Life*, 4-5, 91, 154-57.

96. Melzer, *Natural Goodness*, 90, 101-6, 146-49, 258-60; Christopher Kelly, "On the Naturalness of the Sentiment of Injustice," *L'Esprit Créateur* 52.4 (2012): 68-80, esp. 73, 76-78; cf. Kelly, *Rousseau as Author: Consecrating One's Life to the Truth* (Chicago: University of Chicago Press, 2003), 1, 49, 114, 172; Eve Grace, "Built on Sand: Moral Law in Rousseau's *Second Discourse*," in *The Challenge of Rousseau*, ed. Eve Grace and Christopher Kelly (Cambridge: Cambridge University Press, 2012), esp. 178-80; Meier, *Happiness of the Philosophic Life*, 25-26, 116-17. For exceptions, see Laurence Cooper, *Rousseau, Nature, and the Problem of the Good Life* (University Park: Pennsylvania State University Press, 1999), 51-59, 173, 180-81, 184; Jonathan Marks, *Perfection and Disharmony in the Thought of Jean-Jacques Rousseau* (Cambridge: Cambridge University Press, 2005), 4, 70-74.

97. Esp. Strauss, *Natural Right and History*, 258, 261-63, 292-93; Roger Masters, *The Political Philosophy of Rousseau* (Princeton: Princeton University Press, 1968), 90, 96, 254; Kelly, *Rousseau's Exemplary Life*, 19-26, 209-10, 218-26; Laurence Cooper, *Eros in Plato, Rousseau, and Nietzsche: The Politics of Infinity* (University Park: Pennsylvania State University Press, 2008), 152-63, 176.

98. Starobinski, *Transparency and Obstruction*, 30-33; Wokler, "Todorov's Otherness," *New Literary History* 27.1 (1996): 43-55; Spector, *Au prisme de Rousseau: Usages politiques contemporains* (Oxford: Voltaire Foundation, 2011), chs. 3-4. Spector is useful in discussing how Rawlsians and Straussians put Rousseau in opposite positions regarding the history of liberalism and the status of rational autonomy (see *Au prisme de Rousseau*, 73, 83, 99-101, 104, 111, 136-38, cf. 11).

99. See Cassirer's complaint about the prevalence of biographically dominated studies of Rousseau ("Kant and Rousseau," 58, discussed below, Conclusion, with note 2). A compelling response to the "marvelous assurance of psychoanalysis" is Jean Fabre, "Le Jean-Jacques Rousseau de Lester G. Crocker," *Revue d'histoire littéraire de la France* 75.5 (1975): 799-826, here citing 807.

100. "Rousseau's Two Concepts of Liberty," in *Rousseau, the Age of Enlightenment, and Their Legacies*, ed. Bryan Garsten (Princeton: Princeton University Press, 2012), 181. See, similarly, Rosenblatt, *Rousseau and Geneva*, 1f, and many Straussian responses (below, Chapter 1, note 191).

101. Discussed in Chapter 1, with note 13.

102. See "Kant and Rousseau," 58.

103. For the intellectual categories within the autobiographies, see Roger Masters and Christopher Kelly (below, Chapter 1, note 192). Philippe Lejeune similarly reads *Confessions* Book I in view of the ancient mythology of the four ages, as well as Rousseau's theoretical texts, *Emile* and especially the second *Discourse* (*Le pacte autobiographique* [Paris: Éditions du Seuil, 1975], 88-89, 94-99).

104. E.g., Timothy O'Hagan, *Rousseau* (London: Routledge, 2003), 1-9; Patrick Riley, Introduction to *The Cambridge Companion to Rousseau*, ed. Riley (Cambridge: Cambridge University Press, 2001); John T. Scott, Introduction to *The Major Political Writings of Jean-Jacques Rousseau* (Chicago: University of Chicago Press, 2012), xvi-xxv; David Wootton, Introduction to *Jean-Jacques Rousseau: Basic Political Writings*, 2nd ed., trans. Donald A. Cress (Indianapolis: Hackett, 2011), xii-xix; or, more extensively, Wokler, *A Very Short Introduction*, chs. 1 and 6.

105. Many scholars prefer the three-volume work of Cranston: *Jean-Jacques: The Life and Work of Jean-Jacques Rousseau, 1712–1754* (New York: W. W. Norton, 1983), *The Noble Savage*, and *The Solitary Self: Jean-Jacques Rousseau in Exile and Adversity* (Chicago: University of Chicago Press, 1997). For a first extended study, I would instead recommend Damrosch, *Restless Genius*. Damrosch (5) points to real limits of Cranston; see also below on Cranston's "Lockean" method (Chapter 1, note 14).

106. The First Part was written ca. 1764–1767 (see Chapter 5 below, beginning with note 45), and the Second Part much more rapidly, mostly over four months in the winter of 1769–1770 (Chapter 6, with notes 113-14).

107. In addition, Cranston's untimely death left the final volume of his biography less complete and reliable than the others (discussed below, Chapter 4, note 21).

108. *The Sentiment of Existence*, 78.

CHAPTER 1

1. An exception to the scholarly consensus is Françoise Bocquentin, who argues that the most credible hypothesis is that the children were Thérèse's but not Rousseau's (*Jean-Jacques Rousseau, femme sans enfants?* [Paris: L'Harmattan, 2003]).

2. See Sebastien Mercier in Kelly, *Rousseau's Exemplary Life*, 18, 18n42.

3. OC 1:1416–22, note 1 to p. 345. See also Leigh in CC 2:310, and Alain Grosrichard, *Les Confessions, livres VII à XII* (Paris: GF Flammarion, 2004), 473–74n275.

4. "Enfants de Rousseau," in *Dictionnaire*, 298a.

5. Most scholars offer 1746 or 1747 as the beginning and 1751 or 1752 as the end: Trousson, "Enfants de Rousseau," in *Dictionnaire*, 297b; Leigh, CC 2:145 and 9:18 note c; and Damrosch, *Restless Genius*, 191, 194. Rousseau later claimed the first child was born at some point during the winter of 1746–1747 (letter to Mme de Luxembourg, 12 June 1761, CC 9:14–18, at 15). We have no clear evidence about the birth dates of the last two children (e.g., Charly Guyot, *Plaidoyer pour Thérèse Levasseur* [Neuchâtel: Ides et calendes, 1962], 29); Laurent Müller is rare in using 1753 as the end point ("Marie-Thérèse Levasseur," in *Dictionnaire*, 539b). Some believe there may have been only four, despite Rousseau's testimony of five (cf. CC 44:54–55).

6. Leigh, CC 1:144b; Cranston, *Jean-Jacques*, 239. Similar comments on a 1751 letter are quoted in note 102 below.

7. *Jean-Jacques Rousseau*, 1:188–94, 256–61, 280–81, 2:ix–x, 56–61, 131–35, 235–37, 241, 290.

8. Ibid., 1:191, 259, 2:133–34.

9. Ibid., 1:259, 191–92, 259–60, cf. xii.

10. Ibid., 1:260, 191, cf. 192.

11. *Jean-Jacques Rousseau: The Quest, 1712–1758* (New York: Macmillan, 1968), 174–88.

12. Ibid., 181, 186–87, cf. x. We return to Crocker with notes 180–84 below.

13. Karl Barth, *Protestant Theology in the Nineteenth Century* (1947), trans. Brian Cozens and John Bowden (Grand Rapids: Eerdmans, 2001), 161; Christopher Bertram, *Rousseau and* The Social Contract (London: Routledge, 2004), 11, cf. 5; Eileen Hunt Botting, *Family Feuds: Wollstonecraft, Burke, and Rousseau on the Transformation of the Family* (Albany: State University of New York Press, 2006), 68; Damrosch, "Biographical Note" to *The Essential Writings of Rousseau*, ix; Matthew Gerber, *Bastards: Politics, Family, and Law in Early Modern France* (New York: Oxford University Press, 2012), 124–25, 173; Hartle, *The Modern Self in Rousseau's "Confessions,"* 19, 30–31, 50; Mark Hulliung, *The Autocritique of Enlightenment: Rousseau and the Philosophes* (Cambridge: Harvard University Press, 1994), 233; Kelly, *Rousseau's Exemplary Life*, 11; Meier, *Happiness of the Philosophic Life*, 161, cf. 171; O'Hagan, *Rousseau*, 2; Jean-François Perrin, *Politique du renonçant: Le dernier Rousseau, des* Dialogues *aux* Rêveries (Paris: Éditions Kimé, 2011), 222–24, 330n2–331n8; Patrick Riley, Introduction to *The Cambridge Companion to Rousseau*, 6; Riley, *Character and Conversion in Autobiography: Augustine, Montaigne, Descartes, Rousseau, and Sartre* (Charlottesville: University of Virginia Press, 2004), 11, 91; Wokler, *A Very Short Introduction*, 4–5, 147; Wootton, Introduction to *Basic Political Writings*, xiv. Extending beyond these, Gauthier briefly mentions Rousseau's excuses for his actions and declares them unconvincing (*The Sentiment of Existence*, 130, 180).

14. For the most helpful biographical overview, see Damrosch, *Restless Genius*, 187–95, 455–56, 474–75. In keeping with his "Lockean" method, Maurice Cranston provides context and many of the key sources but minimal analysis (on the method, *Jean-Jacques*, 10, and *The Noble*

Savage, ix; on the children, *Jean-Jacques*, 196–200, 208–12, 244–46, *The Noble Savage*, 246, 285–88, 305, and *The Solitary Self*, 4, 105, 181–83). A biography of Thérèse covers a solid proportion of the evidence, but it omits much and only minimally engages the arguments of Rousseau, since it focuses on whether there were children and whether they were his (Guyot, *Plaidoyer pour Thérèse Levasseur*, 29–47, esp. 31–33 for the key omissions).

15. Discussed in Section 1.6 below.

16. When speaking in my own voice, I use my own (relatively neutral) term, "discarded," rather than the charged term "exposed," to which Rousseau objects (with note 62 below) or Rousseau's preferred term "deposited," which seems too euphemistic. On "abandoned," cf. Perrin, *Politique du renonçant*, 331n6.

17. Edmund Burke, "A Letter to a Member of the National Assembly," 47–50 (discussed above, Introduction, with notes 3–4); Carol Blum, *Rousseau and the Republic of Virtue* (Ithaca: Cornell University Press, 1986), 59, 74–84, 87, 117–18, esp. 77–78; Lejeune, *Le pacte autobiographique*, 155–57; Crocker, *The Quest*, e.g. 185; Starobinski, *Transparency and Obstruction*, 231–32, 285, and "The Accuser and the Accused," *Daedalus* 107.3 (1978): 41–58, at 53, but cf. "La pensée politique de Jean-Jacques Rousseau," 81.

18. See the remarks of Mme de Staël (of 1788), Albert Meynier (of 1912), Albert Schinz (of 1929), and Jean Fabre (1961 and 1975, discussed below, notes 98 and 116), each quoted in Blum, *Rousseau and the Republic of Virtue*, 76–77. Guéhenno may also be placed here.

19. This last clause seems to express the position of several students of Leo Strauss: Roger Masters, Review of *Jean-Jacques Rousseau*, by Guéhenno, *Journal of the History of Philosophy* 5.4 (1967): 373–76, at 375; Joel Schwartz, *The Sexual Politics of Jean-Jacques Rousseau* (Chicago: University of Chicago Press, 1984), 171n55; and Christopher Kelly, "Rousseau's *Confessions*," in *The Cambridge Companion to Rousseau*, ed. Riley, 302–28, at 312, 315 (in connection with natural goodness). We will return to these perspectives in Section 1.6 below.

20. Grant, *Hypocrisy and Integrity*, 111–13, cf. 91; Todorov, *Imperfect Garden*, 102; cf. *Frail Happiness*, 33, with 52–53; and Trousson, *Jean-Jacques Rousseau*, discussed in Section 1.6 below. A related approach is taken by Cassirer in firmly distinguishing personal history from "the objective validity of his doctrines." For instance, "The fact that Rousseau confesses to abandoning his five natural children at a foundling home does not affect the merits of the educational plan in the *Emile*" (*The Question of Jean-Jacques Rousseau*, 15, see also 16). Reisert develops a similar framework for distinguishing personal character from moral teachings but without mentioning the children (see above, Introduction, note 38, and cf. *A Friend of Virtue*, 81n5).

21. Cited as "LF," followed by the paragraph number in brackets (it is translated in CW 5:551–52; the decoded original is in CC 2:142–46).

22. CC 37:205–9.

23. CC 37:248–71, and for Rousseau's copy, which he later modified for posterity, CC 37:272–301.

24. Gagnebin and Raymond, OC 1:1420, note 1 to p. 345. However, writing may have commenced in December 1777 (Perrin, *Politique du renonçant*, 293n25).

25. In Chapter 5 (esp. note 7), we discuss Voltaire's authorship, which Rousseau never came to realize. As for the initial source of the information, Rousseau considers d'Épinay, Friedrich Melchior Grimm, and Diderot as the only possibilities, with Grimm and Diderot the most likely (Conf. IX, 394/470). No current authority points to Diderot, and Cranston seems alone in pointing to Grimm (*The Noble Savage*, 288). To most, it seems that d'Épinay told doctor Théodore Tronchin, who passed it on to Voltaire (cf. Leigh, CC 23:100 note c; Fréderic Eigeldinger, in

Voltaire, *Sentiment des Citoyens*, ed. Eigeldinger [Paris: Honoré Champion, 1997], 82n31; Damrosch, *Restless Genius*, 391). The end of Rousseau's friendship with Tronchin is discussed below, Chapter 6, with notes 42–45.

26. CW 12:48 / CC 23:381. For the fabrications, see R. A. Leigh, "Jean-Jacques Rousseau," *Historical Journal* 12.3 (1969): 549–65, at 551, and the longer quotation below (Chapter 5, with note 14).

27. This annotated reply (6 January 1765) was suppressed by Rousseau after printing began (see Cranston, *The Solitary Self*, 105–6; cf. Conf. XII, 529–30/632f). Trousson asks rhetorically whether this "play on words," "sad denial," and "evasion" was satisfying to Rousseau's conscience (*Jean-Jacques Rousseau*, 586).

28. LF [1, 3].

29. LF [1, 2, and 6] (following note 112 and with note 113); Conf. VIII (299/357, with note 130). This rationale is implied in Conf. VII (287/342f, quoted following note 92) and in Rev. IX (124/1087). The letter to Saint-Germain briefly lists several reasons why Rousseau deposited his children: "example, poverty [*la necessité*], the honor of the one who was dear to me, [and] other powerful reasons" (CC 37:254).

30. LF [4], quoted with note 110.

31. LF [1, 3]; Conf. VII, 289/344; the letter to Saint-Germain on "honor" (CC 37:254, in note 29 above).

32. LF [3].

33. Conf. VII (300f/358), IX (349/415f); Rev. IX (124/1087); cf. LF [3], discussed with note 132.

34. Conf. VIII (300/357); letter to Berthier (CC 37:207); letter to Saint-Germain (CC 37:255); and Rev. IX (124/1087), discussed with notes 137–38.

35. LF [1, 4].

36. LF [5] and cf. "Response to *The Sentiment of the Citizens*" (1765, CW 12:48 note a / CC 23:381n1), quoted with note 27 above.

37. LF [5]; letters to Berthier (CC 37:207) and to Saint-Germain (CC 37:255), discussed with notes 65–66; Conf. VIII (299/357), quoted with note 130.

38. LF [6]; Conf. VIII (299/357), quoted with notes 130–31.

39. Letter to Toussaint-Pierre Lenieps (11 December 1760, CC 7:350–51, at 351), quoted with note 167.

40. Letter to Mme de Luxembourg (12 June 1761, CC 9:15, quoted with note 168), and the indirect avowal in E I (49/262f, quoted with note 169).

41. Conf. XII (497/594), quoted with note 152; and RJJ I (34/70), in note 152.

42. Conf. XII (498/594f), quoted with note 150.

43. Letter to Berthier (CC 37:207, quoted with note 158), letter to Saint-Germain (CC 37:254, in note 159), and cf. letter to Thérèse (12 August 1769, CC 37:120–24, at 122, quoted with note 155).

44. Letter to Saint-Germain (CC 37:255), quoted with note 160.

45. Conf. VII (287–89/342–44), discussed with note 93. The letter to Saint-Germain mentions "*L'exemple*," apparently indicating the customs around him (CC 37:254, in note 29 above).

46. Conf. VIII (299/356f, quoted with note 141), cf. letter to Saint-Germain (CC 37:255), and Rev. IX (123–25/1086–87, discussed with note 122).

47. Conf. VIII (300–301/358–59), quoted with notes 143–44.

48. Letter to Thérèse (12 August 1769, CC 37:122), quoted with note 155; cf. note 82 on "fault."

49. Conf. VIII (301/359), letter to Berthier (CC 37:207), letter to Saint-Germain (CC 37:255), and cf. "Response to *The Sentiment of the Citizens*" (CW 12:48 note a / CC 23:381n1), discussed with note 140.

50. Letter to Berthier (CC 37:207), quoted with note 156.

51. Rev. IX (124/1087), quoted with note 124.

52. *Restless Genius*, 193.

53. For this translation in the context of the foundlings (*enfants trouvés*), see Damrosch, *Restless Genius*, 192.

54. Jean-François Perrin, ed., *Rousseau: Lettres philosophiques* (Cabris: Le Livre de Poche, 2003), 59–60. For related figures, see Leigh, CC 2:145 note b; Damrosch, *Restless Genius*, 192; Trousson, *Jean-Jacques Rousseau*, 188f; and Gerber, *Bastards*, 134, 150, 196–97.

55. See the various scholars in *Family Life in Early Modern Times*, ed. David Kertzer and Marzio Barbagli (New Haven: Yale University Press, 2001), 149–50, 176–79, 215–18, esp. 177, as well as Philip Gorski, *The Disciplinary Revolution: Calvinism and the Rise of the State in Early Modern Europe* (Chicago: University of Chicago Press, 2003), 54, 124.

56. Gagnebin and Raymond, OC 1:1416, note 3 to p. 344.

57. See *Bastards*, 126, 134–44, 152. On unintended consequences, see to similar effect the complaints in the 1770s against the foundling institution, in Damrosch, *Restless Genius*, 192.

58. *Bastards*, 138, 150.

59. "Rousseau and Social Marginality," *Daedalus* 107.3 (1978): 27–40, at 33. See 29–30 for a historical introduction to the two types of marginality Rousseau experienced, those of "the vagabond poor" and the "debutant intellectual."

60. "The High Enlightenment and the Low-Life of Literature in Pre-Revolutionary France," *Past and Present* 51 (1971): 81–115, at 83f. This situation was changing by the time of the late Enlightenment, as successful *philosophes* gained respectability (84).

61. *Jean-Jacques Rousseau*, 189.

62. See with note 27 above, and, on my term "discarded," note 16.

63. Leigh, CC 2:146 note e; Cranston, *Jean-Jacques*, 209, 245n1.

64. [Boucher d'Argis], "Enfant exposé" (1755) and "Exposition d'enfant" (1756), in *Encyclopédie* [University of Chicago: ARTFL Encyclopédie Project, ed. Robert Morrisey, encyclopedie.uchicago.edu], 5:655 and 6:314, respectively). See, similarly, the discussion below of Arrault (with notes 76–78). Cf. Gerber on the rarity and decreasing rates of infanticide in this period (*Bastards*, 136).

65. Letter to Berthier, 17 January 1770, CC 37:207.

66. Letter to Saint-Germain, 26 February 1770, CC 37:255, cf. 279. See also the brief remark in Conf. VIII, 299/357, quoted with note 130 below.

67. Gerber, *Bastards*, 145 and 235n137. The major earlier sources offer similar figures: Leigh, CC 2:146 note f; Cranston, *Jean-Jacques*, 245; Trousson, *Jean-Jacques Rousseau*, 189; Damrosch, *Restless Genius*, 193. Cf. the even higher rates for Toulouse in 1779 (Perrin, *Lettres philosophiques*, 60).

68. Gagnebin and Raymond, OC 1:1416, note 3 to p. 1415.

69. *Restless Genius*, 193.

70. For the promise of the charter, see Gerber, *Bastards*, 144–46, and 149. By contrast, for Grosrichard, "The 30% who survived . . . , did not have complaints about their fate: they were raised in austerity, making little Spartans of them" (*Les Confessions* II, 482n33, 473n274).

71. Leigh, CC 2:146 note f; Trousson, *Jean-Jacques Rousseau*, 189.

72. *Hypocrisy and Integrity*, 112f. For her general stance, see above, Introduction, with note 37.

73. Gagnebin and Raymond infer that Rousseau "must certainly" have seen it (OC 1:1415, note 3 to p. 344); Gerber seems to endorse this claim (*Bastards*, 125, 228n9).

74. *Abregé historique de l'etablissement de l'Hôpital des Enfans-Trouvés* (Paris: Thiboust, 1746), 8–9.

75. *Bastards*, 126f.

76. *Abregé historique*, 9 (partially quoted in OC 1:1416, note 3 to p. 344).

77. Ibid., 11–14.

78. Ibid., esp. 11 on the deaths.

79. Discussed in Guyot, *Plaidoyer pour Thérèse Levasseur*, 40. Cf. DOI I, 135/135.

80. CW 13:726n18 / OC 4:1270, variant a to p. 64, from Favre 11/64, developed into E I, 44/255.

81. For eighteenth-century trends, see Rosenblatt, *Rousseau and Geneva*, 11–17, 34–37, 65–69, 257; for universality, see Christopher Brooke, "Rousseau's Political Philosophy: Stoic and Augustinian Origins," in *The Cambridge Companion to Rousseau*, ed. Riley, 94–123, at 108–12; Riley, *The General Will Before Rousseau: The Transformation of the Divine into the Civic* (Princeton: Princeton University Press, 1986); and Patrick Coleman, *Anger, Gratitude, and the Enlightenment Writer* (New York: Oxford University Press, 2011), 166–70.

82. See, e.g., *Julie* VI.8, 566/689f; E II, 82/306, IV, 325/651; and Philip Stewart and Jean Vaché, CW 6:685n32. For this casuistry in Rousseau's personal case, see note 199 below.

83. See *Autobiography* (written ca. 1771–1789), ed. Leonard W. Labaree et al. (New Haven: Yale University Press, 2003), I, 43, 43n2, 115, 115n7.

84. Ibid., I, 128.

85. Ibid., II, 148. Cf. note 129 below.

86. *Autobiography*, I, 96, 128–29; II, 144–45. For Rousseau's longing, see note 197 below.

87. See *Confessions*, trans. Henry Chadwick (New York: Oxford University Press, 1991), IV.2, VI.15, IX.6; Peter Brown, *Augustine of Hippo: A Biography*, new ed. (Berkeley: University of California Press, 2000), 27f, 50–52, 79–80f; Chadwick's Introduction to *Confessions*, xiii, xvi–xvii; and see the discussion with note 97 below. For Augustine's break with his past, see II.2; VI.11–15; VIII.1, 7, 12; X.29–31.

88. Chadwick, Introduction to *Confessions*, xiii.

89. *Protestant Theology in the Nineteenth Century*, 210; see also 198, 209–10. More generally on Rousseau's "anthropological theme" and his ultimately becoming "a kind of martyr to Pelagianism," see 192–93, 199, 205–12, 218, and cf. note 147 below.

90. Here the main period of the pregnancy is listed; the earlier, article version of this chapter offered the time of birth as spring 1751. The latter is the traditional date, since the *Confessions* moves from the victory in the Dijon essay contest (July 1750) to this third pregnancy, which would apparently place a birth around the following spring (see Conf. VIII, 298f/356, with the spring 1751 birth in Leigh, CC 2:145 note a; Trousson, *Jean-Jacques Rousseau*, 186–87; and Pfister, OC 1:cvi). However, this leaves a surprisingly large gap between the third child and the second, who had been born in late 1747 or sometime in 1748 (note 92 below). It also leaves a questionably rapid pace for the last three births (spring 1751 to the end of 1752, although some have extended the end point to 1753: see note 5 above). It may be for these reasons that some later chronologies offer 1749–1750 as the likely time for the third birth (Raymond Trousson and Frédéric Eigeldinger, *Jean-Jacques Rousseau au jour le jour: Chronologie* [Paris: Honoré Champion, 1998], 54; Leigh, CC 9:19 note c; cf. the 1750 proposal by Coindet reported by Leigh: CC 2:145 note a). In

this light, the *Confessions* passage may be less determinate than it seems at first glance. It is the July 1750 Dijon prize that "reawakened" in him all his heroic and virtuous ideas; but next we are only told that he had to "reflect more" on his own duties because Thérèse "*devint grosse* for the third time" (Conf. VIII, 299/356, translated as "became pregnant" in Kelly, and in Scholar, 347). Rather than following the prize announcement, the pregnancy may precede it by several months, with only its outward signs appearing thereafter (cf., on the first pregnancy, "*engraissoit*," which also likely regards outward signs: Conf. VII, 287/342). Thus, late 1750 could be a plausible birth date for the third child.

91. Following Scholar, 347, slightly modified.

92. He recalled the birth of the oldest child as "the winter of 1746 to 47, or around then" (letter to Luxembourg, 12 June 1761, CC 9:15). The *Confessions* mentions another birth "the following year" (VII, 289/345), which many place around late 1747 to early 1748, or 1748 generally (e.g., Pfister, OC 1:cv; Leigh CC 2:145 note a, 9:18 note c; and Trousson and Eigeldinger, *Rousseau au jour le jour*, 51). However, each of these birth-date estimates might need to be placed a year later if the *Confessions* is correct in recalling autumn 1747 as the time when Rousseau returned from his long retreat at Chenonceaux, surprised to see how advanced Thérèse's first pregnancy was (Conf. VII, 287/342f). The *Confessions* account would better cohere with the 1761 letter if he is actually recalling the autumn of 1746, when apparently he also returned from a trip to Chenonceaux (for these trips, cf. Leigh, CC 2:101–3 with note d; Pfister, OC 1:cv; Charly Guyot, OC 2:1898, notes to pp. 1146 and 1148; and Trousson and Eigeldinger, *Rousseau au jour le jour*, 50–51). Cranston, for one, places this first pregnancy in autumn 1747, and the second pregnancy in summer 1748 (*Jean-Jacques*, 208, 211f).

93. Rousseau frequented this inn from 1744 until at least 1747 (cf. Cranston, *Jean-Jacques*, 195–97, 208).

94. *Jean-Jacques*, 199.

95. Cf. E I, 46/258 on "the worries [*tracas*] of children"; both translations modified. Thérèse still lived with her parents during the birth of her first two children (ca. 1745–spring 1750); for comment, see Pierre-Paul Clément, *Jean-Jacques Rousseau: De l'éros coupable à l'éros glorieux* (Geneva: Slatkine Reprints, 1998 [1976]), 234–35.

96. *Morals and Politics*, 779; for his defense of a qualified intentionalism, see 93–105. See also David Hume, "Of the Standard of Taste" (1757), in *Essays, Moral, Political, and Literary*, ed. Eugene F. Miller (Indianapolis: Liberty Fund, 1987), 245–46.

97. Introduction to Augustine, *Confessions*, xvi. Its customary status is also emphasized by Peter Brown, in the passages cited in note 87 above.

98. Fabre makes a strong appeal to the contextual exculpation, but he wrongly includes all five children under the same moral era (see "Le Jean-Jacques Rousseau de Lester G. Crocker," 808; cf. Blum, *Rousseau and the Republic of Virtue*, 77).

99. Leigh, CC 2:145 note a. In traditional accounts, Rousseau had been working for the Dupins until around February or March 1751 (cf. Chapter 2 below, esp. note 24). It was likely Thérèse's mother who informed Mme Dupin about the children, but it was Dupin's daughter-in-law, Suzanne Dupin de Francueil, who apparently confronted Rousseau about it around this time (Cranston, *Jean-Jacques*, 244). Rousseau's anxiety about the matter is indicated by the fact that he wrote this letter in code, albeit a very simple one (e.g., Damrosch, *Restless Genius*, 194, and Leigh, CC 2:144a).

100. For similar arguments about this effect of his "bad" (or "guilty") conscience in the 1751 letter, see Leigh, CC 2:145a, cf. xxiii; Cranston, *Jean-Jacques*, 245, cf. 238; and Trousson, *Jean-Jacques Rousseau*, 229.

101. The first exception concerns the need to prevent the children from being raised by the Levasseur family (2.c), which Rousseau later claimed he needed to omit here for diplomatic reasons (see the discussion with note 132 below). The second exception concerns the later conspiracy (2.d), which developed in hindsight (see the discussion with note 137 below).

102. E.g., "cruel" (Cranston, *Jean-Jacques*, 245), its "truculence" (Leigh, "Avertissement," CC 2:xxiii); "quite aggressive" (Trousson, *Jean-Jacques Rousseau: En 78 lettres, un parcours intellectuel et humain* [Cabris: Éditions Sulliver, 2010], 53); and "Few pages of Rousseau leave such a painful impression" (Trousson, *Jean-Jacques Rousseau*, 228).

103. See also the linking of full citizenship to marriage in *Corsica* (139/919; cf. the fragments, CW 11:157–58 / OC 3:941–42).

104. John Locke, *Two Treatises of Government* (1690), ed. Peter Laslett (Cambridge: Cambridge University Press, 1988), II, §81; Charles de Secondat, baron de Montesquieu, *Persian Letters* (1721), trans. C. J. Betts (London: Penguin, 2004), nos. 114–17; and Montesquieu, *The Spirit of the Laws* (1748), ed. and trans. Anne M. Cohler, Basia C. Miller, and Harold S. Stone (Cambridge: Cambridge University Press, 1989), XVI.15–16. On the prevalence of concubinage and illegitimacy where neither polygamy nor divorce are permitted, see *The Spirit of the Laws*, XXIII.6, and cf. Hugo Grotius, *The Rights of War and Peace* (1625), ed. Richard Tuck (Indianapolis: Liberty Fund, 2005), II.20 [xxxi] note 2, 1009.

105. For *Bougainville* (1773–1774), see, esp., in *Political Writings*, ed. and trans. John Hope Mason and Robert Wokler (Cambridge: Cambridge University Press, 1992), III, 50–54, and V, 66–71.

106. On the latter, cf. Montesquieu, who finds this unwise legal policy: *Persian Letters*, no. 116.

107. See Arthur Wilson, *Diderot*, 352–53, 590, cf. 44.

108. Wilson, *Diderot*, 37–46, 352–53, 409–10; Damrosch, *Restless Genius*, 189; cf. Gagnebin and Raymond, OC 1:1424, note 1 to p. 347.

109. *On the Inconsistency of Public Opinion Regarding Our Private Actions* (written ca. 1772–1773), in *This Is Not a Story; and Other Stories*, trans. P. N. Furbank (New York: Oxford University Press, 1993), 37–59 / *Madame de la Carlière*, in *Oeuvres*, ed. Versini, 2:539. For the triviality and frequency of adultery, see 51, 53/533, 534.

110. My translation.

111. Cf. Bronisław Baczko, *Rousseau: Solitude et communauté*, trans. Claire Brendhel-Lamhout (Paris: Mouton, 1974), 41, and Starobinski's overall interpretation of Rousseau's discarding, as an expression of his inability to resign himself to a world in which actions have unanticipated, unintended consequences (*Transparency and Obstruction*, 231–32, cf. 249, 285, as well as 21, 41, 106–9 on economics).

112. See also "Political Fragments" IX, CW 4:53 / OC 3:528, quoted with note 79 above.

113. Translation slightly modified. On the necessity of harshness for becoming and remaining wealthy, see the fragment "On Wealth," which was apparently written at some point between 1749 and 1756 (CW 11:8, 12, 15–16 / OC 5:471, 476, 480–81). Cf. E IV, 345/678, and RJJ I, 11/671f. The references to intrigue and infamy likely refer to the work of the Dupin and Francueil family as tax-farmers (cf. note 99 above). Leigh contends that it would be impossible for Rousseau to speak thus in the letter to Francueil about the difficulty of earning his bread if he had already voluntarily resigned a lucrative commission as cashier for that family (CC 2:146 note d, discussed below, Chapter 2, note 24). However, the reasoning about draining "the lifeblood of the needy" (LF [2]) could be taken as eliminating the Dupins' line of work as a moral possibility.

114. See a later, undated letter by François-Joseph de Conzié (CC 1:292–298, at 295), and Diderot's objections to Rousseau's refusal (October 1752) of the king's pension (Conf. VIII, 319f/381).

115. Leigh, CC 2:145a; Trousson, *Jean-Jacques Rousseau*, 229; and Cranston, *The Solitary Self*, 183; cf., similarly, William Kessen, "Rousseau's Children," *Daedalus* 107.3 [1978]: 155–66, at 156.

116. This is part of a broader analysis of the avoidance of drudgery (e.g., Diderot's massive editorial project, the *Encyclopédie*). The discarding of the children is only implicit in Fabre's account here, unlike in Blum's stark presentation of him (see "Deux Frères Ennemis: Diderot et Jean-Jacques," *Diderot Studies* 3 [1961]: 155–213, at 158, 176–79, cf. 194n1, with Blum, *Rousseau and the Republic of Virtue*, 77, which actually translates from Fabre, "Deux Frères Ennemis," 178, not 176, as she cites).

117. Following Scholar, 42. For Fribourg (and the prospect of marrying Anne-Marie Merceret), see Conf. IV, 122/145f.

118. Letter of 23 December 1761, CC 9:344–35, at 345; cf. 344 on Rousseau's experience. On the superiority of being "an honest burgher" or "a good artisan" rather than a wealthy person or a man of letters, see also *Letter to Voltaire* (1756), EPW 235f / OC 4:1063.

119. On the falseness of the claim of necessity, see, e.g., Baczko, "Rousseau and Social Marginality," 33f.

120. With notes 59–60 above.

121. See Hösle's critique of "the Rousseauian conviction that human beings are good by nature, and that it is only society that makes them bad" (*Morals and Politics*, 46, with 46–47n167).

122. We return to the alleged slander below, Chapter 6, with note 125. He appeals to his straightened condition (rationale 1.b), which would have disastrously required him to allow Thérèse's mother to raise the children (2.c, Rev. IX, 79/1087); and what the conspirators would have made of the children (2.d).

123. For testimonies on his relations with children, see Raymond, OC 1:1824–25, note 1 to p. 1087.

124. Modified, following Russell Goulbourne's translation of *Reveries of the Solitary Walker* (New York: Oxford University Press, 2011), 96.

125. Translation modified ("a babe in arms" translates "*un enfant encore en jaquette*," following Goulbourne, *Reveries*, 97). On seeking affection in animals, see below, Chapter 6, with notes 17–19.

126. I follow Trousson in reading rationale 6 in view of the discussion that follows it. After describing the claim that Thérèse's family would have made the children "monsters," Trousson comments: "He indeed must hold on tightly to this conviction, which helps him to cope [*vivre*]. If it were to be done again, he forces himself to say, 'I would do it again.' But suddenly his heart [*poitrine*] breaks: 'Oh! if I still had a few moments of pure affection'" (*Jean-Jacques Rousseau*, 722; similarly, Guéhenno, *Jean-Jacques Rousseau*, 2:290).

127. Cf. the victimological statements of LF [1, 6], quoted following note 112 above, and the rest of [6], including, "I am deprived of the pleasure of seeing them and have never savored the sweetness of paternal embraces."

128. For the antinomian solitude, see Chapter 6 below, especially Sections 6.2–6.4.

129. For "deceived," see Conf. VIII, 299/357; for not accusing or excusing, see VII, 288/343; VIII, 301/359. Cf. his claim, arising from a discussion of his children, that on balance he was too severe rather than too lax in his treatment of himself in the *Confessions* (Rev. IV, 54–55/1035–36).

130. Translation modified, e.g., from *livrant* as "abandoning."

131. Translation modified. At least since 1746, various defenders of the interests of foundlings had referred to them as "children of the state" (Gerber, *Bastards*, 125, 142, 149, 152, including Arrault, *Abregé historique*, 14, cf. 9f).

132. Conf. VIII, 301/358; IX, 349/415. Cf. LF [3].

133. Cf. the general advice about marriage in E V, 408/767, quoted below, Chapter 6, with note 16.

134. Following Scholar, 406, modified. For Thérèse's brother, see Chapter 2, note 31 below. But cf. Clément, *De l'éros coupable*, 236.

135. See his "Epître à M. de L'Étang," a poem perhaps written around the spring of 1752. After depicting the brutal reign of arrogance in Paris and all its oppressions, he continues: "Paris, unfortunate person who lives in you, but a thousand times more unfortunate, is he who lives in you of his own pure choice" (OC 2:1150–53, at 1150; cf. Cranston, *Jean-Jacques*, 259–60).

136. Cf. Clément, *De l'éros coupable*, 230–31.

137. 17 January 1770, CC 37:207. This part of the Berthier letter is repeated almost verbatim in the Saint-Germain letter, with slight corrections added later, which make them even closer (26 February 1770, CC 37:255, cf. 279).

138. *Le fanatisme ou Mahomet le prophète* (1742), summarized by Charles Butterworth, CW 8:296n8. See also Rousseau's discussion of the play in LdA 29–31/272–73/27–29.

139. Heaven is thanked in the *Confessions* and the letters to Berthier and to Saint-Germain, but it is not thanked in the *Reveries*.

140. See Conf. VIII, 301/359; cf. XI, 467/558, the letter to Berthier, 17 January 1770, CC 37:207, and the letter to Saint-Germain, 26 February 1770, CC 37:255, cf. 279. The seed of this contrast is found in the note on the "exposed" children added to *The Sentiment of the Citizens*: "I would rather have done what this author is accusing me of, than to have written such a passage" (CW 12:48 note a / CC 23:381n1).

141. Following Scholar, 347, modified. The contrast of a good heart with a misguided reason is also invoked in explaining Mme de Warens's liberal offering of her sexual favors (Conf. V, 165/197).

142. Following Scholar, 347.

143. Ibid., 348.

144. Ibid., 349.

145. See, e.g., Blum, *Rousseau and the Republic of Virtue*, 81–84; Cooper, *Problem of the Good Life*, 192–94; Patrick Coleman, Introduction to *Confessions*, xxvii; Gagnebin and Raymond, OC 1:1475, note 2 to p. 416; and Starobinski, *Transparency and Obstruction*, e.g., 209–10. However, see Grant's argument that "his emphasis on intentions does not necessarily collapse into limitless subjectivity" (*Hypocrisy and Integrity*, 111, 113).

146. Commenting on Conf. II, 53/63, see Damrosch, "Paranoia and Freedom in Rousseau's Final Decade," in *Rousseau and Freedom*, ed. Christie McDonald and Stanley Hoffman (Cambridge: Cambridge University Press, 2010), 231–44, at 234, and Starobinski, *Transparency and Obstruction*, 245.

147. See Barth (note 89 above) and Raymond, "Les écrits autobiographiques," OC 1:xiv; cf. Neuhouser, *Rousseau's Theodicy of Self-Love*, 266–70, and Laura K. Field's discussion of "the easygoing immoralism of the autobiography" ("Rousseau's *Confessions*: A Pattern for Living," in *The Rousseauian Mind*, ed. Grace and Kelly, 199–209, at 206).

148. "Rousseau and the Peril of Reflection" (1961), in *The Living Eye*, trans. Arthur Goldhammer (Cambridge: Harvard University Press, 1989), 14–77, at 44. On the consequences of this idea, see Starobinski, "The Accuser and the Accused," 55–56.

149. *Transparency and Obstruction*, 17, see also 193–94, 231, 244–45.

150. Following Scholar, 581. Cf. Starobinski, "On Rousseau's Illness," in *Transparency and Obstruction*, 375.

151. 12 June 1761, CC 9:14f, with Leigh, CC 9:17–18 note b. See also Cranston, *Jean-Jacques*, 246. Cf. Deluc's inquest concerning Rousseau's return to the Genevan church, CC 3:325–26. Whatever the causes, it seems likely that his and Thérèse's complete loss of sexual intimacy did not begin until 1758 or 1759 (Clément, *De l'éros coupable*, 445n41, cf. 236–37; Trousson, *En 78 lettres*, 253n1; and Guyot, *Plaidoyer pour Thérèse Levasseur*, 10).

152. Modifying Scholar, 581. The implication is the same in a comment of "the Frenchman," who has "been told that in the *Emile* he [Jean-Jacques] made an almost formal admission, with regrets that would naturally spare him the reproaches of decent people" (RJJ I, 34/703; see also 33/701).

153. *Rousseau: Confessions* (Cambridge: Cambridge University Press, 1987), 25f.

154. He comes closer to expressing guilt in a fragment likely connected with the *Confessions*, which would have commented on the admission in *Emile*: "Every reader will feel, I am sure, that a man who has no remorse for his fault or who wants to hide it from the public would prevent himself from speaking like this" (*Ébauches des Confessions*, no. 18, OC 1:1164, also quoted by Pierre Burgelin, OC 4:1311, note 1 to p. 263).

155. 12 August 1769, CC 37:122.

156. 17 January 1770, CC 37:207.

157. Cf. Conf. VIII, 301 (with note 35)/358 (with variant [a]).

158. CC 37:207.

159. 26 February 1770, CC 37:254, cf. 279, partially translated in Crocker, *The Quest*, 185. The reasons he provides are quoted in note 29 above. For the significance of this letter, see, e.g., Damrosch, "Paranoia and Freedom in Rousseau's Final Decade," 235–36; Trousson, *Jean-Jacques Rousseau*, 680–81, 689–91; and Trousson, *En 78 lettres*, 257.

160. CC 37:255, cf. 279. The latter passage refers to the version that Rousseau extensively revised soon after sending his letter (cf. the discussion below, note 164). The revised version is more aggressive here, replacing the semicolons in the first sentence with exclamation points. Cf., from later in the same letter: "I was human, and I have sinned, I have committed great faults which I have well-expiated, but never has crime approached my heart. I feel myself just, good, virtuous, as much as man can be on earth" (267, cf. 293).

161. Leigh contrasts the letter's claim with the admission in the *Confessions* of the two other faults (CC 37:299 note t; cf. a related understatement in a 1758 letter, discussed below, Chapter 6, with note 71). For Marion, see Conf. II, 70–73/84–87 (revisited in Rev. IV, 51f–53/1032–33). In the *Confessions*, he insists that he is in no way mitigating his crime, but he does attribute it mainly to weakness and claims to be distressed less by the memory of the act than by its likely consequences (i.e., the ruin of an innocent girl). For Le Maître, abandoned while experiencing a seizure by "the one friend on whom he ought to have been able to count," see Conf. III, 108–9/129–30, and IV, 111/132f (here following Scholar, 126).

162. Because (Jean) Foulquier is mentioned as initiating this dinner and is in the correspondence with Rousseau only from October 1764 through February 1765 (cf. CC 50:327), this exchange seems likely to have occurred around the time of *The Sentiment of the Citizens* (December 1764).

163. An exception in the Second Part concerns not coming to the aid of Mme de Warens in her degradation, as leading to the most acute and lasting remorse of his life (see Conf. VIII,

328f/391f). See the discussions in Cranston, *Jean-Jacques*, 320–23, and Damrosch, *Restless Genius*, 245–46.

164. On Rousseau's intentions for his copy of the letter to Saint-Germain, see Leigh, CC 37:269b–70a. For his qualms about publishing his letters (expressed in a very specific context), see his letter to Dom Deschamps, 12 September 1761, CC 9:119–22, at 121, also discussed in Cranston, *The Noble Savage*, 290–91, cf. 298–99. There is a tendency toward greater defensiveness in his books, but *Emile* is a notable exception.

165. See Hermine de Saussure, *Rousseau et les manuscrits des Confessions* (Paris: Éditions E. de Boccard, 1958), 224–26; cf. Conf. X, 455/544.

166. Rationale 2.d, on how his children would have been misled by the conspirators, is also based on events that occurred after the discarding but appeals to the role of fate or heaven, rather than his own behavior or mental states.

167. Letter to Touissaint-Pierre Lenieps, 11 December 1760, CC 7:351, following Cranston's translation (*The Noble Savage*, 246). The use of the Christian term (sin) is rare for Rousseau; we also saw it in the letter to Saint-Germain (CC 37:255, quoted with note 160 above).

168. 12 June 1761, CC 9:15 (cf. Cranston's translations, *Jean-Jacques*, 246, *The Noble Savage*, 286, and *The Solitary Self*, 181f. The passage is also discussed in OC 1:1546, note 1 to p. 558, and Perrin, *Lettres philosophiques*, 64n1). See Cranston's discussion of the context, including how Rousseau came to dissuade Luxembourg from continuing the search for the first child, whereas in the *Confessions* (XI, 467/558) he claimed only that the search proved fruitless (*The Noble Savage*, 285–88; similarly in Trousson, "Enfants de Rousseau," in *Dictionnaire*, 298, and Gagnebin and Raymond, OC 1:1547, note 1 to p. 558).

169. Translation modified, from Bloom's "vitals" for *entrailles* (cf. above, with note 141).

170. It is not known with certainty when work on *Emile* began. Education, public and private, was never far from Rousseau's mind since 1756, and perhaps even since 1754 (John S. Spink, Introduction to "Première version *d'Émile*," in OC 4:lxxvii; cf. Tanguy L'Aminot, "*Émile*," in *Dictionnaire*, 283b). L'Aminot follows Peter Jimack in concluding that Rousseau probably began writing the first fragments and rough drafts in October or November 1757: "*Émile* (manuscrit Favre)," in *Dictionnaire*, 281a. Rousseau describes *Emile* as having cost him "twenty years of meditation and three years of writing" (Conf. VIII, 324/386), and elsewhere as "the work of eight years" (Rousseau to Lenieps, 18 January 1762, CC 10:38–39, at 39, also discussed in Cranston, *The Noble Savage*, 329). He finished editing *Emile* in October 1760 (L'Aminot, "*Émile*," 283b), so this, rather than the May 1762 publication date, is likely to be the reference point for the "three years of writing."

171. See Conf. XII, 497/594, especially the bracketed terms, with note 152 above.

172. See Peter Jimack, *La Genèse et la rédaction de l'Emile de J.-J. Rousseau* (Geneva: Institut et Musée Voltaire, 1960), 253–56, here quoting 254; see also Spink, Introduction, OC 4:lxxvii–lxxix, lxxxv.

173. *Emile* Book V was written in May 1759, according to most sources (e.g., Pfister, OC 1:cx; Spink, OC 4:lxxv; cf. Conf. X, 437/521), but Jimack uses May–July 1759, corresponding to Rousseau's entire stay at the *petit château* that year (*La Genèse et la rédaction de l'Emile*, 39).

174. See also the sustained criticisms of Plato's *Republic*, asserting the necessity of familial sentiments for developing good citizenship (E V, 362f/699f). This seems to be closely anticipated in the early part of the Favre manuscript regarding the development of sensitivity and humanity (Book I, CW 13:13 / OC 4:67 and notes 22–23/b–c; cf. the weaker final version in E I, 46f/259).

175. On the role of the imaginary pupil, see Jimack, *La Genèse et la rédaction de l'Emile*, 258; for the fatherly passages inserted later, see 255–57f; on the dating, see 33–43, and Spink, Introduction,

OC 4:lxxv–lxxvi. Rousseau mentions that the writing of *Emile* was taken up "in earnest" after finishing *Julie* (Conf. X, 432/516), and this seems to indicate late 1758. For Jimack, this comes after the rough drafts and refers to the "Favre manuscript," written from the end of 1758 or the beginning of 1759 until the end of 1759 (perhaps November or December). Finally, the penultimate manuscript "B," and the final manuscript "C," were written from the end of 1759 until September or October 1760 (Jimack, *La Genèse et la rédaction de l'Emile*, 43).

176. Trousson had independently suggested that in the evolution of *Emile*, remorse had already had a strong grip on Rousseau, but it was only through these meditations and imaginings that he came to openly display his pain, no longer closing it up within (*Jean-Jacques Rousseau*, 434).

177. CW 13:15–17 / OC 4:70–71; cf. E I, 48f, 53/262, 268.

178. See *Julie* V.3. This work as a whole was written from 1756 through 1758, but what we know as Parts V and VI apparently date from 1758 (cf. Spink OC 4:lxxv, and Fabre, "Le Jean-Jacques Rousseau de Lester G. Crocker," 810 and 810n18, with letter to d'Houdetot, 13 February 1758, CC 5:29). For a statement of a presumptive obligation to become a father, see *Julie* VI.4, 539/656; cf. VI.3, 538/654. Note, however, that Julie's moral and religious "conversion" during her wedding ceremony is in the earlier section (*Julie* III.18).

179. "Do You See What I See? The Education of the Reader in Rousseau's *Emile*," *Review of Politics* 74.3 (2012): 443–64, at 449–50.

180. *The Quest*, 184. Blum goes even further. She omits any sense of Rousseau's development or oscillation in arguing that abandoning his children never caused him any "inner sensation of wrongdoing" (*Rousseau and the Republic of Virtue*, 78, cf. 80). Throughout her book, she cites extensively from Emile, but she omits its indirect avowal, and does not cite the letters from 1760 and 1770. Cf. the brief mention of the 1761 letter on 74n1.

181. Crocker, *The Quest*, 183; see also 179f, 184.

182. Ibid., 184.

183. Ibid., 182.

184. Ibid., 185, 183, emphasis original.

185. See, esp., DPE 21/260f, and cf. DOI I, 157/159 (quoted following note 109 above), and Blum on the impact of the DPE passage on several French Revolutionaries (*Rousseau and the Republic of Virtue*, 116–17, 183–91). Cf. the awkward hardness of PN 95/963.

186. See Gagnebin and Raymond, OC 1:1419f, note 1 to p. 345, 1430–31, note 2 to p. 356, and note 1 to p. 358.

187. This is my formulation of an objection raised, e.g., by Leigh (CC 2:146 note g) and Coleman (Introduction to *Confessions*, xviii).

188. See *Poland*, ch. 4, esp. 190–91/967–68, on giving the same kind of education to the rich and poor gentry, and on having children play together publicly in physical exercises, even if their parents have opted for domestic education in general.

189. The chapter introduction mentions three major possibilities. Here I omit the polemical interpretation of the discarded children as an illustration of his subjectivism, individualism, and/or narcissism (note 17 above). This is most directly answered in the response to Crocker's *The Quest*, with notes 180–84 above.

190. See Kelly, *Rousseau's Exemplary Life*, 168, 185–86, 204–5, and Schwartz, *Sexual Politics*, 98–99, 105–6, 171n55. The key passages cited in this connection are Conf. IX, 348/414, and DOI I, 155/157f.

191. Masters, review of *Jean-Jacques Rousseau*, by Guéhenno, 374–75; see, similarly, Masters, *Political Philosophy of Rousseau*, ix–x, and Masters and Kelly, Introduction to CW 1:xiii, xix.

Jonathan Marks faults Damrosch's biography on similar grounds ("Rousseau on the Couch," Claremont.org, June 15, 2006). See also Grace and Kelly, Introduction to *The Challenge of Rousseau*, 4. For other anti-reductionist arguments, see above, Introduction, note 100.

192. Masters, review of *Jean-Jacques Rousseau*, by Guéhenno, 374, see also 375–76. Kelly describes his method similarly ("Rousseau's *Confessions*," 308).

193. Masters, review of *Jean-Jacques Rousseau*, by Guéhenno, 375, see also 376.

194. I later find Rousseau aspiring to a variety of solitudes, with importantly different moral implications (Chapter 6 below).

195. This reduction often occurred (see Cranston, *The Noble Savage*, 28–29, 67, 206n; Damrosch, *Restless Genius*, 273, 456; and Reisert, *A Friend of Virtue*, 81n5). Gauthier explores the categories of "sensuous" and "platonic" love, concluding that Rousseau never had either for Thérèse (*The Sentiment of Existence*, 130–31). See also Todorov on the "depersonalization" of Thérèse (*Frail Happiness*, 38–41) and Starobinski on how she "never raised the problem of the *other*" (*Transparency and Obstruction*, 179). For the often-unsatisfying relations with her, see Chapter 6 below, with notes 14–16.

196. *Restless Genius*, 188; see, esp., Conf. VIII, 296–97/353–54, X, 437/521. Much in Clément's analysis would support Damrosch (*De l'éros coupable*, 223–42). However, Clément also distinguishes the love of their early relationship from the "true love" Rousseau claimed to experience with d'Houdetot alone, since this sentiment, in order to become *passion*, is for him inseparable from the "dimension of fantasy" and the "delirium of imagination" (229; on true love, see below, Chapter 2, note 89).

197. On Warens, see, esp., Rev. X, 140f/1098. On aristocratic ladies in general, see Conf. IV, 112f/134. A respectable girl of a self-sufficient class may also have sufficed: see Conf. I, 36f/43f, quoted with note 117 above.

198. *Sexual Politics*, 105–6.

199. Rousseau would not appreciate our application of the term "casuistry" here (cf., on the Jesuit confessor he shared with Warens, Conf. VI, 203/242).

200. See also, in St. Preux's argument for suicide, that among those precluded from it by concrete duties is "a paterfamilias who owes subsistence to his children" (*Julie* III.21, 314/382).

201. George Klosko makes a similar argument for the seriousness of Plato as a political actor (see "Politics and Method in Plato's Political Theory," *Polis* 23.1 [2006]: 328–49).

202. This approach would cohere with the briefer arguments and conclusions of the scholars cited in note 20, ultimately defending Rousseau's standing as a great and constructive moral thinker.

203. Trousson, *Jean-Jacques Rousseau*, 188.

204. Ibid., 190. On judging himself, see the discussions of the indirect avowal in *Emile* (434), the 1761 letter to Luxembourg (488), the 1770 letters (687–88, 690), and the Rev. IX passage (721–22).

205. Trousson, *Jean-Jacques Rousseau*, 227. This relapse approach avoids the mistake of Fabre (cf. note 98 above). See also Trousson, 229, concerning the need to give more complex excuses by the time of the letter to Francueil (discussed above, with note 100). Trousson offers no sustained discussion of the rationales of the *Confessions*. They are only drawn from incidentally in establishing the main intellectual problem and historical narrative (e.g., rationale 5.a on customs [189, quoted with note 61 above], and 5.b on his heart [227f]). Cf. 11, 229.

206. Trousson, *Jean-Jacques Rousseau*, 228–29 on LF, and 721–22 on Rev. (The latter is quoted above, note 126). See also 585f, on Rousseau's response to *The Sentiment of the Citizens*.

207. See Grant, *Hypocrisy and Integrity*, 91 (discussed above, Introduction, note 37).

208. See Scott, "Do You See What I See?" 449–50; discussed with note 179 above.

209. See, esp., the sources in note 145 above.

210. We return to these themes below, esp. Section 3 of the Conclusion.

CHAPTER 2

1. See *Malesherbes* IV, 581/1144 (discussed below, Chapter 6, with note 86). For his frequent mentions in the correspondence of retirement and giving up writing after the publication of *Emile*, see Cranston, *The Noble Savage*, 246, 317, 325, 329, cf. 358; and *The Solitary Self*, 83, 94, 96, cf. 108, 138.

2. Letter to Vincenz Bernhard Tscharner, 29 April 1762, CC 10:225-29, at 226. See also the letter to Jean Ribotte, 28 December 1761, CC 9:363: His severe illness "forced me to throw my last pages to the public in haste, and to quit the pen to never pick it up again."

3. *Emile* is declared "the last" of his writings in an important statement to Duchesne (21 November 1761, discussed below, note 68; see also Cranston, *The Noble Savage*, 329).

4. Introduction to CW 9:xiii. See also Marcel Raymond, "Les écrits autobiographiques," OC 1:xi. On *Corsica* and *Poland*, see below, Chapter 5, with notes 52–53.

5. Gauthier, *The Sentiment of Existence*, 151, 155; Kelly, CW 5:642n18; and *Rousseau's Exemplary Life*, 194 (each discussed below, note 72). See also Starobinski, discussed below, beginning with note 43.

6. John Hope Mason, "The *Lettre à d'Alembert* and Its Place in Rousseau's Thought," in *Rousseau and the Eighteenth Century: Essays in Memory of R. A. Leigh*, ed. Marian Hobson et al. (Oxford: Voltaire Foundation, 1992), 251–69, at 264, 266, and Laurence Cooper, "Nearer My True Self to Thee: Rousseau's New Spirituality—and Ours," *Review of Politics* 74.3 (2012): 465–88, at 478n21 (each discussed below, note 70). James Miller is an outlier, positing the "period of effervescence" as running from 1749–1764 (*Examined Lives*, 254).

7. *The Sentiment of Existence*, 157–59, 163, discussed below, with note 83.

8. See *Rousseau's Exemplary Life*, 13n37, 38–47, 245–48; Masters and Kelly, Introduction to CW 1:xxiii–xxiv, xxvii, citing RJJ 107, 159, 214. See also Grace, "Portraying Nature," 141, and Melzer, *Natural Goodness*, ch. 2.

9. *Rousseau's Exemplary Life*, 190–99, discussed below, beginning with note 54.

10. See, esp., LR 63n/71–72n; "Preface of a Second Letter to Bordes" (written ca. summer 1753), EPW 107/OC 3:103; "Biographical Fragment" (written ca. winter 1755–1756), CW 12:31 / OC 1:1114; *Malesherbes* II, 575/1135; *Beaumont*, 22/928; RJJ III, 209/930.

11. Cassirer, *The Question of Jean-Jacques Rousseau*, e.g., 58, 65, 127; Shklar, *Men and Citizens*, 220–21; Masters, *The Political Philosophy of Rousseau*, 206–7, 248; Masters and Kelly, CW 2:200 notes 3–4; Grace and Kelly, Introduction to *The Challenge of Rousseau*, 1–6, 15. Above all, see Melzer, *Natural Goodness*, esp. 4–9, and the many passages cited there. Cf. Melzer, *Philosophy Between the Lines: The Lost History of Esoteric Writing* (Chicago: University of Chicago Press, 2014), 112–14, 332–34. For a defense of the "provisional assumption" of an author's omniscience and infallibility, see Melzer, *Philosophy Between the Lines*, 297, 311.

12. Melzer is not unaware of genuine inconsistencies in Rousseau's thought (*Natural Goodness*, e.g., 282n36), but his interpretation keeps their significance to an absolute minimum, as do those of Strauss ("On the Intention of Rousseau," 487) and Kelly (*Rousseau as Author*, 99).

13. Wokler, *A Very Short Introduction*, e.g., 32–33, 68, 72, 79, 124–26. See, similarly, Dent, *Rousseau*, 3, 36, 52, 79–82, and Robin Douglass, *Rousseau and Hobbes: Nature, Free Will, and the*

Passions (Oxford: Oxford University Press, 2015), 16, 20. Wokler had earlier set out a sustained argument that Rousseau developed considerably in the period following the first *Discourse* ("The *Discours sur les sciences et les arts* and Its Offspring: Rousseau in Reply to His Critics," in *Reappraisals of Rousseau: Studies in Honor of R. A. Leigh*, ed. Simon Harvey et al. [Totowa, NJ: Barnes & Noble, 1980], 250–78, esp. 250–57, 271).

14. There is also an interlude in Venice (July 1743–August 1744), discussed in Conf. VII. Rousseau names autumn 1741 as his date of arrival in Paris (Conf. VII, 237/282). Many scholars have disputed this, opting instead for 1742 (e.g., Leigh, CC 27:166 note a), but this is not a consensus (cf. Bernard Gagnebin and Marcel Raymond, OC 1:1377, note 6 to p. 282, and Jacques Voisine, ed., *Jean-Jacques Rousseau: Les Confessions* [Paris: Classiques Garnier, 2011], 328n2).

15. Discussed above, Chapter 1, with note 93.

16. Translation modified. Nevertheless, his soul has not given way to "an extravagant softness [*une molesse outrée*]" but still clings to innocence, maintaining that "nothing should be extravagant, not even virtue" (18/1141, translation modified). See the summaries of this phase in Damrosch, *Restless Genius*, 149–68, esp. 151–52; Kelly, Introduction to CW 12:xviii–xix; and, esp., Rosenblatt, *Rousseau and Geneva*, 37–40. For related evidence, see below, Chapter 4, note 227.

17. Gagnebin and Raymond, Introduction to *Les Confessions*, OC 1:xli.

18. Following Renato Galliani, Damrosch concludes that the "event actually occurred in October 1749, not summer," and the "temperature barely reached sixty degrees Fahrenheit," unlike the sweltering heat that Rousseau mentions (*Restless Genius*, 212f, cf. Conf. VIII, 294/350). The Academy of Dijon's question was published in *Mercure de France* in October 1749 (Gagnebin and Raymond, OC 1:1427, note 1 to p. 351). See also Leigh, "Jean-Jacques Rousseau," 551, and Wokler, "The *Discours* and Its Offspring," 257.

19. Gagnebin and Raymond, OC 1:1427, note 2 to p. 351, and 1453, note 1 to p. 390; Leigh, CC 10:57 note d; France, *Rousseau: Confessions*, 93f; Jacques Voisine, "*Quatre lettres à . . . Malesherbes*," in *Dictionnaire*, 780b; Gauthier, *The Sentiment of Existence*, 115, 130. Leigh suggests this may be more stylistic than a matter of fundamental outlook (review of *Oeuvres Complètes*, tome 1, *Modern Language Review* 57.1 [1962]: 104–7, at 106; see also Leigh, CC 10:58 note l). Others have sought to find a deeper authorial intention (Meier, *Happiness of the Philosophic Life*, 186–87; Laura Field, "The Philosopher Doth Protest Too Much: Rousseauian Enlightenment and the Rhetoric of Despair," *Review of Politics* 75.2 [2013]: 221–46, esp. 232–35).

20. Following Scholar, 346.

21. E.g., Pfister, OC 1:cvi, cf. Gagnebin and Raymond, OC 1:1434, note 4 to p. 363. Kelly leaves the chronology more open but may lean toward a later date in stating that Rousseau's "very public personal reform" was "undertaken a few years after the publication of the *First Discourse*" ("Rousseau's *Confessions*," 310–11). Also open are the accounts of Damrosch (*Restless Genius*, 221–22) and Meier (*Happiness of the Philosophic Life*, 52 and 52n11).

22. See also the letter to Claude Anglancier de Saint-Germain, 26 February 1770, CC 37:248–71, at 253f, and a 27 December 1751 letter from d'Alembert, quoted in Leigh, CC 7:429.

23. Rev. III, 30/1014. For Butterworth, the date is "approximate" (CW 8:283n7), and for Meier, "symbolic" (*Happiness of the Philosophic Life*, 52).

24. See Leigh, CC 2:146, note d, and 2:195–96, note a, esp. 196a, for "November 1752 as the probable date of his resignation" of the cashier position (cf. October 1752 in 2:192 note 1, and 2:199 note b). Crocker follows Leigh in this revision (*The Quest*, 228, 231, 357n23, 358n30); Trousson and Eigeldinger seem to find it plausible (see *Rousseau au jour le jour*, 62, cf. 57). Cranston,

however, is not convinced, positing summer 1751 as the "more likely" time of the resignation (*Jean-Jacques*, 250–52, 367nn92–93).

25. See Leigh, CC 2:195b, note a, and "Avertissement," CC 2:xxii. Cf. the *Reveries* on his "intellectual and moral reform": "I carried out this project slowly and with various fresh starts" (III, 33/1016). We have seen a similar approach taken in Trousson's biography (above, Chapter 1, with notes 204–5).

26. The proper response to Thérèse's third pregnancy is considered in this window between the announcement of the Dijon prize (July 1750) and the official "reform" (Conf. VIII, 299–301/356–59, discussed above, Chapter 1, with notes 90–91). See also, on the beautiful Mme de Chenonceaux, Conf. VIII, 302/359f.

27. Even on Leigh's theory, Rousseau may well have left the house of Mme Dupin around January 1751, but this may be distinguished from a possibly later acceptance and resignation of the cashier position (CC 2:195 note a). Cf. Jean-Pierre Le Bouler, "Louis-Claude Dupin de Francueil," in *Dictionnaire*, 356b.

28. Translation modified. Cf. Rev. III, 31/1015.

29. Conf. VIII, 305/363; Rev. III, 31/1014; cf. Conf. VIII, 316f/377f. Excessively long wigs had been condemned in Geneva as a French luxury as early as 1697 (Richard Whatmore, *Against War and Empire: Geneva, Britain, and France in the Eighteenth Century* [New Haven: Yale University Press, 2012], 25).

30. Cranston, *Jean-Jacques*, 169; Trousson, *Jean-Jacques Rousseau*, 230.

31. Cranston confirms that this occurred at Christmas of 1751, when Rousseau was "poorer than ever," although he may have exaggerated the number of shirts stolen (*Jean-Jacques*, 256).

32. In connection with Rousseau's affectations to despise politeness during this period, Cranston observes that he was in fact extremely popular in society, and that his letters reveal that he took active steps to keep up with fashionable friends (*Jean-Jacques*, 249).

33. Gagnebin and Raymond clarify that, although the Second Part was written in haste and with less care than the First Part, it is not a mere rough draft (OC 1:1369, note 1 to p. 273). See, more generally, Gagnebin and Raymond, Introduction to *Les Confessions*, OC 1:xxix; Damrosch, *Restless Genius*, 460; and Susan Jackson, *Rousseau's Occasional Autobiographies* (Columbus: Ohio State University Press, 1992), 2, 16.

34. Following Scholar, 406–7, slightly modified, emphasis added. A similar account is offered, closer to this time period, in the "Biographical Fragment," CW 12:30 / OC 1:1113.

35. A related discussion of Rousseau's mask of citizenship is provided by Gauthier (discussed below, Chapter 3, with notes 7–17).

36. "Rousseau and the Peril of Reflection," 65–67. To "withdraw the image of a Jean-Jacques more virtuous than nature" is thus a leading purpose of the *Confessions* and the *Dialogues* (66). See also 43, 72.

37. *Transparency and Obstruction*, 58, citing Conf. IX, 349f/416. See also *Transparency and Obstruction*, 39.

38. *Transparency and Obstruction*, 59. See also 61, and Gauthier, *The Sentiment of Existence*, 152–55.

39. *Transparency and Obstruction*, 47.

40. Ibid., 49.

41. Ibid., 48; see also 49.

42. "The Accuser and the Accused," 53; cf. 47–49. He cites RJJ II, 127/824. See also *Transparency and Obstruction*, 55.

43. See, e.g., "The Accuser and the Accused," 42, *Transparency and Obstruction*, 45, 204–5, 215, 277, and 34: "Little by little, personal apology [i.e., defense] takes the place of speculative thought." For related biographical discussions of the autobiographical turn, see below, Chapter 5, notes 34–35.

44. Similarly, during ten years of "delirium and fervor," Jean-Jacques was "deluded by the ridiculous hope of making reason and truth triumph over prejudice and lies" (RJJ II, 131/829).

45. Cf. Kelly, *Rousseau as Author*, 110.

46. Letter to Tscharner, 29 April 1762, 226. Kelly cites this page of this letter as evidence that, in some passages, "Rousseau suggests that he had always known the futility" of his goal to vanquish the illusions of the public (*Rousseau as Author*, 190n20, 101).

47. See also Chapter 6, note 87 below.

48. See note 134 below.

49. See the general assessments of Diderot and Hume (above, Introduction, with notes 5–13). For differing views of the reform, see Damrosch, *Restless Genius*, 253–54.

50. D'Alembert, "Jugement sur *Émile*" (1762), in CC 11:274–78, at 275 (modifying Damrosch's translation, *Restless Genius*, 253).

51. Discussed above, Chapter 1, notes 191–92.

52. Note 8 above.

53. *Rousseau's Exemplary Life*, esp. ch. 2.

54. Ibid., 190; on happiness at Les Charmettes, see 147–63. See also "Rousseau's *Confessions*," 324.

55. Quoted in Kelly, *Rousseau's Exemplary Life*, 192.

56. Ibid., 194.

57. Ibid., 199.

58. Ibid., 194, quoting Conf. IX, 295/351. This passage is discussed above, following note 18.

59. Kelly, *Rousseau's Exemplary Life*, 197.

60. See, for instance, Cooper, *Problem of the Good Life*, ch. 1, esp. 25 and 32, as well as 52–53, 124–25, 204n19; cf. Marks, *Perfection and Disharmony*, chs. 1 and 3.

61. See Strauss, *Natural Right and History*, 6; Leo Strauss, *Persecution and the Art of Writing* (Chicago: University of Chicago Press, 1952), 17–18, 33–37; Allan Bloom, "Leo Strauss," in *Giants and Dwarfs: Essays 1960–1990* (New York: Simon and Schuster, 1990), 252; Masters and Kelly, Introduction to CW 1:xx–xxi, and Introduction to CW 2:xvi–xviii; and Meier, *Happiness of the Philosophic Life*, e.g., 4–5, 91, 329. For a general defense of this compromise, see Melzer, *Philosophy Between the Lines*, 3–4, 79, 138–39, 158, 177–78, 185–86, 353–59. However, there is a gap between Straussians who criticize the rational status of justice and moral virtue as such and others who merely criticize political idealism and utopianism (see Michael Zuckert, "Straussians," in *The Cambridge Companion to Leo Strauss*, ed. Steven B. Smith [Cambridge: Cambridge University Press, 2009], 263–86, at 283). For implications on engaging in political life, see below, Chapter 3, note 80; for the solitary Jean-Jacques as the best life, see Conclusion, note 28.

62. Translation modified.

63. *Julie* III.20, 304–5/369f–71; VI.8, 574/699; cf., on acting from "inclination [*gout*]," III.18, 298f/362f.

64. The ancient source is not identified by the editors, but cf. Anaxagoras in Plutarch, *Pericles* ([16] in *Greek Lives*, 161/[36] in *Les vies*, 1:355).

65. See Immanuel Kant, "Conjectural Beginning of Human History," in *Anthropology, History, and Education*, ed. Günter Zöller and Robert B. Louden, trans. Mary Gregor et al. (Cambridge: Cambridge University Press, 2007), AK 8:116–17.

66. See letter to d'Houdetot, 13 February 1758, CC 5:28–31, at 29, and letter to Rey, 14 March 1759, CC 6:44, both discussed in Hope Mason, "The *Lettre à d'Alembert*," 263. See also Cranston, *The Noble Savage*, 285n, and *Julie* Second Preface, 19f/27.

67. See Conf. IX, 339f/404; X, 432/516; the "Notice" to SC, 40/349; letter to Roustan, 23 December 1761, CC 9:344–45, at 345, with Leigh, 345 note d; and letter to Moultou, 18 January 1762, CC 10:39–42, at 41f.

68. See Conf. IX, 475, 480/568, 573; RJJ I, 23/687; and letter to Duchesne, 21 November 1761, CC 9:264–65, at 264f. On the Savoyard Vicar section, see *Beaumont* 46f/960.

69. See Conf. X, 415, 420/495, 502, but cf. his original estimate in LdA 7/256/7, with OC 5:1303–4, variant (a) to p. 6.

70. See Hope Mason, "The *Lettre à d'Alembert*," 264, 266, and Cooper, "Nearer My True Self to Thee," 478n21, both citing Conf. IX, 350/416–17 (quoted above, with note 34).

71. For the combination of personal and philosophical elements in this dispute, see Kelly, *Rousseau as Author*, 8, 12.

72. Gauthier, *The Sentiment of Existence*, 151, 155. See, similarly, Kelly, CW 5:642n18; *Rousseau's Exemplary Life*, 194; Damrosch, "Paranoia and Freedom in Rousseau's Final Decade," 235; and Cooper (on the "period of moral transformation"), *Problem of the Good Life*, 128n20.

73. *The Sentiment of Existence*, 158, quoting Conf. IX, 350/416.

74. Ibid., 157.

75. The Second Part of the *Confessions* was written in 1769–1770; the First Part was written in 1764–1767 (Kelly, "Rousseau's *Confessions*," 306). For more detailed accounts, see below, Chapter 5, with notes 42–49, and Chapter 6, with notes 113–14.

76. The Hermitage is near the town of Montmorency, and the residences of the Luxembourgs are in that town (e.g., Leigh, CC 9:17 note b). Rousseau often refers to the Montlouis simply as "Montmorency"; I will avoid this usage when speaking in my own voice.

77. Quoted above, with note 34.

78. Cf. his discussion of pity for odious men if he possessed the ring of Gyges (Rev. VI, 82/1058).

79. Following Scholar, 407f, modified.

80. I follow Hope Mason's observation that this account "deals principally with his social manner" ("The *Lettre à d'Alembert*," 264).

81. Following Scholar, 408, modified.

82. *Rousseau's Exemplary Life*, 201; see also 203–8.

83. *The Sentiment of Existence*, 159; see also 157–59, 163.

84. Cranston, *The Noble Savage*, 126, and *The Solitary Self*, 96–98; letter to Lenieps, 10 February 1765, CC 23:338–43, at 340; Conf. IX, 376/447, X, 426n/508n; Rev. VI, 80/1056. For an acknowledgment of excessive suspicion, very late in this period, see below, with notes 120–23.

85. Friendliness is opposed to churlishness on the one hand, and flattery or obsequiousness on the other (*Nicomachean Ethics* IV.6; see also IV.5–8). All Aristotle translations are from *The Complete Works of Aristotle*, ed. Jonathan Barnes (Princeton: Princeton University Press, 1995 [1984]).

86. Translation modified.

87. See France, *Rousseau: Confessions*, 64–65; Conf. IX, 374/445; and Rev. X.

88. The first two attributes will be clear from what follows. For "doting," see the description of the decorative paper and ribbons he lavished on the "charming girls" of *Julie* (Conf. IX, 367/436).

89. See also E IV, 214, 329/494, 656; V, 391, 425, 470, 479/743, 791, 853, 866. In *Julie*, the theme is passim through Parts I and II; see, esp., the Second Preface, 10/15f; I.50, 113/138; II.11,

183n/223n; and Julie's polemic against the necessity of love for marriage, III.20, 306/372. See also Clément, *De l'éros coupable*, 229 (discussed above, Chapter 1, note 196).

90. See Conf. VI, 212/253 (on Mme de Larnage), VII, 267/318 (on Zulietta the Venetian courtesan), and IX, 374/445 (on Sophie). For an introduction to the affair with Sophie, see Conf. IX, 363, 369–89, 401–3/431f, 438–64, 478–80; Damrosch, *Restless Genius*, 256–83; or Cranston, *The Noble Savage*, 55–103. She is also discussed below, Chapter 6, note 93.

91. Translation modified, emphasis added.

92. For comment on "ten years of delirium and fervor . . . when Rousseau writes his great works (1750–1760)," see Robert Osmont, OC 1:1684, note 1 to p. 829.

93. In the (apparently earlier) London manuscript (cf. OC 1:xcvi–xcvii), instead of "ten to twelve" years, this is simply ten years. The volume number he mentions refers to later collected works editions, rather than any original books (Osmont, OC 1:1631f, note 1 to p. 687).

94. Cranston, *The Noble Savage*, 300–301.

95. On virtue as force or strength, see the opening of Section 2.1 above. On himself, see Rev. VI, 77/1052f, as well as Conf. VII, 233/277: His literary career set his situation against his inclinations, thus generating "enormous faults, unparalleled misfortunes, and all the virtues, except strength, which can honor adversity." For Kelly, this "can be read to imply that he acquired no real virtues" (*Rousseau's Exemplary Life*, 164n1; cf. CW 5:631n8).

96. Cf. Conf. V, 164/195: "a few slight favors." For the details, including the well-known love triangle involving Saint-Lambert, see IX, 373–75/443–46.

97. For related remarks on his virtue during this period, see *Moral Letters* I, 175/1081 (quoted below, Conclusion, with note 50).

98. Following Scholar, 392. For the difficulties involved, see, e.g., Conf. X, 430–31/514–15.

99. Following Scholar, 516. Simplicity in manners is linked to the reform about aristocratic swords and fancy wigs. On services, see also Section 6.1, esp. with note 74.

100. According to Kelly, Rousseau was obliged to give up copying when he left France in 1762; "He resumed it in 1770 and practiced it until close to the end of his life" (CW 5:643n45). We return to this later phase below (Chapter 6, note 126).

101. See Nicolas Bonhôte, "*Artisan / Ouvrier*," in *Dictionnaire*, esp. 57a.

102. Letter to Lenieps, 18 January 1762, CC 10:38–39, at 39, also discussed in Cranston, *The Noble Savage*, 329. For the money generated from the *Letter to d'Alembert* and *Julie*, and initial payments for *Emile* and the *Social Contract*, see Conf. X, 432/516; XI, 468–70/559–62. We also discuss retirement in relation to duties to society, below, Chapter 6, with note 89.

103. *Rousseau and Geneva*, 100.

104. Ibid., 102, 89; see also ch. 3, as well as Linda Kirk, "Genevan Republicanism," in *Republicanism, Liberty, and Commercial Society, 1649–1776*, ed. David Wootton (Stanford: Stanford University Press, 1994), 270–309, at 283–84, and Whatmore, *Against War and Empire*, 45–47. Richard Tuck directly confirms Rosenblatt here (*The Sleeping Sovereign: The Invention of Modern Democracy* [Cambridge: Cambridge University Press, 2015], 121–24, esp. 122n2).

105. See Tuck, *The Sleeping Sovereign*, 123; and Rosenblatt, *Rousseau and Geneva*, esp. 128, 129f, 131f; cf. 154–55.

106. The best-known case is with Louis XV in October 1752 (see Conf. VIII, 318–20/379–81). Rousseau later refused pensions from Frederick the Great of Prussia (November 1762) and King George III of England (1766; see Zaretsky and Scott, *The Philosophers' Quarrel*, 142–48, 158, 164, 194–95). For a detailed account of the Frederick case, see Avi Lifschitz, "Adrastus versus Diogenes: Frederick the Great and Jean-Jacques Rousseau on Self-Love," in *Engaging with*

Rousseau: Reaction and Interpretation from the Eighteenth Century to the Present, ed. Lifschitz (Cambridge: Cambridge University Press, 2016), 17–32, at 21–23, 32.

107. See, esp., letters of 1 July 1762, in *Letters of David Hume*, 1:363, and of 2 July 1762, in *Letters*, 1:365. For discussion, see Cranston, *The Solitary Self*, 11–12, 62–63, 63n, and Robert Mankin, "Authority, Success, and the Philosopher: Hume vs. Rousseau," in *Better in France? The Circulation of Ideas Across the Channel in the Eighteenth Century*, ed. Frédéric Ogée [Lewisburg: Bucknell University Press, 2005], 177–200, at 185–86.

108. Hume to Mme de Boufflers, 22 January 1763, in *Letters*, 1:372.

109. See letter to Jacob Vernes, [24 June 1761], CC 9:27–28, at 27; *Beaumont* 50, 74n/964, 994–95n; Conf. V, 187/223, IX, 366/436; and Cranston, *The Solitary Self*, 17.

110. Much of what follows runs parallel to Kelly, *Rousseau as Author*, esp. chs. 1–2. For boldness and caution, see 1, 22–24, 46–48, 135. Kelly also points to comparisons with Socrates (24, 164). I offer an alternative account, rather than a direct response. Here there is a greater emphasis placed on the willingness to sacrifice for the benefit of humanity and for substantive philosophical truths that are useful to all. It is unclear to what extent Kelly's Rousseau could accommodate this, given his more subversive and private model of philosophy, as distinguished from authorship (see, esp., 1, 49, 154, 172). My Rousseau also evinces a more positive philosophical inspiration, not merely for a popular audience but in his own life (see Section 2.1 above, esp. following note 60, and Section 2 of the Conclusion).

111. Damrosch, *Restless Genius*, 211–12; Conf. VII–VIII, 292–94/348–51.

112. Cf. Conf. IX, 340f/405f. According to George Havens, Diderot likely advocated "prudence in form" yet "boldness in content," especially on issues such as government, property, war, and the slow evolution of humanity ("Diderot, Rousseau, and the *Discours sur l'Inégalité*," *Diderot Studies* 3 [1961] 219–62, esp. 219–27, 243, 260–62).

113. See Conf. X, 445–46/531–32, with Damrosch, *Restless Genius*, 356–57; Conf. XI, 463–64, 482f/553–54, 576f, with SC III.6, 96/410; Conf. XI, 481/574f, and XII, 495–96/592–93, with E V, 467/849.

114. Letter to Marc-Michel Rey, 29 May 1762, quoted in Jean-Daniel Candaux, OC 3:1666, note 2 to p. 812. Even after the censors turned on him, he defended this book as plainly within the established Genevan freedom to dispute about abstract matters of "natural and political right" (see *Mountain* VI, 235f/812; I, 136/690).

115. See Masters, CW 4:241n42; Leigh, *Unsolved Problems*, 21–22; Damrosch, *Restless Genius*, 356; and the letters to Rey, 11 and 14 March 1762. After providing a softened, abstract version of the note, Rousseau repressed it so late that some first printings included it and others did not; it is in our current versions of SC IV.8 (at 151n/469n).

116. See Zaretsky and Scott, *The Philosophers' Quarrel*, 62–64, and David Beeson and Nicholas Cronk, "Voltaire: Philosopher or *Philosophe*?" in *The Cambridge Companion to Voltaire*, ed. Cronk (Cambridge: Cambridge University Press, 2009), 47–64, at 56–57.

117. For critiques, see Starobinski, *Transparency and Obstruction*, 25, endorsed in Shklar, *Men and Citizens*, 3. However, it has been observed that Voltaire also responded in a lukewarm manner to this case of Rochette, and it was only later in the case of Calas (March 1762–March 1765) that he would respond with the humanitarian zeal that would later characterize him (e.g., Leigh, CC 9:141 note d; Cranston, *The Noble Savage*, 300; and Simon Harvey, Introduction to *Voltaire: Treatise on Tolerance and Other Writings* [Cambridge: Cambridge University Press, 2000], xi–xii).

118. Rousseau to Jean Ribotte, 24 October 1761, CC 9:200–202, at 201. See also Ribotte's appeal to Rousseau, 30 September 1761, CC 9:137–41. The episode is summarized in Cranston, *The Noble Savage*, 299–300, and Damrosch, *Restless Genius*, 356–57.

119. *Emile* was submitted at the beginning of October 1760; the *Social Contract* was submitted on 6 November 1761 (Tanguy L'Aminot, "*Émile*," in *Dictionnaire*, 283b; Cranston, *The Noble Savage*, 300–301).

120. See the accounts of the episode in Cranston, *The Noble Savage*, 315–20; Damrosch, *Restless Genius*, 353; Jackson, *Rousseau's Occasional Autobiographies*, 146–47; and Perrin, "Lire *Les Confessions* avec la correspondance de Rousseau, II," 147–49. Malesherbes's thoughtful analysis (in a letter of 25 December 1761) of Rousseau's troubled condition prompted the four *Letters to Malesherbes* (see CC 9:354–57, also discussed in Cranston, *The Noble Savage*, 321; Jackson, *Rousseau's Occasional Autobiographies*,147; and Perrin, "Lire *Les Confessions*," 149). For an introduction to Malesherbes, see Kelly, *Rousseau as Author*, 12–15.

121. Cranston, *The Noble Savage*, 316. It was actually Jansenists who were influential in the suppression of the Jesuits, and soon of Rousseau (Damrosch, *Restless Genius*, 358). Fear about a possible Jansenist plot to mutilate *Emile* would emerge around February 1762 (Cranston, *The Noble Savage*, 335–36).

122. Rousseau to Malesherbes, 20 November 1761, as translated in Cranston, *The Noble Savage*, 316. See, similarly, Conf. XI, 474–75/566–68. For a comparison of this 1761 acknowledgment of excess suspicion with a similar one of 23 November 1770, see Michael O'Dea, "*Dialogues* and *Rêveries*: Un Monde Idéal Semblable au Nôtre" (1995), in *Jean-Jacques Rousseau: Critical Assessments*, 4 vols., ed. John T. Scott (London: Routledge, 2006), 4:505–29, at 527n13. Rousseau normally claims an overly trusting nature (above, with note 84).

123. Having reversed himself only a few days after the apologies, he was again reassured by 22 December 1761 (Cranston, *The Noble Savage*, 317–19).

124. *Happiness of the Philosophic Life*, 201n15.

125. *The Noble Savage*, 316.

126. See, e.g., Gagnebin and Raymond, OC 1:1230, note 1 to p. 3. On this shift, see also below, Chapter 6, with note 110. For later fears of the mutilation of his works, see below, Chapter 6, with notes 117–19.

127. See *Malesherbes* I, 573/1131, and Conf. XI, 475/568.

128. Rousseau to Moultou, 12 December 1761, as translated in Cranston, *The Noble Savage*, 318.

129. Following Scholar, 556.

130. Ibid., 626. By contrast, fear about the fate of the manuscript of the *Confessions* is palpable in the forewords preceding Parts One and Two of the *Confessions* (see 3, 229/3, 273). These are included in its Geneva manuscript but not its earlier Neuchâtel manuscript or its later Paris manuscript (Kelly, CW 5:598n2, 631n3; Gagnebin and Raymond, OC 1:1230, note 1 to p. 3, and 1369, variant (a) and note 1 to p. 273).

131. "No, there has never been a work as powerful, as luminous, as true on natural religion" (Moultou to Rousseau, 3 February 1762, CC 10:80–83, at 80). However, Moultou questions the public impact of publishing the work, particularly in Geneva and Switzerland, because of its teachings on revelation and miracles (81). See also Cranston, *The Noble Savage*, 341–42.

132. Moultou to Rousseau, 3 February 1762, CC 10:81. Moultou then clairvoyantly warns that there are two bitterly opposed factions in France, which may well unite against Rousseau.

133. See, especially, the anecdote about Charles Duclos (Conf. XI, 471f/563f; Cranston, *The Noble Savage*, 322).

134. See Cranston, *The Noble Savage*, chs. 10–12, esp. 322, 334, 349–55, and Conf. XI, esp. 480f/574. A relative confidence is found even on 5 June 1762: "One says that the *Parlement*

intends to pursue the author, but I do not know that a body so wise and enlightened has committed such a stupidity" (letter to Jean Néaulme, CC 11:24–26, at 25). It seems fair to say that he knew his writings were provocative enough to draw scorn and some possible danger, but he did not anticipate the ensuing disaster as likely. In 1763, following a discussion of the Savoyard Vicar, he concludes: "I knew men too well to expect gratitude from them. I did not know them well enough, I admit, to expect of them what they have done" (*Beaumont* 80/1003). See also, on expecting to suffer but not "the unheard of treatment I have come to experience," his letter to de Moiry, [21 July 1762], CC 12:71–73, at 71. Similar issues emerge with the *Letters Written from the Mountain* (discussed below, Chapter 4, with note 243).

135. Cranston's looser translation indicates the likely meaning: "in my present state of health" (*The Noble Savage*, 334).

136. This refers to Helvétius. However, as Cranston points out, he owed his freedom to a "groveling repudiation of his offending utterances, something Rousseau was the last man to agree to do" (*The Noble Savage*, 334; similarly, Leigh, CC 10:104 note a).

137. Here, Cranston has "that I am not in danger" (*The Noble Savage*, 334), but the original "*je ne risque rien*" seems a likely allusion to the earlier Socratic argument. It would thus suggest not that there is no personal risk but that he cannot be harmed *in the most fundamental regards*. Cf. Socrates' idea that the wicked cannot harm the good, or (at least) cannot harm them in any fundamental respect, and that, in attempting to do so, they harm themselves more (Plato, *Gorgias*, 527c–d; *Apology*, esp. 30c–d, 41c–d; *Crito*, 48a).

138. Rousseau to Moultou, 16 February 1762, CC 10:102–4, at 102–3 (consulting the partial translation in Cranston, *The Noble Savage*, 334).

139. For Socrates against being "inordinately fond of life," and clinging to life at any cost to dignity, see Plato, *Apology*, 34c–35a, 37c, 39a; this applies especially at his advanced age (*Crito*, 43b; *Phaedo*, 117a).

140. For Socrates, see note 137 above.

141. Translation modified. For context, see Chapter 6 below, beginning with note 64.

142. Letter to Jean Néaulme, 5 June 1762, CC 11:24–26, at 24–25, modifying Cranston's translation, *The Noble Savage*, 352, cf. 346.

143. 26 February 1770, CC 37:248–71, at 268.

144. Following Scholar, 626. See also *Beaumont* 22/928. He also strongly distinguishes himself from all authors of his times in his boldness in speaking "the truth, when it is useful to others, without troubling myself about my fortune nor about my safety" (Fragments of the *Letter to Beaumont*, no. 12, CW 9:94 / OC 4:1022).

145. Ruth Grant is among the few who have affirmed certain strengths of his character; she includes disinterestedness and a willingness to sacrifice for truth (*Hypocrisy and Integrity*, 74–77, 113).

146. This is Jackson's phrase, from her helpful study of cases such as the "Preface to *Narcissus*," the Dedication to DOI, the Preface to *Julie*, the *Malesherbes*, and the *Levite of Ephraim* (*Rousseau's Occasional Autobiographies*).

CHAPTER 3

1. See, e.g., Riley, *The General Will Before Rousseau*; Williams, *Rousseau's* Social Contract, 248–50, 253, 263–64; Charly Coleman, "The Value of Dispossession: Rethinking Discourses of Selfhood in Eighteenth-Century France," *Modern Intellectual History* 2.3 (2005): 299–326; and Reisert, *A Friend of Virtue*, 107–14.

2. Translation modified; Bloom has "A philosopher" for "*Tel philosophe*." See also *Geneva Manuscript* I.2, CW 4:81 / OC 3:287.

3. Translation modified. See the discussion below (Section 6.1, esp. with note 35).

4. Letter to Rousseau, 10 March 1757, CC 4:168–69, at 169, my translation (cf. Kelly's translation of the letter, CW 5:558). This passage is also discussed in Cranston, *The Noble Savage*, 47, and Gauthier, *The Sentiment of Existence*, 155. See also the broader argument in Kelly, *Rousseau as Author*, ch. 5. Rousseau does not include the quip in his quotation of Diderot's letter (Conf. IX, 383/456, as pointed out in Cranston, *The Noble Savage*, 47, and Gauthier, *The Sentiment of Existence*, 155).

5. *Satires* II.1–3, 9, invoked in Diderot, "Les Tablettes," 283. The Curii are "representatives of the best type of Roman manhood in the old Republic": Niall Rudd, in *Satires*, trans. Rudd (New York: Oxford University Press, 1999), 147.

6. Juvenal, *Satires*, I.30, 4, modified.

7. *The Sentiment of Existence*, 73.

8. Ibid., 84.

9. Ibid., 78.

10. Ibid., 156.

11. Ibid., citing Conf. VIII, 333/396.

12. *The Sentiment of Existence*, 156.

13. Ibid., 157.

14. Conf. IX, 341/406, quoted in *The Sentiment of Existence*, 159; see also 158.

15. *The Sentiment of Existence*, 158, citation format modified. We have previously found Gauthier's charge about the loss of effervescence and the shift in tone to be exaggerated and overly dichotomous (see Chapter 2, note 72 and the discussion that follows).

16. Quoted in *The Sentiment of Existence*, 173.

17. Ibid., 177; see also 144, 173–77. Less sweepingly, Maurizio Viroli contrasts the impeccable civic devotion of Machiavelli with Rousseau's relative downgrading of political life and final renunciation of his citizenship. See "Rousseau and Machiavelli: Two Interpretations of Republicanism," in *Thinking with Rousseau*, ed. Helena Rosenblatt and Paul Schweigert (Cambridge: Cambridge University Press, 2017), 7–28, at 25–28.

18. For the sweetness of public life, see DPE 16/255; LdA 135–36n/351n/123–24n; and Conf. IV, 121/144, VIII, 329–30/392–93.

19. Cf. "Judgment on the Polysynody," CW 11:97 / OC 3:643, with Patrick Riley, "Rousseau's General Will," in Riley, *The Cambridge Companion to Rousseau*, 124–53, at 131.

20. See, recently, Jared Holley, "Rousseau on Refined Epicureanism and the Problem of Modern Liberty," *European Journal of Political Theory* 17.4 (2018): 411–31, esp. 411–17. For an Epicurean portrayal of Jean-Jacques's character amid the largely Stoic *Emile*, see Dennis Rasmussen, "If Rousseau Were Rich: Another Model of the Good Life," *History of Political Thought* 36.3 (2015): 499–520, esp. 503, 511.

21. See Tocqueville, *Democracy in America* (1835, 1840), 4 vols., ed. Eduardo Nolla, trans. James T. Schleifer (Indianapolis: Liberty Fund, 2010), vol. 2, Part 2, chs. 2–4, and 8. On the deep influence of Rousseau on Tocqueville in general, see Paul Rahe, *Soft Despotism, Democracy's Drift: Montesquieu, Rousseau, Tocqueville, and the Modern Prospect* (New Haven: Yale University Press, 2009), 154, 168–71, and McLendon, *The Psychology of Inequality*, 129–32.

22. Miller, *Dreamer of Democracy*, 54; see also 25, 49–50.

23. "Kant and Rousseau," 9.

24. This later approach is also present in some passages of the *Letters to Malesherbes* (January 1762).

25. See *The Sentiment of Existence*, 155–57.

26. Ibid., 155; see Gauthier's account of the history of invoking this title (144–49). He plausibly suggests that, during the period when most of Rousseau's works (1749–1763) were signed as the Citizen, it applied only to works he thought "will do [Geneva] honor" (146, citing *Julie* Second Preface, 20/27). For the exclusion of *Julie* on these grounds, see above, Chapter 2, note 66. For his renunciation of citizenship (on 12 May 1763), see Section 4.2.

27. Gauthier, *The Sentiment of Existence*, 156, quoted with note 12 above.

28. Ibid., 156 and 156n14. He appeals to Cranston (*The Noble Savage*, 10) and the *Confessions* (see VIII, 331–33/395–97)

29. See Gauthier, *The Sentiment of Existence*, 157.

30. Ibid.

31. *The Noble Savage*, 45, quoted in *The Sentiment of Existence*, 157n15.

32. *The Noble Savage*, 82; see also Gagnebin and Raymond, OC 1:1503, note 1 to p. 475.

33. On the reasons for the 1754 journey, see Leigh, "Avertissement," CC 3:xxi–xxii. Gagnebin and Raymond claim that this zeal was at its height in July 1754 (OC 1:1455, note 3 to p. 392).

34. Miller also cites the "raptures" about the "happy and free people" of Lake Geneva described by St. Preux, after a long period of travel (*Dreamer of Democracy*, 49; see *Julie*, IV.6, 344/419).

35. 20 July 1754, CC 3:16–18, at 16.

36. This dedication was substantially written just before his journey (see Leigh, CC 3:64 note f).

37. Translation modified.

38. Translation modified.

39. See Leigh, "Avertissement," CC 3:xxi.

40. See Leigh, Appendix 138, CC 3:345; Rosenblatt, *Rousseau and Geneva*, 32, 159–63; and Helena Rosenblatt, "Rousseau's Gift to Geneva," *Modern Intellectual History* 3.1 (2006): 65–73, esp. 70–72. See also Rousseau to Jean Perdriau, 28 November 1754, CC 3:55–64, at 56–57. This affair "marked the beginning of the mutual mistrust between Rousseau and the patricians of Geneva" (Leigh, CC 3:63).

41. Cf. DOI Dedication 118/115.

42. Letter to Perdriau, 28 November 1754, CC 3:59–60 (also partially translated in Rosenblatt, *Rousseau and Geneva*, 180).

43. See Conf. VIII, 331f/395, endorsed in Rosenblatt, *Rousseau and Geneva*, 184. An early retrospective captures the ambiguity of weighing several different motives: "For a long time I have fathomed [*pénétre*] the covert hate of the Council, and this is *the true reason, or at least the strongest*, which has prevented me from retiring to Geneva" (Rousseau to Marcet de Mézières, 10 August 1762, CC 12:167–70, at 168, emphasis added).

44. *Against War and Empire*, 58–59. Several others are close to Whatmore here (see Starobinski, OC 3:1286–88, note 1 to p. 111; Cranston, *The Noble Savage*, 7–10; and Miller, *Dreamer of Democracy*, 52–53). Cf. Leigh "Avertissement," CC 3:xxi.

45. Cf. "my distant fellow-citizens [*mes Concitoyens éloignés*]" (DOI Dedication, 118/115).

46. For the limited, dispassionate citizenship that seems to result for Emile, as opposed to the strong citizenship of Rousseau's political writings, see Cooper, *Problem of the Good Life*, 26, 51–52n24, 52–55, 127, 165, 203, and Kelly, *Rousseau as Author*, 92–98.

47. Cf. the "Letter to Philopolis": "If one can, one ought to settle in one's fatherland in order to love and to serve it" (EPW 227 / OC 3:235). This was published posthumously, but apparently written soon after October 1755 (Starobinski, OC 3:1387, 1383).

48. See the "Letter to Philopolis" (EPW 227 / OC 3:235) for a surprisingly cosmopolitan alternative to citizenship for those who may not resettle in their fatherland (*Patrie*). Cf. Seneca *De beata vita*, 21, in *Dialogues and Essays*, 103. Rousseau's very early "Universal Chronology" (ca. 1737) is also highly cosmopolitan (see CW 11:2 / OC 5:488).

49. Cf. Pierre Burgelin OC 4:1699, note 1 to p. 859, and Miller, *Dreamer of Democracy*, 54, 59.

50. Translation modified. Rosenblatt cautiously endorses this: "His desire to be useful to his country may have been part of his reason for staying away" (*Rousseau and Geneva*, 184).

51. See LdA 5–6/254–55/5–6. While this work was being composed, he wrote to a friend that d'Alembert's proposal about the theater "has revived my zeal" (letter to Jacob Vernes, 4 July 1758, CC 5:106–7, at 106).

52. For the reception of the *Letter*, see Rosenblatt, *Rousseau and Geneva*, 227–32, and Whatmore, *Against War and Empire*, 59–60.

53. Cf. Rosenblatt, *Rousseau and Geneva*, 220–22.

54. Ca. 10 November 1758, CC 5:217–19, at 217, following Rosenblatt's translation, *Rousseau and Geneva*, 228.

55. Letter to Rousseau, 13 July 1761, as translated in Rosenblatt, *Rousseau and Geneva*, 232.

56. See also the discussion in Kelly, *Rousseau as Author*, 128.

57. See Conf. IX, 341/406; Leigh, "Avertissement," CC 3:xxi; and "Rousseau's Letter to Voltaire on Optimism (18 August 1756)," in *Studies on Voltaire and the Eighteenth Century*, vol. 30, ed. Theodore Besterman (Geneva: Institut et musée Voltaire, 1964), 247–309, at 264–65.

58. See Cranston, *The Noble Savage*, 10, citing the letter to Jean Jallabert, 20 November 1755, CC 3:206–8.

59. Discussed above, Chapter 2, with note 1 and following.

60. Translation modified, from "the slightest duties." Either translation seems grammatically possible. However, Rousseau goes on to list "a word to say, a letter to write, a visit to make," which seems to emphasize the smallness rather than the universality of the duties in question (*Malesherbes* I, 573/1132). Gagnebin and Raymond also seem to have this meaning in mind when they connect this passage with one in *Confessions* on his "delays in the little duties [*les petits devoirs*]" (OC 1:1848, note 5 to p. 1132, citing Conf. X, 426/509).

61. Rev. VI, 83/1059, quoted with note 16 above.

62. Quoted above, following note 50. This passage also defends his limited solitude as fulfilling duties to the local poor (discussed below, Chapter 6, with note 72).

63. See Conf. IX, 341/406 (quoted with note 56 above), and X, 412/492 (on any sort of "party, faction, cabal"). On the oath, see Conf. V, 181/216, and XII, 510/609 (discussed below, Chapter 4, with notes 223–25).

64. Following Scholar, 387, modified.

65. For alternative, more deflationary accounts of this affair, see Kelly, *Rousseau's Exemplary Life*, 232–35, and Meier, *Happiness of the Philosophic Life*, 171–76.

66. Matthieu Buttafoco to Rousseau, 31 August 1764, CC 21:85–91, at 86. An extensive translation is available in Mark Hill, "Enlightened 'Savages': Rousseau's *Social Contract* and the 'Brave People' of Corsica," *History of Political Thought* 38.3 (2017): 462–93, at 476.

67. Rousseau to Buttafoco, 22 September 1764, CC 21:173–76, at 173.

68. Letter to Alexandre Deleyre, 20 December 1764, CC 22:253–55, at 254.

69. Letter to Buttafoco, CC 21:174. In the *Confessions* account, it is only after more meditation that he increasingly felt the necessity of seeing the island and its people for himself (XII, 544/649).

70. CC 24:27–29, at 28, also discussed in OC 1:1608, note 3 to p. 649. Cf. the discussion of Corsican national character, which includes "primitive virtues" as well as "many vices" contracted from servitude and poor governance (*Corsica* 133–34, 136–37/ 913–14, 917–18).

71. Modifying Scholar, 636f.

72. Similarly, although he announced to Buttafoco in March 1765 that he had renounced the constitutional project, he continued to work on it through that autumn (Jean Roussel, "Projet de constitution pour la Corse," *Dictionnaire* 758a). See the letter to Buttafoco, 24 March 1765, CC 24:299–301, at 300.

73. See Christophe Litwin, Introduction to *Affaires de Corse* (Paris: J. Vrin, 2018), 18. For instance, Rousseau carried his Corsican dossier with him to England (Introduction, 18).

74. Cf. Hill, "Enlightened 'Savages,'" 473, 493; Leigh, CC 21:90; and Cranston, *The Solitary Self*, 143. He came to see this as a plot against him (RJJ III, 220n/944n, with Robert Osmont, OC 1:1733, note 5 to p. 944).

75. Cf. Nicholas White, *Individual and Conflict in Greek Ethics* (Oxford: Clarendon, 2002), and Hulliung, *Autocritique of Enlightenment*, 5, 9, 19, 67, 97.

76. See, for instance, Plato, *Apology*, 28b–c; Aristotle, *Nicomachean Ethics*, e.g., III.7, 1115b11–13, IV.1, 1120a23–25, and IX.8, 1168b25–30, 1169a19–25; and Ryan Balot, "Plato's Protagorean Dialogues: A Skeptical Reassessment," *Review of Politics* 80.1 (2018): 116–20, at 120.

77. Thucydides, *The Peloponnesian War*, trans. Martin Hammond (New York: Oxford University Press, 2009), V.105. This is echoed in E I, 39/248f. Cf. RJJ HPW 251/983: The English nation "has never been cited for any act of justice going contrary to its own interest."

78. See Kelly, *Rousseau's Exemplary Life*, ch. 2, esp. 50–55.

79. E.g., Socrates in Plato, *Apology*, 31c–33a; Plato, *Republic*, IX, 591e–92b; cf. *Republic* I, 347a, V, 473c–e, VI, 499a–c, 501a, and VII, 519c–20e; and (Plato), Letter VII, 324c–26b. Cf. Rousseau, Obs. 42n/46n.

80. For a deflationary interpretation of these ideals, see Melzer on ancient "philosophical politics," understood as engaging in political activity only in order to "secure the practical interests of the theoretical life—the safety and the propagation of philosophy" (*Philosophy Between the Lines*, 88; see 87–88, 143, 185–92). For persecution and writing more generally, see above, Chapter 2, note 61.

81. Plato, *Apology*, 32a.

82. Plutarch, *Dion* ([11] in *Plutarch's Lives*, 2:543/[14] in *Les vies*, 2:998). Here, Plutarch is likely citing (Plato), Letter VII (see, esp., 328c). See also Letter VII, 329b and 347d–e, on defending his friends and the honor of philosophy.

83. See Plato, *Laches*, 181b, *Symposium*, 219e–21c, and *Apology*, 28e; Plutarch, *Alcibiades*, [7] in *Greek Lives*, 227/[11] in *Les vies*, 1:425f; and Diogenes Laertius, *Lives of Eminent Philosophers*, 2 vols., trans. R. D. Hicks (Cambridge: Harvard University Press, 1958–1959), II.23. See also Rousseau, "Comparison of Socrates and Cato," CW 4:14.

84. Plato, *Apology*, 32a–e; Xenophon, *Hellenika*, I.7.7–35; Diogenes Laertius II.24.

85. Letter VII, 334e. Cf. Dion's willingness to perish for his city in *Lives*, 2:563. For Plato's disappointment, see, e.g., Letter VII, 350d–e.

86. Plutarch, *Dion* in *Lives*, 2:567f, and "Live Unknown" [4], in *Selected Essays and Dialogues*, 122. See, similarly, Cicero, *On Obligations* (*De Officiis*), trans. P. G. Walsh [New York: Oxford University Press, 2000], I.155. Rousseau also alludes to this later history (see "Discourse on Heroic Virtue," EPW 306 / OC 2:1263).

87. See, esp., (Plato), Letter VII, 329b.

88. See Yves Touchefeu, "*Écrivains Latins*," in *Dictionnaire*, 274a. Dio Cassius offered a highly critical interpretation of Seneca; Montaigne's response in defense of him is likely to have been convincing to Rousseau (*Essays* II.32, 818). Montaigne (II.32, 818) also endorses Tacitus's more favorable interpretation of Seneca. See Tacitus, *Annals*, trans. J. C. Yardley (New York: Oxford University Press, 2008), esp. XIII.2, XIV.14, 52–57, XV.45, 60–65, and, for the common accusations of hypocrisy, XIII.42, XIV.52, and Griffin, *Seneca*, 5–6, 286, and 292–94. On Tacitus, see *Mountain* VIII, 261n/842n.

89. On the known sources and Rousseau's two attempts to translate Seneca, see Touchefeu, "*Écrivains Latins*," 274, and Trousson, "*Traduction de l'Apolokyntosis de Sénèque*," *Dictionnaire*, 889–90.

90. *De Otio* 3.2 (as *On the Private Life*, in *Moral and Political Essays*, ed. and trans. John M. Cooper and J. F. Procopé [Cambridge: Cambridge University Press, 1995], 174).

91. Seneca, *Letters on Ethics*, 68.2

92. *De Otio* 3.3. The wise person will have perseverance, "but only as long as there is something gained by such perseverance, and as long as one does not have to do or undergo anything unworthy of a good man" (*Letters on Ethics*, 22.8).

93. *De Otio* 3.3. See, similarly, Cicero, *De Officiis*, I.71–72 and 110. In addition, retirement seems to be especially justified on completion of service to the public (e.g., *Letters on Ethics*, 73.4). Cf. *Julie* III.22, 319/388 (quoted below, Chapter 6, with note 84).

94. See Diogenes Laertius II.29, and Xenophon, *Memorabilia*, III.7

95. On the general stance, see, e.g., *Live Unknown*; for "particularly right," see *Rules for Politicians*, 798, in *Selected Essays*, 141; for philosophical leisure, see *How to Profit from Your Enemies*, 87, in *Selected Essays*, 184.

96. Cassirer, "Kant and Rousseau," 9, quoted above, with note 23.

97. In Chapter 6 and in this book's Conclusion, I explore the development, which I place in his later thought, of openly pursuing inclination without regard for duty.

CHAPTER 4

1. See above, Chapter 2, with notes 112–13.

2. See Miller, *Dreamer of Democracy*, 82. For his flouting of conventions of authorial anonymity, see Kelly, *Rousseau as Author*, ch. 1, and below, Chapter 5, with note 3.

3. Derathé, Introduction to *Du contrat social*, OC 3:cx–cxi; Cranston, *The Noble Savage*, 350–51; Miller, *Dreamer of Democracy*, 77.

4. Marie-Hélène Cotoni, "*Lettre à Christophe de Beaumont*," in *Dictionnaire*, 504b; R. A. Leigh, "New Light on the Genesis of the *Lettres de la Montagne*: Rousseau's Marginalia on Tronchin," *Studies on Voltaire and the Eighteenth Century*, vol. 44, ed. Theodore Besterman (Oxfordshire: Voltaire Foundation, 1972), 89–119, at 89; Cranston, *The Noble Savage*, 358. Cf. Rosenblatt, *Rousseau and Geneva*, 271, and Cranston, *The Noble Savage*, 351.

5. Leigh, "New Light on the *Montagne*," 89, and Cotoni, "*Lettre à Christophe de Beaumont*," 504b.

6. *The Solitary Self*, 6; see also 8–9, 13, 27, and the similar observations of Anne-Robert-Jacques Turgot, letter to Tscharner, 27 August 1762, CC 12:257–58, at 258.

7. *Mountain* VI, 234/810, with Jean-Daniel Candaux, OC 3:1665, note 2 to p. 810, and Leigh, "New Light on the *Montagne*," 89.

8. For "reformers," see Whatmore, "'A Lover of Peace More Than Liberty?' The Genevan Rejection of Rousseau's Politics," in *Engaging with Rousseau*, ed. Lifschitz, 1–16, at 2.

9. Whatmore, *Against War and Empire*, 52; see also Leigh, "New Light on the *Montagne*," 93.

10. Rousseau to Isaac-Ami Marcet de Mézières, 10 August 1762, CC 12:167–70, at 169 (discussed below, with note 62).

11. R. A. Leigh, "Rousseau's Political Principles and Genevan Politics: The *Contrat social* and the *Lettres de la montagne*," in *Enlightenment Essays in Memory of Robert Shackleton*, ed. Giles Barber and C. P. Courtney (Oxford: Alden Press, 1988), 131–43, at 134, 137, 143. For these three activist years as uncharacteristic, see Leigh, 133, and Benoît Mély, *Jean-Jacques Rousseau: Un intellectuel en rupture* (Paris: Minerve, 1985), 191.

12. A projected Third Part of the *Confessions*, which would have delved into the fallout with David Hume in England (1766–1767) and countless other troubles, was never written (cf. Conf. XII, 549/656; RJJ II, 154/859).

13. Discussed below, with note 103.

14. See Conf. XII, 510–11, 521–22/609–10, 623–24, discussed below, beginning with note 109.

15. 26 February 1770, CC 37:248–71, at 263f.

16. For Hobbes's view of peace as the fundamental natural law and the only rational basis for moral praise, see, esp., *On the Citizen* (1642), ed. and trans. Richard Tuck and Michael Silverthorne (Cambridge: Cambridge University Press, 1998), Preface, [8], and ch. 3, [32–33]; *Leviathan* (1651), ed. Edwin Curley (Indianapolis: Hackett, 1994), ch. 14, [4], and ch. 15, [40]. For Hobbesian accounts of political authority in the Genevan context, see above, Chapter 2, with note 104.

17. See, recently, Douglass, *Rousseau and Hobbes*, and Richard Tuck, "Rousseau and Hobbes: The Hobbesianism of Rousseau," in *Thinking with Rousseau*, ed. Rosenblatt and Schweigert, 37–62. Tuck (esp. 37–44, 48–52) emphasizes their similarities, whereas Douglass (e.g., 7f, 106f, 121, 189) leans in the opposite direction.

18. Discussed in the opening section of Chapter 3 above. Gauthier is aware of this period but does not engage it: Even though Rousseau "did involve himself extensively in Genevan politics" at this time, "this involvement is largely ignored in the self-construction of the *Confessions*" (*The Sentiment of Existence*, 157n15).

19. See his well-known revisionist republican interpretation of Machiavelli in SC III.6, 95, 95n/409, 409 variant (a); cf. DPE 9/247. For Rousseau's predecessors and contemporaries on this, see Paul Rahe, *Against Throne and Altar: Machiavelli and Political Theory Under the English Republic* (Cambridge: Cambridge University Press, 2008), 5–7, and Derathé, OC 3:1481, notes 4 and 5 to p. 409. Maurizio Viroli also depicts Machiavelli and his republican citizens as devoted to the republic and its foundations, "the rule of law and the common good" (see "Rousseau and Machiavelli," 10–11, 24–25, and 27, citing, e.g., *Discourses on Livy*, I.18 and 55, and III.22).

20. "*Locke en particulier les a traitées exactement dans les mêmes principes que moi*: Revisiting the Relationship Between Locke and Rousseau," in *Locke's Political Liberty: Readings and Misreadings*, ed. Christophe Miqueu and Mason Chamie (Oxford: Voltaire Foundation, 2009), 69–82, at 80.

21. Geneva is also included intermittently in the biographical overview of Cranston (*The Solitary Self*, chs. 1–6). Yet this volume, not fully complete at the time of Cranston's untimely death (cf. ix), is not at the level of Cranston's earlier two volumes, in either thoroughness or reliability. Damrosch's account of this phase of the Genevan controversy is very brief (*Restless*

Genius, 375–76, 388–89). Brooke is therefore right to welcome an early article by Richard Whatmore ("*Locke en particulier*," 80). Whatmore's later book is thematic and not suitable for a chronological narrative, but it provides a major interpretation of Rousseau's relations to Genevan politics (*Against War and Empire*, esp. chs. 1–3). Miller juxtaposes somewhat brief chronological narratives with useful interpretive argument (*Dreamer of Democracy*, chs. 3–5; cf. Miller, *Examined Lives*, 249–50). Trousson's biography also combines a thorough narrative with substantive interpretation (*Jean-Jacques Rousseau*, esp. *Second Partie*, chs. 9–10) as does Mély (*Un intellectuel en rupture*, ch. 5). Finally, Kirk provides a helpful brief overview amid a broader discussion of the history of republicanism ("Genevan Republicanism," esp. 288–96). Much of our account needs to be constructed from the correspondence, making Leigh's commentaries indispensable.

22. See "'A Lover of Peace More Than Liberty'?" esp. 10.

23. Brooke, "*Locke en particulier*," 71; see, esp., 70–74. For some connections, see Jean-Daniel Candaux, OC 3:1667, note 5 to p. 812; Kelly and Grace, CW 9:326n48; and Lee Ward, "John Locke's Influence on Rousseau," in *The Rousseauian Mind*, ed. Grace and Kelly, 65–75.

24. "*Locke en particulier*," 74. See below, with notes 160–62. Istvan Hont posits that the second *Discourse* shows that Rousseau had read Locke's *Second Treatise* "quite carefully" (*Politics in Commercial Society*, 68; see 64-68). However, Hont moves in a very different direction on the right to resistance (see with note 166 below, and Hont, 73: "Revolution was a deeply futile and damaging phenomenon").

25. "*Locke en particulier*," 81–82.

26. Starobinski, OC 3:1353, note 4 to p. 181. Bruno Bernardi observes that filiation is emphasized by Rousseau in exactly two cases: Sidney and Locke ("Rousseau lecteur du *Contrat social*: La fonction critique des principes," in *La Religion, la liberté, la justice: Un commentaire des* Lettres écrites de la montagne *de Jean-Jacques Rousseau* [Paris: Vrin, 2005], 107–26, at 115).

27. 22 June 1762, CC 11:126–28, at 127; also discussed in Cranston, *The Solitary Self*, 7, Miller, *Dreamer of Democracy*, 82f, and Trousson, *Jean-Jacques Rousseau*, 540.

28. 6 July 1762, CC 11:221–24; also discussed in Cranston, *The Solitary Self*, 11.

29. See Leigh, CC 11:223–24 note b, and *Beaumont* 24/930.

30. Letters to Moultou of 11 and 15 July 1762, as discussed in Cranston, *The Solitary Self*, 21.

31. See Rosenblatt, *Rousseau and Geneva*, 269–70; Leigh, "Jean-Jacques Rousseau," 562–63; and Candaux, OC 3:1664, note 3 to p. 809.

32. Letter of 16 June 1762, CC 11:88–91, at 90, consulting Rosenblatt's translation: *Rousseau and Geneva*, 269.

33. Letter of 18 June 1762, as translated in Miller, *Dreamer of Democracy*, 79.

34. SC I.7, II.1, III.1–4, 18, IV.1–2; cf. *Mountain* V, 201–2/770–71, VI, 231–33/806–9, VIII, 257–59/837–40. Richard Tuck has made this distinction the theme of a major historical study, which centers on Rousseau (see *The Sleeping Sovereign*, esp. ix–xi, 1–9, and ch. 3). Whatmore also provides contextual discussion (*Against War and Empire*, 64, 66, 74, 76). See also the discussion below, with note 160.

35. Cf. Whatmore, *Against War and Empire*, 56, and Leigh, "Rousseau's Political Principles," 132–34, 143, with the greater contextual emphasis in Rosenblatt, *Rousseau and Geneva*, 4–8, 269, 280.

36. See the overviews of the various councils in Kirk, "Genevan Republicanism," 274; Whatmore, *Against War and Empire*, 28–29; and Bruno Bernardi et al., *La religion, la liberté, la justice*, 307–9.

37. Whatmore, *Against War and Empire*, 27.

38. See Kirk, "Genevan Republicanism," 274, 279; Rosenblatt, *Rousseau and Geneva*, esp. 17–18, 101–5, 245–50, 269; and Leigh, "New Light on the *Montagne*," 90f.

39. Leigh, "Jean-Jacques Rousseau," 563. For an introduction to the two main narratives about the Genevan constitution, see Whatmore, *Against War and Empire*, 28–32. See also Miller's thoughtful reflections on history, fable, and the appeal to the "ancient constitution" in Rousseau, *Dreamer of Democracy*, 92–104; but cf. Rosenblatt, *Rousseau and Geneva*, 5.

40. Leigh, "New Light on the *Montagne*," 91n2, and Kirk, "Genevan Republicanism," 273.

41. Kirk, "Genevan Republicanism," 273.

42. Ibid., 298, 303–5. Accounts of the four orders are also in d'Alembert, "Geneva" (1757, in *Politics and the Arts*, 142 / CW 10:242 / *Encyclopédie* 7:578b). Whatmore's overview also lists a fifth social order, of "subjects" (*sujets*): see *Against War and Empire*, 26–28.

43. *Rousseau and Geneva*, 30n89.

44. See the discussions of Jacques-François Deluc in Whatmore, *Against War and Empire*, 53, and of Jean Perdriau in Rosenblatt, *Rousseau and Geneva*, 216.

45. Cf. Rosenblatt, *Rousseau and Geneva*, 233, and Whatmore, *Against War and Empire*, 59f. However, Whatmore insists on several important differences between Rousseau and the *représentants* (discussed below, Section 4.4).

46. Discussed above, Chapter 3, with notes 40–44.

47. See the extensive translation of Tronchin's official report to the Small Council on the *Social Contract*, in Miller, *Dreamer of Democracy*, 80–81 ([19 June 1762], CC 11:298–301).

48. See Rosenblatt, *Rousseau and Geneva*, 272–73; Whatmore, *Against War and Empire*, 66–67; Cranston, *The Solitary Self*, 8; and Moultou's letter of 16 June 1762, quoted with note 33 above.

49. See Cranston, *The Solitary Self*, 8–10, 14.

50. See Cranston, *The Solitary Self*, 17, describing a letter, actually of 21 July 1762: CC 12:71–73.

51. Letter to Frédéric-Guillaume de Montmollin, 24 August 1762, CC 12:245–48, at 246.

52. For d'Alembert, Cranston, *The Solitary Self*, 33; for the Calvinists, Rosenblatt, *Rousseau and Geneva*, 272–75, Cranston, *The Solitary Self*, 32–33, 41–43, 46–48, and Leigh, CC 12:247b; for the Small Council, Leigh, "New Light on the *Montagne*," 91. Nonetheless, the liberal vagueness of Rousseau's profession should be evident. Following the controversies of the *Mountain*, in March 1765, Montmollin and the class of pastors of Neuchâtel would (unsuccessfully) demand that Rousseau "declare solemnly to the consistory that he believes in Jesus Christ dead for our offenses and resurrected for our justification" (quoted in Mély, *Un intellectuel en rupture*, 217).

53. Beaumont's *Mandement* against *Emile* was published 28 August 1762. Rousseau began writing his response in October, and sent it to Rey at the beginning of January 1763 (see Cotoni, "*Lettre à Christophe de Beaumont*," 504b, and Cranston, *The Solitary Self*, 57, cf. 64).

54. See Rosenblatt, *Rousseau and Geneva*, 275–76; Whatmore, *Against War and Empire*, 67; and Trousson, *Jean-Jacques Rousseau*, 551, 558–59.

55. "Avertissement," CC 15:xxv.

56. Whatmore, *Against War and Empire*, 68, and Trousson, *Jean-Jacques Rousseau*, 564.

57. Trousson, *Jean-Jacques Rousseau*, 540.

58. Rousseau to Moultou, 24 July 1762, CC 12:99–101, at 99. For the grievances, see the letter forwarded to Moultou but addressed to Marcet de Mézières, 24 July 1762, CC 12:96–99.

59. Letter to Moultou, 24 July 1762, CC 12:99.

60. Ibid.

61. Letter to Moultou, 10 August 1762, CC 12:164–67, at 165.

62. Rousseau to Marcet de Mézières, 10 August 1762, CC 12:167–70, at 169, modifying the translation in Miller, *Dreamer of Democracy*, 83 (also discussed in Rosenblatt, *Rousseau and Geneva*, 275). He was sending Marcet a draft power of attorney concerning the Genevan indictment against Rousseau (Cranston, *The Solitary Self*, 31).

63. For instance, opposition leader Jacques-François Deluc (1698–1780) came to Môtiers in October 1762 to discuss campaign strategy, as well as religion, with Rousseau (see Cranston, *The Solitary Self*, 46–48).

64. For Tronchin's role, see Miller, *Dreamer of Democracy*, 80–82.

65. Ibid., 82.

66. "New Light on the *Montagne*," 90.

67. Cranston, *The Solitary Self*, 53.

68. Trousson, *Jean-Jacques Rousseau*, 558–59.

69. Rosenblatt, *Rousseau and Geneva*, 276.

70. See note 99 below.

71. Letter to Jacob Favre, CC 16:164–67 (also discussed in Miller, *Dreamer of Democracy*, 85, and Rosenblatt, *Rousseau and Geneva*, 276). Favre was the First Syndic (the leading magistrate) of the Republic of Geneva at this time.

72. This was first announced on 10 August 1762 (discussed below, with note 81). See also Gagnebin and Raymond, OC 1:1579–80, note 2 to p. 609.

73. Trousson, *Jean-Jacques Rousseau*, 560.

74. Letter to Favre, CC 16:164.

75. Translation modified. Kelly comments that "Rousseauian political activism" sometimes requires "complete withdrawal from the community as part of the fulfillment of one's civic duty" (*Rousseau as Author*, 135).

76. Letter to Rousseau, [16 May 1763], CC 16:187–88, at 187, following Rosenblatt's translation (*Rousseau and Geneva*, 276).

77. *Jean-Jacques Rousseau*, 561, citing letters from Roustan, Pictet, Minister Pierre Mouchon, and an anonymous Genevan (actually CC 16:187, 189, 195, 218).

78. Mouchon to Rousseau, 17 May 1763, CC 16:195–96, at 195.

79. Anonymous Genevan to Rousseau, [ca. 21 May 1763], CC 16:218.

80. Trousson, *En 78 lettres*, 178n1, and Rosenblatt, *Rousseau and Geneva*, 50f, 148, 181f.

81. 10 August 1762, CC 12:167–70, at 168f. Cf. the partial translation in Cranston, *The Solitary Self*, 31.

82. Marcet de Mézières to Rousseau, 13 August 1762, CC 12:178–79, at 178. Cranston sees this rebuke as politically motivated, since Marcet "wanted to exploit the despotic behaviour of the government toward Rousseau to the advantage of the political opposition" (*The Solitary Self*, 31).

83. CC 12:178–79.

84. Rousseau claims he should be scolded for too much indifference, rather than too much passion, in this affair. He admits he was deeply moved by the first indignity, but once he calmed himself down, "I saw that at bottom this was agitating myself for nothing. For finally . . . , what interest do I have in all this? What benefit has my quality of Citizen of Geneva done for me? What profit, what honor has come to me from it?" (20 August [1762], CC 12:212–17, at 214f). Marcet's next response would again press the case against "taking leave [*congé*] of your Fatherland." The wise person is not impeccable, but judicious reflection will prevent him from stepping over the precipice (27 August 1762, CC 12:252–55, at 253). Moreover, one must "cede to necessity, but not let it beat us down [*abatte*]" (254).

85. Letter to Favre, 12 May 1763, CC 16:164. Instead of "benefits," the first draft has "rights [*droits*]" (CC 16:168).

86. Also discussed in Trousson, *Jean-Jacques Rousseau*, 574.

87. With note 76 above.

88. [16 May 1763], CC 16:187.

89. Ibid., 187f.

90. 7 March 1768, CC 35:179–82, at 180. Cf. Conf. XII, 510/609.

91. CC 35:181 note g.

92. See Deluc to Moultou, 25 May 1763, CC 16:244–45; Rosenblatt, *Rousseau and Geneva*, 277; Leigh, "Avertissement," CC 16:xxv–xxvi; and Bernardi et al., Introduction to *La religion, la liberté, la justice*, 19.

93. CC 16:168, modifying Rosenblatt's translation: *Rousseau and Geneva*, 276.

94. By apparent mistake, in her account of the letter, Rosenblatt quotes from the first draft, rather than from the letter that was sent (cf. *Rousseau and Geneva*, 276, with CC 16:164, 168, and Leigh, CC 16:168a).

95. Letter to Marc Chappuis, 26 May 1763, CC 16:245–47. Chappuis's earlier letter to Rousseau (18 May) had encouraged him to withdraw his renunciation of citizenship and visit the syndics, who may be willing to moderate the severity of their edicts (see Cranston, *The Solitary Self*, 67; Leigh, "New Light on the *Montagne*," 92; and Perrin, *Lettres philosophiques*, 284–85).

96. See Leigh, CC 16:248b, 250; Rosenblatt, *Rousseau and Geneva*, 277; and Cranston, *The Solitary Self*, 67.

97. Letter to Chappuis, CC 16:245, modifying Rosenblatt's translation (*Rousseau and Geneva*, 277).

98. Chappuis's letter to Rousseau (18 May) had argued that "the fatherland in general" had not given him cause for complaint, since "the majority . . . render you justice" (CC 16:197–200, at 198). Cf. Deluc in Miller, *Dreamer of Democracy*, 85.

99. This indicates his reference point is the condemnations of 1762, rather than the (1763) banning of the *Letter to Beaumont* (cf. note 70 above). In later accounts, he claims to have waited "a year" or "more than a year" (*Mountain* IX, 295/884; Conf. XII, 510/609).

100. Leigh notes that in several copies of the letter that circulated, the imperfect tenses here were changed to conditionals—"it would be easy," "it would not at all trouble public order"—thus constituting "a far more marked incitement to sedition" ("Avertissement," CC 16:xxvi–xxvii, with 249, variant 18).

101. Cf. the political principle: "The people's consent has to be presumed from universal silence" (SC II.1, 58/369). This is discussed with SC III.11, 109/424, and DPE 12/250f in Dorina Verli, "Reforming Democracy: Constitutional Crisis and Rousseau's Advice to Geneva," *Review of Politics* 80.3 (2018): 415–38, at 436–37.

102. Letter to Chappuis, CC 16:246 (consulting the partial translation in Rosenblatt, *Rousseau and Geneva*, 277).

103. See Moultou to Rousseau, [25 June 1763], CC 16:338–41, at 338; also discussed in Rosenblatt, *Rousseau and Geneva*, 277.

104. See Rosenblatt, *Rousseau and Geneva*, 277–78; Leigh, "New Light on the *Montagne*," 92–93; Jean Terrasse, "*Lettres écrites de la Montagne*," in *Dictionnaire*, 523a, 527; cf. Gagnebin and Raymond, OC 1:1580, note 1 to p. 610.

105. Letter to Deluc, 25 June 1763, CC 16:335–37, at 336 (also discussed in Rosenblatt, *Rousseau and Geneva*, 279n66).

106. CC 16:336. For a conflict with Deluc around July 1763, see Cranston, *The Solitary Self*, 68–69, and Trousson, *Jean-Jacques Rousseau*, 564.

107. *The Solitary Self*, 73.

108. See Miller, *Dreamer of Democracy*, 123–24, and Rosenblatt, *Rousseau and Geneva*, 274–75.

109. See Conf. XIII, 510f/610, with the analysis of Leigh, CC 16:xxv–xxvii, 65–66, and 250. Trousson also draws this conclusion, adding that in the *Confessions*, he was "a bit worried about taking responsibility for the events which followed" (*Jean-Jacques Rousseau*, 562). See, finally, Mély, *Un intellectuel en rupture*, 191, 214–16.

110. Translation modified.

111. *Mountain* VIII, 263, 263n/844, 844n; Jean-Daniel Candaux, OC 3:1695, note 4 to p. 844.

112. Trousson, *Jean-Jacques Rousseau*, 568.

113. See Miller, *Dreamer of Democracy*, 86.

114. Whatmore, *Against War and Empire*, 61, see also 82–84.

115. *Against War and Empire*, 61. For the defense of the *droit négatif*, see [Tronchin], *Lettres écrites de la campagne*, (Proche Genève: n.p., 1765), *Troisième lettre*.

116. Agreed upon by Trousson, *Jean-Jacques Rousseau*, 568; Leigh, "New Light on the *Montagne*"; Cranston, *The Solitary Self*, 73, 79; Rosenblatt, *Rousseau and Geneva*, 279; and Damrosch, *Restless Genius*, 388. Cf. Conf. XII, 510f/610.

117. Deluc to Rousseau, 30 September 1763, CC 17:288–91, at 289, also discussed in Rosenblatt, *Rousseau and Geneva*, 279. See, similarly, Conf. XII, 511/610.

118. See Trousson, *Jean-Jacques Rousseau*, 569, 572, 575; Whatmore, *Against War and Empire*, 62, 74–75, 85; Miller, *Dreamer of Democracy*, 92–93, but cf. 233n50; and Rosenblatt, *Rousseau and Geneva*, 5.

119. Cranston, *The Solitary Self*, 79. See, similarly, Whatmore, *Against War and Empire*, 62.

120. Rousseau set to work on his response between 20 and 25 October 1763, and he completed the book in May 1764 (Terrasse, "*Lettres écrites de la Montagne*," in *Dictionnaire*, 522b–23a; cf. Gagnebin and Raymond, OC 1:1580, note 5 to p. 610). It was published 18 December 1764.

121. *Mountain* IV, 191–94/759–62; V, 204–5, 216–17/773–75, 788–90.

122. Similarly, in the letter to Marcet, he insists that positive proof is required before "stigmatizing [*flétrir*] the honor of an irreproachable man, before making an attempt on the liberty of a citizen" (24 July 1762, CC 12:96).

123. See *Mountain* I, 134, 136/687, 690, V, 221/794; see also *Beaumont* 21, 27/927, 935.

124. See *Mountain* Foreword, 133/685, VIII, 267/850; see also letter to Deluc, 25 June 1763, CC 16:336.

125. "New Light on the *Montagne*," 94.

126. *Jean-Jacques Rousseau*, 583.

127. Discussed below, with note 243.

128. Quoting Conf. XII, 522/623, translation modified. See also Damrosch, *Restless Genius*, 389, and Trousson, *Jean-Jacques Rousseau*, 587–88, 590, 593. Trousson notes the irony that in Paris it was burned in company with the *Dictionnaire philosophique* of Voltaire (590).

129. For negative religious responses from political allies, see Whatmore, *Against War and Empire*, 73, 94f. Moultou was a notable exception. See Cranston, *The Solitary Self*, 101, cf. 73f.

130. Damrosch, *Restless Genius*, 389. For philosophical criticisms of the "seditious purpose" of the *Mountain*, see below, with notes 234–39. According to Miller, abjuring citizenship freed

Rousseau from the constraint of limiting himself to general principles (*Dreamer of Democracy*, 87; see also Mély, *Un intellectuel en rupture*, 195).

131. Letter of 15 February 1765, quoted in Trousson, *Jean-Jacques Rousseau*, 588f.

132. François-Henri d'Ivernois to Rousseau, 21 December 1764, quoted in Trousson, *Jean-Jacques Rousseau*, 584; also discussed in Cranston, *The Solitary Self*, 100.

133. See Cranston, *The Solitary Self*, 102, and Trousson, *Jean-Jacques Rousseau*, 585. Cf. Bernardi et al., Introduction to *La Religion, la liberté, la justice*, 20. Damrosch oversimplifies in presenting the immediate political effects of *Mountain* as negative, leading the moderates to make peace with the Small Council (*Restless Genius*, 389).

134. See Trousson for the magistrates' fears at this point (*Jean-Jacques Rousseau*, 587).

135. See Mély, *Un intellectuel en rupture*, 186, 189–91, 199–201; Cranston, *The Solitary Self*, 108; and Trousson, *Jean-Jacques Rousseau*, 588.

136. "Genevan Republicanism," 295–96.

137. Leigh, "Rousseau's Political Principles," 137–38. The disgust is also clear in his letter to Lenieps, 10 February 1765, CC 23:338–43, at 338f.

138. Discussed below, Chapter 5, with notes 22–25.

139. Popular movements in Geneva were put down by France in 1734–1738, 1766–1768, and 1782 (Whatmore, *Against War and Empire*, 24–25, 81–83, 90–91; see, more generally, 40, 45, 51, 74, 98, and *Corsica* 136/916f). For the constitutional crises of 1766–1768 and 1782, see Perrin, *Lettres philosophiques*, 286; Leigh, "New Light on the *Montagne*," 90; Kirk, "Genevan Republicanism," 303–5; and Whatmore, *Against War and Empire*, xiv, 3, 6–12. Geneva was annexed by France during its Revolutionary Wars and placed in the federal republic of Switzerland in 1815 (Kirk, "Genevan Republicanism," 306).

140. See Whatmore, *Against War and Empire*, 65, 96.

141. On the appropriation, see Cranston, *The Solitary Self*, 109, and Conf. XII, 522/623f. On the magistrates' framing of his influence, see Whatmore, *Against War and Empire*, 61–62, 82–85, 91.

142. On the new generation, see Whatmore, *Against War and Empire*, 82, 94–95, and "A Lover of Peace More Than Liberty?" esp. 7–16.

143. See *Against War and Empire*, esp. 92–95.

144. Letter to François-Henri d'Ivernois, 29 January 1768, CC 35:62–65, at 62f.

145. Ibid., 63. We return to this advice with notes 208–10.

146. Letter to Moultou, 7 March 1768, CC 35:179–82, at 180f.

147. Whatmore, *Against War and Empire*, 94, citing Rousseau's letter to François-Henri d'Ivernois, 24 March 1768, CC 35:220–22.

148. *Men and Citizens*, 163.

149. *Dreamer of Democracy*, 126–27, 239n16.

150. See *Against War and Empire*, 57–61, 66–69, 78, 92–94; cf. 76.

151. See Leigh, "Rousseau's Political Principles," 140–43; Kirk, "Genevan Republicanism," 298–99, with 273, 303; Rosenblatt, *Rousseau and Geneva*, 107n86; and cf. SC IV.3, 126/442f.

152. Cf. Whatmore on the discovery of "a middle way" and how the *Mountain* supports "the portrayal of Rousseau as an arch-critic of contemporary republican and magisterial politics" (*Against War and Empire*, 78–79).

153. Cf. Whatmore, *Against War and Empire*, 77. For this prerogative of the Small Council, see also with note 115 above.

154. Emphases added.

155. Some of this argument needs to proceed by inference, however, since even though this use of the negative right by the magistrates is novel, the existing Mediation and Edicts do not specifically support the submission of remonstrances to the General Council (cf. *Mountain* VIII, 262, 268/843f, 851).

156. See Leigh on the remonstration of 20 August 1763 ("New Light on the *Montagne*," 93), and *Mountain* VIII, 262–63/843–44f.

157. *Lettres écrites de la campagne, Troisième lettre*, 113–17.

158. *Against War and Empire*, 77, citing OC 3:837–38.

159. *Second Treatise*, §§147, 145.

160. The theoretical distinction is discussed above, with note 34; see also the usage in *Corsica* 127/906.

161. *Rousseau and Geneva*, 250; see 249–51, and, for background, 156, 162, 186, 189–90, 245. The different uses of "democracy," including its positive usage in connection with sovereignty, is also well-argued in Miller (*Dreamer of Democracy*, ch. 5). See, finally, Verli on the fundamentally democratic purpose of Rousseau's qualifications to popular sovereignty, arguing especially from *Mountain* and the *Social Contract* ("Reforming Democracy").

162. See Brooke's comparison, showing how Locke and Rousseau are both "defenders of legislative supremacy in politics" but not in the "uncomplicated" way in which this is often presented ("*Locke en particulier*," 78–81). See also Miller, *Dreamer of Democracy*, and Wokler, "The Enlightenment and the French Revolutionary Birthpangs of Modernity," in *Rousseau, the Age of Enlightenment*, 206.

163. These solicitations are also discussed in letters cited by Gagnebin and Raymond (OC 1:1579, note 1 to p. 609), and in Conf. XII, 510/609.

164. Translation slightly modified.

165. Leigh, "Rousseau's Political Principles," 139. Leigh ends up drawing the "obvious conclusion" that "although Rousseau may have wanted changes which could be brought about only through revolution, he himself was no revolutionary" (139).

166. See Shklar, *Men and Citizens*, 5, 129, 162–64, 213–14; Hont, *Politics in Commercial Society*, 45, 68, 73, 75, 126; and, especially, Melzer, *Natural Goodness*, 261–63, 268. A slightly moderated version is defended in Blaise Bachofen, "Why Rousseau Mistrusts Revolutions: Rousseau's Paradoxical Conservatism," in *Rousseau and Revolution*, ed. Holger Ross Lauritsen and Mikkel Thorup (London: Continuum, 2011), 17–30, esp. 17–23. Whatmore presents his revision as challenging "portrayals of Rousseau as an ideological cause of the French Revolution" (*Against War and Empire*, 56). On these debates, see Jeremy Jennings, *Revolution and the Republic: A History of Political Thought in France Since the Eighteenth Century* (New York: Oxford University Press, 2011), esp. 6–9, 111–33.

167. Wokler, "Preparing the Definitive Edition of the *Correspondance de Rousseau*," in *Rousseau, the Age of Enlightenment*, 138f.

168. "Two Concepts of Liberty," in *Rousseau, the Age of Enlightenment*, 160, 183, and 329n11; see also his *A Very Short Introduction*, 21f. We return to the letter to Wartensleben with note 215 below.

169. *The Sleeping Sovereign*, 203.

170. Thomas Bentley, *Journal of a Visit to Paris, 1776*, ed. Peter France (Sussex: University of Sussex Library, 1977), 60.

171. Ibid., 60–61, with Peter France's Introduction, 15–17.

172. *Natural Goodness*, 270.

173. See also *Mountain* VII, 251–52/830–32. This debate about the tribunes had also taken place in the *Social Contract*, where Rousseau may be replying to Burlamaqui (see SC III.10, 106–7n/421–22n, and IV.5, with Rosenblatt, *Rousseau and Geneva*, 251–52).

174. Also noted by Miller: "The danger here is not intemperate lawmaking and constant turmoil, as patricians like Tronchin pretend" (*Dreamer of Democracy*, 90). Similarly, "Freedom . . . sometimes even warrants enduring a little instability" (87).

175. Cf. *Mountain* VIII, 270/852: "It is sometimes firm, it is never seditious."

176. On weighing peace against liberty, see also *Mountain* VII, 249/828, and VIII, 267, 269/849f, 852.

177. See SC III.9, 106n/420n for a paraphrase of Machiavelli, *Florentine Histories*, Preface. See also the "tranquility of death" in the third paragraph of the note responding to Bayle (E IV, 312n/633n), and the "tempestuous freedom" of "barbarous man" (DOI II, 177/181). The idea is still suggested in the later *Poland* (I, 178/954f, cf. III, 188/965: "divisions, factions, quarrels"). Jean Fabre quotes several related passages (OC 3:1744, note 1 to p. 955).

178. *Rousseau and Geneva*, 253, adding SC I.4, 45/355: "Life is also tranquil in dungeons."

179. See *Discourses on Livy*, trans. Harvey C. Mansfield and Nathan Tarcov (Chicago: University of Chicago Press, 1996), I.4–6 and passim.

180. *Discourses Concerning Government* (1698), ed. Thomas G. West (Indianapolis: Liberty Fund, 1996), II.24, 217–29. In Rousseau's edition, this is "*les séditions, les troubles, et les guerres*": *Discours sur le gouvernement*, 3 vols., trans. P. A. Samson (La Haye: Louïs and Henri van Dole, 1702), e.g., 2:156, 54. See also II.14.

181. *Discourses Concerning Government* II.26, 259.

182. Ibid., 260f.

183. *First Treatise*, §33; cf. the effects of securing impartial "laws of liberty," also "bye the bye" [*sic*]: *Second Treatise*, §42.

184. *Spirit of the Laws* V.14, 61. See also IV.3, VIII.21, XI.5, XIII.2, and *Persian Letters*, nos. 19, 80, and 102. Montesquieu prominently appeals to China here (see, esp., *Spirit of the Laws*, VIII.21). Tocqueville makes similar psychological observations on China (see *Democracy in America*, I 1.5, 154n50, and II 1.10, 786).

185. Letter to Wartensleben, 27 October 1766, CC 30:384–89, at 385, with Leigh CC 30:388 note a.

186. Locke, although different from Rousseau on the question of individual slaves captured in a just war (*Second Treatise*, §§23–24, 172, 178–79), provides a similar voluntarist defense of the rights of conquered peoples (ch. 16, esp. §§175, 192, 196). Montesquieu is close to Rousseau on the question of conquest and slavery (*Spirit of the Laws*, XV.1–9, esp. 2), but he is apparently less voluntarist about subjugated peoples (X.3–4).

187. *Discourses Concerning Government*, III.36, 519–20.

188. Ibid., II.24, 228 / *Discours sur le gouvernement*, 2:81–82.

189. *Second Treatise*, §16.

190. Ibid., §228; see also §176. Cf. Martin Luther King Jr., "Letter from Birmingham City Jail" (1963), in *A Testament of Hope: The Essential Writings and Speeches of Martin Luther King, Jr.*, ed. James Melvin Washington (New York: Harper Collins, 1991), 289–302, at 295.

191. Locke, *Second Treatise*, chs. 2–3, and 17–19. For "extrajudicial" force to punish transgressors of the law, potentially including governing officials, see Sidney, *Discourses Concerning Government*, II.24, 226–27, and from III.36: "All disputes about right do naturally end in force when justice is denied" (524 / *Discours sur le gouvernement*, 3:311).

192. See Kirk, "Genevan Republicanism," 284–87, 304, and with note 195 below.

193. "Genevan Republicanism," 284; see also Rosenblatt, *Rousseau and Geneva*, 146–49.

194. The next paragraph describes another recourse to arms and the intervention of neighboring powers, leading to the Mediation of 1738 (*Mountain* IX, 294/883).

195. In Kirk's discussion of the outbreaks of violence in 1734–1738, the bourgeois militias prevail, while violence remains comparatively low—in the main episode, a dozen people are killed ("Genevan Republicanism," 284–86; cf. Whatmore, *Against War and Empire*, 40, and, on the violence of 1780–1782, Kirk, "Genevan Republicanism," 303–4).

196. This is also referred to as "the Christian maxim," apparently alluding to Romans, ch. 13 (*Mountain* VIII, 262n/843n).

197. See Locke, *Second Treatise*, §230.

198. *Leviathan*, ch. 20, [19], see also ch. 18, [20]. This is similar to the analysis of "seditious opinions" in *On the Citizen*, ch. XII, although cf. XIII.1–2.

199. Although not one of Rousseau's authorities, the position is essentially that of Thomas Aquinas (*Summa theologiae* II–II 42.2 ad 3).

200. Cf. King, "Letter from Birmingham City Jail," 297. Antoine Hatzenberger emphasizes this empirical inevitability of revolution under some circumstances, concluding that, "rather than a revolutionary proper, Rousseau would be more of a *revolutionist*" ("Rousseau and the Revolutions of the Earth: Remarks on a Natural Metaphor," in *Rousseau and Revolution*, ed. Lauritsen and Thorup, 152–60, at 155).

201. See, similarly, *Mountain* VI, 232/808.

202. Obs. 51/56; LR 84f/95; PN 102–4/971–72. More generally, there is a possibility of rebirth amid violent revolutions, but this is rare, and apparently not possible for advanced states (see SC II.8). Cf. Hill, "Enlightened 'Savages,'" 477, 477n69, and Rousseau, "History of the Government of Geneva" (written ca. December 1763–July 1764), CW 9:122 / OC 5:522.

203. See DOI Dedication, 115/113; cf. "Judgment of the Plan for Perpetual Peace," CW 11:60 / OC 3:600; "Fragment," CW 11:49 / OC 3:590; and *Poland* I, 178f/955, VI, 196f/974.

204. *Natural Goodness*, 263; see 262–71.

205. "Two Concepts of Liberty," in *Rousseau, the Age of Enlightenment*, 183. Cf. Wokler with notes 167–68 above.

206. Cf. Mély, who presents evidence that Rousseau wrote repeatedly to the powers who would be responsible for any possible mediation and held out some slight hope that they might intervene justly (*Un intellectuel en rupture*, 186–87, 201–4; for the hope, see also *Mountain* IX, 302/892).

207. Note, however, that the citizens have the right to refuse the syndics (magistrates) proposed to them by the Small Council, but they no longer have selection rights over the Small Council itself (see *Mountain* VII, 246–47, 254f/824–25, 835; IX, 283f/870).

208. Whatmore, *Against War and Empire*, 95.

209. Ibid.

210. "Rousseau's Political Principles," 139.

211. Ibid., 138f.

212. See below, Chapter 5, and Section 6.3, esp. with note 137.

213. Leigh also seems to imply a shift here. After describing why the cause seemed hopeless (with note 211 above), he continues: "In the end, after a long silence, Rousseau took it upon himself to urge peace at any price" ("Rousseau's Political Principles," 139). See his letter to Moultou of 7 March 1768 (CC 35:179–82, discussed above, with note 90).

214. Discussed with note 168 above.

215. CC 30:384–89, at 385, emphases added.

216. Letter to François-Henri d'Ivernois, 7 February 1767, CC 32:116–19, at 116f.

217. Ibid., 117.

218. Letter to d'Ivernois, 6 April 1767, CC 33:11–12, at 12, partially quoted in Leigh, "Rousseau's Political Principles," 139n9.

219. See the quotations above, with notes 144–46.

220. See the sources cited above, Chapter 3, note 46.

221. On the Christianity of the Gospel, see SC IV.8, 147–49/465–67, esp. 148/466; cf. *Mountain* I, 147–49/704–6. This is a Machiavellian critique (see, especially, *Discourses on Livy*, Preface, 6, II.2, 131–32). It is developed in terms close to Rousseau's by Pierre Bayle, whose account is criticized by Montesquieu (*Various Thoughts on the Occasion of a Comet*, trans. Robert C. Bartlett [Albany: State University of New York Press, 2000], §141; Montesquieu, *Spirit of the Laws*, XXIV.6). Rosenblatt offers a revisionist interpretation of the anti-quietist polemic in the *Social Contract*: He is not faulting Christianity, as such, but only the patriciate's dishonest version of it (see *Rousseau and Geneva*, 263–64, 273–76).

222. Cf. "the most absolute quietism" in "Letter to Philopolis," EPW 226 / OC 3:233f.

223. Translation modified, emphasis added. A slightly stronger claim is in a letter of 1768: "Authority and liberty in a continual conflict, carry their quarrels to the point of civil war: I have seen your citizens slit each other's throats within your walls" (letter to d'Ivernois, 9 February, CC 35:100–7, at 101). This refers to the "*combat du perron*" (combat of the steps) of 21 August 1737 (Leigh, CC 35:107 note c).

224. Following Scholar, 211, modified.

225. Translation modified. He alludes to this decision in Conf. V, as a time he "kept this oath on a delicate occasion" (181/216).

226. Although all of the First Part was sketched by October 1765 (below, Chapter 5, note 49), it appears that Book V was not substantially begun until August 1766, with all of the first six books completed by the end of 1767 (cf. Trousson, Introduction to *Les Confessions*, 15–17; Gagnebin and Raymond, OC 1:1316, note 2 to p. 179; and Conf. V, 151/179). Book XII was written around summer 1770 (below, Chapter 6, note 114).

227. A poem he wrote in 1739 alludes to these civic disturbances, faulting the "blind citizens" for disturbing repose and not accepting the benefactions of the French monarch ("The Orchard of Madame de Warens," CW 12:8f / OC 2:1129). This is described by Rosenblatt as part of Rousseau's "anti-Genevan" phase (cf. above, Chapter 2, note 16).

228. OC 3:1698, variant e to p. 851.

229. Following note 190 above.

230. By contrast, Jacques Voisine endorses the account of John S. Spink, that Rousseau must have suppressed this passage "because of the boldness of the alternative proposed in the penultimate phrase (coming close to an analogous passage in the *Social Contract*)" (*Les Confessions*, ed. Voisine, 248–49n1, citing Spink, *Jean-Jacques Rousseau et Genève* [Paris: Boivin, 1934], 33). (The phrase in question seems to be the one on shedding enemy blood.) Although others have linked this draft of the *Mountain* with the *Confessions* accounts, I know of no other attempt to explain this difference. See Trousson, *Les Confessions*, 316n1, and Melzer, *Natural Goodness*, 263n13.

231. The modern language of political left and right do not emerge until the French Revolution, but cf. Leigh on "*la 'gauche' genevoise*" ("*Avertissement*," CC 16:xxviii).

232. According to Mély, Rousseau was now called "seditious" beyond the governmental and ecclesiastical circles (*Un intellectuel en rupture*, 209). Parisian salon opinion about the *Mountain* was overwhelmingly negative, especially after reports of the troubles in Geneva that followed the 6 January 1765 elections (211–14). But several others outside Paris expressed praise for the work (213).

233. *Sentiment of the Citizens*, CW 12:49 / CC 23:382, translation modified. For this anonymous pamphlet, see below, Chapter 5, notes 7–15.

234. On Diderot's general sympathies for the persecuted philosopher, see Wilson, *Diderot*, 445–46, 692. On his attempts to reconcile with Rousseau around this time, see Wilson, *Diderot*, 500–502; Fabre, "Deux frères ennemis," 191–93; and Trousson, *Jean-Jacques Rousseau*, 598.

235. Cf. the similar list in Plato, *Gorgias*, 515c–19b.

236. Letter to Rousseau, 27 August 1762, CC 12:252–55, at 253, with Leigh, 255 note f. This account is based on Plutarch, *Themistocles*, [22–32], esp. [31] in *Greek Lives*. By contrast, according to Thucydides (I.138), Themistocles died of illness rather than poison (discussed in Philip Stadter, *Greek Lives*, 404, note to p. 110).

237. Reported by Grimm in the *Correspondance littéraire, philosophique et critique*, 1 January 1765 (cited here from Raymond Trousson, *Jean-Jacques Rousseau jugé par ses contemporains* [Paris: Honoré Champion, 2000], 394).

238. Letter to Rousseau, 11 February 1765, CC 23:355–56, at 355 (also discussed in Cranston, *The Solitary Self*, 103f, and Trousson, *Jean-Jacques Rousseau*, 589). Our characterization of Mably follows Cranston, 103. Mably is speaking in the past tense because he is defending claims made in a letter of 11 January (the 11 February letter is, in fact, the reply, which Rousseau claims Mably never made: Conf. XII, 520/621; cf. Gagnebin and Raymond, OC 1:1588, note 5 to p. 621, and Leigh, CC 23:292). The 11 January letter mentions "attacks" on the government of Geneva, comparing Rousseau with Herostratus and the Gracchi (CC 23:87–88, at 87).

239. Letter to Mme de Boufflers, ca. January–February 1765, in *Letters of David Hume*, 1:493–94, at 493; also discussed in Cranston, *The Solitary Self*, 101, and Trousson, *Jean-Jacques Rousseau*, 590.

240. For the general omission, see above, note 109.

241. Discussed in the introduction to Chapter 3 above.

242. Chapter 3 above, esp. Section 3.1.

243. *The Solitary Self*, 83. The comment on Paul is *Mountain* I, 146/702f; see also, on Calvin, II, 156, 165n/715, 726n. See above, Chapter 2, note 134, on his earlier element of (misplaced) confidence.

244. "Fiction, or Allegorical Fragment on Revelation" (written ca. 1756–1757), CW 12:172 / OC 4:1052f; "Discourse on Heroic Virtue," EPW 316 / OC 2:1274; *Letter to Franquières*, 15 January 1769; LPW 284 / OC 4:1146. Cf. E SV 307f/626, DPE 16/255, and DSA I, 13/14: "The only precept" he left to his disciples, "the example and the memory of his virtue."

245. *Correspondance littéraire, philosophique et critique*, 15 January 1765, in *Jean-Jacques Rousseau: Mémoire de la critique*, ed. Raymond Trousson (Paris: Presses de l'Université de Paris-Sorbonne, 2000), 330.

246. Trousson, *Jean-Jacques Rousseau*, 558. Apparently, this anticipation was based on an element of philosophical similarity regarding religion. Voltaire would write that Rousseau "has done only one good thing in his life, this is his *Savoyard Vicar*, and this *Vicar* has rendered him miserable for the rest of his days" (letter to d'Alembert, 16 July [1764], CC 20:291–92, at 291).

CHAPTER 5

1. This is a passage that Grimm had in mind in faulting the self-regard of Rousseau (above, Chapter 4, with note 245).

2. Letter to Duchesne, 27 May 1764, CC 20:101–5, at 102. See also Damrosch, *Restless Genius*, 391, and Voltaire to d'Alembert, 16 July [1764], CC 20:291–92, at 291.

3. See Kelly's excellent discussion of this episode in this connection (*Rousseau as Author*, 8–12).

4. Quoting Leigh, "Jean-Jacques Rousseau," 556.

5. Leigh, review of *Voltaire's Correspondence*, vols. 35–40, ed. Theodore Besterman, *Modern Language Review* 57.4 [1962]: 606–12, at 609. Cf. Conf. X, 452/540. See Voltaire's immediate responses, quoted in Gagnebin and Raymond, OC 1:1535–36, note 1 to p. 540, and his 1761 (anonymous) polemic against *Julie* and its author, discussed in Cranston, *The Noble Savage*, 278.

6. Published 27 December 1764, and received by Rousseau on 31 December (*Letters Written from the Mountain* had been published on 18 December). Good overviews of the quarrel surrounding the pamphlet are in Zaretsky and Scott, *The Philosophers' Quarrel*, 67–71; Damrosch, *Restless Genius*, 390–92; Cranston, *The Solitary Self*, 102–5; and Trousson, *Jean-Jacques Rousseau*, 584–86. The pamphlet was also meant to undermine Rousseau's Genevan cause (Leigh, "Jean-Jacques Rousseau," 552). See the above discussions of the pamphlet itself (Chapter 1, note 25) and of Rousseau's annotated response to it (Chapter 1, with note 27).

7. Cranston, *The Solitary Self*, 102–3; Damrosch, *Restless Genius*, 391; cf. Whatmore, *Against War and Empire*, 63. See also Conf. XII, 529–31/632–34. For Rousseau's ironic confidence that it is easy to see Voltaire's blows as they come, see the letter to Lenieps, 10 February 1765, CC 23:338–43, at 340.

8. In signed testimony in the letter from Jacob Vernes to Pierre-Alexandre Du Peyrou, 9 January 1790, CC 23:384–85, at 384. See also Damrosch, *Restless Genius*, 391–92.

9. "The Enlightenment Hostilities of Voltaire and Rousseau," in *Rousseau, the Age of Enlightenment*, 81.

10. *Sentiment of the Citizens*, CW 12:45–46 / CC 23:378–79, translation modified.

11. Ibid., 46/379, translation modified.

12. Ibid., 48f/381f. In his annotated response, Rousseau insists on the "painful sacrifices" he has made "not to disturb the peace of my fatherland" (see *Sentiment of the Citizens*, 48, note d/382n).

13. Translation modified. Being dressed as a "*saltimbanque*" (also a charlatan or "snake-oil salesman") refers to the Armenian caftan, which he began wearing in late 1762 to help treat his urinary condition (cf. Cranston, *The Noble Savage*, 339). It is portrayed in a well-known painting by Allan Ramsay, which Rousseau came to see as driven by the conspiracy, making him look like "a petty impostor, a petty liar, a petty swindler [*un petit escroc*], a denizen of taverns and low places" (see RJJ II, 94/782; Damrosch, *Restless Genius*, 423; and Mankin, "Authority, Success, and the Philosopher," 188–92).

14. *Sentiment of the Citizens*, 47f/380f, translation modified.

15. For the distortions, see Leigh, "Jean-Jacques Rousseau," 551, and Wokler, "The Enlightenment Hostilities," 81.

16. Wokler, "The Enlightenment Hostilities," 87.

17. "On Rousseau's Illness," in *Transparency and Obstruction*, 374; see 372–75.

18. See Damrosch, *Restless Genius*, 392–97, and Cranston, *The Solitary Self*, 129–33. See Rousseau's parody of the kind of religious fanaticism that gave rise to the stoning: "The Vision of Pierre of the Mountain, Called the Seer" (published September 1765; CW 9:307–14 / OC 2:1232–38). We return to the Island of Saint-Pierre in the introduction to Chapter 6.

19. *The Solitary Self*, 103; see also xii, 104, 183.

20. *Against War and Empire*, 63. Another commonly observed stage of mental decline begins with the English exile (1766–1767, discussed below, Chapter 6, with notes 110–12).

21. An election on 7 February (discussed above, Chapter 4, with note 135).

22. Letter to Lenieps, 10 February 1765, CC 23:338–43, at 339 (also discussed in Cranston, *The Solitary Self*, 109). This resolution was almost broken in mid-February 1765, when he began writing a long letter to an opposition leader, Jacques Vieusseux, "to try one last time to mobilize opinion" (Trousson, *Jean-Jacques Rousseau*, 590).

23. CC 23:339, consulting Damrosch's translation: *Restless Genius*, 389.

24. Letter to François-Henri d'Ivernois, 22 February 1765, CC 24:74–75, at 74 (also discussed in Whatmore, *Against War and Empire*, 63).

25. Letter to Jean-André and Guillaume-Antoine Deluc, 24 February 1765, CC 24:87–88, at 87 (consulting Cranston's translation: *The Solitary Self*, 109).

26. The major exception seems to be several letters written to the remonstrators in February–March 1768, counseling peace during their constitutional crisis (discussed in Sections 4.4 and 4.6 above).

27. Letter to Duclos, 13 January 1765, CC 23:99–100.

28. See Leigh's argument against Jean Guéhenno's view that "it was the shock of reading this pamphlet which made Rousseau decide to write his *Confessions*" ("Jean-Jacques Rousseau," 552). Gagnebin and Raymond cite Voltaire's pamphlet and the crisis of the end of 1761 as the usual views of the origins of the *Confessions*, before explaining that this "forgets a bit," as there is a much longer prehistory (Introduction to *Les Confessions*, OC 1:xvi).

29. See CC 9:368–70, at 368; Leigh CC 9:360 note e; Gagnebin and Raymond, OC 1:1524–25, note 3 to p. 516; Perrin, "Lire *Les Confessions*," 147, 150–51; and cf. Conf. X, 433/516. For the collecting of documents to this purpose while in Montmorency, see Conf. XI, 487/582, and XII, 508/607.

30. See Conf. XI, 469/560f, XII, 521/622, and Gagnebin and Raymond, OC 1:1525, note 3 to p. 516. On retirement and leisurely writing, see above, Chapter 2, note 1, and the discussion that follows.

31. For oscillations between writing a "life" and a "portrait"—the *Malesherbes* is an outstanding example of the latter—see Gagnebin and Raymond, OC 1:xxii–xxiii, xxxii.

32. See Conf. X, 433/517; letter to Moultou, 20 January 1763, CC 15:70–73, at 70; and letter to Rey, 27 April 1765, CC 25:188–90, at 189. For the financial considerations, see the letter to Rey, 18 March 1765, CC 24:234–39, at 235–36.

33. CC 25:189.

34. Starobinski, "Rousseau and the Search for Origins," in *Transparency and Obstruction*, 274 (see also above, Chapter 2, note 43); Cranston, *The Solitary Self*, xii.

35. Damrosch, *Restless Genius*, 253.

36. 26 October 1762, CC 13:249–50, at 249.

37. CC 13:250 note a.

38. See *Malesherbes* 572/1130, with Leigh, CC 10:8a, and Jacques Voisine, "*Quatre Lettres à M. le Président de Malesherbes*," in *Dictionnaire*, 779a. The subtitle of the Neuchâtel Preamble is similar (CW 5:585 / OC 1:1148).

39. Letter to Marc-Michel Rey, 16 November 1762, CC 14:54–56, at 55 (also discussed in Kelly, Introduction to CW 5:xviii–xix).

40. CC 14:55, with Leigh, 56 note e.

41. Letter to Duchesne, 20 January 1763, CC 15:73–75, at 75.

42. OC 1:xxii; cf. his myth of "earthly paradise," xlii.

43. Kelly, "Rousseau's *Confessions*," 303, 305; see also 314, and *Beaumont* 53/967f.

44. Letter to Moultou, 20 January 1763, CC 15:70–73, at 70 (also discussed in Gagnebin and Raymond, OC 1:xxii).

45. See Gagnebin and Raymond, OC 1:xxii–xxiv.

46. Letter to Duclos, 13 January 1765, CC 23:99–100, at 99. The "false friends" refers to those who passed on the secret about his children (here mentioning *la Dame d'Épinay*; see above, Chapter 1, note 25). This letter to Duclos is also discussed in Trousson, *Jean-Jacques Rousseau*, 586.

47. 18 March 1765, CC 24:235–36.

48. Letter to Rey, 27 April 1765, CC 25:189 (also discussed in Kelly, Introduction to CW 5:xix).

49. See the letter to Du Peyrou, entrusting him with a copy of the manuscript (ca. 23 October 1765, CC 27:165–66): "It would be impossible for anyone except myself to decipher this draft which contains the history of my youth up to my departure for Paris in 1741" (165, following Cranston's translation, *The Solitary Self*, 139). Leigh confirms this as demonstrating that by the date of the letter, Rousseau "had sketched out all the first part of his autobiography" (CC 166, note a).

50. Cranston, *The Solitary Self*, 108. Gagnebin and Raymond similarly argue that, despite the considerable efforts made through 1764, the "decisive event" of *The Sentiment of the Citizens* made him throw himself into the work (OC 1:xxiii–xxiv).

51. For the completion of the First Part of the *Confessions*, see below, Chapter 6, with notes 136–47. For the writing of the Second Part, see below, Chapter 6, with notes 113–14.

52. Discussed above, Chapter 3, with notes 72–73.

53. Cf. Perrin, *Politique du renonçant*, 314n28; Gourevitch, LPW 310; Cranston, *The Solitary Self*, 177; and below, Chapter 6, with notes 148–50. The writings on botany are a more leisurely activity, apparently more so than the writing of the memoirs (cf. Conf. XII, 538f/643, and above, Chapter 2, notes 1–3). Cf. the *Dictionary of Music* (1767), discussed above, Chapter 2, with note 4.

54. For the various purposes of the autobiographies, including self-knowledge and self-justification, see France, *Rousseau: Confessions*, 24. For reminiscence versus confessions, see Cranston, *The Solitary Self*, 108.

55. OC 1:xxiv–xxv; cf. xliv.

56. Introduction to *Les Confessions*, 38.

57. Following Scholar, 505, modified. This is supported by the contemporary "My Portrait" (quoted following note 29 above).

58. Following Scholar, 505. This is a case where an argument in the Neuchâtel Preamble (CW 5:586 / OC 1:1149f), but missing from the definitive Preamble, found its way into the main text of the *Confessions*.

59. Letter to Moultou, 20 January 1763, CC 15:70.

60. Following the translation in Kelly, CW 5:599n3, from Persius, *Satires*, III.30. See also RJJ II, 190/905.

61. Letter to Rey, 27 April 1765, CC 25:189.

62. Letter to Duclos, 13 January 1765, CC 23:100 (also partially quoted in Cranston, *The Solitary Self*, 107f, and Damrosch, *Restless Genius*, 392).

CHAPTER 6

1. Among several parallels noted by Raymond (OC 1:1799–1800), see, esp., *Julie* IV.10, 383f/466f, and DOI I, 143/144. See also Gourevitch, EPW 358, note to I [21], and Starobinski's links between the depiction of adult humans in the *Discourse* and Buffon's depictions of animals and human infants (OC 3:1321, note 3 to p. 144).

2. See the sources cited above, Introduction, note 97.

3. Quotation from Kelly and Masters, Introduction to CW 1:xiii. See also Philippe Lejeune, *On Autobiography*, ed. Paul John Eakin, trans. Katherine Leary (Minneapolis: University of Minnesota Press, 1989), 48–50.

4. Introduction to *The Cambridge Companion to Rousseau*, 6.

5. Translation modified.

6. Translation slightly modified.

7. For Rousseau's regrets about his final solitary condition, see Todorov, *Frail Happiness*, 31–32, 57–58, and *Imperfect Garden*, 97–105; Neuhouser, *Rousseau's Theodicy of Self-Love*, 85–86; and, more tentatively, Zaretsky and Scott, *The Philosophers' Quarrel*, 238n37. Todorov also appeals to this passage in his critique of Allan Bloom ("Professors of Desire," *New Republic*, October 4, 1993, 38–43, at 40c). See also the arguments against solitude as the most fundamental ideal in Joseph Reisert, "Authenticity, Justice, and Virtue in Taylor and Rousseau," *Polity* 33.2 (2000): 305–30, at 313–14, 321–25, 330; Williams, "The Platonic Soul of the *Reveries*," 96–97, 113–14, 123; and McLendon, *The Psychology of Inequality*, 123. Gauthier appeals to this passage not in support of a moralistic Rousseau but one in search of loving union (*The Sentiment of Existence*, 165, 172).

8. Translation modified. In the account of this island in the *Confessions*, he provides one of his most sweeping claims against having further commerce with mortals (Conf. XII, 534f/638, quoted with note 24 below). Yet he also claims that assisting in "one of those little rural tasks, the harvesting of vegetables and fruits," recalled "the sweet life I had led in Les Charmettes" (539f/644, following Scholar, 630). Finally, he favorably mentions the gatherings for dances (534/637).

9. "*Dialogues* and *Rêveries*," 522–24, 528n20, citing Rev. V, 70/1048. John Scott, who may be described as a moderate Straussian, has also questioned whether *Reveries* V in fact depicts the optimal and sustained wholeness that it is often taken to (see "Rousseau's Quixotic Quest in the *Rêveries du promeneur solitaire*," in *The Nature of Rousseau's* Rêveries, ed. John C. O'Neal [Oxford: Voltaire Foundation, 2008], 139–52, at 145–47).

10. This theme is also helpfully explored, especially regarding moral and political idealism, throughout Miller, *Dreamer of Democracy*, esp. ch. 1.

11. See the many quotations from works and letters in Gagnebin and Raymond, OC 1:1241–42, note 1 to p. 13, as well as Cranston, *The Noble Savage*, 106, 231, 327, and *The Solitary Self*, 65–66, cf. 152.

12. Following Scholar, 521. See, similarly, "My Portrait" (ca. 1758–1762), no. 18, CW 12:39 / OC 1:1124. On solitude as a happy yet second choice, see France, *Rousseau: Confessions*, 77.

13. On masturbation, see Conf. III, 91/109; cf. E IV, 334/663, and *Julie* II.15, 194–95/236–37. On supplements and compensation in general, see, e.g., Starobinski, *Transparency and Obstruction*, 263–65, and "Rousseau and the Peril of Reflection," 32–33.

14. See Conf. VII, 278–79/331–33; cf. IX, 347–50/413–16, and the discussion above, Chapter 1, note 190. Several relevant passages are discussed in Todorov, *Imperfect Garden*, 97–105, esp. 97, and *Frail Happiness*, ch. 3, esp. 31–32.

15. See Conf. VII, 278–79/331–33, and IX, 347–50/413–16; see also the discussion above, Chapter 1, note 195.

16. Cf. *Julie* II.27, 250/306; Conf. IX, 354/421; and E V, 408f/767f, quoted above, Chapter 1, with note 133.

17. Cranston, *Jean-Jacques*, 343.

18. Cranston, *The Noble Savage*, 199, 162, 206, cf. 293.

19. Notes for the *Reveries*, no. 12, CW 12:52 / OC 1:1168; also discussed in Todorov, *Frail Happiness*, 37–38. See also the *Reveries* on turning to the affection of animals since it has been denied him by humans (IX, 126/1089, quoted with Chapter 1, note 125 above).

20. SC I.7, 53/364; cf. DPE 9/248. For the autobiographical extension, see Fiona Miller, "Forced into Freedom: Rousseau's Strange Self-Portrait in the *Rêveries*," in *The Nature of Rousseau's* Rêveries, ed. O'Neal, 129–38.

21. See above, Section 2.1, and below, Section 2 of the Conclusion.

22. *Rousseau's Exemplary Life*, 203–4.

23. Ibid., 50.

24. Following Scholar, 625.

25. Ibid., 585f. Cf. 519/620.

26. See above, Chapter 2, note 19.

27. Emphasis added. For the *Confessions*, see note 8 above.

28. Letter to Rousseau, 30 August 1755, CW 3:102 / CC 3:156–62, at 157.

29. Voltaire to d'Alembert, 4 May 1759, as translated in Cranston, *The Noble Savage*, 165. See, similarly, 278, and Cranston, *The Solitary Self*, 7. For later receptions of Rousseau linking him with Diogenes the Cynic, including favorable ones of the Cynics as "enthusiasts of virtue," see Michael Sonenscher, *Sans-Culottes: An Eighteenth-Century Emblem in the French Revolution* (Princeton: Princeton University Press, 2008), 21–28, and ch. 3.

30. Fabre, "Deux frères ennemis," 165.

31. For overviews of this quarrel, see Cranston, *The Noble Savage*, 47–53; Damrosch, *Restless Genius*, 288–94; and Wilson, *Diderot*, 254–59.

32. Translation modified.

33. Cf., e.g., Chouillet and Chouillet, in *Le Fils naturel*, 62n45; Wilson, *Diderot*, 255; and Fabre, "Deux frères ennemis," 180.

34. *Le fils naturel*, IV.3, 61. See, however, his immediately preceding remarks on how friendship had delivered him in the past.

35. *Le fils naturel*, IV.3, 61f. On the ruin of happiness through "the awareness of a bad action," see also V.3, 74. For comment, see Damrosch, *Restless Genius*, 292, and McLendon, *The Psychology of Inequality*, 46.

36. See, especially, Diderot's letter of 10 March 1757, CC 4:168–70, at 169 (translated in Cranston, *The Noble Savage*, 47), and Conf. IX, 382/455.

37. *Diderot*, 259; on the concern about Thérèse's mother, see Cranston, *The Noble Savage*, 48–52.

38. Wilson, *Diderot*, 255.

39. "Un questionnement radical de la civilité des Lumières: La question de l'amitié dans la correspondance de Rousseau durant la crise des années 1757–1758," in *Jean-Jacques Rousseau en 2012*, ed. Michael O'Dea (Oxford: Voltaire Foundation, 2012), 9–28, at 10.

40. LdA 7/255f/7, with the note. See Cranston for the shock of Rousseau's friends upon reading the denunciation: Saint-Lambert (*The Noble Savage*, 141), Deleyre (144), and Diderot himself (151).

41. For *le monde* as high society and worldly sociability, see Antoine Lilti, *The World of the Salons: Sociability and Worldliness in Eighteenth-Century Paris*, trans. Lydia G. Cochrane (New York: Oxford University Press, 2015), e.g., 4–9.

42. Tronchin to Rousseau, 4 April 1759, CC 6:54–56, at 54 (following Cranston's translation: *The Noble Savage*, 163).

43. CC 6:54.

44. Jean-Daniel Candaux, "Théodore Tronchin," in *Dictionnaire*, 894b.

45. See Cranston, *The Noble Savage*, 163–65; for their later hostilities, see Candaux, "Théodore Tronchin," 895a.

46. Above, Chapter 1, note 25.

47. See E II, 105n/340–41n; Conf. IX, 382–87/455–61, esp. 382/455; and RJJ II, 99–100/788–89. In the long *Confessions* passage discussing the episode, the only direct response made in his present voice is the one concerning non-harm (382/455), although other responses also emerge in the lengthy quotations from letters that follow.

48. See Conf. I, 34f/41; V, 187f/224; VI, 189/225. See also the 1746 or 1747 poem, "*L'allée de Silvie*," at OC 2:1146; the (ca. 1758–1759?) "On the Art of Enjoying and Other Fragments," at CW 12:57 / OC 1:1173; and *Malesherbes* III, 578/1138.

49. See Baczko on the solitary person's experiences of religion, morality, and nature (*Solitude et communauté*, 232–63), and Neidleman on solitude and the search for truth (*Rousseau's Ethics of Truth*, chs. 2 and 4).

50. "Preface of a Second Letter to Bordes," EPW 107 / OC 3:103.

51. "Remarks on the *Letters on the English and the French* by Beat de Muralt," CW 12:274 / OC 2:1318.

52. For the letter of 16 March 1757 as unsent, see Leigh CC 4:180b; Rousseau to d'Épinay, [17 March 1757], CC 3:186–88, at 186; and the discussion in Cranston, *The Noble Savage*, 50–51. The summary of the letter in the *Confessions* (IX, 385/459) does not mention that it was unsent (see Gagnebin and Raymond, OC 1:1493, note 2 to p. 459). It quotes only one of the letter's nine paragraphs, omitting the offensive parts, including the thesis that "in our altercations you were always the aggressor" (to Diderot, [16 March 1757], CC 4:178–80, at 178; see, similarly, 4:183).

53. Letter to Rousseau, [14 March 1757], CC 4:172–75, at 173. The first sentence follows the translation in Conf. IX, 385/459; the second sentence is not included in the *Confessions.*

54. Since there are four liards in a sou, Rousseau is saying that giving 8 liards in Montmorency has greater moral value than 100 liards in Paris.

55. Cf. *Letter to Voltaire* (1756), EPW 234 / OC 4:1062; *Julie* Second Preface, 9, 14/14, 20; and Leigh, CC 4:180 note a.

56. Letter to Diderot, [16 March 1757], CC 4:179. The last sentence is not included in the *Confessions*; otherwise, I follow the translation in Conf. IX, 385/459.

57. Letter to d'Épinay, 13 March [1757], CC 4:171–72, at 171; cf. Cranston's translation, *The Noble Savage*, 49; see also 48–50.

58. [16 March 1757], CC 4:182–84, at 183, following Damrosch's translation: *Restless Genius*, 293. On their prospects for friendship, see also, from the unsent letter: "You have not changed? Do not flatter yourself about that. If you had always been what you are, I can only feel quite sad to believe that I would have become your friend; I am quite sure, at least, that you would never have become mine" (CC 4:178).

59. Cf. Damrosch, *Restless Genius*, 291.

60. *The World of the Salons*, 121.

61. See ibid., 121–22.

62. I.125, 1103, modifying the translation in Lilti, *The World of the Salons*, 122.

63. *Essai sur les règnes*, II.5, 1118. According to Laurent Versini, Rousseau is "evidently" in mind here: 1118n1.

64. See LdA 36–45/277–83f/34–42. For a much richer discussion of this challenging passage, as well as of Molière's play itself, see Grant, *Hypocrisy and Integrity*, ch. 3, esp. 69–78.

65. See *The Misanthrope*, in *The Misanthrope, Tartuffe, and Other Plays*, ed. and trans. Maya Slater (New York: Oxford University Press, 2001), esp. I.1, 12, V.1, and V.4, 272–73; cf. III.3.

66. Translation modified. Alceste's "dominant passion" is "a violent hatred of vice, born from an ardent love of virtue and soured by the continual spectacle of men's viciousness" (LdA 39/279/36).

67. See LdA 39–45/279–83/33–41, and, esp., 39/279/36 and 41f/281/38, which point to their hypocritical egotism and disregard for the hungry.

68. The Heraclitus approach is clear in the account of disgust and pity for human vice in *Emile* (IV, 236–37, 244, 265/525–26, 535–36, 564). Rousseau thus departs from Seneca, who invokes these predecessors and recommends seeing "the vices of the mob" as ludicrous rather than hateful (*On the Tranquility of the Mind*, XV, in *Dialogues and Essays*, 135; this essay is cited in E V, 466/848).

69. Malesherbes to Rousseau, 25 December 1761, CC 9:354–57, at 355.

70. Letter to Tronchin, 28 April 1758, CC 6:77–79, at 78, modifying the partial translation in Cranston, *The Noble Savage*, 163; see also 164.

71. CC 6:79 note d; for Marion, see above, Chapter 1, with note 161.

72. Translation modified. This paragraph goes on to discuss civic duties (see also above, Chapter 3, following note 50). Perrin also marks this passage as an amplification of the defense made in the unsent letter to Diderot (*Politique du renonçant*, 221, 330n1). For grateful recollections by the country people of Montmorency about Rousseau's generosity and advocacy, see Damrosch, *Restless Genius*, 309.

73. Rev. VI, 74–78/1050–54, discussed following note 158 below.

74. Following Scholar, 611, modified. See also, in discussing his earlier plans for retirement, his intention to go with Thérèse to "live together in the depths of some province . . . continuing to do all the good I could around me" (Conf. XI, 469/560f). Similar language is in X, 442/527 (quoted above, Chapter 2, with note 99).

75. Letter to Jean Sarasin, 25 September 1762, as translated in Cranston, *The Solitary Self*, 42.

76. Letter to Sarasin, 15 January 1765, as described in Cranston, *The Solitary Self*, 104; cf. 110.

77. This is implied in RJJ II, 190–91/905–6 (discussed below, with note 154). See also Cranston's discussion of the time at Wootton in England: "At first, because of his strange dress and taciturn ways, he alarmed the local cottagers, but Thérèse and he were so generous to the poor that they soon became very popular figures" (*The Solitary Self*, 169; Thérèse's relations with the servants in her house were a very different matter, 170). Based on separate evidence, Robert Osmont also confirms that Rousseau visited poor people during his walks there, and the memory of him in Staffordshire was "quite enduring" (OC 1:1713, note 4 to p. 905). Cf. Damrosch, *Restless Genius*, 415, 431.

78. Shklar, "Jean-Jacques Rousseau and Equality" (1978), in *Political Thought and Political Thinkers*, ed. Stanley Hoffmann (Chicago: University of Chicago Press, 1998), 276–93, at 290.

79. *Hypocrisy and Integrity*, 169.

80. Ibid., 168f, with citations reformatted.

81. After describing an argument Julie used to challenge her lover to devote his life to the poor and humble, Shklar comments: "Rousseau was obviously questioning himself also at this point" (*Men and Citizens*, 99).

82. Above, Chapter 2, with notes 1–3.

83. See also Obs. 46/51; LR 81/91; PN 97/965; and LdA 16/262/15.

84. Translation modified.

85. Twice in the *Confessions*, Rousseau discusses retirement from economic or political ambition in connection with "the advice that Cineas once offered to Pyrrhus" (Conf. XI, 461/551; cf. V, 158/188f, E IV, 242/533, and *Poland* XI, 224/1003). See Plutarch, *Pyrrhus*, [14] in *Hellenistic Lives*, 228–29; for Plutarch's agreement, see [13], 227. For other ancient sources on retirement, see Section 3.3 above, esp. note 93. For Montaigne, see "On Solitude," *Essays*, I.39, 271–72.

86. Translation modified. His retirement seems to be partially justified by his illness and his belief that he will soon die (*Malesherbes* II, 576/1136f; cf. I, 573/1132f). Nonetheless, "If I lived another hundred years I would not write a line for the press" (IV, 581/1144).

87. See also "My Portrait," no. 2, CW 12:36 / OC 1:1120 (quoted above, Chapter 5, following note 29); Conf. IX, 339/404; and RJJ II, 101/791. His doubts about the usefulness of his writings seem to become more severe by the time of his autobiographies (see above, Chapter 2, note 44).

88. See the appeal in the same paragraph to the moral and political benefits of his writings (*Malesherbes* IV, 580/1143, partially quoted above in connection with Geneva, Chapter 3, following note 50).

89. Despite his normal aversion to earning a living as an author, Rousseau sometimes allowed an exception for living off of already published works (above, Chapter 2, with notes 100–102).

90. The same paragraph begins with the argument we have seen on the merits of serving the peasants of Montmorency (IV, 580/1143, quoted above, with note 72). See also 580f/1143. None of the argument suggests that these duties could be definitively discharged.

91. On the projected Third Part of the *Confessions*, see above, Chapter 4, note 12.

92. Of the forty volumes in the *Correspondance complète* dedicated to his lifespan, only the first ten are mainly pre-exile. Cf., on the Swiss exile, István Cseppentő, "L'Expression de l'exil dans la correspondance (1762–1765)," *Annales de la Société Jean-Jacques Rousseau* 47 (2007): 229–43, at 229f.

93. See Conf. IX, 397/473; X, 410, 454f/489, 543f; and XII, 545/650. Sophie was introduced above, Chapter 2, note 90.

94. Scholar and Kelly both follow the main Geneva manuscript here, translating *les douceurs de la liberté*. Here I follow the (later) Paris manuscript ("*les douceurs de la société*"), agreeing with Cranston that the Geneva version "must be a mistake of transcription" (*The Noble Savage*, 374n3).

95. Following Scholar, 492, slightly modified.

96. See, esp., Conf. X, 437/522; see also 446/533, and *Malesherbes* IV, 582/1145f. While his relations with Mme de Luxembourg gave rise to some anxiety, he was much at ease with her husband (see Conf. X, 447/534, and XII, 518/618).

97. Conf. XII, 515/616; see also X, 437/522, and *Malesherbes* IV, 582/1145f.

98. E.g., Lord Keith (Conf. XII, 499f/597, cf. 548/654); Isabelle d'Ivernois (503/601); Du Peyrou (504/602f); and the self-styled Baron de Sauttern (515/616).

99. Letter, 7 May 1764, in "Letters to 'Henriette,'" trans. Christopher Kelly, in *On Women, Love, and Family*, ed. Kelly and Eve Grace (Hanover: University Press of New England, 2009), 149–56, at 152 / CC 20:21.

100. Above, note 8 and with note 24.

101. Zaretsky and Scott, *The Philosophers' Quarrel*, e.g., 137.

102. For the disastrous quarrel with Hume, see Zaretsky and Scott, *The Philosophers' Quarrel*, esp. 134–69; Cranston, *The Solitary Self*, ch. 8, esp. 165–68; and Rasmussen, *The Infidel and the Professor*, ch. 7.

103. Letter to Mirabeau, 31 January 1767, CC 22:81–86, at 83. We discuss this letter more extensively below, beginning with note 129.

104. For this sense of persecution, see the letter to Mirabeau, CC 22:83, and Marcel Raymond on the *Letter to Beaumont* (OC 1:1763, note 1 to p. 995).

105. Several related passages are cited in Raymond, OC 1:1763–64, note 1 to p. 995.

106. E.g., Lilti, "The Writing of Paranoia," 53–55, 75–76; and, for "truly formidable paranoia" by 1772–1774, Wokler, *A Very Short Introduction*, 145–46. Note, however, that this is different from a global, debilitating mental disorder such as schizophrenia, which reduces speech to incoherent rambling (Lilti, "The Writing of Paranoia," 75). Related issues are discussed above, Introduction, with notes 35–36.

107. See Mostefai, *Écrivain polémique*, 98, and Lilti, "The Writing of Paranoia," 55.

108. Leigh, "Avertissement," CC 37:xxiv, describing the period from 1769–1770.

109. See Damrosch, *Restless Genius*, 452–53, 469–71, 478, and Leigh's account of his relationships with his three literary executors, the marquis de Girardin, Paul-Claude Moultou, and Pierre-Alexandre Du Peyrou (*Unsolved Problems*, 114–18).

110. "*Dialogues* and *Rêveries*," 506. Damrosch also considers this a deeper "succumbing to paranoia" than occurred during the brief Jesuit episode in 1761 (*Restless Genius*, 421; discussed above, Chapter 2, with notes 120–23). Cf. Ernest Mossner, *The Life of David Hume*, 2nd ed. (Oxford: Clarendon Press, 1980), 525.

111. *The Philosophers' Quarrel*, 153, 163, quoting letters of 26 June and 10 July 1766.

112. Ibid., 178, quoting a letter of 1 August 1766.

113. *Jean-Jacques Rousseau*, 685–86; see also Leigh, "Avertissement," CC 37:xxiii–xxiv, and Conf. XII, 509/608.

114. Introduction to *Les Confessions*, OC 1:xxviii–xxx. Hermine de Saussure argues that the writing through Book XI occurred in the fall of 1769, being completed by December. The copying was completed by February 1770 (*Rousseau et les manuscrits des Confessions*, 241–42, 224–27). Rousseau left Monquin on 10 April 1770, having either some or all of Book XII completed as well. That final book may not have been completed until that summer, when he was living in Paris (cf. Gagnebin and Raymond, OC 1:xxx, cxv; Eigeldinger and Trousson, *Rousseau au jour le jour*, 358; Jacques Voisine, "*Les Confessions*," in *Dictionnaire*, 154). A contrasting account of the origins of the Second Part is explored below, with notes 142–146.

115. The lantern image likely invokes Diogenes the Cynic (cf. DOI II, 186/192).

116. "The Writing of Paranoia," 66.

117. This hope is framed providentially and as a prayer: see RJJ 2/659, the lengthy reported quote from Jean-Jacques himself on III, 227–28/952–54, and the portion of RJJ HPW written before the episode at Notre Dame, 247/979. Cf. "Declaration Relative to Different Reprints of His Works" (written January 1774), CW 12:68 / OC 1:1187.

118. The event is dated to 24 February 1776 (RJJ HPW 248/979). It is apparently in July 1776 that he wrote the "History of the Preceding Writing" (Osmont, OC 1:1748, note 1 to p. 977). Wokler claims the book was "drafted mainly between 1772 and 1774" (*A Very Short Introduction*, 145).

119. Cf. also the prayer on RJJ 2/659.

120. For Kelly, this is the "final cure," which is anticipated in the *Confessions*. See *Rousseau's Exemplary Life*, 235.

121. See Damrosch, *Restless Genius*, 484f, and Arnaud Tripet, "*Les Reveries du Promeneur Solitaire*," in *Dictionnaire*, 808f. By contrast, Charles Butterworth suggests the attempt (in May 1776) to distribute the circular letter in Paris (CW 8:276n3).

122. For these continuities, against the approach of setting apart "the *Rêveries* as a miracle of old age in which Rousseau escapes from his obsessions and finds an entirely new voice," see O'Dea, "*Dialogues* and *Rêveries*," esp. 505–6, 520–22. See also Marcel Raymond, Introduction to *Les Rêveries du Promeneur solitaire*, OC 1:lxxxii.

123. Cf. Rev. VIII, 113/1077: "As long as I could judge men, or at least some men, favorably, the judgments they held about me could not be uninteresting to me."

124. For the severe injuries inflicted upon him by a Great Dane racing in front of a carriage, and his recovery, see Rev. II, 15–21/1004–10. He distances himself from the conspiratorial conclusions of 17f/1007, but not those of 19f/1009f.

125. For his response on his affection for children, see above, Chapter 1, with notes 122–26.

126. See Conf. XII, 503/601; RJJ II, 138, 143/838f, 845; this copying reveals the "empire of habit and taste for manual work" (133, 167n/832, 875n). For the thousands of musical pages he copied since returning to Paris in 1770, see Damrosch, *Restless Genius*, 468f, and Osmont, OC 1:1684–85, 1702. For his earlier turn to copying, see above (Chapter 2, note 100), and for earning his own bread, note 170 below.

127. Damrosch makes a similar argument about Rousseau's "*oisiveté* as constructive idleness" (see *Restless Genius*, 294). But Damrosch may overstate the case in claiming that this applies ever since the break with Diderot (*Restless Genius*, 294), thus including the final years.

128. Translation modified. The account seems at least somewhat exaggerated compared to the contemporary letters (see Cranston, *The Solitary Self*, 133–38).

129. Letter to Mirabeau, 31 January 1767, CC 22:81–86, at 83. For a useful summary of the related series of letters and their context, see Michael Sonenscher, *Before the Deluge: Public Debt, Inequality, and the Intellectual Origins of the French Revolution* (Princeton: Princeton University Press, 2007), 237–40. The 31 January letter is written in a beautiful final copy, almost in calligraphy (Leigh CC 22:84a). See also Damrosch, *Restless Genius*, 416.

130. CC 22:83.

131. Ibid.

132. Ibid.; also discussed in Neidleman, "Rousseau's Philosophy of Truth," 831. As for the "very small number" of friends, this amplifies a complaint made early in the Swiss exile: "separated by insurmountable obstacles from the few friends who remain to me" (letter to George Keith, 27 November 1762, quoted in Cseppentő, "L'Expression de l'exil," 232).

133. For interpretations of Rousseau as Epicurean, see above, Chapter 3, note 20.

134. Letter to Mirabeau, CC 22:82.

135. Letter to Hugh Blair, 25 March 1766, in *Letters of David Hume*, 2:29.

136. Letter to General Conway, [18 May 1767], CC 33:63–68, at 65 (also quoted in Gagnebin and Raymond, OC 1:xxvi). See the discussion in Zaretsky and Scott, *The Philosophers' Quarrel*, 195–97.

137. Sonenscher, *Before the Deluge*, 238, describing a letter of 9 June 1767.

138. He ended up partially reading the book sent to him (see Sonenscher, *Before the Deluge*, 238; Gourevitch, LPW 319; and the letter, 26 July 1767, LPW 270 / CC 33:238–46, at 238).

139. "The Writing of Paranoia," 75.

140. Ibid.

141. Translation modified. He was still "in my first botanical fervor" when on the island of Saint-Pierre, having learned botany with Dr. Jean-Antoine d'Ivernois in Môtiers, with his first passion for it developing in summer 1764 (Rev. V, 64f/1042; Conf. XII, 528/631; Cranston, *The Solitary Self*, 89, 106f; and Cseppentő, "L'expression de l'exil," 233). Botanizing continued in England; when he sold his books there, he kept the ones on botany (Osmont, OC 1:1687, note 5 to p. 832, appealing to a letter of 2 March 1767).

142. Letter to Rey, 23 November 1769, CC 37:176–79, at 177.

143. Ibid.

144. 15 November 1769, CC 37:174–76, at 174. He must quit the "innocent and amiable distraction" of botany (175).

145. See Gagnebin and Raymond, OC 1:xxix–xxx, and cf. Raymond, OC 1:lxxxiv.

146. The language of fulfilling the "indispensable duty" of this enterprise is also in Conf. VIII, 335/399f.

147. See Gagnebin and Raymond, OC 1:xxvi–xxviii, and the opening sentence of Conf. VII, 233/277; an account of this panic is in Damrosch, *Restless Genius*, 450–53. Here the origins of the Second Part seem duty-driven, but compare Trousson's fear-centered account (above, with note 113). In this case, paranoid fear and an elevated sense of duty seem coterminous.

148. See Damrosch, *Restless Genius*, 474–76, and Osmont, OC 1:1668, note 1 to p. 792.

149. Above, Chapter 5, note 53.

150. Cf. RJJ II, 136/836, as a "*devoir d'humanité*," and *Poland* I, 177/953: "my zeal for his fatherland."

151. Raymond provides the essential summary: Botany was taken back up in the summer of 1771 and abandoned in August 1773 (apparently in connection with work on the *Dialogues*). It resumed at the beginning of the summer of 1777, the apparent time of *Reveries* VII (see OC 1:1807–8, note 3 to p. 1060; for August 1773, see Osmont, OC 1:1686, note 3 to p. 832). From August 1771 to May 1773, he wrote what was later published as the *Lettres [élémentaires] sur la botanique à Madame Delessert* (Henry Cheyron, in *Dictionnaire*, 528b). The discussion of botany in the *Dialogues* is brief (RJJ II, 132f–35/832–35), including a comment that he gave his herbarium and sold his botanical books to Daniel Malthus, which apparently occurred around 1775 (RJJ II, 134n/832, with Osmont, OC 1:1685, note 5 to p. 832).

152. See, similarly, Rev. VII, 90, 97, 99/1061, 1068, 1070.

153. See *Frail Happiness*, 52–53, citing Conf. IX, 393/468.

154. The *Reveries* similarly observes: "During my brief periods of prosperity, many people turned to me for help, and doing everything I could for them, I never turned any of them away" (VI, 75/1051, following Goulbourne, *Reveries*, 60).

155. Translation modified.

156. Cf. the use of this Latin phrase in the original autobiographical enterprise (above, Chapter 5, with notes 59–60).

157. See RJJ II, 191/906f, and Rev. VI, 76, 79/1052, 1055. However, there are examples of generosity which are written of, and apparently occurred, during these later periods (see the girls and the wafers in IX, 127f–29/1090–91f). Cf. his accounts of his rising suspicion, despite a trusting nature (discussed above, Chapter 2, with note 84).

158. For similarly strong remarks on the impossibility of doing good deeds amid his circumstances, such that "the best thing he can do from now on is to abstain entirely from acting," see RJJ III, 234, 235f/962, 963f. It is here that the author adds an exception regarding "the just defense of my honor" (234n/962n1, quoted above, with note 119).

159. Cf. Conf. V, 160/190, on all "subjection and constraint." For connections with virtue, see below, Conclusion, with note 31.

160. See, esp., Rev. VIII, 112, 114/1075, 1077f.

161. Tronchin died in 1781 (*Dictionnaire*, 894b), before the publication of any of the autobiographical writings besides Book I of the *Dialogues* (published 1780).

162. See Section 1 of the Introduction above, esp. with note 33.

163. Starobinski, "The Accuser and the Accused," esp. 53–56. For the totalitarian mindset that "is to be read in his attitude," see 55f.

164. Discussed above, Section 2.1, esp. with notes 36–42.

165. Discussed above, Chapter 2, note 11, and below, Section 3 of the Conclusion. This is different from the psychological consistency perceived by Starobinski.

166. This passage is discussed more fully above, Chapter 3, note 2.

167. James Harris, *Hume: An Intellectual Biography* (Cambridge: Cambridge University Press, 2015), 464, 572n26. See also Knud Haakonssen, "The History of Eighteenth-Century Philosophy: History or Philosophy?" in *The Cambridge History of Eighteenth-Century Philosophy*, 2 vols., ed. Haakonssen (Cambridge: Cambridge University Press, 2006), 1:3–25, at 16–17.

168. We return to this in Section 3 of the Conclusion.

169. See "Letter on Virtue, the Individual, and Society" (ca. Spring 1757), trans. Arthur Goldhammer, *New York Review of Books*, May 15, 2003, 31–32, at 32b / "*Lettre sur la vertu, l'individu et la société*," ed. Jean Starobinski and Charles Wirz, *Annales de la Société Jean-Jacques Rousseau* 41 (1997), 313–27, at 325f. See also *Julie* III.22, 321/391, and E V, 473/858.

170. On earning his bread in the final phase by copying music, and thereby needing neither charity nor intrigue, see RJJ II, 127, 137f, 148/824, 837f, 851 (for other motivations, see above, with note 126). At the beginning of his final year, soon before departing from Paris for the more natural surroundings of Ermenonville, his hand had become "too shaky to keep up with music copying" (Damrosch, *Restless Genius*, 487).

171. We return to this in Section 3 of the Conclusion.

172. The charges from Diderot and Grimm are in Wilson, *Diderot*, 296–98, and Cranston, *The Noble Savage*, 83, 90–91. For d'Épinay, see the letter of ca. 26 September 1757 (quoted below, Conclusion, with note 18).

173. Discussed above, Chapter 1, with notes 145–49.

174. *Theory of Moral Sentiments* (1759–1790), ed. D. D. Raphael and A. L. Macfie (Indianapolis: Liberty Fund, 1982), II.iii.3.3, also discussed in Ryan Patrick Hanley, "Adam Smith on Living a Life," in *Adam Smith: His Life, Thought, and Legacy*, ed. Hanley (Princeton: Princeton University Press, 2016), 123–37, at 129–30. Hanley contrasts Smith's moral solution with Rousseau's resistance to charitable giving, seen as connected with his ideal of solitude ("Commerce and Corruption: Rousseau's Diagnosis and Adam Smith's Cure," *European Journal of Political Theory* 7.2 [2008]: 137–58, at 138, 148–49).

CONCLUSION

1. Above, Introduction, Section 2.

2. Cassirer, *The Question of Jean-Jacques Rousseau*, 39–40, 95–96, 127–28; Cassirer, "Kant and Rousseau," 55–59; Peter Gay's Introduction to *The Question of Jean-Jacques Rousseau*, 15–17.

3. Todorov, *Frail Happiness*, 95.

4. Todorov, *Imperfect Garden*, 99; see also 97–105; Todorov, *Frail Happiness*, 57–58, ch. 3, esp. 34, 49–53; and the more general discussion of solitude above, in the introduction to Chapter 6, esp. note 7. See, similarly, Neuhouser, *Rousseau's Theodicy of Self-Love*, 35, 35n13, 85–87, and Reisert, *A Friend of Virtue*, 89n15, 110n6.

5. Grace, "Portraying Nature," 142. See, similarly, Meier, *Happiness of the Philosophic Life*, 165, and Gauthier, *The Sentiment of Existence*, 73 (quoted above, Chapter 3, with note 7).

6. For the *Discourse on Inequality* as the most philosophically fundamental, see Conf. IX, 341/407, as interpreted by Strauss, *Natural Right and History*, 264; Masters, *The Political Philosophy of Rousseau*, xv, 105–6; and Grace, "Built on Sand," 168–71. For its links with the *Reveries*, see Grace, "Portraying Nature," esp. 142–45, 156–59; Grace, "Built on Sand," esp. 170–72, 178–80; and Meier, *Happiness of the Philosophic Life*, ix, 3–4, 45, 93, 165, 196.

7. See Kelly, *Rousseau's Exemplary Life*, e.g. 38–47, 245–48 (discussed above, Chapter 2, note 8 and with note 52). On forcing to be free, see above, Chapter 6, with note 20.

8. Fuller assessments are provided in my two companion articles in the *Political Science Reviewer*: "A Veiled Antinomian? On Straussian and Subversive Interpretations of Rousseau's Life and Thought," 43.1 (2019): 137–66; "A Flawed Moralist? On Kantian and Other Constructive Interpretations of Rousseau's Life and Thought," forthcoming.

9. Discussed above, Introduction, with notes 38–39.

10. Cranston, *Jean-Jacques*, 326–30, cf. 348. See also Rosenblatt, *Rousseau and Geneva*, e.g., 220–22, 227–33. Similar accommodations were offered from Pastor Montmollin, ca. 1762–1764, regarding Rousseau's interest in taking communion; this would change following the *Letters Written from the Mountain* (cf. above, Chapter 4, note 52).

11. *Maxims* (1665–1678), bilingual ed., Stuart D. Warner and Stéphane Douard (South Bend: St. Augustine's Press, 2001), no. 218, p. 43. For Rousseau's approaches to La Rochefoucauld, see *Julie*, III.20, 307n/373n, and Conf. III, 93/112; cf. ML IV, 190/1101.

12. See Augustine, *Confessions*, IV.2, VI.15, IX.6 (discussed above, Chapter 1, note 87).

13. See the discussions above about the indirect avowal in E I, 49/262f (Section 1.5), and the letter to Berthier, 17 January 1770, CC 37:207 (Chapter 1, with note 158).

14. See Crocker, *The Quest*, 179.

15. See Grant, *Hypocrisy and Integrity*, 91, 111–13 (discussed above, Introduction, with note 37). Cf. Rousseau's warning to Diderot about the dangerous uses to which Diderot's idea of his own natural goodness may be put (letter of 2 March 1758, CC 5:47–49, at 48, also discussed in Cranston, *The Noble Savage*, 126).

16. Jennifer Herdt, *Putting on Virtue: The Legacy of the Splendid Vices* (Chicago: University of Chicago Press, 2008), 304–5; see also 297, 415–16n28.

17. See, esp., Kelly, "Rousseau's *Confessions*," 312–15.

18. Letter to Rousseau, 26 September 1757, CW 5:560 / CC 4:262–66, at 263; see also 562/265. For related charges by Diderot and Grimm, see above, Chapter 6, note 172.

19. This is in keeping with our "apprentice in practical wisdom" model (above, Introduction, with notes 25–27).

20. *Maxims*, no. 230, p. 45.

21. See Section 1 of the Introduction.

22. See also *Julie* V.2, 441/538, and *Constitutional Project for Corsica*, separate fragments, CW 11:156 / OC 3:940f; cf., briefly in the main text of *Corsica*, 152/935. Strauss ("On the Intention of Rousseau," 458f) connects this theme with Montesquieu, *The Spirit of the Laws*, V.3.

23. Letter to Usteri, 18 July 1763, LPW 267 / CC 17:62–67, at 64.

24. Already in the *Observations* (1751), Cromwell is the example of the irredeemability of the hypocrite (47/52). Cf. Montesquieu, *The Spirit of the Laws* III.1, 22. Leigh cites Abbé Prévost's *Clèveland* as an earlier source for Cromwell's "bad press in France during this era" (CC 17:66 note b).

25. See Obs. 46f/51; LR 65/74; PN 103, 103n/972, 972n; and LdA 64/298/59 (discussed in Matthew D. Mendham, "Enlightened Gentleness as Soft Indifference: Rousseau's Critique of

Cultural Modernization," *History of Political Thought* 31.4 [2010]: 605–37, at 629–30). Other intellectuals appealed to La Rochefoucauld against Rousseau on this front (e.g., King Stanislas, *Reply to the Discourse*, CW 2:34 / *Mémoire de la critique*, ed. Trousson, 47; Charles Bordes, *Discourse on the Advantages of the Sciences and Arts*, CW 2:99–101 / *Mémoire de la critique*, 71–73). Rousseau's critique of hypocrisy and worldly moderation is effectively brought out by Grant's discussion of his response to Molière (*Hypocrisy and Integrity*, ch. 3).

26. See *Julie* IV.6, 349/424, and VI.5, 541/658. See also Grant, *Hypocrisy and Integrity*, 58–62, 155, 161–62, and, esp., 174. The theme of transparency is Starobinski's, but he would not allow for this limitation.

27. Above, Introduction, with notes 37–42.

28. See Strauss, *What Is Political Philosophy?*, 53; Masters, *The Political Philosophy of Rousseau*, 13, 90–91, 96, 103, 254; Stephen Salkever, "Interpreting Rousseau's Paradoxes," *Eighteenth-Century Studies* 11.2 (1977–1978): 204–26, at 208–9, 223–26, esp. 223n64, 225n70; Kelly, *Rousseau's Exemplary Life*, 39, 117, 140, 162, 245–48; Melzer, *Natural Goodness*, 90–94, 113, 279; Marks, *Perfection and Disharmony*, 70, 178; and cf. Clifford Orwin, "Rousseau Between Two Liberalisms: His Critique of the Older Liberalism and His Contribution to the Newer One," in *The Liberal Tradition in Focus*, ed. João Carlos Espada et al. (Lanham: Lexington, 2000), 53–65, at 62. A moderated form is in Cooper, *Problem of the Good Life*, esp. 47–59; cf. Cooper, *Eros in Plato, Rousseau, and Nietzsche*, 139–40, 148–49, 166–69, 175–76.

29. See Strauss, *Natural Right and History*, 254–55; on all society as a form of bondage, see also Strauss, "On the Intention of Rousseau," 474, 480. For related interpretations on the tensions between reason and social norms, see above, Chapter 2, note 61. Céline Spector objects that, by "passing in silence the pages which praise the moral amelioration of humanity in society [e.g., SC I.8], *Natural Right and History* darkens the tableau of the city of the *Social Contract*" (*Au prisme de Rousseau*, 79).

30. See Gauthier, *The Sentiment of Existence*, esp. 144, 173–77 (discussed above, Chapter 3, with notes 16–17).

31. For related observations on civic life, see also above, Chapter 3, with note 16; on constraint, see Chapter 6, with note 159.

32. See *Rousseau's Exemplary Life*, ch. 2, esp. 49–56 on Cato and social utility. See also the discussion in Kelly, *Rousseau as Author* (155–71) of Rousseau's relation to earlier exemplary figures in "Fiction, or Allegorical Fragment on Revelation" (written ca. 1756–1757).

33. See above, Chapter 6, note 7, and the discussions above of Cassirer (note 2), Grant (note 14), and Reisert (Introduction, with notes 38–39).

34. "Interpreting Rousseau's Paradoxes," 223n64.

35. See *Malesherbes* IV, 580/1143, quoted above, Chapter 3, following note 50 (on politics and truth), and Chapter 6, with note 72 (on assisting neighbors).

36. Following Scholar, 352.

37. Ibid., 353. Kelly cites Conf. VIII, 303–4 as the evidence for his claim that "almost from the beginning of his literary career, Rousseau had presented himself as the virtual embodiment of the principles contained in his writings, a living example of the truth of what he said" (CW 5:xix).

38. Burke, "A Letter to a Member of the National Assembly," 49 (quoted above, Introduction, with note 3).

39. See Masters and Kelly, Introduction to CW 1:xxi (quoted above, Introduction, with note 40). Their support would seem to be the claim that he is good but not virtuous (RJJ II, 127/824, cited in xxiv). Cooper is less emphatic: "He never showed much virtue in his life,"

though "for one lengthy stretch [1756–1762] he was imbued with the *love* of virtue" ("Nearer My True Self to Thee," 478, 478n21, also discussed above, Chapter 2, with note 70).

40. Reisert refers to a letter to Sophie (17 December 1757) in support of the more modest claim that Rousseau "tended to think about his own personal relationships in the terms his intellectual system made available to him" (*A Friend of Virtue*, 81). See also Grant's balanced discussion of his character (*Hypocrisy and Integrity*, 74–77, 91, 111–13, discussed above, Introduction, with note 37, and Chapter 2, note 145).

41. For the dismissal, see, e.g., *Obs.* 35–36/39–40, and "Letter About a New Refutation" (May 1752), EPW 88 / OC 3:100. Masters appeals to these passages as decisive evidence for bracketing questions of personal inconsistency (*The Political Philosophy of Rousseau*, ix–x).

42. This is Rousseau's preliminary dismissal of the ad hominem in PN 94/962; see, more generally, 93–95/960–63.

43. Cf. Socrates' charge on the frivolousness of Meletus and related interlocutors (*Apology* 24c, 26b, 26e–27a, *Euthyphro* 15d).

44. Translation modified, emphasis added.

45. See above on the conditions of writing with integrity (Chapter 2, with notes 100–102). There are a few residual claims of virtue, e.g., the Frenchman's conclusion: "I believe that J.J. is innocent and virtuous" (RJJ III, 221/945).

46. Discussed above, Chapter 1, following note 161.

47. See Leigh's discussion of how "Rousseau refused gifts, from strangers and friends alike, with an ungracious pertinacity that did not make for smooth social relations." Yet to find this "extremely suspicious and in some way discreditable" would be to overlook his essence: "an overwhelming sense of the pervasive ease of corruption, a craving for purity and an obsessive desire to preserve his all-too vulnerable integrity" ("Jean-Jacques Rousseau," 551).

48. Letter to Jean Perdriau, 29 November 1754, CC 3:57–64, at 59–60. The claims that follow, on sacrificing out of zealous citizenship, are quoted above (Chapter 3, with note 42). He may err from "indiscreet zeal," but he relies on his "disinterestedness" and "the uprightness of his heart" more than on his enlightenment; he "seeks even my happiness only in that of others" (57).

49. Letter of 25 March 1758, CC 5:63–65, at 63f, following Cranston's translation (*The Noble Savage*, 130).

50. For the *Confessions* account of dealing with these passions for Sophie, see above, Chapter 2, with notes 96–97.

51. Letter to Hume, 10 July 1766, in David Hume, *A Concise and Genuine Account of the Dispute Between Mr. Hume and Mr. Rousseau* (London: T. Becket and P. A. De Hondt, 1766), pp. 34–83 / CC 33:29–54. In the following references, the bracketed numbers refer to the paragraphs, as indicated in CC.

52. This refers to Rousseau's recollection that he heard Hume speaking menacingly in his sleep, "*Je tiens J. J. Rousseau*!" (Letter to Hume, [58, 60], 78, 80/44, 45). Hume objected that he did not think he was in the habit of dreaming in French. See the account in Damrosch, *Restless Genius*, 422–24.

53. Letter to Hume, [62], 81f/45f, translation modified. Cf. also [35], 35f/40, on the costliness of doing his duty in refusing the King of England's pension, as orchestrated by Hume.

54. In the letter to Mirabeau, 31 January 1767 (above, Chapter 6, note 129 and following).

55. See, e.g., Conf. I, 8/9, III, 77/91f, and VI, 217–21/259–64 (discussed in the opening of Section 2.1 above). This theme may be clearer in the First Part of the *Confessions* than the Second. Cf., e.g., Conf. IX, 350/416 (quoted in Chapter 2, with note 34).

56. See Introduction, Section 1, especially with notes 61–62, where 1764 is provided as a conservative end date for his virtue. Here the *perception* of virtue extends through 1766, but, given the actual quarrel with Hume, the self-understanding may conflict too much with the reality.

57. See also Section 2.1 above.

58. See Sections 6.2–6.4 above, and Blum's response to Pierre Burgelin's appeal to set aside Rousseau's life and focus only on his work: "This posture of willful ignorance is difficult to maintain . . . because 'Rousseau's life' is a *problem* almost exclusively because of its literary representation by Rousseau" (*Rousseau and the Republic of Virtue*, 77; cf. Grace, "Portraying Nature," 141).

59. Emphasis added. For other shifts, see above, Chapter 1, with note 162, Section 2.2, Sections 4.4–4.6, and Chapter 6.

60. See Hösle on the need to distinguish clearly between discerning an author's intention and the (potentially more important) work of interpretations that go beyond it (*The Philosophical Dialogue: A Poetics and a Hermeneutics*, trans. Steven Rendall [Notre Dame: University of Notre Dame Press, 2012], 136–38, 459–60).

61. For love without obligation, see Gauthier (discussed above, Introduction, note 93). For the implications of the "deepest premises," see Nathan Tarcov and Thomas Pangle on the unfolding of modern political philosophy in general ("Leo Strauss and the History of Political Philosophy," in *History of Political Philosophy*, 3rd ed., ed. Leo Strauss and Joseph Cropsey [Chicago: University of Chicago Press, 1987], 907–38, at 910). See, similarly, Melzer's discussion of the Rousseauian view of sincerity as the highest good, which sometimes extends "Rousseau's ideas beyond his own formulations of them—yet not beyond the general tendency of his thought, or so I believe" ("Rousseau and the Modern Cult of Sincerity," in *The Legacy of Rousseau*, ed. Clifford Orwin and Nathan Tarcov [Chicago: University of Chicago Press, 1997], 274–95, at 288).

62. Differences in emphasis can be accounted for by the subtler coherentist views (see Melzer, *Natural Goodness*, 7–8, 12). Kelly effectively develops the claim in the Second Preface to *Julie* that Rousseau changed methods, not goals (*Rousseau as Author*, 98–104). The difference may be that in these coherentist views, differences in emphasis always serve a strategic and rhetorical purpose, based on a consistent philosophical intention. See Strauss, "On the Intention of Rousseau," 455f: "Rousseau himself said that all his writings express the same principles. There are then no other Rousseauan principles than those underlying his short discourse on the sciences and arts, however imperfectly he may have expressed them." For Masters and Kelly, "His entire body of work is internally consistent and guided by a single purpose" (Introduction to CW 1:xviii). Todorov's interpretive method is to similar effect (see *Frail Happiness*, 3, 19, 28–29, 57–58, and Scott and Zaretsky's Introduction, xxiii).

63. O'Hagan similarly posits a "powerful recurring tension at the heart of a unitary systematic project" in Rousseau. However, he explicitly avoids discussing the autobiographies and the later developments of the thought. See *Rousseau*, xi–xii, 271–72, and ch. 1, esp. 19–20, 27–28.

64. See Conf. VIII, 309, 326n/368, 389n, IX, 340n, 368/405n, 437f; letter to Claude Anglancier de Saint-Germain, 26 February 1770, CC 37:272–301, at 281, 281n, 286, 286n; and RJJ II, 149/852. For comment, see Havens, "Diderot, Rousseau, and the *Discours sur l'Inégalité*."

65. Cf. "Letter to Philopolis" (written ca. late 1755): "In my Epistle Dedicatory I congratulated my fatherland for having one of the best governments that can be; in the body of the Discourse I showed that there could be very few good governments; I do not see the contradiction you find in this" (EPW 227 / OC 3:235). On pseudo-progress in the second *Discourse*, see Conf. VIII, 326/388.

66. Chapter 6, with notes 142–50.

67. The disappointment with a new self-absorption was already expressed regarding *Beaumont* and *Mountain* (above, Chapter 4, with notes 245–46).

68. Above, Introduction, with notes 33–36.

69. The difference between a portrait and a "life," or biography, is above, Chapter 5, note 31. For Plutarch, see above, Introduction, with notes 29–31. Once fully committed to the *Confessions* project, it is more speculative whether Rousseau ever aspired to Plutarch's restraint, or whether he thought it was enough to avoid Montaigne's error of deceitfully "plastering" over one's faults (cf. Chapter 5, with notes 57–61 on Montaigne). Even the First and Second Parts of the *Confessions* may be importantly different here. I suggest a contrast between the case of Marion and the later discussions of Rousseau's abandoned children (on Marion, Conf. II, 71–73/85–87, discussed in Chapter 1, with note 161; on the children, cf. the outline with notes 28–51).

70. This is particularly the case if the deeds could have been discussed in the manner of *Émile* or the 1770 letter to Berthier, rather than the *Confessions*. See notes 12–17, above.

71. See the epigraphs by the comte de Buffon and the comtesse d'Houdetot (above, Introduction).

INDEX

ACKNOWLEDGMENTS

I have accumulated many debts in writing this book over nearly a decade. Of my mentors in graduate school, Vittorio Hösle and Mary Keys were pivotal for their support and contributions to my intellectual formation. Eileen Hunt Botting provided my first introduction to Rousseau. Michael Zuckert has been exceedingly generous to me over the years, including sponsoring a workshop for this book manuscript in the spring of 2018. Ryan Patrick Hanley was our selected discussant, and he provided indispensable guidance for improving the manuscript as it neared its final phase.

Many Rousseau scholars have benefited me and my work; I owe special debts of gratitude to Clifford Orwin and Joseph Reisert. They have surely known "the pleasure of doing good." Vickie Sullivan, Dennis Rasmussen, David Lay Williams, and Christophe Litwin have also provided insight and support at key junctures.

Of many supportive and learned colleagues, I particularly thank Paul Rahe for his guidance and advocacy in the later stages of this project. Concerning a much earlier stage, I thank Jonathan W. White—a Lincoln scholar—for first suggesting (summer of 2013) that it sounded like I was writing a second book, rather than still revising an earlier project.

This book has also been advanced by the work of research assistants, who braved some obscure corners of Rousseau and Enlightenment studies on my behalf. I thank Rachael Behr, Christian Winter, and, especially, Casey Wheatland.

The Institute for Humane Studies has generously provided a subvention for this book. I have also benefited from research grants provided by Hillsdale College and by Christopher Newport University.

At Penn Press, Damon Linker was an ideal acquisitions editor, at once insightful and supportive. On the production side, Noreen O'Connor-Abel and Kathleen McQueen spared me from more than a few errors.

My deepest debts of gratitude are to my family. My wife, Katie, and our children—Sophia, David, Josephine, and Stephen—graciously endured my distractions and exhaustions during the peak years of laboring on this project. The book is dedicated to my parents, Joann and Don, for the profound devotion and care they have always provided to their children and grandchildren. They will never "shed bitter tears" or need to "find consolation" for doing otherwise.

* * *

An earlier version of Chapter 1 appeared in *History of European Ideas* ("Rousseau's Discarded Children: The Panoply of Excuses and the Question of Hypocrisy," 41, no. 1, 2015; ©Taylor & Francis Ltd., www.tandfonline.com). An earlier version of Chapter 4 appeared in *History of Political Thought* ("A Lover of Peace or a Vile Insurgent? Rousseau, Geneva, and the Right to Revolution, c. 1762–8," 41, no. 1, 2020). Brief portions of the Introduction and the Conclusion appeared in *Political Science Reviewer* ("A Veiled Antinomian? On Straussian and Subversive Interpretations of Rousseau's Life and Thought," 43, no. 1, 2019; "A Flawed Moralist? On Kantian and Other Constructive Interpretations of Rousseau's Life and Thought," forthcoming). I thank each journal for permission to reprint.

Lightning Source UK Ltd.
Milton Keynes UK
UKHW010655280121
377821UK00001B/23